Economics of International Environmental Agreements

International environmental agreements provide a basis for countries to address ecological problems on a global scale. However, countries are heterogeneous with respect to their economic structures and to the problems relating to the environment that they encounter. Therefore, economic externalities and global environmental conflicts are common and can cause problems in implementation and compliance with international agreements.

Economics of International Environmental Agreements illuminates those issues and factors that might cause some countries or firms to take different positions on common problems. This book explores why international environmental agreements deal with some problems successfully but fail with others. The chapters address issues that are global in nature, such as: transboundary pollution, provision of global public goods, individual preferences of inequality-aversion, global cooperation, self-enforcing international environmental agreements, emission standards, abatement costs, environmental quota, technology agreement and adoption and international institutions. They examine the necessary conditions for the improved performance of international environmental agreements, how cooperation among countries can be improved and the incentives that can be created for voluntary compliance with international environmental agreements.

This text is of great importance to academics, students and policy makers who are interested in environmental economics, policy and politics, as well as environmental law.

M. Özgür Kayalıca is a professor of Economics at Istanbul Technical University, Turkey. One of his main research interests is environmental economics, especially the environment and trade issues, with game theoretic applications.

Selim Çağatay is a professor of Economics at Akdeniz University, Turkey. His research focuses on sustainable development, migration and applied policy analysis.

Hakan Mıhçı is a professor of Economics at Hacettepe University, Turkey. One of his main research interests is development economics, especially human development and environment-related issues.

Routledge Explorations in Environmental Economics

Edited by Nick Hanley
University of Stirling, UK

For a full list of titles in this series, please visit www.routledge.com/series/REEE

Economics of International Environmental Agreements

A Critical Approach

**Edited by M. Özgür Kayalıca,
Selim Çağatay and Hakan Mıhçı**

Routledge
Taylor & Francis Group

LONDON AND NEW YORK

First published 2017
by Routledge

2 Park Square, Milton Park, Abingdon, Oxfordshire OX14 4RN
52 Vanderbilt Avenue, New York, NY 10017

Routledge is an imprint of the Taylor & Francis Group, an informa business

First issued in paperback 2019

British Library Cataloguing-in-Publication Data
A catalogue record for this book is available from the British Library

Library of Congress Cataloging-in-Publication Data
Names: Çağatay, Selim, editor. | Kayalıca, M. Özgür, editor. |
Mıhçı, Hakan, editor.
Title: Economics of international environmental agreements : a critical approach / edited by Selim Çağatay, M. Özgür Kayalıca and Hakan Mıhçı.
Description: 1 Edition. | New York : Routledge, 2017. | Includes index.
Identifiers: LCCN 2016043507 | ISBN 9781138650657 (hardback) |
ISBN 9781315625195 (ebook)
Subjects: LCSH: Environmental law, International–Compliance costs. |
Environmental policy–International cooperation–Economic aspects. |
Sustainable development. | Environmental economics.
Classification: LCC HC79.E5 E28223 2017 | DDC 333.7–dc23
LC record available at https://lccn.loc.gov/2016043507

ISBN: 978-1-138-65065-7 (hbk)
ISBN: 978-0-367-87722-4 (pbk)

Typeset in Times New Roman
by Out of House Publishing

Contents

Figures

Tables

Contributors

Sarah Al Doyaili-Wangler Friedrich-Schiller-University, Jena, Germany.

Yasemin Atalay PhD Researcher at Institute for Environmental Studies (IVM) at VU University Amsterdam.

Soham Baksi Department of Economics, University of Winnipeg, Canada.

Hassan Benchekroun Department of Economics, CIREQ, McGill University, Montreal, Canada.

Michel Cavagnac Toulouse School of Economics (TSE), Université des Sciences Sociales, Manufacture des Tabacs (Bâtiment S).

Amrita Ray Chaudhuri Department of Economics, University of Winnipeg, Canada and CentER, TILEC, Tilburg University, The Netherlands.

Guillaume Cheikbossian Université de Montpellier & TSE, Faculté d'Economie, France.

Selim Çağatay Department of Economics, Akdeniz University, Antalya, Turkey.

Klaus Eisenack Humboldt-Universität zu Berlin, Germany.

Narod Erkol Istanbul Bilgi University, Business Administration Department, Eyüp, Istanbul, Turkey.

Rafael Salvador Espinosa Ramirez Department of Economics, University of Guadalajara, Guadalajara, Mexico.

Toshiyuki Fujita Faculty of Economics, Kyushu University, Japan.

Luis Gautier University of Texas at Tyler, USA.

Achim Hagen Carl von Ossietzky University Oldenburg, Germany and Humboldt-Universität zu Berlin, Germany.

Leonhard Kähler Carl von Ossietzky University Oldenburg, Germany.

Chisa Kajita Faculty of Economics, Kyushu University.

Gülgün Kayakutlu Department of Industrial Engineering, Istanbul Technical University, Macka, Istanbul, Turkey.

M. Özgür Kayalıca Department of Management Engineering, and TEDRC (Technology and Economic Development Research Centre), Istanbul Technical University, Macka, Istanbul, Turkey.

Merve Kumaş TEDRC (Technology and Economic Development Research Centre), Istanbul Technical University, Macka, Istanbul, Turkey.

Sajal Lahiri Department of Economics, Southern Illinois University Carbondale, USA.

Yu-Hsuan Lin Department of Economics, the Catholic University of Korea, South Korea.

Walid Marrouch Department of Economics, Lebanese American University, Beirut, Lebanon.

Hakan Mıhçı Department of Economics, Hacettepe University, Ankara, Turkey.

Yingyi Tsai Department of Applied Economics, National University of Kaohsiung, Taiwan.

Onur Tutulmaz Visiting scholar, Faculty of Environmental Studies, York University, Toronto, Canada.

Leo Wangler Institute for Innovation and Technology, Berlin, Germany.

Benan Zeki Orbay Istanbul Bilgi University, Business Administration Department, Eyüp, Istanbul, Turkey.

Introduction

M. Özgür Kayalıca, Selim Çağatay and Hakan Mıhçı

Pacta sunt servanda
Agreements must be kept

Human beings depend on the environment and the environment depends on human beings. The relationship between the two has not been smooth and does not seem to continue happily unless humans realize that resources of the Mother Nature are not finite. According to Intergovernmental Panel on Climate Change (IPCC 2013), it is extremely likely that human influence has been the dominant cause of the observed warming since the mid-twentieth century. It continues and reports that warming in the climate system is unequivocal. Moreover, the effects will persist for many centuries even if emissions of CO_2 stop.

It has been almost over 50 years since the environmental problems have entered the global agenda as a common enemy. Most of the important environmental problems are global in nature, such as ozone depletion, transboundary (cross-border) pollution, marine pollution and climate change, etc. Global problems require solutions globally achieved through international agreements on environment. This makes the countries depend on each other. In other words, there is interdependence, in particular a strategic one, amongst the countries. Economic models, mostly game theoretic ones, show that due to free rider problems countries may be reluctant to cooperate for global environmental issues. Instead, with self-interest they create too much pollution. This is the very well-known prisoners' dilemma.[1]

While environmental treaties date back to the end of the nineteenth century, the vast majority of Multilateral Environment Agreements (MEAs) have been adopted since the 1972 United Nations Conference on the Human Environment (UNCHE), often referred to as the Stockholm Conference (UNEP 2007). According to International Environmental Agreements (IEAs) Database Project, there are around 1,200 Multilateral Environmental Agreements (MEA) and over 1,500 Bilateral Environmental Agreements (BEAs).[2] A racing number of efforts to make agreements has proved that governments are quite aware that many environmental problems are transboundary rather than being local and that international cooperative behaviour is necessary.

In spite of the huge number of international agreements, not very much has been reached in terms of cooperative success. As stated in the press, 'governments spend years negotiating environmental agreements, but then willfully ignore them. It's a dismal record' (Guardian 2012). Sadly, empirical works show results in parallel with the prisoners' dilemma (Kellenberg and Levinson 2014).[3]

International environmental agreements provide a basis for countries to address environmental problems on a global scale. However, countries are heterogeneous with respect to their economic structures and to environmental problems they encounter. Therefore, economic externalities and international environmental conflicts are common and cause problems in implementation and compliance with international agreements.

This book at your hand is mainly concerned with illuminating those issues/factors that might cause some countries to take different positions on common problems. In other words, the book attempts to explore why IEAs deal with some problems successfully and do fail in some others. Needless to say, there are several books, volumes or reports in the literature on IEAs.

These works, most of which are non-economics, focus on a variety of issues and in different contexts around IEAs. While some of them provide a review of agreements with respect to their coverage, others are more thematic focusing on a single environmental concern. There are country specific ones as well as the ones which evaluate the legal status, regulatory processes and governance in a set of countries. Amongst others several (Andresan *et al.* 2012; Barrett 2007; Carraro 1999; Desai 2010; Dinar and Rapoport 2013; Nordhaus 2013; Victor *et al.* 1998) are directly and/or indirectly related to the current work.

Carraro (1999), an often-cited reference book in the field, might be the one that shares most common ground with the present study. Nonetheless, it is slightly dated. Barrett (2007) addresses a number of the key global changes today (global public goods) such as global climate change through making use of the game theory. Yet another researcher, Nordhaus (2013), provides an extensive work on the economics of global warming. Moreover, he discusses the policies and institutions for slowing detrimental climate changes.

Desai (2010) is a general and introductory study covering mostly institutional aspects of environmental agreements. However, Victor *et al.* (1998) are more concerned about effectiveness and implementation of the IEAs. Therefore, they are more concerned about the degree such agreements lead to changes in behaviour and the process that turns commitments into action. Meanwhile, Andresan *et al.* (2012) mainly deal with the politics of such agreements and handle environmental issues on a global scale. They are interested in understanding why IEAs deal with some problems successfully while others are ignored. Their book covers a diverse set of environmental problems such as long-distance air pollution, ozone-depleting and greenhouse gases, ocean management, biological diversity, agricultural plant diversity and forest stewardship. In a relatively recent edited book, Dinar and Rapoport's (2013) main objective is to illustrate the usefulness of game theory and experimental economics in policy making at multiple levels and for various aspects of IEAs over climate change, international water management, common pool resources, public goods, international fisheries, international trade and collective action, protest and revolt.

The chapters of this book address issues that are global in nature, such as: transboundary pollution, provision of global public goods, individual preferences of inequality-aversion, global cooperation, self-enforcing IEAs, emission standards, abatement costs, environmental quota, technology agreement and adoption and international institutions. The book also attempts to discuss how performance of IEAs can be improved. In this respect, as a permanent solution to the problem, the final part of the book also talks about alternative but quite radical, expansive and high technology embodied methodologies to control gas emissions such as emission catching methods, pumping carbon emissions underground, carbon capturing and injecting sulphur to the atmosphere. This book aims to bring the main challenges of international agreements in sharper focus, by juxtaposing the treatment of different angles to cooperation in a single volume. In the majority of the chapters, game theoretical modelling is extensively employed.

The main concern of the current book is to find answers to the following two questions: 'What determines the success of IEAs in achieving the foreseen goals?' and/or if we put the question the other way round 'which factors cause IEAs to fail in achieving the goals?'

We group and explore those factors based on the sources causing them. Five main sources are detected and these sources shaped the structure of the book accordingly. These sources are: stability of IEAs, country heterogeneity, firm heterogeneity, technology adoption and international institutions.

Furthermore, the book explores various aspects of 'stability of IEAs'. One aspect is the heterogeneity of countries that are partners in an IEA. The stability of IEAs can be less likely in the case of heterogeneous countries as such those countries may avoid a multi-country agreement and may prefer to sign a bilateral agreement among them. In the spirit of a political economy survey, Chapter 1 offers valuable insights on compliance with international agreements in general and IEAs in particular. In this chapter, Doyaili and Wangler especially focus on implementations of environmental agreements by countries after IEAs have been negotiated and approved by the associated parties. This is a survey where it is assumed that there is not automatic compliance by the countries once the IEA has been set. Instead, the chosen compliance level is the result of a complex domestic policy-making process, which is influenced by national and international determinants. The model of Dai (2006) is followed in order to lay a groundwork introducing major determinants. The theoretical and empirical literature is surveyed considering the international consequences of the domestic compliance decision, and combines it with the national policy-making process, which is shaped by political institutions and actors, their preferences and interests. The main contribution of the chapter, among others, is to provide a political economy framework to the current literature.

Another aspect is the endogenous and exogenous factors that determine stability. Endogenous determinants are internal and depend on national institutions. Exogenous determinants are dependent on factors that are external to individual countries' decision-making processes. Detecting those factors will help to get an understanding on countries' compliance with IEAs, and consequently, the stability of IEAs. In a simple model of free trade with three heterogeneous countries, Chapter 2 analyses the stability of IEAs among the countries with unequal market size and transboundary pollution emitted by producers in each country. The governments in each country are concerned with the environmental damage, consumer surplus and producer surplus of such policy coordination. In a context of free trade, Cavagnac and Cheikbossian in this chapter assume the existence of production taxes as the sole policy instrument at governments' disposal, and these taxes are the instrument to be coordinated among countries. Thus, this chapter examines the problem of coordinating environmental policies in the context of free trade, where the result is going to depend on the imperfect competition à la Cournot among firms, and the unbalanced trade given by the unequal market size of the countries. It is going to consider the feasibility of both partial and global international environmental agreements modelled as a simple coalition formation game.

The last aspect is related to preferences of individuals regarding inequality-aversion that affects stability of coalitions. A lower degree of inequality-aversion means the subjects are more likely to act strategically by violating the internal constraint and punish the free riders, whilst those with a high degree of inequality-aversion are less likely to violate the internal constraint by leaving the coalition. Chapter 3 emphasizes the complex nature of the cross-boundary environmental issues and pulls attention to the necessity of collaboration between states that are part of an environmental agreement. In this chapter, Lin attempts to address the influence of social preferences on individual incentives for participating in a climate coalition. While a growing number of studies propose the assumption of rational self-interest to explain individual decision makers' behaviour, several others suggest that the role of social preferences on individual incentives should be taken into account in an interactive game.

This experimental study builds a heterogeneous model with the concern of inequality aversion in which each agent has a clear dominant strategy for whether or not to participate in a coalition and the model is used to answer the questions of whether the concern about payoffs of others change the subjects' decisions, and whether individuals' social preferences affect their own incentives for participating in a public good game. The experiment is designed in two parts and offers two strengths. The first part identifies individual inequality-averse attitudes by taking either a certain fair payoff or an all-or-nothing payoff. In the second part, the subjects are given particular payoff tables and they decide whether or not to join the coalition. The first strength of the chapter is that it investigates incentives for participating in an IEA in the existence of one or more stable coalitions. The second strength is that under the assumption that the preference for inequality aversion would influence the equilibrium differently from the egoistic preference, the study indicates that a coalition would be formed differently when individuals care about other agents' payoffs.

The game theoretic analysis of IEAs with heterogeneous countries is a largely unresolved issue. Regarding effects of 'country heterogeneity' on performance of IEAs, the book identifies three factors. The first is the transnational approach that might become a necessity in case of heterogeneous countries. These are multi-level approaches that better represent variety of interests; that facilitate more efficient coordination of collective action; that build trust and commitment.

Chapter 4 specifically focuses on the dangerous interference of anthropogenic greenhouse gas emissions with the climate and so far unsatisfactory efforts to find cooperative solutions on an international level. From the above perspective, the chapter highlights the complementary approaches for global emissions reductions such as minilateralism, climate clubs, building blocks approaches and explains the behaviour of lobby groups, NGOs and city alliances. The main aim of Hagen, Kähler and Eisenack in this chapter is stated to be exploring transnational initiatives or patterns of cooperation and their effectiveness. A transnational environmental agreement is defined based on the condition that it should have heterogeneous contracting parties. Knowing that global public goods suffer from free rider incentives, the chapter tries to find out which factors seem to be the major, and therefore, lead to sign a non-universal transnational environmental agreement, and if they do so, why shouldn't they not just pretend to reduce greenhouse gas emissions?

Due to the limited number of academic studies that address transnational environmental agreements, the chapter reports on the global governance literature and empirical examples of emerging transnational climate agreements, and then devotes itself to an overview of the existing economic literature on the scope and limits of IEAs. Building on these two pillars, the chapter follows up with two proposals for game theoretic models. The models analyse the strategic effects of climate clubs and city alliances as examples for transnational environmental agreements. Then, these approaches are contextualized in an outlook on promising future research.

The second factor in country heterogeneity arises in the case of transboundary pollution, which might harm the incentives to participate in a self-enforcing IEA. Dealing with transboundary pollution is hard, and requires international environmental cooperation and agreements. When there is heterogeneity amongst countries in terms of the damage they face from pollution, it is even harder. These differences in disutility will eventually affect international trade as well. Baksi and Chaudhuri, in Chapter 5, examine countries' incentives to cooperate in regulating emissions of a transboundary pollutant. The analysis is based on how the extent of heterogeneity and freer trade affect the sustainability of international cooperation.

Unless it is multilaterally agreed, imposing more stringent environmental policies could harm those countries that agreed and imposed tighter policies by making their firms lose international competitiveness. This explains why some developed countries are reluctant to sign and some withdraw from such treaties. In addition, more severe policies may shift production of dirty industries to developing countries, which in turn would harm the mitigation of transboundary pollutants at the global level. Baksi and Chaudhuri remind us that the use of border tax adjustments (BTAs) based on differences in environmental regulations between trading countries may solve such problems (see Böhringer *et al.* 2015, 2016; Eyland and Zaccour 2012, 2014; Ghosh *et al.* 2012).

In order to analyse the above issues, they use an oligopoly model of trade in a polluting good between two countries, North and South, which differ in terms of their pollution damage parameter (higher in the North). There exists transboundary pollution as a by-product of production. Each country imposes a pollution tax on its domestic firm, where the tax rate can be chosen either cooperatively or non-cooperatively. Markets are assumed to be imperfectly competitive. Each country has an incentive to strategically distort its non-cooperative pollution tax in order to give its domestic firm a competitive advantage and capture rents from the other country. They analyse the sustainability of environmental cooperation between the two countries within an infinitely repeated game framework, where cooperation is self-sustained through the use of trigger strategies.

The third factor in country heterogeneity is the case where a developed country faces a developing one, i.e., a North vs South type of model like the previous chapter. However, this work specifies the heterogeneity through labour intensity and different degrees of damage from pollution. In Chapter 6, Orbay and Erkol construct a North (developed country)–South (developing country) type of model to examine the effects of labour intensity and marginal damage of pollution on government policies and location choice. The focus of the chapter is on how location choice of a firm from a developed country directly and indirectly depends on exogenous factors, such as labour intensity and marginal damage of pollution in an environment where government policies are chosen observing the location choice. It is straightforward that when labour intensity is high, the employment effect of production is more substantial, thus, the host country's policies change accordingly and thus, labour intensity indirectly affects location choice. Besides, labour intensity directly affects location decision because with a lower wage rate in the host country, production becomes cheaper with more labour intensity. Noting this, they construct a two-country theoretical model with two firms located in each of these countries.

They further assume that the firm located in South has a less efficient production technology than the firm located in North. Each of these firms pollutes the local environment, and there is no transboundary pollution. Both firms use two types of inputs, labour and other local inputs in fixed proportions. Labour is assumed to be cheaper in South. In the first stage of the game, North Firm decides where to locate. Its choices are to produce at home or to move the production facility to the South country. In the second stage, South and North countries reveal the level of government policy. Firms decide their country specific production levels à la Cournot in the third stage. The chapter also analyses how the social welfare levels of the countries and environmental pollution levels change when the countries determine a uniform cooperative government policy.

Under the title of 'firm heterogeneity', one of the issues that the book focuses on is the presence of foreign penetration, which affects optimal pollution policies. It has long been argued that many polluting industries migrated to countries with less strict environmental restrictions (see Low and Yeats 1992; Lucas *et al.* 1992). Huge flows of FDI, especially during the 1990s and 2000s into countries with low controls on emissions have been alleged to create pollution havens. However, empirical evidence does not support this strongly (see Jeppesen *et al.* 2002 for an excellent survey). According to the pollution haven hypothesis, FDI inflows are seen as the result of low standards while one can also argue that FDI inflows may also be the reason for low standards.

In Chapter 7, Lahiri and Tsai question the latter. For a given amount of FDI, a country weighs the marginal benefits and costs of environmental restrictions, and then decides on the optimal level of policy. An inflow of FDI can alter these benefits and/or costs, and thus, the level of optimal policy. They consider a Cournot oligopolistic market for a non-tradable commodity. A number of domestic and foreign firms serve the market. They assume that the number of foreign firms is exogenous. The analysis is based on two scenarios namely when there is free entry and exit of domestic firms and when there is not. Both sets of firms create pollution while producing and possess an abatement technology.

The second issue regarding the firm heterogeneity is the abatement levels in agreements, which may influence firm compliance in case of firm heterogeneity in abatement costs. Losing competitiveness to foreign competition has been used as an argument by many countries to avoid implementing environmental policies. Countries may engage in laxer environmental policy in order to avoid losing to foreign competition and attract profits. In Chapter 8, Gautier looks at the elements of strategic environmental policy, with particular attention to policy reform and its impact on global emissions.

He also examines the policy reform of reducing emissions under imperfect competition by incorporating changes in costs (both abatement and production costs) into the policy reform of emission taxes. This is important because as cost structures change, governments may adjust optimal taxation, thus having an impact on the extent to which policy reform may reduce global emissions. Additionally, this study presents a model with asymmetries in pollution abatement and production costs, and demand functions in a general setting. This chapter is built on a two-country model where firms compete in a Cournot fashion, face an emission tax and exhibit heterogeneous abatement costs. The heterogeneity in costs is captured through two channels. First, marginal abatement costs may differ across countries. Second, there is heterogeneity in costs through a cost parameter, assumed to be exogenous, which changes the level of the cost functions for any level of output and emissions, i.e. shifts costs for any level of output and emissions.

For the last chapter of this part, the book focuses on production generated pollution externalities and optimal emission standards in the case of heterogeneous firms as well as heterogeneous countries. Concerns about firm competitiveness, trade and environmental degradation play an important role in the development of policy in Chapter 9. Different countries may exhibit firm heterogeneity and differences in country size, which in turn affect the ability of countries to (i) negotiate the implementation of environmental/trade policies in an international context, and (ii) address local environmental degradation. With these in mind, Espinosa and Kayalica develop a partial equilibrium model of pollution quotas and reciprocal dumping where firms with different levels of costs behave à la Cournot and where countries differ in size. The cooperative and non-cooperative equilibria are characterized and conditions derived under which stringent/laxer pollution quotas are set by each country.

'The relationship between environmental technology and international cooperation' is covered in three different contexts. In the first one, in Chapter 10, firms decide whether to sign an agreement and to conduct R&D collectively where the role of R&D is to reduce the cost of technology adoption. An international technology agreement is a mechanism that is used to promote multilateral technological collaboration in the R&D phase that is required to overcome the high technology cost incurred by each nation and free rider problem due to knowledge spillover. This agreement is a joint-research project that is carried out by the group of countries who are voluntary participants. Kajita and Fujita, in this chapter, first explore and review the international technology agreements (ITAs) from various angles, and discuss the efficiency of them in terms of climate agreements. The main aim of the chapter is stated to be investigating the impacts of R&D costs on the effectiveness of an ITA. The chapter further considers a game in which players are countries, and their strategies include technology-related R&D and its adoption. ITA members collectively decide whether to conduct R&D under exogenously determined R&D costs. The proposed model is solved first where each country decides whether to join an ITA, and second signatories collectively decide whether to conduct R&D, third each country independently decides whether to adopt the technology.

A well-established result in the literature on IEAs is that when the gains from cooperation are large, the incentive of an individual country to free ride and not participate in the IEA is also large. From that perspective, in the second context of the 'relationship between environmental technology and international cooperation', the relation between adoption technology and free riding is searched. Mitigation and adaptation are two-pronged policy responses to climate change and hand in hand with IEAs. While mitigation tries to reduce emissions, the latter deals with adapting to the current levels. According to the United Nations Framework Convention on Climate Change (UNFCCC 2006), most methods of adaptation involve some form of technology – which in the broadest sense includes not just materials or equipment but also diverse forms of knowledge. Chapter 11 investigates the relationship between adaptation technology and the likelihood of sustaining a self-enforcing IEA over emissions. Benchekroun, Marrouch and Chaudhuri model an increase in the efficiency of adaptation technology as a reduction in the marginal cost of providing adaptive measures. The model is set on a game theoretic framework incorporating adaptation and participation in a global agreement on emission reduction.

The chapter's contribution to the vast literature on adaptation is to see how adaptation affects the incentives of an individual country to participate in a global effort to abet emissions. Considering an exogenous decrease in the marginal cost of adaptation allows them to focus on the impact of the arrival of a new technology, and abstract from the game of investment in R&D to invent the new technology. The chapter considers a fixed cost of not participating in an IEA borne by each non-signatory. If this fixed cost is sufficiently large, it is possible to construct a stable coalition of any size. They are interested in the comparative statics with respect to the adaptation cost parameter, and they use the fixed cost parameter to move around the baseline that the comparative static analysis is applied to.

Chapter 12 presents the final work regarding the relationship between environmental technology and international cooperation. Kumas, Kayalica and Kayakutlu develop a theoretical model in which there are two countries, labelled A and B, and each country has one firm located in it. The firm in each country produces a homogeneous product, and it serves both domestic and foreign markets in the form of intra-industry trade. The model assumes that production activities generate pollution and there is transboundary (cross-border) pollution between the countries. It is also assumed that the domestic firms differ from each other in terms of their abatement technology level (i.e. one of the firms has inferior environmental technology). The intention of the model is to analyse the impact of asymmetric technology levels on the optimal environmental quota and welfare for non-cooperative and cooperative solutions.

The last part of the book starts with Chapter 13 and explores a case study to understand how successfully international energy is governed. This part also examines what sort of an institutional framework will be efficient and effective during the inevitable energy transition. Atalay, in this chapter, focuses on the rapid uptake of renewable energy, which would require numerous new, technology-intensive and rather unconventional governance and management mechanisms. A large-scale consolidation of renewable energy resource use would mean a paradigm shift in the international energy govern-ance as well, especially when all the embedded characteristics, rules, norms, regulations, actors and institutions of the current international energy regime are considered. An energy transition will also mean a transition in the inter-national institutional structure, in the sense that the dominance of fossil fuel-centred institutions will be broken, and participation and compliance in the renewable energy sector are fostered.

After introducing the current challenges of fragmented international energy governance, this chapter attempts to explain how and to what extent the International Renewable Energy Agency is addressing the energy chal-lenges we are facing today.

Then, in Chapter 14, the impact of 'international institutions' on IEAs with a general and forward-looking approach is introduced. The past experience is evaluated to create messages to improve performance of IEAs in the future. In this chapter, Tutulmaz and Çağatay look at the climate change problem from various angles and with a critical eye since very little success has been achieved so far to cope with this problem. The chapter identifies the problem as quite a 'complex' one, and argues that until very recently some of the scientists (a minority) were still not convinced that climate change is an imminent problem for the world. From this perspective, the study first attempts to clarify scientific realities such as the earth's different climate ages in its past geological time scale; the earth and the life on it has survived and adapted; human causa-tion in climate change and global warming, etc. that are used as arguments in this dispute. The chapter later summarizes the institutional timeline of climate change briefly, that is, bilateral and multilateral environmental agreements signed mostly in the pre-Paris period. The carrying capacity of the earth is also discussed in the chapter, and consequently, the effects of carbon emissions on the carbon cycle are evaluated. With a forward-looking perspective, the chapter concludes by referring to alternative channels/methods that should be searched to cope with the problem of climate change.

Notes

1 For more on this issue, see a recent paper by de Zeeuw (2015). Also, see Caparrós (2016), and Ioannidis *et al.* (2000) for excellent surveys.
2 http://iea.uoregon.edu/pages/view_treaty.php?t=1992-ClimateChange.EN. txt&par=view_treaty_html.
3 The first chapter of the book provides a fairly extensive survey.

References

Andresan, S., Boasson, E. L. and Hønneland, G. (eds) (2012), *International Environmental Agreements: An Introduction*, London and New York: Routledge.
Barrett, S. (2007), *Why Cooperate? The Incentive to Supply Global Public Goods*, Oxford: Oxford University Press.

Böhringer, C., Müller, A. and Schneider, J. (2015), 'Carbon Tariffs Revisited', *Journal of the Association of Environmental and Resource Economists*, 2 (4): 629–672.

Böhringer, C., Carbone, J. C. and Rutherford, T. F. (2016), 'The Strategic Value of Carbon Tariffs', *American Economic Journal: Economic Policy*, 8 (1): 28–51.

Caparrós, A. (2016), 'Bargaining and International Environmental Agreements', *Environmental and Resource Economics*, 65 (5). doi:10.1007/s10640-016-9999-0.

Carraro, C. (ed.) (1999), *International Environmental Agreements on Climate Change*, Berlin: Springer.

Dai, X. (2006), 'The Conditional Nature of Democratic Compliance', *Journal of Conflict Resolution*, 50 (5): 690–713.

Desai, B. H. (2010), *Multilateral Environmental Agreements*, Cambridge: Cambridge University Press.

de Zeeuw, A. (2015), 'International Environmental Agreements', *Annual Review of Resource Economics*, 7: 151–168.

Dinar, A. and Rapoport, A. (eds) (2013), *Analyzing Global Environmental Issues, Theoretical and Experimental Applications and Their Policy Implications*, London: Routledge.

Eyland, T. and Zaccour, G. (2012), 'Strategic Effects of a Border Tax Adjustment', *International Game Theory Review*, 14 (3): 1–22.

Eyland, T. and Zaccour, G. (2014), 'Carbon Tariffs and Cooperative Outcomes', *Energy Policy*, 65: 718–728.

Ghosh, M., Luo, D. Siddiqui, M. S. and Zhu, Y. (2012), 'Border Tax Adjustments in the Climate Policy Context: CO_2 versus Broad-based GHG Emission Targeting', *Energy Economics*, 34: 154–167.

Guardian (2012), Retrieved from Guardian Website on 31 August 2016: www.theguardian.com/environment/blog/2012/jun/07/earth-treaties-environmental-agreements.

Ioannidis, A., Papandreou, A. and Sartzetakis, E. (2000), International Environmental Agreements: A Literature Review, *working paper*, GREEN, Université Laval, Chaier de Recherche du GREEN, 00-08.

IPCC (2013), 'IPCC Press Release', 27 September. Retrieved from IPCC Web site on 31 August 2016: www.ipcc.ch/news_and_events/docs/ar5/press_release_ar5_wg1_en.pdf.

Jeppesen, T., List, J. A. and Folmer, H. (2002), 'Environmental Regulations and New Plant Location Decisions: Evidence from a Meta-analysis', *Journal of Regional Science*, 42 (1): 19–49.

Kellenberg, D. and Levinson, A. (2014), 'Waste of Effort? International Environmental Agreements', *Journal of the Association of Environmental and Resource Economists*, 1 (1/2): 135–169.

Low, P. and Yeats, A. (1992), 'Do Dirty Industries Migrate?' in P. Low (ed.), *International Trade and the Environment*, Washington, DC: The World Bank, 89–103.

Lucas, R. E. B., Wheeler, D. and Hettige, H. (1992), 'Economic Development, Environmental Regulation and the International Migration of Toxic Industrial Pollution: 1960–1988' in P. Low (ed.), *International Trade and the Environment*, Washington, DC: The World Bank, 67–86.

Nordhaus, W.D. (2013), *The Climate Casino: Risk, Uncertainty, and Economics for a Worming World*, New Haven, CT: Yale University Press.

UNEP (2007), *Multilateral Environment Agreement: Negotiator's Handbook*, University of Joensuu, UNEP Course Series 5, Finland.

UNFCCC (2006), *The United Nations Framework Convention on Climate Change Handbook*, Bonn, Germany: Climate Change Secretariat.

Victor, D. G., Raustiala, K. and Skolnikoff, E. B. (eds) (1998), *The Implementation and Effectiveness of International Environmental Commitments: Theory and Practice*, Cambridge, Mass.: MIT Press.

Part I
Stability
External and internal

1 What drives compliance with international environmental agreements?

A political economy analysis of international and national determinants

Sarah Al Doyaili-Wangler and Leo Wangler

1 Introduction

This chapter takes a closer look on implementation of and more precisely compliance with international environmental agreements (IEAs). Barrett (1998a) considers IEA formation as a process consisting of five stages – pre-negotiation, negotiation, ratification, implementation and renegotiation. Each of the stages is crucial to the success and effect of the other stages as well as the whole IEA. After an IEA enters into force and becomes legally binding, parties have to implement the agreement. For most IEAs, national environmental laws and regulations have to be passed and enforced (Barrett 1998a: 322). However, passing of national legislation is not sufficient for compliance with the commitment made by signing and ratifying the IEA. Laws and regulations have to be designed as such that national IEA goals can be achieved. Therefore, we follow Young (1979) in stating that 'compliance can be said to occur when the actual behavior of a given subject conforms to prescribed behavior, and non-compliance or violation occurs when actual behavior departs significantly from prescribed behavior' (104, cited in Simmons 1998: 77).

The majority of formal models analysing the implementation stage assume that countries will comply with the IEA without considering international and national processes influencing the compliance decision (Wangler *et al.* 2013). Instead of automatically complying, the chosen compliance level is the result of a complex domestic policy-making process, which is influenced by national and international determinants. The aim of this survey is to give more insights on these determinants generated by theoretical and empirical literature on compliance with international agreements and IEAs in particular. In order to do so, we present the mechanics of a formal model by Dai (2006) to lay a groundwork, which allows us to introduce major determinants. The model considers international consequences of the domestic compliance decision and combines it with the national policy-making process, which is shaped by political institutions and actors, their preferences and interests.

The remainder of the chapter is organized as follows. Section 2 considers theoretical background and presents the basic mechanics of the model by Dai (2006). In sections 3 and 4 we derive international and national determinants of compliance. The last section concludes.

2   Theoretical background

Literature on international cooperation in general has gained importance over the last decades. Gilligan and Johns (2012) distinguish three generations of formal models on international cooperation. First generation models explained compliance with international agreements in anarchy through basic repeated prisoner's dilemma models and hegemonic theory (Gilligan and Johns 2012). As IEAs are not enforceable by a third party, parties to the IEA will comply as long as benefits from complying are greater than benefits from reneging (Simmons 2010: 275). In these models reciprocity and reputation are modelled as main drivers of compliance. Countries comply in order to keep a reputation as a credible partner in international cooperation or to avoid sanctions (Axelrod 1984; Keohane 1984). These early models treat states as unitary actors and the state's utility from cooperation as exogenous. In models of later generations, it is viewed endogenously as the result of domestic bargaining processes. This allows the introduction of public choice decision-making processes into the models. Carraro and Siniscalco (1998) and Folmer *et al.* (1998) were among the first authors to highlight the necessity to include preferences of domestic actors (in particular government, voters and interest groups) in the context of IEAs (Kroll and Shogren 2008: 564). Models following this approach include actors of national policy-making processes and generate insights on the role of regime-type and domestic institutions.

We contribute to this political economy approach with our survey. As theoretical basis, we refer to a formal model introduced by Dai (2006). It is not our goal to recite the whole model but rather to take the basic mechanics to lay a groundwork, which allows us to introduce major international and national determinants of IEA compliance.

According to Dai (2006), the level of compliance (c) is chosen by national policy-makers,[1] in the form of deciding on environmental policies that are sufficient to fulfil national commitments. Thereby, the policy-maker's main goal is to maximize her own utility (UG) and she will choose c accordingly. The policy-maker's utility is influenced by two main factors – social welfare (SW) and the probability of re-election (PR). Equation 1 depicts this relationship.

$$UG = SW + PR$$

Domestic social welfare is defined as the sum of the utilities of different groups within the society ($\sum_{i=1}^{N} U_i(c)$). In case of compliance with IEAs, basically two domestic groups can be distinguished ($i \in \{1,2\}$) – one group with a preference for compliance and a second group with a preference against. This implies that each domestic group, and for that matter each individual constituent, has a preference for a certain ideal level of compliance (c_i). The utility of each group ($U_i(c)$) depends on the deviation of the government's compliance level from the group specific optimum ($c-c_i$) as well as on international consequences of the chosen compliance level (μc, *with* $\mu \in [0,1]$). Other countries react to the country's compliance behaviour in the form of rewards, sanctions or concessions in future international negotiations. If μ converges to 1, reciprocity or reputational effects at the international level are highest and domestic constituents gain from the chosen compliance level.

This leads to the following equation 2:

$$U_i(c) = \mu c - (c - c_i)^2$$

Equation 2 can be interpreted as follows: Group *i*'s utility increases the closer the government's compliance level is to the compliance level preferred by group *i* and the greater international gains from national compliance.

As can be seen in equation 1, the government's utility is not only shaped by the social welfare component but also by the value ascribed to the expected probability of re-election. In general it is to be assumed that policy-makers seek re-election (Dai 2006: 698). To reach this aim enough votes have to be gained to generate a winning coalition (Chyzh 2014). To secure these votes, the compliance level will be according to the preferences of the subgroup of voters needed to stay in office. Two major factors determine the probability of staying in office: On the one hand, voter preferences and factors influencing these preferences play a significant role. On the other hand, domestic institutional settings (e.g. regime type, electoral institutions) influence how different domestic preferences and interests participate within the compliance process. Thus, the structure presented by this model allows the derivation of different drivers of compliance on the international as well as national level. First, it can give insights on how international consequences resonate nationally and then influence compliance behaviour. Second, it considers relevant actors of the domestic policy-making process – namely policy-makers and domestic constituents. Third, it allows explaining the role of domestic political institutions. In the remainder of this chapter we take a closer look at these three facts by providing further theoretical and empirical insights. Section 3 starts with evidence from the international level and expands on the concepts of reciprocity, reputation and the role of IEA design. Section 4 is dedicated to the domestic compliance process. It takes a closer look at how domestic institutions and actors with their different preferences and interests shape the policy-makers' compliance decision.

3   International determinants of compliance

On the international level, a country's decision to comply or not has consequences mostly in the form of reactions by other participating countries which in turn lead to domestic costs or benefits that influence social welfare. In most of the cases, global environmental problems and solutions are characterized by a high degree of uncertainty. For one thing, these uncertainties are of a scientific nature and concern causes and consequences of these problems (especially in the context of climate change) (Koremenos *et al.* 2001: 779). For another thing they are of an economic nature as there are regional and intergenerational discrepancies between costs and benefits of international environmental cooperation. Stavins (2011: 49) states that '[f]or virtually any jurisdiction, the benefits it reaps from its climate-policy actions will be less than the costs it incurs'. Subsequently, in combination with the lack of a third-party enforcer, there are strong incentives to free-ride and to take advantage without participating in the provision of the public good. Therefore, trust and repetition are essential in explaining cooperation in the context of IEAs. Mechanisms such as reputation and reciprocity are based upon them and are additional determinants facilitating IEA enforcement.

3.1   Reputation

According to Henkin (1979), a reputation for honouring international commitments is crucial in foreign and international politics. Reasons can be, first, that it may be a basic principle of a certain nation's international policy to be perceived as a credible partner. Second, a certain reputation can have economic and political consequences – in the form of material benefits or the security of future cooperation. It allows other parties to predict this state's future behaviour (von Stein 2013: 481). For example, policy-makers comply with the IMF's Article VIII in order to be observed by market actors as credible in honouring property rights (Simmons 2000). In the context of security alliances, there is a higher probability to enter future alliances for states that complied in the past (Gibler 2008). The wish to secure future cooperation of other parties in various international policy areas, including additional environmental treaties, may drive states to comply with IEAs. A formalisation of this argument can be found in McEvoy and Stranlund (2009) who model reputation effects of non-compliance with IEAs.

   However, it remains unknown if a reputation for compliance with IEAs indeed influences a country's reputation in other areas (Fisher 1981; Downs and Jones 2002) and if having a good reputation drives compliance. Furthermore, the objective to uphold a certain reputation can also lead to obvious non-compliance. Some countries use this to signal the value they give to national interests (Keohane 1997). Empirical evidence on reputation is scarce and exists mainly in the form of anecdotal evidence. The main reason is difficulties in measuring reputational effects. A promising approach by Tomz (2008) draws on interviews and surveys (von Stein 2013).

3.2 IEA design

The most crucial determinant on the national level is the IEA and its design itself. The IEA design is the result of comprehensive and intensive negotiations. This phase is characterized by strategic behaviour and the countries' aim to influence the design according to their own interests and motives (Wagner 2001; Mitchell 2003). With the drafting of the design there are essential decisions to be made including the decision on the extent of formalisation (hard versus soft law), on rules for signing and ratification stages (e.g. minimum participation rules) and on mechanisms that are designed to prevent or sanction non-compliance (Barrett 1998a; Wagner 2001; Guzman 2005; Al Doyaili and Wangler 2013). All decisions made during this process have implications on participation, compliance and effectiveness with/of the IEA. In general there are trade-offs between the depth of an IEA on the one hand and participation,[2] compliance and effectiveness on the other hand. These trade-offs influence decisions regarding the IEA design (von Stein 2008; Al Doyaili and Wangler 2013).

Hard law versus soft law

The most obvious division of IEAs can be made with concern to the degree of formalisation. Soft law is characterized by the lack of binding obligations. These agreements merely state common goals, norms and principles. In contrast, hard law IEAs are characterized by a high degree of formalisation. Specific goals and rules that are binding under international law are agreed upon. The non-binding character of soft law IEAs will most certainly lead to a high rate of participation and a lower level of compliance (von Stein 2008; Al Doyaili and Wangler 2013). However, it is uncertain how compliance can be defined in this case. Is it the provision of any level of the public good that is in the scope of the common goal? Al Doyaili and Wangler (2013) are able to give evidence for non-Annex I countries of the Kyoto Protocol. These countries did not commit to specific GHG emission limitation goals and, thus, for them the Kyoto Protocol can be defined as soft law. The authors were able to find quantitative empirical evidence that non-Annex I countries were among the countries participating in environmental public good provision.

In the context of hard law IEAs, participation and compliance depend on the magnitude of the binding goals and on mechanisms that induce, monitor and enforce compliance. The stricter (deeper) the goals, the lower the expected participation and compliance but the higher the effectiveness. If the (individual) IEA goal exceeds the level of what the country would have provided voluntarily, the incentive for treaty violation increases. Thus, the higher the depth of an agreement the greater the need for positive and negative inducements incorporated into the design (von Stein 2008; Al Doyaili and Wangler 2013; Bernauer, Kalbhenn *et al.* 2013).

Transparency mechanisms

Transparency mechanisms include reporting, review and monitoring requirements. These mechanisms fulfil two tasks. First, they aim to discourage reneging through increasing obligation. Second, transparency mechanisms provide information on the compliance behaviour of other parties to counteract the prisoner's dilemma situation and to detect and sanction free-riding (Vigneron 1997: 603). These mechanisms increase the costs of reneging and when included and used thoroughly, they are crucial in fostering compliance. However, they have to be created during the negotiation process and states choose to include weaker transparency institutions the deeper the agreement is in order to reduce costs of non-compliance in advance (Raustiala 2004: 56). Furthermore, in most of the IEAs transparency is reliant on self-reporting of IEA parties and has to be questioned to say the least (Finus 2000).

Empirical evidence, that transparency is a relevant compliance-inducing driver, is given by Mitchell (1994). He compares two subregimes of the International Convention for the Prevention of Pollution of the Seas by Oil, and finds significant differences for the level of compliance for both regimes. The subregime that induced higher compliance was characterized by a design setting that increased transparency. Weiss and Jacobson (1998) present a collection of case-studies studying compliance with five different IEAs (World Heritage Convention, Convention on International Trade in Endangered Species (CITES), International Tropical Timber Agreement (ITTA), London Convention on ocean dumping, Montreal Protocol on Substances that Deplete the Ozone Layer) in eight diverse countries (Japan, Russia, USA, Brazil, India, China, Hungary, Cameroon) and the European Union. They give insights on the design of reporting, review and monitoring mechanisms within these IEAs. Especially the *Montreal Protocol on Substances That Deplete the Ozone Layer* from 1987 is named as a positive example for fostering compliance through its extensive monitoring system. The Vienna Convention fulfils the monitoring task. Participating countries meet regularly and scientific analyses are presented. Parties have to report on their compliance process and the measures that were implemented (Jacobson and Weiss 1995: 136).

Transparency mechanisms can only have the wanted consequences if the design incorporates mechanisms that sanction detected non-compliance. Inducement mechanisms prove to be crucial IEA design elements. However, these do not only sanction non-compliance but are also aimed at preventing it or benefitting compliant states (sticks and carrots) (Vigneron 1997). The next subsection will present some insights on inducement mechanisms.

Inducement mechanisms

Inducement mechanisms build on the concept of reciprocity, which has long been seen as a major driver of compliance (Axelrod 1984; Keohane 1984;

Tingley and Tomz 2014). Tingley and Tomz (2014) distinguish two forms of reciprocity – intrinsic and extrinsic. In the case of intrinsic reciprocity, countries use tit for tat strategies to react to the compliance behaviour of other IEA members. They will implement environmental regulations when other parties do and they refrain from complying to punish non-compliance.

Extrinsic reciprocity links compliance behaviour in one policy area to rewards or punishments from other policy areas (Tingley and Tomz 2014). A series of authors propose this so-called issue linkage as an instrument to coerce treaty participation as well as compliance (e.g. Tollison and Willett 1979; Lohmann 1997; Koremenos *et al.* 2001; Leebron 2002; Poast 2013). Theoretically, issue linkage solutions are modelled into prisoner's dilemma models with the result that these models are transformed into coordination games (Folmer *et al.* 1993; Carraro and Siniscalco 1995; Cesar and Zeuw 1996; Barrett 1998a).

Possible positive inducements include trade or aid concessions or cooperation in another area. Aid cuts, economic sanctions or financial transfers are ways to punish non-compliance. Furthermore, it is crucial to distinguish the reasons for non-compliance. There are countries that are not willing to comply and countries that lack necessary capacity. For the latter, inducements in form of monetary or technical assistance can be included in order to support compliance efforts. In most cases, emerging and developing countries are crucial to the success of IEAs but often lack the capacity to implement regulations or let alone technological measures for environmental protection (Koremenos *et al.*, 2001: 786). Within the Montreal Protocol, for example, monetary and technological assistance is offered to countries that lack the capacity to fulfil the requirements of the agreement (e.g. Russian in 1996) (Vigneron 1997; Barrett 1998b). Overall, extrinsic reciprocity is viewed as a successful determinate of participation and compliance for this specific IEA. It also includes a punishment mechanism in form of trade sanctions for certain chemical substances as well as goods containing them for non-participating and non-complying countries (Barrett 1998b: 36). Chayes and Chayes (1995), however, argue against the use of inducement mechanisms, especially as a routine measure of enforcement. In any case, a number of conditions have to be given to ensure the effect of reciprocity. First and foremost, imitated non-compliance as punishment for reneging has to address the reneging country only (von Stein 2013: 479). Due to the supranational public good characteristic of IEAs, non-compliance as retaliation is not an appropriate measure, as it affects all parties. Measures such as economic or diplomatic sanctions are more appropriate (Barrett 2007; Tingley and Tomz 2014). Second, it is a question of how credible the threat of punishment is. Complying parties, often, do not have the flexibility to punish free-riders. It is highly unlikely that already established environmental regulations get annulled (Tingley and Tomz 2014: 348). Third, inducements should be applied evenly. Treaty violations of the same extent might not be punished to the same extent. In addition, disagreements on whether a sanction should be imposed and to what extent among IEA parties inhibit straightforward sanctioning (von Stein 2013: 479). More powerful parties have advantages at eluding as well as imposing sanctions. The inclusion of dispute settlement procedures (DSP) is a possible measure to overcome this problem.[3] Furthermore, from a normative point of view, it is questionable if issue-linkage should be used as an instrument at all. For example, linking environmental issues to international trade bears the threat that the environmental argument is misused by vested interests putting in danger the general achievements in trade liberalisation.[4] If we consider the so-called *Tinbergen rule* (Tinbergen 1952) on policy assignment and apply it to the global policy level, the responsibility for different policy areas (trade, health, environment and so on) should be carried out separately.

If we go back to the theoretical background developed in section 2, section 3 considered the μc part of equation 2. If the aforementioned determinants come to play non-compliance with the IEA will lead to reputational loss or sanctions that reduce μc and subsequently social welfare. Even though these losses affect the country as a whole, domestic costs and benefits of compliance or non-compliance are distributed unevenly among domestic actors (Dai 2006). Consequently, domestic actors have different preferences for and interests in the level of compliance. Rent seeking will occur. Depending on the domestic institutional setting concerning, e.g. the rule of law, separation of powers or the electoral system, these preferences and interests come to play and shape the national compliance decision. The next section takes a look on how different political regime types and institutions facilitate the influence of domestic preferences and interests.

4   National determinants

4.1   Role of domestic institutions

Democracy versus autocracy

A series of authors come to the result that democracies are more credible in keeping their international promises (e.g. Fearon 1994; Gaubatz 1996; McGillivray and Smith 2005) and in providing environmental public goods (e.g. Congleton 1992; Payne 1995; Bernauer and Koubi 2009).[5] Countries exhibiting democratic characteristics such as a strong prevalence of the rule of law, independent judiciary (Ho 2002: 659), or a high transparency for political decisions (Cowhey 1993: 299; Weiss and Jacobson 1999: 39) are more likely to comply with international commitments. Democratic institutions allow domestic citizens and non-state actors to detect non-compliance and to push government action towards stricter environmental regulations (domestic audience costs) (Fearon 1994; Weiss and Jacobson 1999). A central role is given to competitive and regularly held elections, which enable domestic constituents to punish policy-makers for breaking their international commitments by voting them out of office (Weiss and Jacobson 1998; McGillivray and Smith 2000, 2005; Mansfield *et al.* 2002). According to the selectorate theory developed by Bueno De Mesquita *et al.* (2002) and Bueno de Mesquita *et al.* (2003), the extent of public goods provision can be ascribed first, to the number of domestic actors that 'have an institutional say in choosing leaders' (Bueno De Mesquita *et al.* 2002: 559), the selectorate, and second to the number of supporters needed to stay in office, the winning coalition. Hereby, the latter one is a subgroup of the first. In democracies, the size of the winning coalition is determined by electoral rules, and is significantly higher than in autocracies where it consists of a small number of powerful elite members. This leads to an underprovision of public goods in favour of private goods in autocracies. In the context of compliance with international agreements, this means that there is a higher probability that cheating in international cooperation and its consequences stay undetected or unpunished by constituents, and subsequently, the level of compliance will be lower than in democracies (McGillivray and Smith 2005; Chyzh 2014).

However, anecdotal and empirical evidence show that compliance behaviour of different regime types is much more ambiguous than these arguments let it appear. In general, studies concentrating on the compliance behaviour of autocratic states are scarce (Chyzh 2014: 7). Chyzh (2014) takes a more detailed look on institutional settings in autocracies and differentiates certain types of authoritarian states. She comes to the result that some of these authoritarian regimes show no differences in their compliance behaviour than democratic regimes. Similarly, the assumption that democracies in general are more credible in fulfilling their international commitments is highly questionable. On the contrary, according to Gartzke and Gleditsch (2004), the regular change of leadership can also lead to less consistency in international cooperation. Differences of the institutional design in democracies concerning the size of winning coalition, legislative power, presidential versus parliamentary systems, the existence of federalism or the number of political parties influence the compliance process and can explain ambiguous results (e.g. Weiss and Jacobson 1999; Martin 2000; Fredriksson and Wollscheid 2006; Bernauer and Koubi 2009; Böhmelt *et al.* 2015). Furthermore, domestic audience costs theory does not account for different preferences and interests of non-state actors instead they assume that with the right institutional setting non-compliance is punished either way (Tomz 2002; Dai 2006). First, IEA compliance has wealth redistribution effects, which affects domestic actors unevenly (Dai 2006: 691). Subsequently, actors facing the costs of compliance have little interest in punishing the incumbent. Second, in most cases IEAs are very intricate and constituents may not be able to understand the IEA and the consequences in its entirety. Third, especially in the case of environmental problems voters might value other political issues (economic policy, unemployment) as more important and their voting decision is mainly influenced by these topics (Tomz 2002: 2). In summary, democratic compliance behaviour is conditional on domestic preferences and interests. Therefore, it is necessary to combine the influence of the domestic institutional setting with an analysis of prevalent preferences and interests of domestic actors (Dai 2006). The model by Dai (2006) presented in section 2 consists of these components. It models how the existence of competitive and regular elections facilitates the influence of opposing domestic interests. The next subsection will go into more detail and present the basic mechanics of the model.

A closer look on electoral institutions and preferences of domestic constituents

Electoral institutions are the key factor in Dai (2006)'s model. As we recall, incumbent policy-makers decide on the level of compliance under the assumption that they want to maximise their own utility. This utility is shaped by social welfare and the probability of re-election. The re-election probability depends on how regularly elections are held, the policy-makers' chance to win the election, and how binding election results are. Electoral institutions in different regime types vary along these factors, with a pure democracy on the one end and a pure autocracy on the other end. The first is characterised by competitive elections, which are held regularly and lead to binding results. The chance of winning the election depends on the voting behaviour of domestic citizens and how they evaluate past performance. In contrast, elections in autocracies are either non-existent, non-competitive or non-binding. The incumbent's fate does not depend on the chance of winning the election (Dai 2006: 697).

Two opposing interests are considered within the model – one with a preference for compliance and one group with a preference for reneging. For the purpose of this survey we extend these two groups and consider them to entail not only interest groups but also domestic voters. The chance of re-election depends on each group's 'informational status' and 'electoral leverage' (Dai 2006: 699). Policy-makers anticipate both and choose the level of compliance accordingly. The more regularly elections are held the higher the accountability to voters. In summary, democratic institutions alone do not lead to a higher credibility of IEA commitments. A country will comply if the pro-compliance group is better informed and its votes are decisive for the incumbent's chance of re-election. The next section will take a closer look at the role domestic actors play, how domestic voters form their preferences for or against compliance and how interest groups influence policy-makers.

A similar model can also be considered for autocratic countries. In this case the above-mentioned selectorate is not equal to the electorate but to a number of domestic actors (military or party personnel) that is able to influence the incumbent's fate (Bueno De Mesquita *et al.* 2002: 561). Here the incumbent as well has to set the level of compliance as such that she can receive the support of a winning coalition. Therefore, preferences and interests of these actors influence the compliance outcome. The difference to democratic states is that the winning coalition is much smaller; the way of influence is not going through electoral systems, and therefore will facilitate vested interests instead of public ones. However, theoretically this allows explaining differences in autocratic compliance behaviour and challenges the simplified attribution that democracies are in advantage concerning commitment credibility (Chyzh 2014).

4.2 Role of domestic actors

Domestic voters

For one, economic interests resulting from employment status, industry of employment and income situation shape individual preferences (Dai 2006; Bechtel *et al.* 2014). The higher unemployment in general or employment in to-be regulated industries the lower preference for the respective environmental regulation or climate policy (Horbach 1992; Kahn and Kotchen 2010). Bechtel *et al.* (2014) give empirical evidence on the relationship of an individual's economic well-being and their stance on international cooperation concerning climate change. Individuals grouped into the highest income quartile, show stronger support for cooperation than individuals in other quartiles. According to Raustiala (1997: 731), members and supporters of environmental non-governmental organizations (ENGOs) belong to the politically interested, middle-income part of the society. There are a number of articles analysing additional non-economic factors (e.g. level of education, age, political ideology, climate change exposure) influencing an individuals' concern for the environment (Inglehart 1995; Brechin 2003; Franzen and Meyer 2010; Kvaloy *et al.* 2012). Furthermore, voters' preferences are also shaped by personal and social norms and values (Ostrom 2000). Considering the characteristics of international environmental problems – e.g. regional and intergenerational mismatch between costs and benefits of IEA compliance – values such as altruism and reciprocity are especially relevant (Bechtel *et al.* 2014). To arrive at an ideal level of compliance (c_i) economic interest, personal and social values and the level of concern for the environment are balanced and weighted against preferences for other policy issues such as unemployment, health, pensions and general economic policy (Al Doyaili-Wangler 2016: 6). The above-mentioned case studies presented by Weiss and Jacobson (1998) show that public support for compliance can be a crucial factor. Al Doyaili-Wangler (2016) is able to provide evidence that a high domestic public concern for the environment, namely climate change, positively influences national compliance behaviour of Annex I countries with the Kyoto Protocol.

Literature on the role of interest groups within the policy-making process, e.g. the seminal work *The Logic of Collective Action* by Olson (1965), shows that the outcome of the policy-making process is not only shaped by voter preferences but also by interests represented by lobby groups. Interest group activity can lead to policy outcomes different to the outcomes preferred by a majority of voters.

Interest groups and non-governmental organizations

Interest groups exist in different shapes and sizes and are formed to further their members' common interests and agendas. 'Some seek to further the objectives of their members as factors of production or producers' (e.g. labour unions, different business and industry associations). 'Others seek to influence public policy and public opinion' (e.g. environmental or human rights groups) (Mueller 2003: 473). These groups have different possibilities to shape national decision in their own favour. They directly (supporting policy-making) and indirectly (lobbying, campaigning, funding elections) shape the policy-making process in order to influence subsequent wealth redistributions in their favour (Dai 2006; Böhmelt *et al.* 2015). In comparison to agreements of other policy issues (e.g. human rights, health), regulations made in order to fulfil IEA commitments address domestic non-state actors. Subsequent costs are initially mainly in disadvantage to industry sectors that will be affected by environmental regulations (e.g. fossil fuel producers, car manufacturers) and their stakeholders. Thus, lobby groups representing these interests have strong incentives to foster non-compliance (Simmons 2010: 286). In contrast, environemental non-governmental organizations (ENGOs) lobby for adherence to treaty commitments.

Essential to interest group activity is the acquisition, editing and distribution of information (Grossman and Helpman 2001). Especially when considering the characteristics of environmental problems and IEAs, providing information is a crucial tool for the success of interest group activities (Böhmelt *et al.* 2015). Overall, the interest group that is better informed and organized will be better in influencing the policy-making process (Dai 2006). Homogenous well-endowed industry interest groups are in an advantageous position over ENGOs that represent heterogeneous public ones (Olson 1965). They facilitate the influence of vested interests as well which leads to the implementation of policy regulations that are not in the interest of the majority of voters (Al Doyaili-Wangler 2016).

Quantitative empirical studies systematically analysing the relationship between interest group activity and compliance with IEA are scarce. The majority of this literature studies national IEA ratification (Roberts *et al.* 2004, Fredriksson *et al.* 2007, von Stein 2008, Bernauer, Böhmelt and Koubi 2013). Fredriksson *et al.* (2005) and Binder and Neumayer (2005) concentrate on the influence of national environmental regulations for the lead content in gasoline and for air pollution, respectively. Both are able to find a positive link between the number of ENGOs and the reduction of the level of lead and air pollution and the contrary result for the number of industry interest groups. These results show that certain interest group activities affect domestic environmental regulations. However, they do not allow conclusions to be drawn on the fulfilment of IEA commitments. A number of studies give empirical evidence on the role of interest groups. Dai (2007) analyses domestic ENGO activity and compliance with the *Long-Range Transboundary Air Pollution Convention* from 1985 and finds a positive link between the two. Bernhagen (2008) presents similar results. The author studies the influence of environmental as well as business interest groups on IEA compliance in general and with the UNFCCC in particular. Al Doyaili-Wangler (2016) gives evidence that countries with strong industry interest groups provide a lower level of compliance with the Kyoto Protocol. The overall thin quantitative empirical results on interest group influence can be explained by difficulties with operationalizing their strength. Common indicators use production, export and employment data for certain industries to account for these industries' relevance and strength as well as number of ENGOs active within the countries for ENGO influence (e.g. Fredriksson *et al.* 2005, 2007; Al Doyaili-Wangler 2016). Especially, indicators for ENGO strength have disadvantages, as the number of ENGOs does not give insights on how well informed and organized they are.

States are not only influenced by domestic ENGO activity but also by transnational ENGOs. See for example Vigneron (1997) and Gulbrandsen and Andresen (2004) for further insights. Böhmelt *et al.* (2015) present relevant literature on the impact of ENGOs in international environmental policy.

5 Conclusion and further remarks

It is the aim of this chapter to give a survey on political economy literature, which allows deriving major international and national drivers of compliance with IEAs. We built our analysis on the basis of a formal model by Dai (2006). Without claiming to be complete, we identified reputational effects and IEA design (including transparency and inducement instruments) on the international level and domestic institutions and actors on the national level as major determinants of IEA compliance. Specific country characteristics such as employment situation, household incomes or level of education influence national preferences and interests. Two points became apparent during our literature research for this survey.

First, overall systematic (empirical) evidence on determinants of compliance with IEAs is limited. Exceptions are case studies like the ones presented by Victor *et al.* (1998) or Weiss and Jacobson (1999). While these works present a comprehensive qualitative analysis of various different determinants on both levels, the number of countries studied is necessarily low. Results and derived conclusions have to be handled carefully and a generalisation should be avoided. It is necessary to complement these results with comprehensive quantitative studies. However, most of these studies are concerned with cooperation in general (e.g. Neumayer 2002; Bättig *et al.* 2008; Al Doyaili and Wangler 2013; Bernauer and Böhmelt 2013), ratification of IEAs (e.g. Fredriksson and Ujhelyi 2005; von Stein 2008; Leinaweaver 2012) or domestic environmental policy (e.g. Congleton 1992; Binder and Neumayer 2005; Fredriksson *et al.*

2005; Fredriksson and Wollscheid 2006) but only a small number with compliance as defined within this survey (e.g. Bernhagen 2008; Al Doyaili-Wangler 2016). A major explanation is difficulties with quantification of compliance and above derived determinants. To find an appropriate indicator for compliance proves to be complicated especially if there is no precise compliance goal the behaviour of IEA parties can be compared to. For a great number of IEAs, reporting on national compliance is incomplete or non-existent. Additionally, it is hardly possible to ascribe changes in environmental behaviour such as emission reductions to specific determinants (Bernhagen 2008: 89). Often used indicators simply measure physical output and output changes but do not compare them to the commitment made within the IEA.

Second, the literature on autocratic compliance with international agreements in general is limited and on IEAs in particular basically non-existent. As Chyzh (2014: 21) puts it, autocracies are used as a 'mere reference category' and a more detailed analysis that distinguishes among different authoritarian regime types is necessary to 'challenge the existing stereotype regarding the democratic credibility advantage over autocracies'. So far, the literature mostly considers only non-IEA topics (Weeks 2008; Chyzh 2014; Mattes and Rodríguez 2014) or ratification behaviour (Leinaweaver 2012) and domestic environmental policy in general (Klick 2002).

Furthermore, insights on compliance and its drivers do not allow for deductions on effectiveness and efficiency of IEAs. Downs *et al.* (1996) rightly ask: 'Is the good news about compliance good news about cooperation?' Often IEAs are designed as such that parties are certain they will be able to adhere to their commitments. In this case, the depth of the IEA is not great enough for behavioural changes to exceed the extent of voluntary changes that parties would have done without the agreement. Compliance with the IEA will be high but the agreement ineffective in what it is supposed to achieve – a lasting and substantial change of current behaviour (Gilligan and Johns 2012: 7.9). Aichele and Felbermayr (2012: 351) for example analyse the Kyoto Protocol ratification period and its effects on worldwide GHG emissions. Even though national emissions of dedicated countries declined by approx. 7 per cent, national carbon footprints rose because of increased net carbon imports. The authors conclude that positively spoken the agreement had no effect and negatively spoken even an adverse effect through a 'substantial relocation of production (carbon leakage)'.

Finally, from an economic perspective IEAs and their results have to be assessed in regard to efficiency aspects. IEAs and national compliance strategies are most likely to be inefficient. There are two major reasons for this result. First, national policy-makers are tempted to implement command and control policies instead of superior market based instruments. Second, even though market based instruments are used to comply, policy targets are set on non-optimal levels. Kirchgässner and Schneider (2003) ascribe this to the influence of domestic actors (voters, politicians, public bureaucracy, regulated industries and related interest groups). Inefficiencies also result from the design of the IEA itself. For example, in case of GHG emission reductions, an international emission trading system would be in advantage over specific limitation goals. However, IEAs can only be efficient if there is compliance. Therefore, research on compliance and its determinants has relevance and aforementioned gaps need to be addressed in further studies.

Notes

1 For our purposes and in the context of this model, the term policy-makers refers to national actors with legislative power. Depending on the specific regime type, this includes ruling parties, the chief policy-maker or dictators.
2 See Bernauer, Kalbhenn *et al.* (2013) for an extensive quantitative analysis of the depth versus participation trade-off for more than 200 IEAs.
3 See Vigneron (1997) for thoughts on IEAs and DSPs.
4 See Reeve (2002: 298) and Karp and Zhao (2010), for some information and discussion on linking global environmental topics and multilateral trading agreements.
5 For more information on contrasting arguments of democratic environmental good provision, see Gleditsch and Sverdrup (2002: 47) or Li and Reuveny (2006: 936).

References

Aichele, R. and Felbermayr, G. (2012), 'Kyoto and the Carbon Footprint of Nations', *Journal of Environmental Economics and Management*, 63 (3): 336–354.

Al Doyaili, S. and Wangler, L. (2013), 'International Climate Policy: Does it Matter? An Empirical Assessment', *Journal of Environmental Economics and Policy*, 2 (3): 288–302.

Al Doyaili-Wangler, S. (2016), Democracy, Interest Groups and Compliance with the Kyoto Protocol. Friedrich-Schiller-University Jena, working paper.

Axelrod, R. M. (1984), *The Evolution of Cooperation*, New York: Basic Books.

Barrett, S. (1998a), 'On the Theory and Diplomacy of Environmental Treaty-making', *Environmental and Resource Economics*, 11 (3): 317–333.

Barrett, S. (1998b), 'Political Economy of the Kyoto Protocol', *Oxford Review of Economic Policy*, 14 (4): 20–39.

Barrett, S. (2007), *Why Cooperate?: The Incentive to Supply Global Public Goods*, Oxford: Oxford University Press.

Bättig, M. B., Brander, S. and Imboden, D. M. (2008), 'Measuring Countries' Cooperation within the International Climate Change Regime', *Environmental Science & Policy*, 11 (6): 478–489.

Bechtel, M. M., Genovese, F. and Scheve, K. (2014), Interests, Norms, and Mass Support for Global Climate Cooperation, Retrieved from SSRN Web site: http://dx.doi.org/10.2139/ssrn.2528466.

Bernauer, T. and Böhmelt, T. (2013), 'National Climate Policies in International Comparison: The Climate Change Cooperation Index', *Environmental Science & Policy*, 25: 196–206.

Bernauer, T. and Koubi, V. (2009), 'Effects of Political Institutions on Air Quality', *Ecological Economics*, 68 (5): 1355–1365.

Bernauer, T., Böhmelt, T. and Koubi, V. (2013), 'Is there a Democracy–Civil Society Paradox in Global Environmental Governance?', *Global Environmental Politics*, 13 (1): 88–107.

Bernauer, T., Kalbhenn, A., Koubi, V. and Spilker, G. (2013), 'Is there a 'Depth Versus Participation' Dilemma in International Cooperation?', *The Review of International Organizations*, 8 (4): 477–497.

Bernhagen, P. (2008), 'Business and International Environmental Agreements: Domestic Sources of Participation and Compliance by Advanced Industrialized Democracies', *Global Environmental Politics*, 8 (1): 78–110.

Binder, S. and Neumayer, E. (2005), 'Environmental Pressure Group Strength and Air Pollution: An Empirical Analysis', *Ecological Economics*, 55 (4): 527–538.

Böhmelt, T., Bernauer, T. and Koubi, V. (2015), 'The Marginal Impact of ENGOs in Different Types of Democratic Systems', *European Political Science Review*, 7 (1): 93–118.

Brechin, S. R. (2003), 'Comparative Public Opinion and Knowledge on Global Climatic Change and the Kyoto Protocol: The US Versus the World?', *International Journal of Sociology and Social Policy*, 23 (10): 106–134.

Bueno De Mesquita, B., Morrow, J. D., Siverson, R. M. and Smith, A. (2002), 'Political Institutions, Policy Choice and the Survival of Leaders', *British Journal of Political Science*, 32 (4): 559–590.

Bueno de Mesquita, B., Smith, A., Siverson, R. M. and Morrow, J. D. (2003), *The Logic of Political Survival*, Cambridge, Mass.: MIT Press.

Carraro, C. and Siniscalco, D. (1995), R&D Cooperation and the Stability of International Environmental Agreements, *CEPR Discussion Paper 1154*.

Carraro, C. and Siniscalco, D. (1998), 'International Environmental Agreements: Incentives and Political Economy', *European Economic Review*, 42 (3): 561–572.

Cesar, H. S. and Zeuw, A. D. (1996), 'Issue Linkage in Global Environmental Problems', *in* A. Xepapadeas (ed.), *Economic Policy for the Environment and Natural Resources: Techniques for the Management and Control of Pollution*, Cheltenham: Edward Elgar Publishing, 158–173.

Chayes, A. and Chayes, A. H. (1995), *The New Sovereignty: Compliance with International Regulatory Agreements*, Cambridge, Mass.: Harvard University Press.

Chyzh, O. (2014), 'Can You Trust a Dictator: A Strategic Model of Authoritarian Regimes' Signing and Compliance with International Treaties', *Conflict Management and Peace Science*, 31 (1): 3–27.

Congleton, R. D. (1992), 'Political Institutions and Pollution Control', *Review of Economics & Statistics*, 74 (3): 412–421.

Cowhey, P. F. (1993), 'Domestic Institutions and the Credibility of International Commitment: Japan and the United States', *International Organization*, 47 (2): 299–326.

Dai, X. (2006), 'The Conditional Nature of Democratic Compliance', *Journal of Conflict Resolution*, 50 (5): 690–713.

Dai, X. (2007), *International Institutions and National Policies*, Cambridge: Cambridge University Press.

Downs, G. W. and Jones, M. A. (2002), 'Reputation, Compliance, and International Law', *The Journal of Legal Studies*, 31 (1): 95–S114.

Downs, G. W., Rocke, D. M. and Barsoom, P. N. (1996), 'Is the Good News About Compliance Good News About Cooperation?', *International Organization*, 50 (03): 379–406.

Fearon, J. D. (1994), 'Domestic Political Audiences and the Escalation of International Disputes', *American Political Science Review*, 88 (3): 577–592.

Finus, M. (2000), Game Theory and International Environmental Cooperation: A Survey with an Application to the Kyoto-Protocol. Fondazione Eni Enrico Mattei.

Fisher, R. (1981), *Improving Compliance with International Law*, Charlottesville: University of Virginia Press.

Folmer, H., Mouche, P. v. and Ragland, S. (1993), 'Interconnected Games and International Environmental Problems', *Environmental and Resource Economics*, 3 (4): 313–335.

Folmer, H., Hanley, N. and Mißfeldt, F. (1998), 'Game-Theoretic Modelling of Environmental and Resource Problems: An Introduction', *in* H. Folmer and N. Hanley (eds), *Game Theory and the Environment*, Cheltenham: Edward Elgar Publishing, 1–29.

Franzen, A. and Meyer, R. (2010), 'Environmental Attitudes in Cross-National Perspective: A Multilevel Analysis of the ISSP 1993 and 2000', *European Sociological Review*, 26 (2): 219–234.

Fredriksson, P. G. and Ujhelyi, G. (2005), 'Political Institutions, Interest Groups, and the Ratification of International Environmental Agreements'. Retrieved from Harvard University, Department of Economics Web site: www.people.fas.harvard. edu/~ujhelyi/ratify.pdf.

Fredriksson, P. G. and Wollscheid, J. R. (2006), 'Democratic Institutions Versus Autocratic Regimes: The Case of Environmental Policy', *Public Choice*, 130 (3–4): 381–393.

Fredriksson, P. G., Neumayer, E., Damania, R. and Gates, S. (2005), 'Environmentalism, Democracy, and Pollution Control', *Journal of Environmental Economics and Management*, 49 (2): 343–365.

Fredriksson, P. G., Neumayer, E. and Ujhelyi, G. (2007), 'Kyoto Protocol Cooperation: Does Government Corruption Facilitate Environmental Lobbying?', *Public Choice*, 133 (1): 231–251.

Gartzke, E. and Gleditsch, K. S. (2004), 'Why Democracies May Actually Be Less Reliable Allies', *American Journal of Political Science*, 48 (4): 775–795.

Gaubatz, K. T. (1996), 'Democratic States and Commitment in International Relations', *International Organization*, 50 (1): 109–139.

Gibler, D. M. (2008), 'The Costs of Reneging: Reputation and Alliance Formation', *Journal of Conflict Resolution*, 52 (3): 426–454.

Gilligan, M. J. and Johns, L. (2012), 'Formal Models of International Institutions', *Annual Review of Political Science*, 15 (1): 7.1–7.23.

Gleditsch, N. P. and Sverdrup, B. O. (2002), 'Democracy and the Environment', *in* E. Page and M. Redclift (eds), *Human Security and the Environment: International Comparisons*, Cheltenham: Edward Elgar Publishing, 45–70.

Grossman, G. M. and Helpman, E. (2001), *Special Interest Politics*, Cambridge, Mass.: MIT Press.

Gulbrandsen, L. H. and Andresen, S. (2004), 'NGO Influence in the Implementation of the Kyoto Protocol: Compliance, Flexibility Mechanisms, and Sinks', *Global Environmental Politics*, 4 (4): 54–75.

Guzman, A. T. (2005), 'The Design of International Agreements', *European Journal of International Law*, 16 (4): 579–612.

Henkin, L. (1979), *How Nations Behave: Law and Foreign Policy,* 2. Edn, New York: Columbia University Press.

Ho, D. E. (2002), 'Compliance and International Soft Law: Why Do Countries Implement the Basle Accord?', *Journal of International Economic Law*, 5 (3): 647–688.

Horbach, J. (1992), *Neue politische Ökonomie und Umweltpolitik*, Frankfurt: Fischer.

Inglehart, R. (1995), 'Public Support for Environmental Protection: Objective Problems and Subjective Values in 43 Societies', *PS: Political Science and Politics*, 28 (1): 57–72.

Jacobson, H. K. and Weiss, E. B. (1995), 'Strengthening Compliance with International Environmental Accords: Preliminary Observations from Collaborative Project', *Global Governance*, 1 (2): 119–148.

Kahn, M. E. and Kotchen, M. J. (2010), Environmental Concern and Business Cycle: The Chilling Effect of Recession, *NBER Working Paper Series*.

Karp, L. and Zhao, J. (2010), 'International Environmental Agreements: Emissions Trade, Safety Valves and Escape Clauses', *Revue Économique*, 61 (1): 135–160.

Keohane, R. O. (1984), *After Hegemony: Cooperation and Discord in the World Political Economy*, Princeton, NJ: Princeton University Press.

Keohane, R. O. (1997), 'International Relations and International Law: Two Optics', *Harvard International Law Journal*, 38 (2): 487–502.

Kirchgässner, G. and Schneider, F. (2003), 'On the Political Economy of Environmental Policy', *Public Choice*, 115 (3): 369–396.

Klick, J. (2002), *Autocrats and the Environment or It's Easy Being Green*, Arlington, Va.: George Mason University School of Law.

Koremenos, B., Lipson, C. and Snidal, D. (2001), 'The Rational Design of International Institutions', *International Organization*, 55 (4): 761–799.

Kroll, S. and Shogren, J. F. (2008), 'Domestic Politics and Climate Change: International Public Goods in Two-Level Games', *Cambridge Review of International Affairs*, 21 (4): 563–583.

Kvaloy, B., Finseraas, H. and Listhaug, O. (2012), 'The Publics' Concern for Global Warming: A Cross-National Study of 47 Countries', *Journal of Peace Research*, 49 (1): 11–22.

Leebron, D. W. (2002), 'Linkages', *American Journal of International Law*, 96 (5): 5–27.

Leinaweaver, J. (2012), Autocratic Ratification: Environmental Cooperation to Prolong Survival, Retrieved from https://ssrn.com/abstract=2084866.

Li, Q. and Reuveny, R. (2006), 'Democracy and Environmental Degradation', *International Studies Quarterly*, 50 (4): 935–956.

Lohmann, S. (1997), 'Issue Linkage', *Journal of Conflict Resolution*, 41 (1): 38–67.

McEvoy, D. M. and Stranlund, J. K. (2009), 'Self-Enforcing International Environmental Agreements with Costly Monitoring for Compliance', *Environmental and Resource Economics*, 42 (4): 491–508.

McGillivray, F. and Smith, A. (2000), 'Trust and Cooperation Through Agent-specific Punishments', *International Organization*, 54 (4): 809–824.

McGillivray, F. and Smith, A. (2005), 'The Impact of Leadership Turnover and Domestic Institutions on International Cooperation', *The Journal of Conflict Resolution*, 49 (5): 639–660.

Mansfield, E. D., Milner, H. V. and Rosendorff, B. P. (2002), 'Why Democracies Cooperate More: Electoral Control and International Trade Agreements', *International Organization*, 56 (3): 477–513.

Martin, L. L. (2000), *Democratic Commitments: Legislatures and International Cooperation*, Princeton, NJ: Princeton University Press.

Mattes, M. and Rodríguez, M. (2014), 'Autocracies and International Cooperation', *International Studies Quarterly*, 58 (3): 527–538.

Mitchell, R. B. (1994), 'Regime Design Matters: Intentional Oil Pollution and Treaty Compliance', *International Organization*, 48 (3): 425–458.

Mitchell, R. B. (2003), 'International Environmental Agreements: A Survey of their Features, Formation, and Effects', *Annual Review of Environment and Resources*, 28 (1): 429–461.

Mueller, D. C. (2003), *Public Choice III*, Cambridge: Cambridge University Press.

Neumayer, E. (2002), 'Do Democracies Exhibit Stronger International Environmental Commitment? A Cross-Country Analysis', *Journal of Peace Research*, 39 (2): 139–164.

Olson, M. (1965), *The Logic of Collective Action: Public Goods and the Theory of Groups*, Cambridge, Mass.: Harvard University Press.

Ostrom, E. (2000), 'Collective Action and the Evolution of Social Norms', *The Journal of Economic Perspectives*, 14 (3): 137–158.

Payne, R. A. (1995), 'Freedom and the Environment', *Journal of Democracy*, 6 (3): 41–55.

Poast, P. (2013), 'Can Issue Linkage Improve Treaty Credibility?: Buffer State Alliances as a "Hard Case"', *Journal of Conflict Resolution*, 57 (5): 739–764.

Raustiala, K. (1997), 'States, NGOs, and International Environmental Institutions', *International Studies Quarterly*, 41 (4): 719–740.

Raustiala, K. (2004), 'Form and Substance in International Agreements'. Retrieved from SSRN Web site: http://dx.doi.org/10.2139/ssrn.505842.

Reeve, R. (2002), *Policing International Trade in Endangered Species: The CITES Treaty and Compliance*, London: Earthscan Publication.

Roberts, J. T., Parks, B. C. and Vásquez, A. A. (2004), 'Who Ratifies Environmental Treaties and Why? Institutionalism, Structuralism and Participation by 192 Nations in 22 Treaties', *Global Environmental Politics*, 4 (3): 22–64.

Simmons, B. A. (1998), 'Compliance with International Agreements', *Annual Review of Political Science*, 1 (1): 75–93.

Simmons, B. A. (2000), 'International Law and State Behavior: Commitment and Compliance in International Monetary Affairs', *The American Political Science Review*, 94 (4): 819–835.

Simmons, B. (2010), 'Treaty Compliance and Violation', *Annual Review of Political Science*, 13 (1): 273–296.

Stavins, R. (2011), *The National Context of U.S. State Policies for a Global Commons Problem*, Roskilde, Denmark: UNEP.

Tinbergen, J. (1952), *On the Theory of Economic Policy*, Amsterdam: North-Holland Publication Company.

Tingley, D. and Tomz, M. (2014), 'Conditional Cooperation and Climate Change', *Comparative Political Studies*, 47 (3): 344–368.

Tollison, R. D. and Willett, T. D. (1979), 'An Economic Theory of Mutually Advantageous Issue Linkages in International Negotiations', *International Organization*, 33 (4): 425–449.

Tomz, M. (2002), Democratic Default: Domestic Audiences and Compliance with International Agreements, Paper delivered at the 2002 Annual Meeting of the American Political Science Association, Boston, August.

Tomz, M. (2008), Reputation and the Effect of International Law on Preferences and Beliefs, Paper presented at the annual meeting of the ISA's 49th Annual Convention, Bridging Multiple Divides, San Francisco, CA, USA.

Victor, D. G., Raustiala, K. and Skolnikoff, E. B. (1998), *The Implementation and Effectiveness of International Environmental Commitments: Theory and Practice*, Cambridge, Mass.: MIT Press.

Vigneron, G. (1997), 'Compliance and International Environmental Agreements: a Case Study of the 1995 United Nations Straddling Fish Stocks Agreement', *The Georgetown International Environmental Law Review*, 10: 581–623.

von Stein, J. (2008), 'The International Law and Politics of Climate Change: Ratification of the United Nations Framework Convention and the Kyoto Protocol', *The Journal of Conflict Resolution*, 52 (2): 243–268.

von Stein, J. (2013), 'The Engines of Compliance', *in* J. L. Dunoff and M. A. Pollack (eds), *Interdisciplinary Perspectives on International Law and International Relations: The State of the Art*, Cambridge: Cambridge University Press, 477–501.

Wagner, U. J. (2001), 'The Design of Stable International Environmental Agreements: Economic Theory and Political Economy', *Journal of Economic Surveys*, 15 (3): 377–411.

Wangler, L., Altamirano-Cabrera, J.-C. and Weikard, H.-P. (2013), 'The Political Economy of International Environmental Agreements: A Survey', *International Environmental Agreements: Politics, Law and Economics*, 3: 387–403.

Weeks, J. L. (2008), 'Autocratic Audience Costs: Regime Type and Signaling Resolve', *International Organization*, 62 (01): 35–64.

Weiss, E. B. and Jacobson, H. K. (1998), *Engaging Countries: Strengthening Compliance with International Environmental Accords*, Cambridge, Mass.: MIT Press.

Weiss, E. B. and Jacobson, H. K. (1999), 'Getting Countries to Comply with International Agreements', *Environment: Science and Policy for Sustainable Development*, 41 (6): 16–20.

Young, O. (1979), *Compliance and Public Authority: A Theory with International Applications*, Baltimore: Johns Hopkins University Press.

2 Stable environmental agreements and international trade in asymmetric oligopoly markets

Michel Cavagnac and Guillaume Cheikbossian

1 Introduction

Some of the most serious environmental problems that urgently call for solutions are those related to transboundary pollution, greenhouse gas emissions and climate change. The Copenhagen accord in December 2009 recognizes the scientific case for keeping temperature rises to no more than 2° Celsius, but did not contain any commitments to emission reductions to achieve that goal. The last Climate Change Conference of the United Nations that took place in Doha in December 2012 (Qatar) resulted in several documents collectively titled 'The Doha Climate Gateway'. It is basically an extension of the Kyoto Protocol until 2020, but which is limited in scope to only 15 per cent of the global carbon dioxide emissions. This is due to the lack of participation of important developed countries like the United States and other key countries which decided to drop out of the Kyoto Protocol (notably Canada, Japan, New Zealand and Russia).[1] This is also due to the fact that developing countries – like China which managed to hang on to its developing country status while becoming the world's number one emitter – are not subject to any emissions reductions under the Kyoto Protocol. Even at the European level, obtaining a general environmental agreement is quite difficult. For example, there have been several attempts to introduce a unitary carbon tax across all EU member states from the beginning of the 1990s. But it has never materialized, as countries – like the UK – were unwilling to render national competencies on taxation to Brussels.[2]

It has long been recognized that the difficulty of coordinating environmental policies among sovereign countries is inherent to the global trend of trade liberalization. This is because in the context of free trade, governments are reluctant to abandon sovereignty on environmental policies because they can use these policies for trade related goals. Conrad (1993) and Barrett (1994a) were the first to show that under imperfect (Cournot) competition in world markets, governments have an incentive to strategically use environmental policies in order to implicitly subsidize their exports. This leads to weak environmental standards or to pollution taxes below the Pigovian level – what is called 'environmental dumping' – especially when pollution is transboundary (Kennedy 1994).

In this chapter, we examine the problem of coordinating environmental policies between several sovereign countries facing a global pollution problem in the context of free trade and imperfect competition in world markets. We extend the standard analysis of strategic environmental policies into several complementary directions. First, we assume that trade occurs between countries – not in a third market. Governments are thus concerned – in addition to the environmental damage – not only with the producer surplus but also with the consumer surplus. Related to this, we also assume that countries are heterogeneous in terms of market sizes. Therefore, trade is unbalanced and so countries may have conflicting interests depending on whether they are net exporters or net importers. Finally, we consider a three-country world economy in order to analyse the feasibility of both partial and global international environmental agreements. The motivation for such departures from the standard analysis is that international environmental negotiations – at the European or at worldwide level – typically involve countries with converging interests that may sometimes decide to speak with one voice. One can mention for example the *Association of Independent Latin American and Caribbean States* (AILAC) – that brings together Colombia, Costa Rica, Chile, Peru, Guatemala and Panama – or the *Climate and Clean Air Coalition* (CCAC) – founded by the United States, Bangladesh, Canada, Ghana, Mexico and Sweden – among other blocks of countries around the negotiating table during the last climate change conference in Doha.

More specifically, the model employed in this chapter is the following. There are three countries of unequal population size and in each one of them, there is a single firm producing a homogeneous good. Production of this good generates pollution emissions that spread perfectly across the national borders. Furthermore, free trade prevails and the three firms compete à la Cournot in all three countries. Finally, a production – or emission – tax is the sole policy instrument at governments' disposal. Tax rates can be negative since they are set to correct for two distortions as the market is characterized by both over-production due to the environmental damage and under-production due to oligopoly pricing. In any cases, there are gains to coordinating environmental (tax) policies and our objective is to determine with the help of a simple coalition formation game whether – and which – stable cooperative arrangement(s) can be reached to exploit these gains.

Our analysis of such arrangements is framed by a three stage game. In the first stage, countries choose their coalition partners. A coalition forms if there is unanimity with respect to a partnership plan, which means that each country would like to join precisely the other(s) in a coalition. In the second stage, each coalition commits to tax polluting production at a rate that maximizes the coalition's aggregate welfare. Finally, in the third stage, firms decide (non-cooperatively) on quantities, taxes are levied, international trade occurs and consumption takes place. In this set-up, we then define a stable cooperative arrangement as an equilibrium coalition structure which is immune to any – unilateral or multilateral – deviations. We also assume that the cooperative arrangement (if any) prescribes that the fiscal revenues raised remain in the country of origin. In other words, there are no transfer payments between countries. We note that transfers have a sound theoretical justification to foster cooperation and enhance efficiency when countries are heterogeneous (see, e.g., Eyckmans and Finus 2006; Weikard 2009), but that they are hardly observed in reality.

The main result is that if two countries can benefit from being part of a subcoalition, then the grand coalition is less likely to emerge as an equilibrium coalition structure, whilst the three countries would have agreed to join the grand coalition if the sole alternative was the singleton coalition. Furthermore, the grand coalition can be blocked not only by one country – called the outsider – but also by a subcoalition of two countries.

Intuitively, when a subcoalition of two countries is formed, it gives rise to a strategic advantage for the outsider. Indeed, this last can take advantage of the internalization of the pollution externality by the coalition – which results in a more stringent policy and then in increased production costs for the firms of the coalition – to make its own firm more competitive. But it is also possible that the two countries of the subcoalition prefer the third country to stay outside the coalition and free-ride on them. This happens when the damage parameter and the population size of the outsider are both relatively large. This is because, in this case, the formation of the grand coalition would lead to a significant decrease in produced and consumed quantities – due to the internalization of the pollution externality over all three countries – which in turn would lead to a strong decrease in export revenues for the two relatively small countries of the subcoalition. Certainly, with a two-coalition structure, the two members of the coalition lose market shares to the benefit of the outsider, but the market size is also much larger than under the grand coalition and a large market size mostly benefits small countries.

This chapter contributes to and connects two different strands of the literature: the one on strategic environmental policies and the other on international environmental agreements (IEAs). In general, since Conrad (1993) and Barrett (1994a), the first strand of literature considers that two symmetric countries compete in a third country. Kennedy (1994) analyses strategic environmental policies in a 'reciprocal-market' model and Bárcena-Ruiz and Campo (2012) extend the analysis by considering (partial) cross-ownership of firms. Still in a 'reciprocal-market' model, Tanguay (2001) and Lai and Hu (2008) consider that governments can also use import tariffs (or exports subsidies) and focus on the impact of trade liberalization on the global environment. Duval and Hamilton (2002) maintain the assumption of free trade but consider a two-country model with asymmetric number of consumers and firms as well as asymmetric pollution diffusion across countries. Unlike the above mentioned papers, we focus on the issue of stability of global *and* partial environmental agreements between three countries, which are heterogeneous in terms of market size.

The earliest works on IEAs (Hoel 1992; Carraro and Siniscalco 1993; Barrett 1994b) analyse a global emission-abatement game and characterize equilibrium IEAs by applying the internal-external stability concept developed for cartel theory (d'Aspremont *et al.* 1983). These works have been extended in many directions including that of heterogeneous countries participating in an IEA (see, e.g., McGinty 2007).[3] We also investigate the stability of IEAs but our analysis is based on the literature on endogenous coalition formation in games with externalities (see, Bloch 1996; Yi 1996). Some authors have also applied this approach to the analysis of IEAs (see, e.g., Carraro and Marchiori 2003) but, again, the analyses rely on a global emission-abatement game with reduced-form specifications.[4] Few exceptions are given by Eichner and Pethig (2013, 2014) who study the formation of IEAs in a micro-founded model with international trade. Like them, we explicitly consider consumption, production and trade. We must also mention that our framework is more specific but that, unlike them, our world economy consists of (three) heterogenous countries and is characterized by imperfect competition among producers in the world market.

In Section 2, we present the general framework. Section 3, 4 and 5 derive the outcome of the international policy game under respectively the grand coalition, the singleton and the coalition structure with only two countries forming a coalition. In Section 6, we give a precise definition of a stable environmental agreement and then derive the outcome of the coalition formation game, depending on the parameter reflecting the pollution externality and that reflecting the asymmetry in population sizes.

2   The model

2.1   *The households*

We consider a world composed of three countries, $N = \{A, B, C\}$. There are n_i consumers in country i and we normalize total population to 1, i.e. $n_A + n_B + n_C = 1$. Two goods are consumed in each country. The numeraire good Y is produced by competitive firms, while good X is produced under conditions of imperfect competition. Pollution is generated as a by-product of the production of X and this pollution cross borders. The Y industry does not pollute. An individual consumer in country i (for $i = A, B, C$) has the quadratic utility function:

$$u_i = \alpha x_i - (1/2) x_i^2 + y_i - \mathcal{D}(X) \tag{1}$$

where x_i and y_i are per capita consumption levels of X and Y respectively in country i, and where $\mathcal{D}(X)$ is the environmental damage incurred by the consumer. This damage is a function of world production of X (which is identically denoted as X). Finally, α corresponds to the maximal marginal utility of X.

An individual is assumed to own L units of labour and we assume that total endowment of labour – also equal to L since world population is normalized to 1 – is large enough to support production of good X and Y demanded by the three countries. The numeraire good Y is produced according to a one-to-one production function. The production of good X under conditions of imperfect competition will be more precise in the next sub-section. In addition, in each country, all revenues that the government obtains from taxation are distributed equally and in a lump-sum fashion across the population. (If these revenues are negative, this implies that each government can impose lump-sum taxes on its population.) Denoting the per capita tax revenues by T_i and by p_i is the consumer price of good X in country i, the budget constraint facing a representative household in each country i is then:

$$y_i + p_i x_i = L + T_i. \tag{2}$$

Maximization of (1) subject to the budget constraint (2) yields the representative household's inverse demand of good X, that is $\alpha - x_i = p_i$, for $i = A, B, C$. A convenient feature of the quadratic utility function (1) is that the individual's tax return does not enter the demand for good X since at the margin, income changes affect only the demand for the numeraire good Y. Aggregating over households in each country yields the following market demand curves for each country i:

$$X_i = n_i x_i = n_i (\alpha - p_i), \tag{3}$$

where X_i represents aggregate consumption of good X in country i.

2.2 The firms and the environmental damage

There is in each country a monopolist that produces good X[5]. More specifically, the X firm produces with a constant marginal cost m and with fixed costs F (all in terms of units of labour).

For all firms, production leads to the emission of the same pollutant which is perfectly transboundary. We assume that one unit of pollution is produced by one unit of X whether production takes place in the home country or in the foreign countries. We also assume that pollution is a pure public bad so that consumers in all countries are equally harmed by the pollution released from any country. More specifically, pollution generates environmental damage in each country according to the following form

$$\mathcal{D}(X) = \beta \left[X^A + X^B + X^C \right], \tag{4}$$

where X^i represents the production of the firm located in country i and where $\beta \in (0, \alpha)$ is a parameter that captures the marginal environmental damage caused by the production of X^6. We suppose that this marginal environmental damage cannot be higher than the maximal marginal utility of the consumption of good X given by α, otherwise production of X would never be socially desirable – i.e. even though the three countries form the grand coalition and maximize joint welfare, as one can see from Equation (13).

The three countries constitute a single market. Each firm can export in the two other markets at no shipping costs. X_i being the demand for good X in country i, the aggregate demand in the integrated economy is

$$X_A + X_B + X_C = \alpha - p. \tag{5}$$

In equilibrium, aggregate demand equals aggregate supply, i.e. $X^A + X^B + X^C$.

Each government can charge a tax on the production of X that is produced by the domestic firm. Let t_i be the per-unit production tax (or subsidy if t_i is negative) set by the government of country i. The profit function of the firm located in country i is

$$\pi^i = \left[\alpha - \left(X^i + X^j + X^k \right) \right] X^i - mX^i - t_i X^i - F, \quad i \neq j \neq k. \tag{6}$$

Since an increase in the marginal cost m is equivalent to a decrease in α, we set $m = 0$ for sake of simplicity.[7]

Differentiating this profit expression with respect to X^i, and setting the derivative equal to zero yields the following best response functions of the firms, that is $R_i(X^{-i}) = \max\left\{0, \left(\alpha - t_i - X^{-i} \right)/2 \right\}$ for $i = A, B, C$ and where X^{-i} denotes total production minus that of the firm located in country i[8]. The (interior) Nash equilibrium in quantities is then given by (for $i = A, B, C$)

$$X^i = \frac{\alpha - 3t_i + t_j + t_k}{4}, \quad i \neq j \neq k. \tag{7}$$

Firms i's production is decreasing in the domestic tax rate and increasing in the tax rate faced by its competitors. In equilibrium, aggregate supply, i.e. $X^A + X^B + X^C$, equals aggregate demand, i.e. $X_A + X_B + X_C$. Since total population is normalized to 1, aggregate supply or aggregate demand also corresponds to individual consumption of good X in either country, that is

$$x_A = x_B = x_C = x = \left[3\alpha - \left(t_A + t_B + t_C \right) \right]/4. \tag{8}$$

Expressions (5), (7) and (8) complete the output stage of the model.

We can now express the domestic welfare of each country as the sum of net consumer surplus which includes the environmental damage and tax revenues – such that $n_i T_i = t_i X^i$ – plus profits, that is

$$W_i = n_i \left[\frac{1}{2} x_i^2 + L - \beta \left(X^A + X^B + X^C \right) \right] + \pi^i + t_i X^i. \tag{9}$$

To simplify the analyse of the results, we shall use another expression of the domestic welfare of each country. First, recall that aggregate production equals aggregate and individual consumption, and so we denote by $p(x) = \alpha - x$, the market price. Now, adding and subtracting the term $n_i p(x)x$ – i.e. the value of domestic consumption in country i – into (9), we can express the welfare level of country i as follows

$$W_i = \underbrace{n_i \left[\frac{1}{2} x^2 + (p(x) - \beta)x + L \right]}_{CS_i} + \underbrace{p(x)(X^i - n_i x)}_{EX_i} - F, \tag{10}$$

The first term – denoted CS_i – corresponds to the *gross* consumer surplus, whereas the second term – denoted EX_i – corresponds to the value of external trade, which can be positive (negative) if country i is a net exporter (importer).[9]

We want to determine whether there exist stable cooperative arrangements among the three countries to deal with the two market failures: the pollution externality and the imperfect competition in global markets. To this end, as already specified in the introduction, we consider the following three-stage game. In the first stage, countries decide on their membership in a coalition. In the second stage, each coalition sets a tax rate on polluting production. Finally, in the third stage, firms play the Cournot-Nash game described just above, international trade occurs and consumption takes place.

We now turn to the second stage at which countries are already aligned into coalition structures. A coalition structure is a partition of the set of countries and there are three types of possible coalition structures: the singleton coalition denoted $\mathcal{B}_S$, the grand coalition denoted $\mathcal{B}_G$ and the structure which involves a coalition between only two countries i and j, while country k remains a singleton. This coalition structure will be denoted $\mathcal{B}_{(i,j)} \equiv \{\{i,j\},\{k\}\}$. We first analyse the case where no arrangement has been agreed in the first stage of the game, what corresponds to the singleton coalition $\mathcal{B}_S$.

3   Global agreement: the grand coalition $\mathcal{B}_G$

Suppose first that the three countries are willing to form the grand coalition which means that they jointly decide to tax polluting production in all three countries at rates that maximize the sum of the welfare functions given by (9). Note however that coalition members retain the responsibility to levy taxes and that all revenues raised remain in the country of origin.

Since the countries form an integrated market and since environmental damage is linear in pollution, there is a unique common tax rate that maximizes the (grand) coalition's aggregate welfare. Actually, uniform (tax) solutions are frequently viewed as efficient means to tackle a (pure) global environmental problem and furthermore often constitute a typical feature of many IEAs to reduce the emission of pollutants (see, e.g., Hoel 1992; Finus and Rundshagen 1998).

Therefore, we can set $t_A = t_B = t_C = t$, which implies that $X^A = X^B = X^C$ and $\pi^A = \pi^B = \pi^C = \pi$. Then, the aggregate welfare of the grand coalition is given by

$$W = \left[\frac{1}{2}x^2 + L - \beta x\right] + 3\pi + tx,$$

(11)

since $X^A + X^B + X^C = x$. Using (8), we have $x = \frac{3}{4}(\alpha - t)$ and the profit of each firm is then $\pi = (\alpha - t)^2/16 - F$. Differentiating W with respect to t and setting the derivative equal to 0, we obtain the following pollution tax rate under the grand coalition $\mathcal{B}_G$[10],

$$t(\mathcal{B}_G) = \frac{4\beta - \alpha}{3}.$$

(12)

This common pollution tax rate is set to correct for two distortions as the market is characterized by both over-production due to the negative externality and under-production due to oligopoly pricing. Then, the policy of the grand coalition levies a second-best tax below the marginal cost of pollution (equal to β) which can be, in principle, either positive or negative.[11]

From (8), individual consumption of good X in each country is $x(\mathcal{B}_G) = \alpha - \beta$ and the equilibrium price is $p(\mathcal{B}_G) = \beta$. In equilibrium, the three firms have an equal market share of the integrated economy, and then each produces $X^i(\mathcal{B}_G) = (\alpha - \beta)/3$. The gross consumer surplus for country i is $CS_i(\mathcal{B}_G) = [(1/2)(\alpha - \beta)^2 + L]n_i$, and the value of its external trade is $EX_i(\mathcal{B}_G) = [\beta(\alpha - \beta)/3](1 - 3n_i)$. Substituting the above expressions into (10), we obtain the aggregate welfare of country i in the grand coalition, i.e.

$$W_i(\mathcal{B}_G) = \frac{1}{6}(\alpha - \beta)\left[2\beta + 3n_i(\alpha - 3\beta)\right] + n_i L - F.$$

(13)

4   No agreement: the singleton coalition structure $\mathcal{B}_S$

Consider now the singleton coalition structure which corresponds to the situation where the three countries play a Nash game in tax rates. In other words, each country chooses its tax rate on production so as to maximize domestic welfare, taking as given the other countries' tax rates and anticipating the behaviour of both the firms and the consumers.

Substituting (6), (7) and (8) into (9), differentiating this expression with respect to t_i, and setting the derivative equal to zero yields the following best response function in tax rates for country i (for $i = A, B, C$),[12]

$$t_i\left(t_j, t_k\right) = \frac{4\beta n_i - \alpha(2 + 3n_i) - (2 - n_i)(t_j + t_k)}{6 - n_i}, \quad i \neq j \neq k. \tag{14}$$

This function is downward sloping as it is typically the case in a Cournot oligopoly model of international trade à la Brander and Spencer (1985).

Solving this system of best response functions, we obtain the following equilibrium tax rates under the singleton coalition $\mathcal{B}_S$ (for $i = A, B, C$),

$$t_i\left(\mathcal{B}_S\right) = \frac{(10\beta - 9\alpha)n_i - 2\beta}{9}. \tag{15}$$

Using (8) and (15), the per capita consumption level of X in each country is $x(\mathcal{B}_S) = \alpha - \beta/9$ and the equilibrium price is $p(\mathcal{B}_S) = \beta/9$. In equilibrium, aggregate demand (i.e. $x(\mathcal{B}_S)$) is equal to aggregate production, and substituting (15) into (7), we obtain the production of the firm located in country i, i.e. $X^i(\mathcal{B}_S) = [(9\alpha - 10\beta)n_i + 3\beta]/9$. The gross surplus for country i is $CS_i(\mathcal{B}_S) = [(1/162)(9\alpha - 17\beta)(9\alpha - \beta) + L]n_i$, and the value of its external trade is $EX_i(\mathcal{B}_S) = (\beta^2/27)(1 - 3n_i)$. Substituting these expressions into the welfare function given by (10), we obtain the welfare of each country when the singleton coalition structure prevails, that is

$$W_i\left(\mathcal{B}_S\right) = \frac{1}{162}\left[(6 - n_i)\beta^2 + 81\alpha n_i(\alpha - 2\beta)\right] + n_i L - F. \tag{16}$$

To conclude this section, we consider the difference in equilibrium tax rates. First observe that the tax rates are negative, so that countries always subsidize domestic production even though increased production involves more pollution.[13] This result is the logic consequence of combining imperfect competition with an integrated international market (see, e.g., Brander 1995). Now, suppose that the marginal cost of environmental damage is not too high, i.e. $\beta < (9/10)\alpha$, and that, for example, $n_A > n_B > n_C$. This implies from (15) that $t_A(\mathcal{B}_S) < t_B(\mathcal{B}_S) < t_C(\mathcal{B}_S)$. Hence, when $\beta < (9/10)\alpha$, a small country has an incentive to set a lower subsidy rate than the other(s). The explanation is related to the openness of the economies. Indeed, the national monopolists compete against each other in a single market and without governmental regulation, each would get an equal share of the market implying that a relatively small country would be a net exporter. A small country has thus some intrinsic advantage to capture oligopoly rents from foreign consumers and, consequently, has less need to subsidize its firm in order to gain a competitive advantage over its trading partner.[14] Inversely, a large country has an incentive to reduce its imports and hence to set a higher subsidy rate than smaller countries so as to increase domestic production.

However, increasing production also reduces the gross consumer surplus to the extent of both the marginal cost of pollution β and the size of the population. Indeed, the marginal gross consumer surplus in country i – i.e. $CS_i^m = \partial CS_i / \partial x$ – is negative, that is $CS_i^m = n_i[p(\mathcal{B}_S) - \beta] = -n_i(8\beta/9)$ since $p(\mathcal{B}_S) = \beta/9$. Therefore, when the marginal cost of environmental damage is relatively high, i.e. $\beta \geq (9/10)\alpha$, a large country sets a lower subsidy rate than smaller countries at the Nash equilibrium.

5   Partial agreement: the coalition structure $\mathcal{B}_{(i,j)}$

Suppose now that two countries – say countries i and j – form a coalition and choose a common tax rate, denoted t_{ij}, so as to maximize their joint-welfare $W_i + W_j$, where W_i and W_j are given by (9). As for the grand coalition, each coalition partner still has the responsibility to levy and collect taxes on its own territory and there is a unique common tax rate maximizing the subcoalition's aggregate welfare. The third country – i.e. country k – remains a singleton.

In the last stage of the game, the three firms still maximize their individual profits independently of each other, given t_{ij} and t_k. From (7) with $t_i = t_j = t_{ij}$, we have the following equilibrium quantities

$$X^i = X^j = \frac{\alpha - 2t_{ij} + t_k}{4}, \quad X^k = \frac{\alpha - 3t_k + 2t_{ij}}{4}. \tag{17}$$

Again, since the market is integrated, there is only one price p and therefore individual consumption of good X is identical in the three countries and is given (using (8)) by

$$x = \left[3\alpha - \left(2t_{ij} + t_k\right)\right]/4. \tag{18}$$

It follows that the equilibrium market price is $p = (\alpha + 2t_{ij} + t_k)/4$. The profit of each firm of the coalition is $\pi^i = \pi^j = (\alpha - 2t_{ij} + t_k)^2 / 16 - F$, while the profit of the firm located in country k is $\pi^k = (\alpha - 3t_k + 2t_{ij})^2 / 16 - F$.

In the second stage of the game, the coalition and country k choose their pollution tax rates independently of each other so as to maximize their respective welfare. Substituting (17), (18) and profits into (9), and maximizing $W_i + W_j$ with respect to t_{ij} yields[15]

$$t_{ij}(t_k) = \frac{(n_i + n_j)(4\beta - 3\alpha + t_k)}{2\left[4 - (n_i + n_j)\right]}. \tag{19}$$

Observe that the best response function of the coalition is upward sloping. The explanation is the following. Suppose that country k increases its tax rate (or decreases its subsidy rate) by dt_k. Then, the firm located in country k reduces its production level while each firm of the coalition increases its production (see eq. (17)). The key point is that the two firms of the coalition act independently of each other in the oligopoly game. Facing the increased competition between its firms, the coalition best reacts to an increase in tax rate (respectively, a decrease in subsidy rate) in the third country by increasing its own tax rate (respectively, decreasing its own subsidy rate) so as to internalize the market externality between the two firms located on its territory. In turn, it makes the two firms of the coalition act as if they were a single producer.

Similarly, substituting (17), (18) and profits into (9), and maximizing W_k with respect to t_k yields

$$t_k(t_{ij}) = \frac{4\beta n_k - \alpha(2 + 3n_k) - 2(2 - n_k)t_{ij}}{6 - n_k}.$$

(20)

In contrast to the best response function of the coalition, that of the country outside the coalition is still downward sloping.

Solving this system, we obtain the following equilibrium tax rates under the coalition structure $\mathcal{B}_{(i,j)}$,

$$t_{ij}\left(\mathcal{B}_{(i,j)}\right) = -\frac{(5\alpha - 6\beta)(n_i + n_j)}{10},$$

$$t_k\left(\mathcal{B}_{(i,j)}\right) = -\frac{(5\alpha - 6\beta)n_k + 2\beta}{5}.$$

(21)

When marginal cost of environmental damage is not too high (i.e. $\beta < (5/6)\alpha$), tax rates under a partial agreement are again negative.

To conclude this section, we now determine the welfare level of each country. Using (18) and (21), the per capita consumption level of X in each country is $x(\mathcal{B}_{(i,j)}) = \alpha - \beta/5$, while the market price is $p(\mathcal{B}_{(i,j)}) = \beta/5$. Substituting (21) into (17), we obtain $X^i(\mathcal{B}_{(i,j)}) = X^j(\mathcal{B}_{(i,j)}) = [5\alpha(n_i + n_j) + 2\beta[1 - 3(n_i + n_j)]]/10$ and $X^k(\mathcal{B}_{(i,j)}) = [5\alpha n_k + 3\beta(1 - 2n_k)]/5$.

The gross surplus for country i is $CS_i(\mathcal{B}_{(i,j)}) = [(1/50)(5\alpha - 9\beta) + L]n_i$. Finally, the value of exports for country i is $EX_i(\mathcal{B}_{(i,j)}) = (\beta/50)[5\alpha(n_j - n_i) - 2\beta(2n_i + 3n_j - 1)]$, while that of country j, i.e. $EX_j(\mathcal{B}_{(i,j)})$, is given by permuting n_i and n_j into $EX_j(\mathcal{B}_{(i,j)})$. It follows that $EX_k(\mathcal{B}_{(i,j)}) = -(EX_i(\mathcal{B}_{(i,j)}) + EX_j(\mathcal{B}_{(i,j)})) = -(\beta^2/25)[5(n_i + n_j) - 2]$. Substituting these expressions into the welfare functions given by (10), one can obtain

$$W_i\left(\mathcal{B}_{(i,j)}\right) = \frac{1}{50}\left[25\alpha^2 n_i - 5\alpha\beta(11n_i - n_j) + \beta^2\left(5n_i - 6n_j + 2\right)\right] + n_i L - F, \quad i \neq j,$$

$$W_k\left(\mathcal{B}_{(i,j)}\right) = \frac{1}{50}\left[25\alpha^2 n_k - 50\alpha\beta n_k + \beta^2\left(6 - n_k\right)\right] + n_k L - F,$$

(22)

and $W_j(\mathcal{B}_{(i,j)})$ is obtained by permuting n_i and n_j into $W_i(\mathcal{B}_{(i,j)})$. Calculating the difference between aggregate welfare for the two countries i and j when they form a subcoalition and when no coalition is formed, we obtain

$$\left(W_i\left(\mathcal{B}_{(i,j)}\right)+W_j\left(\mathcal{B}_{(i,j)}\right)\right)-\left(W_i\left(\mathcal{B}_S\right)+W_j\left(\mathcal{B}_S\right)\right)=\left(\frac{2\beta}{45}\right)^2\left[3-7\left(n_i+n_j\right)\right]. \quad (23)$$

Therefore, a two-country coalition increases the joint-welfare of the two participating members with respect to the singleton coalition if and only if $n_i+n_j \leq 3/7$. In other words, two countries would collectively benefit from being part of a coalition only if total population size is lower than that of the country outside the coalition.

6   IEAs and coalition formation

6.1   Preliminaries

We now characterize the outcome of the first stage of the game at which each country decides on its membership in an International Environmental Agreement (IEA), in cognizance of the subsequent stages. A strategy for country i is a choice of a coalition S_i to which i wants to belong. Formally, the set of strategies for country i is given by: $\forall i \in N, \Sigma_i = \{S_i \mid S_i \in N \text{ and } i \in S_i\}$. A strategy profile is denoted $s = (S_A, S_B, S_C) \in \pounds$, where $\pounds$ stands for the set of all strategy profiles (i.e. $\Sigma \equiv \Sigma_A \times \Sigma_B \times \Sigma_C$).

A *coalition-structure rule* is given by a function, $\Psi : \Sigma \rightarrow \mathcal{B}$, that assigns to any $s \in \Sigma$ a coalition structure $\mathcal{B} = \Psi(s)$. We restrict attention to the coalition-structure rule which prescribes that a coalition forms if and only if there is *unanimity* with respect to a partnership plan. For example, if $s = (\{A,B,C\};\{A,B,C\};\{C\})$, then no coalition is formed because countries A and B choose country C as a partner, but country C is not available as a partner. If however $s = (\{A,B\};\{A,B\};\{A,B,C\})$, then countries A and B form a coalition – since they agree on the partnership plan – but country C remains a singleton. We identify a coalition structure $\mathcal{B}$ as an *equilibrium coalition structure* if $\mathcal{B} = \Psi(s)$ for an *equilibrium* strategy profile s of the coalition-formation game.

The equilibrium concept used in this chapter is that of coalition-proof Nash equilibrium (CPNE) due to Bernheim *et al.* (1987). Roughly, a strategy profile is *coalition-proof* if it is immune to *self-enforcing* deviations by any coalition, and a deviation is self-enforcing if there is no further profitable deviation available to a subcoalition of players. In other words, a strategy profile is coalition-proof if there does not exist a credible deviation for a subset of countries.

In the following and for the sake of clarity, we distinguish between two cases. We first consider the case where the coalition structure $\mathcal{B}_{(i,j)}$ does not increase the joint-welfare of the two coalition partners, i.e. $n_i + n_j > 3/7 \, \forall i \neq j$ (see eq. (23)). Subsequently, we will consider the situation where there exists a couple of countries i and j such that the coalition structure $\mathcal{B}_{(i,j)}$ does increase the joint-welfare of the two coalition partners $(n_i + n_j \leq 3/7)$.

6.2 The grand coalition $\mathcal{B}_G$ versus the singleton coalition $\mathcal{B}_S$

When $n_i + n_j > 3/7$, country i or j or both are worse off under the coalition structure $\mathcal{B}_{(i,j)}$ than under the singleton coalition $\mathcal{B}_S$ and, hence, $\mathcal{B}_{(i,j)}$ cannot be supported by a CPNE as we will see in Proposition 1. Hence, in this section, we only determine the preference ordering of the three countries over the two alternatives $\mathcal{B}_G$ and $\mathcal{B}_S$. Calculating the difference between $W_i(\mathcal{B}_G)$ given by (13) and $W_i(\mathcal{B}_S)$ given by (16) for each country $i = A, B, C$, we obtain

$$W_i(\mathcal{B}_G) - W_i(\mathcal{B}_S) = \frac{\beta}{81}\left[27\alpha(1-3n_i) - 2\beta(15-61n_i)\right]. \tag{24}$$

To simplify the exposition, let $\hat{\beta}(n_i)$ such that $W_i(\mathcal{B}_G) = W_i(\mathcal{B}_S)$, i.e. $\hat{\beta}(n_i) = (27\alpha/2)(1-3n_i)/(15-61n_i)$.

We then have the following lemma which in fact holds independently of the country-size distribution.[16]

Lemma 1: *The preference ordering for country $i = A, B, C$ over $\mathcal{B}_G$ and $\mathcal{B}_S$ is:* (i) $W_i(\mathcal{B}_S) \geq W_i(\mathcal{B}_G)$ *if* $n_i \leq 3/41$ *and* $\beta \geq \hat{\beta}(n_i)$ *or* $n_i \geq 1/3$ *and* $\beta \leq \hat{\beta}(n_i)$; (ii) $W_i(\mathcal{B}_G) \geq W_i(\mathcal{B}_S)$ *for all other configurations of the parameters.*

Corollary 1: *If $n_i \in [3/41, 1/3]$, then country i (for $i = A, B, C$) prefers $\mathcal{B}_G$ to $\mathcal{B}_S$ independently of β.*

From Lemma 1, we can now state the following Proposition.

Proposition 1: *Suppose that $n_i + n_j > 3/7 \, \forall i, j = A, B, C$ and $i \neq j$. The unique equilibrium coalition structure is:* (i) $\mathcal{B}_S$ *if there is at least one country i for which $n_i \leq 3/41$ and $\beta \geq \hat{\beta}(n_i)$ or $n_i \geq 1/3$ and $\beta \leq \hat{\beta}(n_i)$; (ii) $\mathcal{B}_G$ in all other cases.*

To interpret these results, recall that each country's welfare can be written as the sum of gross consumer surplus plus the value of exports minus production costs as shown by (10). Under the singleton coalition, the *marginal* gross consumer surplus is $p(\mathcal{B}_S) - \beta$, which is negative since $p(\mathcal{B}_S) = \beta/9$, and becomes nil under the grand coalition since $p(\mathcal{B}_G) = \beta$. Then, the gross consumer surplus of each country is increased in proportion to its population size.[17]

Now consider the impact of the formation of the grand coalition on the external trade of each country and consider first that $n_i \leq 1/3$. We have seen that, under the singleton coalition $\mathcal{B}_S$, a small country sets a lower subsidy rate than larger countries provided that the parameter reflecting the environmental damage is not too high (i.e. $\beta < (9/10)\alpha$). In this case, since the grand coalition sets a common tax (or subsidy) rate, the domestic firm of a relatively small country becomes more competitive and then benefits from increased export revenues.[18] Hence, the grand coalition increases both the gross surplus and the value of external trade of a net exporting country (whose relative size is lower than $1/3$) with respect to the singleton coalition.

Suppose now the damage parameter is very high (i.e. $\beta \geq (9/10)\alpha$). In this case, a relatively small country (i.e. $n_i \leq 1/3$) sets a larger subsidy rate than larger countries under the singleton coalition and then becomes less competitive under the grand coalition with a common tax rate, thus losing market shares and export revenues. Therefore, for this country to prefer the grand coalition, it must be the case that the gross surplus gain due to the formation of the grand coalition is large enough to compensate losses in export revenues, implying that its population size must be sufficiently important. To be more specific, a sufficient condition for country i to prefers B_G to B_S is that $n_i \geq 3/41$. In sum, country i prefers to join the grand coalition than to remain a singleton whenever $n_i \in [3/41, 1/3]$ independently of the size of the damage parameter as stated in Corollary 1. We also note that for the special case of symmetric market sizes – i.e. $n_A = n_B = n_C = 1/3$ – all countries prefer full cooperation over the Nash outcome.

When $n_i \notin [3/41, 1/3]$, country i may also prefer to join the grand coalition than to remain a singleton depending on the extent of the pollution externality, as stated in Lemma 1. Indeed, for country i to prefer to remain a singleton when $n_i < 3/41$ (respectively, $n_i > 1/3$), it must be the case that the pollution externality is larger (respectively, lower) than $\beta(n_i)$. Consider first that $n_i < 3/41$ and $\beta \geq \beta(n_i)$, which implies that $\beta > (9/10)\alpha$. In this case, the significant decrease in consumed quantities resulting from the formation of the grand coalition – because of a high β – has a strong negative impact on the external trade (i.e. on exports) of the small country i, all the more this country cannot longer set a higher subsidy rate than larger countries.[19] This negative impact on the external trade dominates the positive impact on the gross consumer surplus, and so in this case country i prefers B_S to B_G.

Consider now that $n_i > 1/3$ and $\beta \leq \hat{\beta}(n_i)$, which implies $\beta < (9/10)\alpha$. In this case, under B_G, the large country i cannot longer undercut smaller countries by setting a higher subsidy rate, and consumed quantities do not decrease sufficiently to avoid an increase in import costs. This increased cost cannot be compensated by the gain in gross surplus when the grand coalition is formed compared to the singleton coalition.

6.3   *The possibility of subcoalitions* $B_{(i,j)}$

Suppose now that there exists a couple of countries i and j such that the coalition structure $B_{(i,j)}$ increases the joint-welfare of the two coalition members with respect to the singleton coalition, i.e. $n_i + n_j \leq 3/7$. It should be noted that this does not necessarily imply that both countries will agree with this partnership plan.

6.3.1 The coalition $\mathcal{B}_{(i,j)}$ versus the singleton coalition $\mathcal{B}_S$

We first compare for each country its preference ordering over the coalition structures $\mathcal{B}_{(i,j)}$ and $\mathcal{B}_S$. Using (16) and (22), the welfare difference for country i between $\mathcal{B}_{(i,j)}$ and $\mathcal{B}_S$ is given by

$$W_i\left(\mathcal{B}_{(i,j)}\right) - W_i\left(\mathcal{B}_S\right) = \frac{\beta}{4050}\begin{bmatrix} 2\beta\left(6+215n_i-243n_j\right) \\ -405\alpha\left(n_i-n_j\right) \end{bmatrix}, i \neq j. \tag{25}$$

The respective welfare difference for country j – i.e. $W_j(\mathcal{B}_{(i,j)}) - W_j(\mathcal{B}_S)$ – is given by permuting n_i and n_j into (25).

This welfare difference can be positive or negative depending on the country size asymmetry as well as on the value of the marginal environmental damage. For example, if β is relatively small and if $(n_i - n_j)$ is positive and relatively large, then the formation of the subcoalition would be detrimental to the larger country.

To simplify our analysis, we now assume throughout the rest of the chapter that $n_i = n_j = n$ implying that $n_k = 1 - 2n$. In this case, the welfare difference for countries i and j when they form a coalition and when they do not is given by

$$W_i\left(\mathcal{B}_{(i,j)}\right) - W_i\left(\mathcal{B}_S\right) = W_j\left(\mathcal{B}_{(i,j)}\right) - W_j\left(\mathcal{B}_S\right) = 2\left(\frac{\beta}{45}\right)^2 [3-14n]. \tag{26}$$

The welfare difference for the country outside the coalition is given by

$$W_k\left(\mathcal{B}_{(i,j)}\right) - W_k\left(\mathcal{B}_S\right) = 28\left(\frac{\beta}{45}\right)^2 [5+2n]. \tag{27}$$

We can now state – directly from (26) and (27) – the following lemma.

Lemma 2: *Suppose $n_i = n_j = n \leq 3/14$ which implies $n_k = 1 - 2n \geq 4/7$. Hence, all countries prefer the coalition structure $\mathcal{B}_{(i,j)}$ to the singleton coalition $\mathcal{B}_S$, independently of the extent of the pollution externality.*

When the coalition structure $\mathcal{B}_{(i,j)}$ forms, it increases the market price from $p(\mathcal{B}_S) = \beta/9$ to $p(\mathcal{B}_{(i,j)}) = \beta/5$, reducing total consumed quantities by $4\beta/45$. Again, this leads to an increase in the gross consumer surplus of each country in proportion to its population size, that is $CS_i(\mathcal{B}_{(i,j)}) - CS_i(\mathcal{B}_S) = 152(\beta/45)^2 n$ for country i (or j) while for country k, n must be replaced by $(1-2n)$.

Now, let us evaluate the impact of the formation of the coalition structure $\mathcal{B}_{(i,j)}$ on each country's external trade. As shown before, the value of external trade for country i (or j) under $\mathcal{B}_S$ is $EX_i(\mathcal{B}_S) = (\beta^2/27)(1-3n)$, while it amounts to $EX_i(\mathcal{B}_{(i,j)}) = (\beta^2/25)(1-5n)$ under $\mathcal{B}_{(i,j)}$. Calculating the difference, we have $EX_i(\mathcal{B}_{(i,j)}) - EX_i(\mathcal{B}_S) = -(2\beta^2/675)(30n-1)$, implying that $EX_k(\mathcal{B}_{(i,j)}) - EX_k(\mathcal{B}_S) = (4\beta^2/675)(30n-1)$.

It appears that the formation of the subcoalition has most often a negative impact on the value of the external trade of the two coalition members. This is indeed the case if population size in country i (or j) is not too small, i.e. $n \geq 1/30$. The reason is that the two coalition members set a lower subsidy rate, and then their domestic firms are less competitive, under the coalition structure $B_{(i,j)}$ than under the singleton coalition B_S, while the reverse holds for the outsider. Hence, when $n \geq 1/30$, the formation of the subcoalition induces for each coalition member a decrease in export revenues and an increase in gross surplus, but the latter effect is stronger provided the population size of each coalition member is small enough (i.e. $n \leq 3/14$).

This is somewhat surprising because the gain in gross surplus due to the formation of the subcoalition is increasing in country size. The explanation is the following. The larger the population size of each coalition member, the greater is the impact of the pollution externality on the joint consumer surplus and the lower is the incentive to subsidize production. Country k best responds to a decreasing subsidy rate in the coalition by increasing its own subsidy rate to take advantage of the increased cost incurred by the firms of the coalition. In fact, the strategic response of country k is inversely related to its size, as one can infer from (20). It follows that the larger the population sizes of countries i and j and the lower the size of country k, the greater is the incentive for country k to increase its subsidy rate, and this negative effect on the competitiveness of countries i and j overcomes their gains in gross surplus for $n > 3/14$.

Now, suppose that the population sizes of country i and j are very small, i.e. $n < 1/30 < 3/14$. In this case, the two coalition partners record an increase in export revenues following the formation of the subcoalition. Intuitively, when country size is very small, export quantities are sufficiently large for the decrease in export quantities to be compensated by the increase in the export price. Since coalition members also register an increase in gross surplus, they unambiguously prefer to form a subcoalition than to remain singletons.

Finally, consider the impact of the formation of the coalition on the value of external trade of the country that remains outside the coalition, i.e. country k. If $n < 1/30$, then country k experiences an increase in import costs but it also experiences a huge gain in gross surplus since country size is very large $(1 - 2n > 14/15)$. If $n \geq 1/30$, then the formation of the coalition between countries i and j leads to both a decrease in import costs and to an increase in gross surplus for country k. As a result, country k always benefits from the formation of the coalition structure $B_{(i,j)}$.

6.3.2   Equilibrium coalition structures

We need to determine each country's preference ordering over the three coalition structures in case two small countries prefer cooperation among them over the Nash outcome (i.e. $n \leq 3/14$). First, Lemma 1 determines each country's preference ordering over B_G and B_S independently of the country-size distribution, and so this lemma remains valid when $n_i = n_j = n \leq 3/14$

and $n_k = 1 - 2n \geq 4/7$. Second, Lemma 2 states that when $n_i = n_j = n \leq 3/14$ *all* countries prefer the coalition structure $\mathcal{B}_{(i,j)}$ to the singleton coalition $\mathcal{B}_S$. Therefore, we just need to calculate the welfare difference between $\mathcal{B}_{(i,j)}$ and $\mathcal{B}_G$ for each country.

When countries i and j form a subcoalition and $n_i = n_j = n$, the welfare level of each country is given (from (22)) by

$$W_i\left(\mathcal{B}_{(i,j)}\right) = W_j\left(\mathcal{B}_{(i,j)}\right) = \frac{1}{50}\left[25\alpha(\alpha - 2\beta)n + \beta^2(2 - n)\right] + nL - F,$$

$$W_k\left(\mathcal{B}_{(i,j)}\right) = \frac{1}{50}\left[25\alpha(\alpha - 2\beta)(1 - 2n) + \beta^2(5 + 2n)\right] + (1 - 2n)L - F. \tag{28}$$

Using (13) and (28), the welfare difference between $\mathcal{B}_G$ and $\mathcal{B}_{(i,j)}$ for country i (or j) is thus given by

$$W_i(\mathcal{B}_G) - W_i\left(\mathcal{B}_{(i,j)}\right) = \frac{\beta}{75}\left[25\alpha(1 - 3n) - 2\beta(14 - 57n)\right], \tag{29}$$

while the difference in welfare between $\mathcal{B}_G$ and $\mathcal{B}_{(i,j)}$ for country k is given by

$$W_k(\mathcal{B}_G) - W_k\left(\mathcal{B}_{(i,j)}\right) = \frac{2\beta}{75}\left[-25\alpha(1 - 3n) + 2\beta(20 - 57n)\right]. \tag{30}$$

To simplify the exposition of the results, let $\hat{\beta}_{ij}(n)$ such that – for country i or j – $W_i(\mathcal{B}_G) = W_i(\mathcal{B}_{(i,j)})$, i.e. $\hat{\beta}_{ij}(n) = (25\alpha/2)(1 - 3n)/(14 - 57n)$. Similarly, let $\hat{\beta}_k(n)$ such that $W_k(\mathcal{B}_G) = W_k(\mathcal{B}_{(i,j)})$ i.e. $\hat{\beta}_k(n) = (25\alpha/2)(1 - 3n)/(20 - 57n)$.

We can now determine – directly from (29) and (30) – the preferences of each country between $\mathcal{B}_{(i,j)}$ and $\mathcal{B}_G$.

Lemma 3: *Suppose* $n_i = n_j = n \leq 3/14$ *implying* $n_k = 1 - 2n \geq 4/7$. (i) *The preferences for country* i – *or country* j – *are:* $W_i(\mathcal{B}_G) \geq W_i(\mathcal{B}_{(i,j)})$ *if* $\beta \leq \hat{\beta}_{ij}(n)$ *and* $W_i(\mathcal{B}_{(i,j)}) \geq W_i(\mathcal{B}_G)$ *if* $\beta \geq \hat{\beta}_{ij}(n)$ *(implying* $n \leq 1/13$*).* (ii) *The preferences for country* k *are:* $W_k(\mathcal{B}_G) \geq W_k(\mathcal{B}_{(i,j)})$ *if* $\beta \geq \hat{\beta}_k(n)$ *and* $W_k(\mathcal{B}_{(i,j)}) \geq W_k(\mathcal{B}_G)$ *if* $\beta \leq \hat{\beta}_k(n)$.

We mention first that the market price under the coalition structure $\mathcal{B}_{(i,j)}$, i.e. $p(\mathcal{B}_{(i,j)}) = \beta/5$, is lower than that under the grand coalition where it is equal to the marginal cost of pollution, i.e. $p(\mathcal{B}_G) = \beta$. This leads to an increase in the gross surplus of each country in proportion to its population size.[20]

Now, let evaluate the difference in the value of external trade between the two coalition structures $\mathcal{B}_{(i,j)}$ and $\mathcal{B}_G$ for each country, starting with country k. Again, when countries i and j form a coalition, country k sets a higher subsidy rate than the two coalition members, i.e. $t_k(\mathcal{B}_{(i,j)}) < t_{ij}(\mathcal{B}_{(i,j)})$ for any $n_k > 4/7$, as one can infer from (21). Now, if country k joins the grand coalition and sets the same subsidy (or tax) rate than its partners, it becomes less competitive and then may suffer from increased import costs. We indeed have

$EX_k(\mathcal{B}_G) - EX_k(\mathcal{B}_{(i,j)}) = -(2\beta/75)[25\alpha(1-3n)-2\beta(14-45n)]$, which is negative for any $\beta \leq \bar{\beta}(n)$ with $\bar{\beta}(n) = (25\alpha/2)(1-3n)/(14-45n)$. If the environmental damage is even lower than $\bar{\beta}(n)$, i.e. $\beta \leq \hat{\beta}_k(n) < \bar{\beta}(n)$, then the increase in gross surplus following the accession to the grand coalition is not sufficient to compensate the increased import costs and, hence, country k prefers to be an outsider under the coalition structure $\mathcal{B}_{(i,j)}$ than to join the grand coalition (as stated in (ii) of Lemma 3). As β increases it becomes more profitable for country k to join the grand coalition. Indeed, the greater β the lower are consumed quantities under $\mathcal{B}_G$ compared to $\mathcal{B}_{(i,j)}$, which alleviates the increased import costs and further contributes to the increase in gross surplus. Hence, when the damage parameter is sufficiently large (i.e. $\beta \geq \hat{\beta}_k(n)$), preferences of country k are reversed and it prefers to join the grand coalition than to be an outsider (as stated in (ii) of Lemma 3). If β further increases and becomes larger than $\bar{\beta}(n)$, country k experiences both a large increase in gross surplus and a decrease in import costs by acceding to the grand coalition.

We now consider the preference ordering between $\mathcal{B}_{(i,j)}$ and $\mathcal{B}_G$ for country i or j. The difference in the value of external trade between $\mathcal{B}_{(i,j)}$ and $\mathcal{B}_G$ for country i, or j, is $EX_i(\mathcal{B}_G) - EX_i(\mathcal{B}_{(i,j)}) = (\beta/75)[25\alpha(1-3n)-2\beta(14-45n)]$, which is negative for any $\beta \geq \bar{\beta}(n)$. The argument is symmetric to that for country k. When the environmental damage is relatively large, the decrease in produced and consumed quantities due to the formation of the grand coalition is sufficiently large for countries i and j to register a decrease in export revenues even though country k can no longer set a higher subsidy rate than countries i and j. If the pollution externality is even larger than $\bar{\beta}(n)$, i.e. $\beta \geq \hat{\beta}_{ij}(n) > \bar{\beta}(n)$, the decrease in export revenues cannot be compensated by the increase in gross surplus, and then countries i and j prefer the coalition structure $\mathcal{B}_{(i,j)}$ to the grand coalition (as stated in (i) of Lemma 3). In fact, one can observe that $\hat{\beta}_{ij}(n)$ is increasing in n and that it is equal to α in $n = 1/13$. Since $\beta \leq \alpha$, $\beta \geq \hat{\beta}_{ij}(n)$ can hold only if $n \leq 1/13$ – as stated in (i) of Lemma 3 – so that the formation of the grand coalition has a limited impact on the gross consumer surplus of country i (or j), due to its small size.

Now, when the pollution externality decreases below $\beta \leq \hat{\beta}_{ij}(n)$, then the negative impact on export revenues due to the formation of the grand coalition is small enough to be compensated by the increase in gross surplus. Therefore, for $\beta \leq \hat{\beta}_{ij}(n)$, countries i and j prefer $\mathcal{B}_G$ to $\mathcal{B}_{(i,j)}$, as stated in (i) of Lemma 3. In fact, if β is even lower than $\hat{\beta}_{ij}(n)$, i.e. $\beta \leq \bar{\beta}(n) < \hat{\beta}_{ij}(n)$, the formation of the grand coalition leads to an increase in both export revenues and gross surplus for countries i and j.

We can now state the following Proposition.

Proposition 2: *Suppose* $n_i = n_j = n \leq 3/14$ *implying* $n_k = 1 - 2n \geq 4/7$. *The unique equilibrium coalition structure is:* (i) $\mathcal{B}_{(i,j)}$ *if* $\beta \leq \hat{\beta}_k(n)$ *or if* $\beta \geq \hat{\beta}_{ij}(n)$; (ii) $\mathcal{B}_G$ *if* $\hat{\beta}_k(n) \leq \beta \leq \hat{\beta}_{ij}(n)$.

We now turn to the interpretation of Propositions 1 and 2 together.

6.4   Interpretation of the results

To jointly interpret Propositions 1 and 2, we consider – with the help of the figure just below – increasing values of the parameter $\beta \in [0, \alpha]$, reflecting the extent of the pollution externality. The threshold values $\hat{\beta}(n)$ or $\hat{\beta}(1-2n)$ are given just above Lemma 1 (with n_i replaced by n or by $1-2n$), while $\hat{\beta}_{ij}(n)$ and $\hat{\beta}_k(n)$ are given just above Lemma 3. Equilibrium coalition structures depend on whether $n \geq 3/14$ so that countries i and j always prefer $\mathcal{B}_S$ to $\mathcal{B}_{(i,j)}$ or $n \leq 3/14$ so that countries i and j (as well as country k) always prefer $\mathcal{B}_{(i,j)}$ to $\mathcal{B}_S$.

Suppose first that the environmental damage due to production of X is 'very' low. In this case, the larger country (i.e. country k) sets a higher subsidy rate than countries i and j under the singleton coalition B_S. Therefore, the formation of a grand coalition B_G with a common subsidy (or tax) rate, results in a loss (respectively, gain) of competitiveness for country k (respectively, country i or j). Moreover, since the damage parameter is relatively low, the environmental policy under B_G slightly decreases produced and consumed quantities compared to B_S. In turn, for the larger country k, the significant increase in import costs cannot compensate the moderate gain in gross consumer surplus. Countries i and j would like to form the grand coalition than to remain singletons because B_G increases both their gross surplus and their export revenues, but country k is not available as a partner when β is low.

As the damage parameter increases, the grand coalition sets a more stringent (environmental) policy, and so produced and consumed quantities decrease more significantly. For the larger country, the formation of the grand coalition is then less costly in terms of imports costs, while the gain in gross surplus becomes more important. There is thus a threshold value of β, i.e. $\hat{\beta}(1-2n)$, above which the larger country becomes available as a partner in the grand coalition, provided countries i and j have no interest in forming a subcoalition (i.e. $n \geq 3/14$).

If, however, the coalition structure $B_{(i,j)}$ is welfare-improving for countries i and j, then country k may prefer to remain a singleton even though $\beta \geq \hat{\beta}(1-2n)$. The reason is that the coalition structure $B_{(i,j)}$ gives rise to a strategic advantage for country k. Indeed, recall that under the coalition structure $B_{(i,j)}$, the two coalition members set a lower subsidy rate than under B_S so as to internalize the pollution externality (on joint consumer surplus) and the market externality between the domestic firms. In turn, the larger country undercuts the coalition by setting a higher subsidy rate in order to

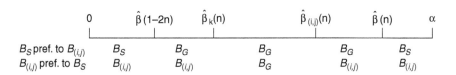

Figure 2.1 Equilibrium coalition structures

take advantage of the increased costs incurred by the firms of the coalition, thus making its own firm more competitive in the integrated market. As a result, for the larger country to resign its competitive advantage and to join the grand coalition, it requires greater benefits from internalizing the pollution externality and hence a higher β, i.e. $\beta \geq \hat{\beta}_k(n) > \hat{\beta}(1-2n)$.

Now let consider again that countries i and j do not have interest in forming a subcoalition. In this case, as just mentioned above, country k agrees to form the grand coalition for any $\beta \geq \hat{\beta}(1-2n)$. Countries i and j also agree to join the grand coalition except if the damage parameter is 'very' large. Indeed, recall that in that case, smaller countries set higher subsidy rates than the larger country under the singleton coalition B_S. It follows that the formation of the grand coalition implies, for those countries, a decrease in competitiveness and in export revenues, especially since produced and consumed quantities sharply decrease as a result of a large value of β. As the damage parameter decreases, this negative impact on the external trade of countries i and j becomes less important compared to the gain gross surplus. There is thus a threshold value of β, i.e. $\hat{\beta}(n)$, below which countries i and j agree to form the grand coalition.

Now, let consider that countries i and j prefer the coalition structure $B_{(i,j)}$ to the singleton coalition B_S (i.e. $n \leq 3/14$). In this case – for countries i and j to join country k in the grand coalition – the environmental pollution externality must be even lower than $\hat{\beta}(n)$, i.e. $\beta \leq \hat{\beta}_{ij}(n) < \hat{\beta}(n)$. In other words, when $\beta > \hat{\beta}_{ij}(n)$, countries i and j are better off by letting country k stay outside the coalition and free-ride on them. The explanation is the following. First, recall that $\beta > \hat{\beta}_{ij}(n)$ necessarily implies that $n < 1/13$. So, if the population size of the subcoalition is relatively small, B_G has a limited positive impact on the gross consumer surplus of each coalition member and, if the environmental damage is relatively high, B_G has a strong impact on their external trade. Indeed, the greater β the lower are produced and consumed quantities under B_G compared to $B_{(i,j)}$.

Obviously, under B_G, the common subsidy (or tax) rate implies that all firms have equal market shares, whereas letting country k be an outsider (under $B_{(i,j)}$) implies a competitive framework. Furthermore, we have seen that the formation of the subcoalition gives rise to a strategic response of the outsider that increases its own subsidy rate to increase domestic production. However, for the outsider, increasing production also reduces the gross surplus especially when both β and population size are large. Hence, for high values of β and n_k, country k is not willing to substantially increase its subsidy rate so that it captures a moderate competitive advantage over the two coalition members. As a result, in this case, countries i and j sign up together without country k. The resulting coalition structure $B_{(i,j)}$, when $\beta > \hat{\beta}_{ij}(n)$, avoids the strong decrease in export markets that would arise with the grand coalition B_G, while the losses in market shares (for countries i and j) remain moderate since the subsidy policy of country k is slightly aggressive due to its large size.

In conclusion, when the coalition structure $B_{(i,j)}$ is a profitable alternative for countries i and j to the singleton coalition B_S, the parameter reflecting the pollution externality must lie within a restricted range (i.e. $[\hat{\beta}_k(n), \hat{\beta}_{ij}(n)]$) for the grand coalition B_G to be the (unique) equilibrium coalition structure.

7   Conclusion

Our analysis suggests that a multi-step process is less likely to give rise to a global international environmental agreement than a one-step process. Indeed, once a first group of countries sign an IEA, it modifies the incentives of all countries to sign a global agreement and, actually, it makes them more demanding than if a preliminary restricted agreement was not signed. In addition, the further enlargement of the initial coalition may be blocked, not only by the outsider(s), but also by the insiders depending on the size of the pollution externality and on the country-size asymmetry. Overall, the grand coalition is less likely to emerge when subcoalitions are profitable which implies – in the context of our model – a strong country-size asymmetry. To deal with this asymmetry problem, this suggests that the European Union should speak with one voice with the other big producers-polluters (such as the USA, China or India) to push forward a (real) global environmental agreement.

Let us again make clear that the simplicity of the framework analysed in this chapter is attractive but that a number of criticisms could be formulated. In particular, a limitation of our analysis is that the marginal environmental damage caused by production was assumed to be the same in each country. This assumption seems reasonable to analyse strategic interactions amongst advanced industrial countries. But it is less convincing to analyse strategic interactions between, for example, countries of the EU and emerging and developing countries. More importantly, we assumed – from empirical evidence – that side payments are not used by governments. The possibility to make (or receive) transfers would certainly modify the incentives to sign an IEA, but not necessarily in the expected direction.[21] Clearly, the chapter leaves questions that need to be addressed in future research.

8   Appendix

8.1   Proof of Lemma 1

We have $W_i(B_S) \geq W_i(B_G)$ whenever $\Delta_i(n_i, \alpha, \beta) \equiv 27\alpha(1 - 3n_i) - 2\beta(15 - 61n_i) \leq 0$. Suppose first that $(15 - 61n_i) \geq 0$ or $n_i \leq 15/61 < 1/3$. Then $\Delta_i(n_i, \alpha, \beta) \leq 0$ for any $\beta \geq \hat{\beta}(n_i) \equiv (27\alpha/2)(1 - 3n_i)/(15 - 61n_i)$. $\hat{\beta}(n_i)$ is increasing in n_i and is equal to α in $n_i = 3/41$. Yet, one must have $\beta \leq \alpha$. Therefore, when $n_i \leq 15/61$, $\beta \geq \hat{\beta}(n_i)$ can be satisfied only if $n_i \leq 3/41 < 15/61$. Suppose now that $(15 - 61n_i) \leq 0$ or $n_i \geq 15/61$. In this case, $\Delta_i(n_i, \alpha, \beta) \leq 0$ for any $\beta \leq \hat{\beta}(n_i)$. $\hat{\beta}(n_i)$ is negative for any $n_i \in [15/61, 1/3]$ and becomes positive from $n_i = 1/3$. Since $\beta \geq 0$, $\beta \leq \hat{\beta}(n_i)$ for $n_i \geq 15/61$ can be satisfied only if $n_i \geq 1/3 > 15/61$. Corollary 1 directly follows from this.

8.2   Proof of Lemma 3

(i) $W_i(\mathcal{B}_{(i,j)}) \geq W_i(\mathcal{B}_G)$ whenever $25\alpha(1-3n) - 2\beta(14-57n) \leq 0$. One has $n \leq 3/14 < 14/57$. Hence $14-57n > 0$ and $W_i(\mathcal{B}_{(i,j)}) \geq W_i(\mathcal{B}_G)$ for any $\beta \geq \beta_{ij}(n) \equiv (25\alpha/2)(1-3n)/(14-57n)$. $\beta_{ij}(n)$ is increasing in n and is equal to α in $n = 1/13$. Yet, one must have $\beta \leq \alpha$. Therefore, $\beta \geq \beta_{ij}(n)$ can be satisfied only if $n \leq 1/13$.

(ii) $W_k(\mathcal{B}_{(i,j)}) \geq W_k(\mathcal{B}_G)$ whenever $-25\alpha(1-3n) + 2\beta(20-57n) \leq 0$. One has $n \leq 3/14 < 20/57$. Hence $20-57n > 0$ and $W_k(\mathcal{B}_{(i,j)}) \geq W_k(\mathcal{B}_G)$ for any $\beta \leq \beta_k(n) \equiv (25\alpha/2)(1-3n)/(20-57n)$. One must also verify that $\beta_k(n) \geq 0$, which is indeed the case for any $n \leq 3/14$. This is because $\beta_k(n)$ is decreasing in n and is equal to $(125/218)\alpha > 0$ in $n = 3/14$, implying that $\beta_k(n)$ is positive for any $n \leq 3/14$.

8.3   Proof of Proposition 1

From (23), when $n_i + n_j > 3/7 \; \forall i, j = A, B, C$ and $i \neq j$, we must have at least one country – say country i – for which $W_i(\mathcal{B}_{(i,j)}) < W_i(\mathcal{B}_S)$. This implies that $\mathcal{B}_{(i,j)}$ cannot be an equilibrium coalition structure. Indeed, for $\mathcal{B}_{(i,j)}$ to be an equilibrium coalition structure, the strategy profile $s^* = (S_i^*, S_j^*, S_k^*)$ with $S_i^* = S_j^* = \{i, j\}$ must be a CPNE. But when $W_i(\mathcal{B}_{(i,j)}) < W_i(\mathcal{B}_S)$, country i has a profitable deviation to $S_i = \{i\}$, giving rise to the singleton coalition $\mathcal{B}_S$. Therefore, there are only two coalition structures that are equilibrium candidates in the first stage of the game: $\mathcal{B}_G$ and $\mathcal{B}_S$.

For the grand coalition to be an equilibrium structure, it must be the case that $\hat{s} = (\hat{S}_i, \hat{S}_j, \hat{S}_k)$ with $\hat{S}_i = \hat{S}_j = \hat{S}_k = \{i, j, k\}$ is a CPNE. Therefore, if there is one country – say country i – for which $n_i \leq 3/41$ and $\beta \geq \hat{\beta}(n_i)$ or $n_i \geq 1/3$ and $\beta \leq \hat{\beta}(n_i)$, then this country prefers (from Lemma 1) to remain a singleton than to join the grand coalition. This country would then deviate from the strategy profile $\hat{s}$ to $S_i = \{i\}$, thus giving rise to $\Psi(S_i, \hat{S}_j, \hat{S}_k) = \mathcal{B}_S$. Such a deviation is immune to further profitable joint deviation – here by countries j and k – because $n_j + n_k > 3/7$ which implies that country j (or k) prefers to be a singleton than to form a two-country coalition. Finally, unilateral deviation by country j or country k would have no effect on the resultant coalition structure $\mathcal{B}_S$. Therefore, $\mathcal{B}_S$ is the unique equilibrium coalition structure. In all other parameter configurations – i.e. $n_i \in [3/41, 1/3]$, or $n_i \leq 3/41$ and $\beta \leq \hat{\beta}(n_i)$ or $n_i \geq 1/3$ and $\beta \geq \hat{\beta}(n_i)$ – all countries prefer $\mathcal{B}_G$ to $\mathcal{B}_S$ and at least one country (i or j) is worse off under $\mathcal{B}_{(i,j)}$ than under $\mathcal{B}_S$. Therefore, $\hat{s}$ being immune to any deviation – unilateral or multilateral – it is the unique CPNE, resulting in the formation of the grand coalition $\mathcal{B}_G$.

8.4   Proof of Proposition 2

Consider first that $\beta \leq \hat{\beta}(1-2n) < \hat{\beta}_k(n)$. Then Lemma 3 implies for country k that $W_k(\mathcal{B}_{(i,j)}) \geq W_k(\mathcal{B}_G)$, while it implies for countries i and j that

$W_i(\mathcal{B}_G) \geq W_i(\mathcal{B}_{(i,j)})$. In this case any strategy profile $s^* = (S_i^*, S_j^*, S_k^*)$ with $S_i^* = S_j^* = \{i,j\}$ is a CPNE and gives rise to the coalition structure $\mathcal{B}_{(i,j)}$ regardless of S_k^*. Countries i and j prefer the grand coalition $\mathcal{B}_G$ to the coalition structure $\mathcal{B}_{(i,j)}$, but – by Lemma 1 – country k prefers to remain a singleton than to join the grand coalition. Hence, $\hat{s} = (\hat{S}_i, \hat{S}_j, \hat{S}_k)$ with $\hat{S}_i = \hat{S}_j = \hat{S}_k = \{i,j,k\}$ – which is the unique strategy profile giving rise to $\mathcal{B}_G$ – is not a CPNE because country k has an incentive to deviate from $\hat{s}$ to $S_k = \{k\}$. Therefore, countries i and j do not have any incentive to deviate from s^* because any deviation – unilateral or multilateral from $S_i^* = S_j^* = \{i,j\}$ – would result in the singleton coalition which is dominated by $\mathcal{B}_{(i,j)}$ for countries i and j. Finally, a unilateral deviation by country k from s^* has no effect on the resultant coalition structure. Therefore, if $\beta \leq \hat{\beta}(1-2n)$, the unique equilibrium coalition structure is $\mathcal{B}_{(i,j)}$.

Consider now that $\hat{\beta}(1-2n) < \beta \leq \hat{\beta}_k(n)$. Then Lemma 3 implies for country k that $W_k(\mathcal{B}_{(i,j)}) \geq W_k(\mathcal{B}_G)$, while it implies for countries i and j that $W_i(\mathcal{B}_G) \geq W_i(\mathcal{B}_{(i,j)})$. The coalition structure $\mathcal{B}_S$ cannot be supported by a CPNE since countries i and j have a profitable joint deviation to $S_i^* = S_j^* = \{i,j\}$ giving rise to the coalition structure $\mathcal{B}_{(i,j)}$, irrespective of country k's choice. In fact, the coalition structure $\mathcal{B}_{(i,j)}$ can result from four strategy profiles: $s = (\{i,j\},\{i,j\},\{k\})$, $s = (\{i,j\},\{i,j\},\{i,k\})$, $s = (\{i,j\},\{i,j\},\{j,k\})$ or $s = (\{i,j\},\{i,j\},\{i,j,k\})$. The first three strategy profiles constitute a CPNE. However, the strategy profile $s = (\{i,j\},\{i,j\},\{i,j,k\})$ is not a CPNE because countries i and j have a joint profitable deviation to $S_i = S_j = \{i,j,k\}$ so as to perform the grand coalition that gives them a higher welfare than $\mathcal{B}_{(i,j)}$. But the resulting strategy profile $\hat{s} = (\{i,j,k\},\{i,j,k\},\{i,j,k\})$ is not a CPNE because country k would have a profitable deviation to any other strategy than $S_k = \{i,j,k\}$ so as to induce *ultimately* the coalition structure $\mathcal{B}_{(i,j)}$, which is most preferred by country k. Indeed, a unilateral deviation from $\hat{s}$ by country k would lead to the singleton coalition $\mathcal{B}_S$, which in turn would lead to a further joint deviation by countries i and j to $S_i^* = S_j^* = \{i,j\}$. This is because $S_i^* = S_j^* = \{i,j\}$ leads to the coalition structure $\mathcal{B}_{(i,j)}$ that is preferred by both countries i and j to the singleton coalition $\mathcal{B}_S$. To summarize, for any $\beta \leq \hat{\beta}_k(n)$, the unique equilibrium coalition structure is $\mathcal{B}_{(i,j)}$.

This is also the case when $\beta \geq \hat{\beta}_{ij}(n)$. Indeed, in this case, country k prefers the coalition structure $\mathcal{B}_G$ to $\mathcal{B}_{(i,j)}$ but countries i and j prefer the coalition structure $\mathcal{B}_{(i,j)}$ to $\mathcal{B}_G$ (Lemma 3) so that they will not accept country k as a coalition partner. Since countries i and j also prefer $\mathcal{B}_{(i,j)}$ to the singleton coalition – by Lemma 2 – the unique coalition structure supported by a CPNE is again $\mathcal{B}_{(i,j)}$. To summarize, $\mathcal{B}_{(i,j)}$ is the unique equilibrium coalition structure for any $\beta \notin [\hat{\beta}_k(n), \hat{\beta}_{ij}(n)]$, as stated in (i) of Proposition 2.

If $\hat{\beta}_k(n) \leq \beta \leq \hat{\beta}_{ij}(n)$, then all three countries prefer the grand coalition structure $\mathcal{B}_G$ to $\mathcal{B}_{(i,j)}$ (Lemma 3) and prefer the coalition structure $\mathcal{B}_{(i,j)}$ to $\mathcal{B}_S$ (Lemma 2). In other words, there is unanimity to form the grand coalition $\mathcal{B}_G$ and hence $\hat{s} = (\hat{S}_i, \hat{S}_j, \hat{S}_k)$ is the unique CPNE which then leads to $\mathcal{B}_G$, as stated in (ii) of Proposition 2.

Acknowledgements

We thank an anonymous referee for helpful comments, seminar participants at University of Savoie Mont-Blanc, University of Montpellier, Toulouse School of Economics, and conference participants at the Econometric Society European Meeting in Malaga and at the World Congress of Environmental and Resource Economics in Istanbul (WCERE 2014).

Notes

1 See   www.birdlife.org/community/2012/12/climate-change-talks-end-with-doha-climate-gateway/.
2 Note though that in conjunction with the Kyoto Protocol, the European Union Emission Trading Scheme (or EU ETS), which is the largest multi-national green-house gas emissions system, was launched in January 2005. Nevertheless, this system covers only half of the European CO_2 emissions.
3 For surveys of this large literature, see Barrett (2007) or Finus (2008).
4 Still using reduced-form specifications, more recent analyses have applied the 'farsightedness concept' to the stability of IEAs (see, e.g., de Zeeuw 2008; Ray and Vohra 2014; and Benchekroun and Ray Chaudhuri 2015, for a survey of the recent literature on coalition formation games). We must insist that the contribution of our analysis is rather that the value function of each of the three countries (for every coalition structure) is derived from an underlying trade framework with imperfect competition and pollution externalities.
5 Monopoly can emerge as an equilibrium market structure if firm-specific fixed costs are sufficiently high to make entry for a second firm unprofitable in each market (see, Horstmann and Markusen 1992).
6 We had initially worked with a quadratic function for the environmental damage, but it did not change the qualitative results. Our restriction to a linear environmental damage function only makes the analysis more readable.
7 We also assume, throughout the analysis, that profits are always strictly positive in all three countries, i.e. profit margin implied by the choice of the (exogenous) parameters α and β is sufficiently large to cover the fixed costs F.
8 This stage of the game corresponds to a standard Cournot oligopoly model with linear demand functions and, hence, second-order conditions are satisfied.
9 Equivalently, each country's welfare can be written as the difference between gross consumer surplus CS_i and total costs denoted TC_i, i.e. $W_i = CS_i - TC_i$. These costs are the sum of production costs (in terms of labour), i.e. $mX^i + F = F$ since $m = 0$, plus the costs of imports, i.e. $p(x)(n_i x - X^i)$.
10 Given the equilibrium outcome in the third stage of the game, the aggregate welfare function is concave in t. We indeed have $\partial^2 W / \partial t^2 = -9/16$.
11 The marginal variation of the gross consumer surplus is $\alpha - x - \beta$ and is positive as long as $x < \alpha - \beta$. Without environmental regulation, the aggregate supply – which equals x – is $3\alpha/4$ (see (8)). Hence, the common tax rate is negative as long as $3\alpha/4 < \alpha - \beta$ or $4\beta - \alpha < 0$.
12 Each country's welfare function induced by the equilibrium outcome in the third stage of the game is concave in the domestic tax rate. We indeed have $\partial^2 W_i / \partial t_i^2 = -(1/16)(6 - n_i) < 0$. Therefore, there does exist a (pure-strategy subgame-perfect) Nash equilibrium in tax rates under the singleton coalition structure.
13 $t_i(\mathcal{B}_S) > 0$ requires that $\beta(10n_i - 2) - 9\alpha n_i > 0$, which could be satisfied for $n_i > 0.2$. However, we have that $\beta < \alpha$. Therefore, if the previous inequality is satisfied, we must also have $\alpha(10n_i - 2) - 9\alpha n_i > 0$. This last inequality reduces to $\alpha(n_i - 2) > 0$,

which cannot be satisfied. It follows that $t_i(\mathcal{B}_S)$ is always negative. Moreover, the use of a quadratic function for the environmental damage does not change the sign of tax rates: they are still negative.

14 This effect is similar to the terms-of-trade effect identified by (among others) Krutilla (1991).

15 The aggregate welfare of the subcoalition, induced by the Cournot Nash equilibrium, is concave in t_{ij} since $\partial^2 (W_i + W_j)/\partial t_{ij}^2 = -(1/4)[4 - (n_i + n_j)] < 0$. This is also the case for the welfare function of country k, since $\partial^2 W_k/\partial t_k^2 = (-1/16)(6 - n_k)$. Therefore, there does exist a (pure-strategy subgame-perfect) Nash equilibrium in tax rates under the coalition structure $\mathcal{B}_{(i,j)}$.

16 All the proofs are in the Appendix.

17 Indeed, the difference in the gross consumer surplus between $\mathcal{B}_G$ and $\mathcal{B}_S$ for country i is given by $CS_i(\mathcal{B}_G) - CS_i(\mathcal{B}_S) = (32\beta^2/81)n_i$.

18 We indeed have $EX_i(\mathcal{B}_G) - EX_i(\mathcal{B}_S) = (\beta/27)(9\alpha - 10\beta)(1 - 3n_i)$, which is positive when $\beta < (9/10)\alpha$ and $n_i \leq 1/3$.

19 Recall that under $\mathcal{B}_S$ a small country undercuts its competitors when $\beta > (9/10)\alpha$.

20 We indeed have $CS_i(\mathcal{B}_G) - CS_i(\mathcal{B}_{(i,j)}) = (8\beta^2/25)n$ for country i (or j) while for country k, n must be replaced by $(1 - 2n)$.

21 For example, Hoel and Schneider (1997) in a reduced-form model show that side payments may substantially reduce the incentives to join an IEA.

References

Bárcena-Ruiz, J.C. and Campo, M.L. (2012), 'Partial Cross-Ownership and Strategic Environmental Policy', *Resource and Energy Economics* 34 (2): 198–210.

Barrett, S. (1994a), 'Strategic Environmental Policy and International Trade', *Journal of Public Economics* 54 (3): 325–338.

Barrett, S. (1994b), 'Self-enforcing International Environmental Agreements', *Oxford Economic Papers* 46: 878–894.

Barrett, S. (2007), *Why Cooperate? The Incentive to Supply Global Public Goods*, Oxford: Oxford University Press.

Benchekroun, H. and Ray Chaudhuri, A. (2015), 'Cleaner Technologies and the Stability of International Environmental Agreements', *Journal of Public Economic Theory* 17 (6): 887–915.

Bernheim, B.D., Peleg B. and Whinston, M.D. (1987), 'Coalition-Proof Nash Equilibria I. Concepts', *Journal of Economic Theory* 42 (1): 1–12.

Bloch, F. (1996), 'Sequential Formation of Coalitions in Games with Externalities and Fixed Payoff Division', *Games and Economic Behavior* 14 (1): 90–123.

Brander, J.A. (1995), 'Strategic Trade Policy', in G. Grossman and K. Rogoff (eds), *Handbook of International Economics* vol. III, Amsterdam: North-Holland, 1395–1455.

Brander, J.A. and Spencer, B.J. (1985), 'Export Subsidies and International Market Share Rivalry', *Journal of International Economics* 18 (1–2): 83–100.

Carraro, C. and Marchiori, C. (2003), 'Stable Coalitions', in C. Carraro (ed.), *The Endogenous Formation of Economic Coalitions*, Cheltenham: E. Elgar.

Carraro, C. and Siniscalco, D. (1993), 'Strategies for the International Protection of the Environment', *Journal of Public Economics* 52 (3): 309–328.

Conrad, K. (1993), 'Taxes and Subsidies for Pollution-Intensive Industries as Trade Policy', *Journal of Environmental Economics and Management* 25 (2): 121–135.

D'Aspremont, C., Jacquemin, J., Gabszewicz, J. and Weymark, J. (1983), 'On the Stability of Collusive Price Leadership', *Canadian Journal of Economics* 16 (1): 17–25.

Duval, Y. and Hamilton, S. (2002), 'Strategic Environmental Policy and International Trade in Asymmetric Oligopoly Markets', *International Tax and Public Finance* 9 (3): 259–271.

Eichner, T. and Pethig, R. (2013), 'Self-Enforcing Environmental Agreements and International Trade', *Journal of Public Economics* 102: 37–50.

Eichner, T. and Pethig, R. (2014), 'Self-Enforcing Agreements and Capital Mobility', *Regional Science and Urban Economics* 48: 120–132.

Eyckmans, J. and Finus M. (2006), 'Coalition Formation in a Global Warming Game: How the Design of Protocols Affects the Success of Environmental Treaty-making', *Natural Resource Modeling* 19 (3): 323–358.

Finus, M. (2008), 'Game Theoretic Research on the Design of International Environmental Agreements: Insights, Critical Remarks and Future Challenges', *International Review of Environmental and Resource Economics* 2: 1–39.

Finus, M. and Rundshagen, B. (1998), 'Toward a Positive Theory of Coalition Formation and Instrumental Choice in Global Pollution Control', *Public Choice* 96 (1): 145–186.

Hoel, M. (1992), 'International Environmental Conventions: The Case of Uniform Reductions of Emissions', *Environmental and Resource Economics* 2 (2): 141–159.

Hoel, M. and Schneider, K. (1997), 'Incentives to Participate in an International Environmental Agreement', *Environmental and Resource Economics* 9 (2): 153–170.

Horstmann, I.J. and Markusen, J.R. (1992), 'Endogenous Market Structures in International Trade (Natura Facit Saltum)', *Journal of International Economics* 32 (1–2): 109–129.

Kennedy, P. (1994), 'Equilibrium Pollution Taxes in Open Economies with Imperfect Competition', *Journal of Environmental Economics and Management* 27 (1): 49–63.

Krutilla, K. (1991), 'Environmental Regulation in an Open Economy', *Journal of Environmental Economics and Management* 20 (2): 127–142.

Lai, Y-B. and Hu, C-H. (2008), 'Trade Agreements, Domestic Environmental Regulation, and Transboundary Pollution', *Resource and Energy Economics* 30 (2): 209–228.

McGinty, M. (2007), 'International Environmental Agreements among Asymmetric Nations', *Oxford University Press* 52 (1): 45–62.

Ray, D. and Vohra, R. (2014), 'Coalition Formation', in H.P. Young and S. Zamir (eds), *Handbook of Game Theory with Economic Applications* Vol IV, Amsterdam: North-Holland, 239–326.

Tanguay, G.A. (2001), 'Strategic Environmental Policies under International Duopolistic Competition', *International Tax and Public Finance* 8 (5): 793–811.

Weikard, H.P. (2009), 'Cartel Stability under Optimal Sharing Rule', *The Manchester School* 77 (5): 575–593.

Yi, S-S. (1996), 'Endogenous Formation of Customs Unions under Imperfect Competition: Open Regionalism is Good', *Journal of International Economics* 41 (1–2): 153–177.

de Zeeuw, A.J. (2008), 'Dynamic Effects on the Stability of International Environmental Agreements', *Journal of Environmental Economics and Management, Elsevier* 55 (2): 163–174.

3 The effects of inequality aversion on the formation of climate coalition

Theory and experimental evidence

Yu-Hsuan Lin

1 Introduction

It is widely recognized that the ecosystem on earth has changed dramatically over the last few decades due to rapid economic and industrial development. In particular, cross-boundary environmental issues (such as climate change) are usually so complex and so widespread that they require collaboration between states. In this respect, international environmental agreements (IEAs) are constructed to regulate and manage the current situation. According to previous studies (Mitchell 2003), there are over 700 multilateral agreements and over 1,000 bilateral agreements. IEAs have become the most important mechanism for solving the international environmental problems.

Since Barrett's study in 1994 (Barrett 1994), a large number of studies have explored the structures of and variations in IEAs (such as Barrett 2001; Bratberg *et al.* 2005; Eyckmans and Finus 2006 and Bahn *et al.* 2009). In light of the Nash prediction, as long as coalitions are stabilized both internally and externally, stable coalition combinations exist. However, predicted coalitions without any policy mechanism are usually small. Recent experimental studies (Kosfeld *et al.* 2009; Burger and Kolstad 2010) have pointed out that actual coalition formations are usually larger than Nash predictions.

A growing number of experimental studies have proposed that this challenge is due to the fundamental assumption of rational self-interest (Willinger and Ziegelmeyer 2001). In light of the assumption of self-interest, rational agents would choose their own highest payoff. This assumption has been widely employed in the majority of studies of IEAs (e.g. Breton *et al.* 2010). Such assumption is not enough to explain individual decision makers' behaviours in an interactive game. Several (Charness and Rabin 2002; Kosfeld *et al.* 2009; Dannenberg *et al.* 2012) have suggested that the role of social preferences (also known as other-regarding preferences) should be taken into account in order to address this limitation.

In regards to social preferences in the provision of public goods, Kosfeld *et al.* (2009) employed the inequality-averse preference (proposed by Fehr and Schmidt 1999) and confirmed with laboratory-based evidence that inequality-averse behaviour existed. They claimed that the coalition size could be larger than a Nash equilibrium outcome, and even the full cooperation is a possible outcome. On the other hand, Kolstad (2014) adopted Charness and Rabin's (2002) social preference theory, which suggested that agents primarily care about three things: private payoff, fairness in payoffs, and overall efficiency. In contrast to Kosfeld *et al.* (2009), Kolstad (2014) argued that such social preference reduced the equilibrium size of a coalition of agents formed to provide the public good.

Although the influence of social preferences on coalition formation might be explained by the literature mentioned earlier (e.g. Kosfeld *et al.* 2009; McEvoy *et al.* 2014), the influence on individual incentives for participating in a coalition has not yet been properly explored. The design with uniform pay-offs limited the prediction of individuals' membership statuses. For example, multiple stable coalition combinations might have existed when an identical payoff table was provided, so individual decisions were difficult to predict. In this study, we attempted to address this gap by developing a particular treat-ment with a unique equilibrium coalition. Each agent had a clear dominant strategy for whether or not to participate in a coalition.

This design offered two primary strengths. First, we endeavoured to investigate incentives for participating in IEAs in this study. If there was more than one stable coalition, the individual decisions were difficult to predict. However, if we had a coalition with a unique equilibrium, it would provide a suitable environment to observe individual decisions when every player had a best strategy to choose. Second, the hypothesis of this study assumed that the preference for inequality aversion would influence the equilibrium differently from the egoistic preference. This indicates that a coalition would be formed differently when individuals care about other agents' payoffs. This design provides detailed observations on the individual decision-making process.

In order to investigate individual incentives, we answered the following questions in this study: Does the concern about payoffs of others change the subjects' decisions? How do individuals' social preferences affect their own incentives for participating in a public good game?

In order to answer these questions, the experiment was designed in two parts. The first part aimed to identify individual inequality-averse attitudes by taking either a certain fair payoff or an all-or-nothing payoff. The second part was a public good game. The subjects were given particular payoff tables and decided whether or not to join the coalition.

Our theoretical findings predicted that, when inequality aversion was taken into account, the stability of the coalition formation depended on the indi-vidual inequality-averse attitudes. When agents had strong inequality-averse attitudes, they would not only pursue their own payoffs, but also those of others. However, this hypothesis was not supported as a means to predict individual decisions using the experimental results. When subjects had eco-nomic incentives to free ride, inequality-averse individuals were more likely to free ride rather than work toward a fair outcome.

The outline of the chapter is as follows. In the next section, a heterogeneous model with the concern of inequality aversion was built. Section 3 introduces two experiments that were based on the theory built in Section 2. Then, Section 4 reports the experimental results and implications. The final section concludes.

2 The model

Suppose N countries with different marginal benefits of the total abatement considered participation in a climate coalition, and then n countries joined while the rest did not.[1] According to their marginal benefits, which were in the range of 0 to 1,[2] the signatories were ranked from high to low as $\gamma_1 > \ldots > \gamma_n$ and the non-signatories were ranked from high to low as $\gamma_{n+1} > \ldots > \gamma_N$. The unit cost of abatement for each country was standardized to be 1.

Each country decided whether to join an IEA or not and their payoffs depended on their membership status. In a profitable n-member coalition, a non-signatory j maximized its payoff π_j by choosing its abatement level (x_j) as $\max_{x_j} \pi_j = (-x_j) + \gamma_j X \ \forall j = n+1, \ldots, N$, where x_j is j's abatement level and its marginal benefit rate is γ_j. Since this study focused on individual participation, the level of abatement (x_j) was normalized in the range between 0 (implies fully polluted) and 1 (implies fully abated). X was the total abatement, which included n signatories' aggregate reduction ($\sum_{i=1}^{n} x_s$)[3] and ($N - n$) non-signatories' aggregate reduction ($\sum_{j=n+1}^{N} x_j$). The optimal abatement level for a non-signatory j was no abatement ($x_j = 0$). Therefore, j's payoff was as follows:

$$\pi_j = \gamma_j X. \tag{3.1}$$

On the other hand, all of the signatories acted as one in order to maximize the coalition payoff. The n-member coalition payoff (Π_s) was the *pre-redistribution* payoff of all of the members ($\pi_i, \forall i = 1, \ldots, n$). Each signatory shared the coalition payoff equally, as the common abatement (x_s). The coalition payoff was optimized with respect to x_s as follows:

$$\max_{x_s} \Pi_s = \sum_{i=1}^{n} \pi_s$$

$$= \sum_{i=1}^{n} \left[(-x_s) + \gamma_i X \right]. \tag{3.2}$$

As mentioned earlier, a profitable n-member coalition requires that the aggregate marginal benefit of signatories be greater than 1 ($\sum_{i=1}^{n} \gamma_i > 1$). From (3.2), the optimal abatement for a signatory i was full abatement ($x_s = 1$).

Regarding the distribution of the coalition payoff, Burger and Kolstad (2010) noted that the majority-voting rule, unanimity and joint payoff maximization all led to an equivalent outcome under the assumption of homogeneous agents. However, with heterogeneous agents, they suggested that majority-voting reflected the interests of the median voter and might not reach a joint payoff maximum. Although wealth transfer among members of a coalition is often suggested as being politically infeasible, Kolstad (2014) stated that 'sharing the wealth' within the coalition might be appropriate. In addition, in order to achieve the goal of maximizing a pre-distributed coalition payoff, each signatory should share the same responsibility at international conventions. It was reasonable to assume that the coalition payoff was equally shared by all of the signatories. Any signatory i in an n-member coalition had a *post*-redistribution payoff as follows:[4]

$$\pi_s = \frac{1}{n}\Pi_s = (-1) + \sum_{i=1}^{n} \gamma_i \tag{3.3}$$

Turning to the membership game, countries were asked to simultaneously decide whether to participate in a coalition or not. Following D'Aspremont *et al.* (1983), when countries were self-interested, a stable coalition existed when the internal and the external constraints were satisfied as follows:

$$\pi_i^n(n^*) > \pi_j^n(n^*-1), \tag{3.4}$$

$$\pi_j^N(n^*) > \pi_i^N(n^*+1). \tag{3.5}$$

The internal constraint (3.4) denoted that a signatory did not have an incentive to leave the n^*-member coalition and n^* was the stable number to maintain the coalition. If it was satisfied, then everyone would like to participate in the coalition. The external constraint (3.5) indicated that a non-signatory did not have any incentives to participate in a coalition as the (n^*+1) th member. If it was satisfied, all of the non-signatories did not want to participate.

As (3.4) and (3.5) were satisfied, there might exist multiple stable coalitions. Taking examples of experimental studies, such as Kosfeld *et al.* (2009) and Burger and Kolstad (2010), there existed several stable coalition combinations. These studies failed to foresee individual decisions in the membership game. Individuals might make different decisions over time in their experimental settings. In this study, to have better prediction on individual decisions with social preferences, we focused on the cases of unique coalition. To do so, both internal and external constraints and the following unique equilibrium condition should be satisfied:

$$\gamma_{n^*} > \sum_{j=n^*+1}^{N} \gamma_j \tag{3.6}$$

The condition categorized countries into two groups: countries with large marginal benefits were critical to form a profitable coalition; those with small marginal benefits were non-critical. The condition (3.6) implied that any critical country could not be replaced by all of the non-critical countries. In other words, critical countries would participate in a coalition because they were necessary members and non-critical countries would not participate because they could take advantage from free riding. The condition ensured that the formation was the only stable profitable coalition. While we acknowledge this is indeed a strong condition, in order to identify the individual incentives to participate in the coalition, this condition provided better observation of the individual decisions in the membership game.

2.1 Inequality-averse preference in a coalition game

As mentioned in the introduction, self-interested preference has failed to illustrate the provision of public goods. In this study, we incorporated inequality-averse preferences by following Fehr and Schmidt (1999). The magnitude of inequality-aversion indicated the level of dislike for unfair outcomes. With this concept, a country k pursued its welfare function as follows:

$$u_k = \pi_k - \frac{\alpha_k}{N-1}\sum_{k'}\max\left(\pi_{k'} - \pi_k, 0\right) - \frac{\beta_k}{N-1}\sum_{k'}\max\left(\pi_k - \pi_{k'}, 0\right) \quad (3.7)$$

where k' was any other country except k. The first term is the payoff of country k. The second and third terms represent the average payoff gap from the other country k' with the disadvantage-loss parameter α_k and advantage-loss parameter β_k, respectively. Both of the parameters presented an inequality-averse magnitude of k and were between 0 (inequality-neutral) and 1 (strongly inequality-averse).

As previously mentioned, when countries were self-interested and the constraints of (3.4), (3.5) and (3.6) were satisfied, a stable n^*-member coalition existed. However, when countries were inequality-averse, the coalition formation was dependent on the individual inequality-averse magnitudes. The coalition formation could become either a stable n^*-member coalition, unstable or a stable coalition larger than n^*.

When all of the countries were inequality-neutral or weakly inequality-averse, a stable n^*-member coalition existed. When any critical country was strongly inequality-averse, that country would leave and break a profitable coalition internally. Therefore, the formation became unstable. In the last circumstance, when any non-critical country was strongly inequality-averse, that country would participate and expand the coalition. Therefore, the formation was stable and larger than n^*.

Intuitively, there were a number of effects with inequality-aversion. First, egalitarianism reduces the individual welfare when the payoffs among the countries were not equal. A coalition could be enlarged by a non-critical egalitarian country, when it sought for smaller advantage loss. Second, the transfer mechanism where signatories shared the same coalition payoff could minimize the payoff gap among the countries. However, except for a grand coalition, signatories always suffered the disadvantage loss from non-signatories. An expanding IEA tended to exacerbate the payoff gap between the signatories and the non-signatories. Egalitarian signatories could punish free-rider behaviour by turning down a profitable IEA. In other words, the effects of inequality-aversion could shape the stability and the formation of IEAs both internally and externally.

3   Experiment design and procedure

The experiment was conducted at the Centre for Experimental Economics (EXEC) laboratory at the University of York (UK) and programmed with z-Tree (Fischbacher 2007). Fifty subjects were invited through the Online Recruitment System (ORSEE) (Greiner 2004). They were students from different countries and studied various disciplines. In order to understand the coalition formation, we mimicked the diversity in the real world where decision makers have different nationalities and multidisciplinary knowledge in this experiment.

In order to ensure data quality, the subjects had to comprehend the rules of the game as much as possible. They were not allowed to exchange information and no conversation was allowed (except for asking the experimenter to clarify the questions) during the experiment. The experimenter introduced the rules and gave the participants time to read through the instructions thoroughly and to accomplish the controlled questions. At the beginning of each part of the experiment, four control questions were asked in order to test the subjects' understanding. A new part would only start if all of the subjects had answered all of the control questions correctly.

A pre-experimental questionnaire was conducted in order to gather demographic information, including the subjects' degree disciplines, age (the year they were born), ethnicity, political orientation and their level of belief in a religion.

Regarding the subjects' educational background, 11 subjects were recruited from economics; 8 subjects were from the humanities; 13 subjects were from science; 1 subject was from law; 9 subjects were from engineering; 1 subject was from psychology; and 7 subjects were from other disciplines. With respect to their ethnicities: 32 subjects were white; 15 were Asian or Asian British; 2 were Black, African, Caribbean or Black British; and 1 fell into the category of any other ethnic groups. In addition, their average age was 25 years old (the oldest being 45 and the youngest being 21).

Another two questions collected information about their self-evaluated preferences. The question regarding religion identified the subjects' belief attitude on a scale ranging from 1 (not religious at all) to 5 (extremely religious). The distribution showed that 20 subjects considered themselves to be atheists. Meanwhile, 6, 8, 9 and 7 subjects considered themselves to be religious, as mild belief, median belief, strong belief and pure religionists, respectively. The distribution of the level of religious attitude showed that the subjects were primarily considered as mild belief. The last question aimed to indicate the subjects' political preference (level one indicates left, level two indicates centre-left, level three indicates neutral, level four indicates centre-right and level five indicates right). The distribution showed that 7 subjects self-identified themselves as left wing; 10 as centre-left; 25 as neutral; 7 as centre-right; and 1 as right wing.

The experiment was comprised of two parts and its procedures were designed as follows.

3.1 An inequality-averse preference test

In this test, we aimed to examine the individuals' attitudes towards inequality-aversion. In order to extract information from a purified environment, the subjects were paired without knowing their partners or their partners' decisions. Each subject had two roles: dictator and receiver. A receiver passively earned allowance from the dictator's decision. A dictator, on the other hand, decided to share a £5 allowance with his/her receiver. There were two ways to share as shown in Table 3.1. Option 1 shared the allowance equally, while option 2 allocated the allowance unjustly with an all-or-nothing allocation at a certain probability.

Option 1 was a fair allocation where the dictator's utility was not affected by unfair loss. On the other hand, the all-or-nothing allocation in option 2 indicated two extreme cases. As described in (3.7), an inequality-averse agent considered both advantage-loss and disadvantage-loss. The range of the two extremities could be normalised.[5] In round 1, the all-or-nothing allocation would be taken by a rational subject because the outcome was definitely better than that from option 1. By contrast, in the final round, the outcome for the fair allocation was better than that for the all-or-nothing allocation. For each subject with a consistent preference, there existed a point with a certain probability where the subject would switch from the all-or-nothing allocation to the fair allocation. The switch point indicated the individuals' attitudes toward inequality-aversion.

When the subjects were inequality-neutral (or self-interested), then their utilities were the same as their monetary payoffs. In other words, they would switch when the expected outcome of all-or-nothing allocation was equal to that of fair allocation. When subjects were inequality-averse, their utilities were lower than their monetary payoffs. They were more likely to take an equal allocation in order to avoid extremely unfair consequences.[6]

It is important to bear in mind that this test could be characterized by strategic uncertainty due to the fact that a series of probabilities were involved. The subjects' risk attitudes might have been involved in their decisions. In other words, it might have been difficult to distinguish the risk-aversion and

Table 3.1 Inequality-aversion test

Round	Option 1	Option 2
1	(£2.5, £2.5) for sure	(£0, £5) with probability 0%; (£5, £0) with probability 100%
2	(£2.5, £2.5) for sure	(£0, £5) with probability 10%; (£5, £0) with probability 90%
3	(£2.5, £2.5) for sure	(£0, £5) with probability 20%; (£5, £0) with probability 80%
4	(£2.5, £2.5) for sure	(£0, £5) with probability 30%; (£5, £0) with probability 70%
5	(£2.5, £2.5) for sure	(£0, £5) with probability 40%; (£5, £0) with probability 60%
6	(£2.5, £2.5) for sure	(£0, £5) with probability 50%; (£5, £0) with probability 50%
7	(£2.5, £2.5) for sure	(£0, £5) with probability 60%; (£5, £0) with probability 40%
8	(£2.5, £2.5) for sure	(£0, £5) with probability 70%; (£5, £0) with probability 30%
9	(£2.5, £2.5) for sure	(£0, £5) with probability 80%; (£5, £0) with probability 20%
10	(£2.5, £2.5) for sure	(£0, £5) with probability 90%; (£5, £0) with probability 10%
11	(£2.5, £2.5) for sure	(£0, £5) with probability 100%; (£5, £0) with probability 0%

inequality-aversion in this study. This issue might be avoided by employing two separate games in order to indicate the attitudes toward disadvantage- and advantage-aversion, such as those developed by Blanco *et al.* (2011) and Yang *et al.* (2012). However, this study was superior for two reasons. First, the two games created another bigger issue in that the measurement of two attitudes might have been biased. Second, there was a significant positive correlation between the inequality-aversion and risk-aversion (Kroll and Davidovitz 2003; Carlsson *et al.* 2005). It was unnecessary to distinguish the inequality-aversion from the risk-aversion.

3.2   *Coalition game experiment*

In this section, the subjects were randomly assigned different roles in a group of five anonymous persons for the entire session. In order to purify the sample, it was a public goods game without any environmentally related content in the instructions. As described in (3.1) and (3.2), the payoffs depended on the marginal benefit of the total abatement. In this study, we built eight treatments of various marginal benefits as shown in Tables 3.2a and 3.2b. Each group played four treatments for a session. They were designed for stable coalitions of 2–4 critical players. As explained earlier, based on the assumption of self-interest, the unique-equilibrium design could help to identify individual

Table 3.2a List of parameters of marginal benefit for players in treatments 1–4

Rounds	Player 1	Player 2	Player 3	Player 4	Player 5
1–15	0.675*	0.375*	0.125	0.1	0.075
16–30	0.075	0.15*	0.25*	0.3*	0.35*
31–45	0.4*	0.65*	0.075	0.1	0.125
46–60	0.05	0.1	0.4*	0.35*	0.3*

* means critical players

Table 3.2b List of parameters of marginal benefit for players in treatments 5–8

Rounds	Player 1	Player 2	Player 3	Player 4	Player 5
1–15	0.075	0.1	0.45*	0.35*	0.25*
16–30	0.125	0.1	0.15	0.5*	0.55*
31–45	0.45*	0.6*	0.05	0.2	0.1
46–60	0.45*	0.25*	0.2*	0.15*	0.05

* means critical players

decisions. As illustrated earlier, critical players were essential for a profitable coalition, while non-critical players had the incentive to free ride.

When the subjects had strong inequality-averse attitudes, then the critical players might have had the incentive to break the coalition internally. On the other hand, non-critical players might have given up the free-riding benefit by participating in a coalition. In this study, we assigned each subject a particular payoff table, which contained all of the possible payoffs with the corresponding coalition combinations.[7] The payoff depended on the given parameters and the coalition formation. For any unprofitable coalition, all of the subjects in the group gained nothing in return. The possible payoffs for the subjects ranged from £0 up to £24.

4 Experimental results

The results for the inequality-averse test demonstrated that 31 out of the 50 subjects had clearly switched from the all-or-nothing allocation to the fair allocation. In particular, two subjects stuck with the fair allocation for the entire session. Their behaviours indicated their individual attitude toward inequality-aversion.

Table 3.3 presents the number of fair allocations taken in each round. Initially, most of the subjects preferred the all-or-nothing allocation. Then, their decisions switched to the fair allocation in rounds 3, 4 and 6.

Table 3.4 shows the ordinary least squares (OLS) estimation of the inequality-averse attitudes. The dependent variable was the number of times that the fair allocation was taken. The independent variables were the factors

Table 3.3 Number of fair allocations taken

Round	1	2	3	4	5	6	7	8	9	10	11
Number of fair allocations taken	10	11	8	23	33	35	48	48	47	48	46

Table 3.4 OLS estimation for inequality-averse attitudes

Variable	Estimation		
Constant term	−137.84		
	(122.70)		
Age	0.07		
	(0.06)		
Political attitude	0.05		
	(0.31)		
Religious attitude	−0.17		
	(0.19)		
Total observations	50	R-square	0.042

selected from the questionnaire, which included the subjects' ages, political attitudes and religious attitudes. The results showed that these factors were insignificant to the individual inequality-averse attitudes.

Regarding the coalition formation in the membership game, profitable coalitions were formed in 387 out of 600 rounds, and the formation was usually larger than the self-interested equilibrium size. The actual coalition formation matched the self-interested equilibrium in only 112 rounds. The coalitions were usually neither stable nor convergent to a particular coalition. With the same treatments, the coalition formation varied in different groups. For example, group 6 and group 8 both took treatments 5–8. Group 6 formed profitable coalitions in 47 rounds, but group 8 achieved profitable coalitions in only 12 rounds.

In this study, we predicted the individual incentives of participating in a coalition by employing the subjects' inequality-averse attitudes and historical decisions in the membership game. On the other hand, benchmark self-interested predictions were built by employing only the historical data in the membership game. The inequality-averse predictions matched the actual decisions by 1,838 over 2,800 observations (65.6 per cent). In the sample of 1,540 observations of critical subjects, the inequality-averse predictions matched the actual outcome for 77.2 per cent of the observations. On the other hand, the inequality-averse predictions matched for 51.5 per cent of the 1,260 observations. With individual inequality-averse predictions, the predicted coalition formation was shown as unstable, but it was usually larger than the actual formation.

Turning now to the factors that might have affected the individual decisions, the maximum likelihood estimation of the binary probit regressions (Probit MLE) were employed as shown in Table 3.5. The variables included the decision made during the previous round, the times of taking the fair

Table 3.5 Probit estimations of the probability of joining a coalition

Variable	Probit MLE(1)	Probit MLE(2)	Probit MLE(3)	Probit MLE(4)	Probit MLE(5)
Constant Term	8.98 (12.36)	0.52*** (0.16)	−1.69 (20.99)	−0.49*** (0.15)	16.57 (18.65)
Past Decision	1.23*** (0.07)		1.34*** (0.13)		1.00*** (0.09)
Inequality-Averse Attitude	0.04** (0.02)	0.07*** (0.02)	0.05** (0.02)	0.05*** (0.02)	0.03 (0.09)
Age	−0.004 (0.006)		0.001 (0.01)		−0.008 (0.009)
Political Attitude	0.05 (0.03)		−0.13** (0.05)		0.22*** (0.05)
Religious Attitude	−0.05** (0.02)		0.03 (0.03)		−0.17*** (0.03)
Critical player dummy	0.76*** (0.06)				
Marginal Benefit					−6.37*** (1.11)
Past Group Contribution	−0.20* (0.12)		−0.26 (0.21)		−0.34** (0.15)
Total Observations	2,520	1,500	1,400	1,200	1,120
Observations of Joining	1,692	1,279	1,185	555	507
Log Likelihood	−1219.83	−621.21	−513.39	−824.28	−771.30

Note: Each cell contains coefficient and the standard error in parenthesis. *, ** and *** are significant at 10%, 5% and 1%, respectively.

allocation, the year the subjects were born, the political attitudes from left to right, the religious attitudes from atheist to religious, the dummy variable of being critical players, the marginal benefit of the total contribution, and the group contribution in the previous round.

Although the experimental design allowed for the existence of inequality acceptors, as predicted in the assumption of the theory, the degree of inequality-aversion was unlikely to be negative. As mentioned in Footnote 7, five negative inequality-averse subjects were excluded from the sample observation. We examined 45 subjects that had various attitudes toward inequality-aversion. The estimation of Probit MLE(1) covered all of the observations of the 2,520 individual decisions due to the observations in the first round being excluded. Among these observations, the subjects decided to join 1,692 times, while they did not decide to join 828 times.

The inequality-averse attitudes, the dummy variable of being critical players, and the decision made in the previous round had significant positive effects on the decisions. This interesting result showed that the strongly inequality-averse subjects were more likely to participate in a coalition. It implied that subjects participated as the experimental design suggested, and that their decisions were consistent. Having said that, the group contribution to the participation was significantly negative due to the fact that the free-riding incentive was higher when the coalition was expanded. Another interesting result was that the subjects with a weaker religious belief were more likely to participate.

This experimental design used a number of critical players to form a profitable coalition. Those critical players were essential in order to stabilize the coalition internally. Probit MLE(2) and Probit MLE(3) examined the observations of the critical players. Eighty-five per cent out of the 1,500 observations participated in a coalition as the design suggested. Their decisions were consistent with the past decisions. On the other hand, the experimental results showed that the coalition instability was caused by the subjects with low degrees of inequality-aversion rather than those with high degrees of inequality-aversion. As discussed in the theoretical section, egalitarians might break a coalition internally. In contrast, the experimental evidence showed that stronger inequality-aversion led subjects to stabilize the coalition internally.

Interestingly, pro-left-wingers were more likely to participate. That being said, subjects had stronger incentives to form a profitable coalition when they were egalitarians or pro-left-wingers. Perhaps a low profit, but safe action appeared to be more favourable than a risky strategy of punishing and forcing free riders to participate.

Having discussed the critical players, the non-critical players were assessed by the estimations of Probit MLE(4) and Probit MLE(5). Those non-critical subjects had the free-riding incentives. The results showed that such incentives were rejected for nearly half of the 1,200 observations. Again, the decisions were consistent with the historical data. Besides, egalitarian subjects were more likely to compromise and cooperate. Subjects with stronger attitudes towards inequality-aversion, such as taking the fair allocation for more than six rounds, were more likely to participate in a coalition.

Apart from the inequality-averse attitudes, the estimation of Probit MLE(5) examined the factors. In contrast to the experimental evidence of the study by Burger and Kolstad (2010), the results of this study did not support their earlier finding that higher marginal benefits would significantly increase a coalition size and, consequently, the total contribution. The results suggest that the free-riding incentive for non-critical players could be mitigated by a lower marginal benefit. In other words, the marginal benefit to the total abatement had a significantly negative effect on the willingness of participation. The estimation showed that the marginal benefit to the total abatement had a significantly negative effect on the willingness of participation. It was intuitive that the non-critical players would not participate when the incentive was high.

In addition, individual political and religious attitudes had significant effects on the willingness of participation. When they were non-critical players, the pro-left-wingers were more likely to free ride. In comparison to the results when they were critical players, the pro-left-wingers played strategically by punishing and cooperating. On the other hand, the religionists were more likely to cooperate by joining a coalition.

5   Conclusions

In this chapter, we examined the impacts of inequality-averse attitudes on the individual incentives of participating in international environmental agreements using a laboratory experiment. Theoretically, when countries are self-interested, stable coalitions exist if signatories have no incentive to leave and non-signatories have no incentive to join. In particular, we focused on a coalition with a unique equilibrium. Any signatory was a critical member to the coalition and could not be replaced by non-signatories. Having introduced the benchmark model, we considered the individuals' attitudes toward inequality-aversion in this study. When countries had a strong inequality-averse attitude, egalitarians could break the coalition internally or externally. Therefore, the coalition formation might enlarge, remain the same as the results of the benchmark, or become unstable.

A set of experiments was conducted in order to validate this hypothesis. The first test measured the individuals' attitudes towards inequality-aversion. The second test was a public good game, which mimicked the international environmental convention. Subjects were given different payoff tables and asked whether or not they would join a coalition. Regarding the coalition formation in the membership game, the formation was usually larger than the self-interested equilibrium size. Under such conditions, the coalition formation was still difficult to predict, and even in this study, we employed the predictions with the individuals' inequality-averse attitudes. The predicted formation was unstable and usually larger than the actual formation.

Turning back to the research question, one may suggest that the inequality-averse attitudes had significant positive impacts on the incentives of participation. In particular, when the subjects were non-critical players, the egalitarians were likely to give up the free-riding benefit by joining a coalition. This result could explain why the coalition formation was usually larger than the Nash equilibrium.

Some significant factors could be illustrated intuitively. The subjects were rational since they behaved consistently and pursued economic incentives. In addition, a larger coalition formation and a higher marginal benefit both could lead to a higher free-riding incentive for non-critical players. Apart from that, other factors may not have been intuitive. According to their self-examination in the questionnaire, the pro-left-wingers behaved strategically. When they were critical players, they punished free riders by not joining a coalition. When they were non-critical players, they compromised by joining a coalition. On the other hand, those who held strong religious beliefs were less likely to be cooperative, especially when they could free ride.

In conclusion, individual inequality-averse attitudes could be the reason for large coalition formation. No matter whether they were critical players or not, a stronger attitude towards inequality-aversion led to more willingness to participate in a coalition. The results of this study also suggested that the individual motivation could be affected by their political and religious attitudes.

The implications could advise policy makers on constructing a climate coalition for a better future.

Notes

1 Any coalition needs at least two members, so $n \in [2, N]$.
2 The meaningful range of the marginal benefit of total abatement was between 0 and 1. When the marginal benefit was above the upper bound, an IEA was unnecessary, because the countries already had the incentive to abate fully. When the aggregate marginal benefit was lower than the lower bound, then a profitable IEA was also non-existent, because all of the players would pollute anyway.
3 The aggregate emission abatement would be $\sum_{i=1}^{n} x_s = nx_s$, because members in the coalition moved as one.
4 It was worth noting that a rule of the coalition requires coalition members use transfers to equalize the net payoffs between agents. Such a rule achieved a less unequal distribution of payoffs through transferring. This assumption implied that for the primary purpose of this chapter, it was difficult to separate out the issue of IEA formation and its impact on fairness from the fact that the IEA was itself a mechanism for achieving a less unequal distribution of payoffs through using transfers. Countries with higher marginal benefits of total abatement were more likely to leave the coalition *ex post*, because those countries could earn higher payoffs for being non-signatories. However, in this study, we assumed that countries had the full information when they agreed to participate in an IEA. Therefore, they knew the consequences of being signatories and non-signatories. Signatories would commit to stay in the coalition and make transfers to equalize individual payoffs. We acknowledge that this is a strong assumption. However, considering each member had the same right to determine the members' abatement, every signatory would share equal responsibility. Therefore, our design for sharing the pre-distributed coalition payoff was still an adequate solution.
5 The range between two extreme unfair outcomes was normalized, so both the advantage- and disadvantage-losses could be merged as one inequality-averse indicator. Although a subject might suffer more from disadvantage than advantage, two reasons supported this technique. In practice, it is not easy to find a subject's preference without standardizing the unit of the utility. In the literature, the experimental evidence showed that the disadvantage factor was not necessarily smaller than the advantage factor (Dannenberg *et al.* 2012 and Yang *et al.* 2012).
6 Inequality acceptors, which never chose an equal allocation, could be possible, but they were uncommon in reality (as seen in the experimental results later). They could be observed in this experimental design. Therefore, we excluded those inequality acceptors from our analyses, similar to Fehr and Schmidt (1999).
7 A possible coalition combination requires at least two players. Therefore, there were $(2^5 - 5 - 1) = 26$ possible coalition combinations.

References

Bahn, O., M. Breton, L. Sbragia and Zaccour, G. (2009), 'Stability of International Environmental Agreements: An Illustration with Asymmetrical Countries', *International Transactions in Operational Research*, 16 (3): 307–324.
Barrett, S. (1994), 'Self-Enforcing International Environmental Agreements', *Oxford Economic Paper*, 46: 878–894.

Barrett, S. (2001), 'International Cooperation for Sale', *European Economic Review*, 45 (10): 1835–1850.

Blanco, M., Engelmann, D. and Normann, H.T. (2011), 'A Within-Subject Analysis of Other-Regarding Preferences', *Games and Economic Behavior*, 72 (2): 321–338.

Bratberg, E., Tjotta, S. and Oines, T. (2005), 'Do Voluntary International Environmental Agreements Work?', *Journal of Environmental Economics and Management*, 50 (3): 583–597.

Breton, M., Sbragia, L. and Zaccour, G. (2010), 'A Dynamic Model for International Environmental Agreements', *Environmental and Resource Economics*, 45: 25–48.

Burger, N. E. and Kolstad, C. D. (2010), International Environmental Agreements: Theory Meets Experimental Evidence. Working paper, University of California at Santa Barbara.

Carlsson, F., Daruvala, D. and Johansson-Stenman, O. (2005), 'Are People Inequality-Averse, or Just Risk-Averse?', *Economica*, 72: 375–396.

Charness, G. and Rabin, M. (2002), 'Understanding Social Preferences With Simple Tests', *The Quarterly Journal of Economics*, 117 (3): 817–869.

Dannenberg, A., Riechmann, T., Sturm, B. and Vogt, C. (2012), 'Inequality Aversion and the House Money Effect', *Experimental Economics*, 15: 460–484.

D'Aspremont, C., Jacquemin, A., Gabszewicz, J. and Weymark, J. (1983), 'On the Stability of Collusive Price Leadership', *Canadian Journal of Economics*, 16 (1): 17–25.

Eyckmans, J. and Finus, M. (2006), 'New Roads to International Environmental Agreements: The Case of Global Warming', *Environmental Economics and Policy Studies*, 7 (4): 391–414.

Fehr, E. and Schmidt, K. M. (1999), 'A Theory of Fairness, Competition, and Cooperation', *The Quarterly Journal of Economics*, 114 (3): 817–868.

Fischbacher, U. (2007), 'z-Tree: Zutich Toolbox for Ready-made Economic Experiments', *Experimental Economics*, 10 (2): 171–178.

Greiner, B. (2004), 'The Online Recruitment System ORSEE 2.0 – A Guide for the Organization of Experiments in Economics', Department of Economics, University of Cologne.

Kolstad, C. D. (2014), International Environmental Agreements among Heterogeneous Countries with Social Preferences, NBER Working Paper No. 20204.

Kosfeld, M., Okada, A. and Riedl, A. (2009), 'Institution Formation in Public Goods Games', *American Economic Review*, 99 (4): 1335–1355.

Kroll, Y. and Davidovitz, L. (2003), 'Inequality Aversion versus Risk Aversion', *Economica*, 70 (227): 19–29.

McEvoy, D. M., Cherry, T. L. and Stranlund, J. K. (2014), 'International Environmental Agreements with Endogenous Minimum Participation and the Role of Inequality.' In *Toward a New Climate Agreement: Conflict, Resolution and Governance*, T. L. Cherry, J. Hovi and D. M. McEvoy (eds), London and New York: Routledge, 93–105.

Mitchell, R. B. (2003), 'International Environmental Agreements: a Survey of Their Features, Formation, and Effects', *Annual Review of Environment and Resources*, 28: 429–461.

Willinger, M. and Ziegelmeyer, A. (2001), 'Strength of the Social Dilemma in A Public Goods Experiment: An Exploration of the Error Hypothesis', *Experimental Economics*, 4 (2): 131–144.

Yang, Y., Onderstal, S. and Schram, A. (2012), 'Inequity Aversion Revisited', Discussion Paper.

Part II
Heterogeneous countries

4 Transnational environmental agreements with heterogeneous actors

Achim Hagen, Leonhard Kähler and Klaus Eisenack

1 Introduction

There is unequivocal scientific agreement on the dangerous interference of anthropogenic greenhouse gas emissions with the climate. But efforts to find cooperative solutions on an international level have been mostly unsatisfactory so far. The recent UN climate negotiations in Paris have led to some agreement about global targets, but not about the individual nations' contributions to the global public good. This state of affairs motivates the search for complementary approaches for global emissions reductions. Some suggestions are in the air. For example, some authors think about minilateralism (Eckersley 2012), climate clubs (Widerberg and Stenson 2013; Falkner 2015) or a building blocks approach (Stewart *et al.* 2013). Lobby groups and NGOs influence climate and energy policy. City alliances grow in parallel to nation state based coalitions. This chapter aims at exploring some of such transnational initiatives or patterns of cooperation. Although there has been some research on those patterns in the global governance literature (related to political science), we aim at making this topic conducive for economic analysis, in particular game theory. How can such patterns of cooperation be explained? Can we expect cooperation to be effective?

In this chapter, we call a contract that stipulates rules for contributions to a global environmental good 'transnational environmental agreement' (TEA) if it has heterogeneous contracting parties, i.e. of different type. Parties can be national, subnational, international, or of different quality. Such contracts can be explicit or implicit. They might directly aim at emissions reductions, or only indirectly (e.g. by stipulating monitoring procedures). We chose the term 'transnational' to generalize from the established 'international' environmental agreement (IEA) framing. Transnational agreements are not undertaken within single jurisdictions (which would not be international either), but the main actors involved do not necessarily need to be national governments (cf. Andonova *et al.* 2009; Hale and Roger 2014).

TEAs are not an invention from the theory. For example, the C40 Cities Climate Leadership Group (C40 2015) with more than 80 megacities (from the South and the North) took leadership in signing the Greenhouse Gas

Protocol for Cities in 2014. As of December 2015, the number of signatories increased to 428 cities (GHG Protocol 2015). Weischer *et al.* (2012) map 17 climate clubs, being non-universal and partially overlapping agreements of nation states that cooperate on climate change. In total, 122 countries are members of at least one of those clubs. Some of these clubs include non-nation state partners. A first study roughly estimates that non-state initiatives might reduce greenhouse gas emissions by three gigatons in 2020 (UNEP 2015). Although the empirical fact that many TEAs already exist might seem impressive at the first glance, some sceptical questions warrant attention. It is well known, after all, that global public goods suffer from freerider incentives. So what does motivate actors then to be frontrunners and sign a non-universal TEA? And if they do so for some reason, why shouldn't they not just pretend to reduce greenhouse gas emissions? These questions will be further explored in this chapter.

There are only few papers in economic journals that address TEAs, some of which are discussed in more detail below. The theme of city alliances seems to be broadly neglected (but see Sippel 2010; Millard-Ball 2012 for some data analysis). Subnational emission reductions are not analysed, to our knowledge, from the perspective of cooperation between actors from different countries. The exception is the game theoretic literature on environmental agreements that explains non-universal cooperation (more on that below). Studies that admit for multiple climate clubs are sparse (e.g. Asheim *et al.* 2006; Finus 2008; Hagen and Eisenack 2015). National lobby groups are addressed by Marchiori et al. (2016), Habla and Winkler (2013) and Hagen *et al.* (2016), but not from a transnational perspective (for a literature review on the political economy of the formation of international environmental agreements, see Wangler *et al.* 2013). The chapter is not intended to fill all these gaps, but contributes by arguing for the relevance of this research field. It provides structure in transferring insights from global governance research, where much more has been published on transnational climate governance than in economics, to game theory. First, we report on the global governance literature and empirical examples of emerging transnational climate agreements. Then we give an overview of the existing economic literature on the scope and limits of international environmental agreements. Building on these two pillars, we follow up with two proposals for game theoretic models. They analyse strategic effects of climate clubs and city alliances as examples for TEAs. We then take a look at the larger picture again and contextualize these approaches in an outlook on promising future research.

2   Current transnational approaches in the global governance literature

This section puts together some selected and documented empirical observations of transnational environmental agreements, and summarizes relevant publications from the global governance literature. Climate clubs can be understood as 'Club-like arrangements between states that share common climate-related concerns, and sometimes in partnership with non-state actors such as companies and Non-Governmental Organizations' (Widerberg and Stenson 2013: 1). Climate clubs are also coined as 'minilateralism' (Eckersley 2012). They are currently analysed in the discourse on fragmented global governance (e.g. Biermann *et al.* 2009; Keohane and Victor 2011; Isailovic *et al.* 2013). This literature acknowledges that there is no monolithic and rational global governance architecture, but a carpet of loosely coupled international institutional arrangements and regimes, not all being universal but many overlapping. Although they may address multiple issues, their scope can be synergistic, cooperative or conflictive. One set of overarching questions addresses the conditions under which fragmentation is conducive or detrimental to regime effectiveness (e.g. Gehring and Oberthür 2008; Biermann *et al.* 2009).

Weischer *et al.* (2012) analyse existing climate clubs and explore their contribution to climate action as well as the incentives for becoming club members and taking action. Similarly, Widerberg and Stenson (2013) find different types of clubs, from political and technical dialogue forums to country strategy and project implementation groups. Examples are the Asia-Pacific Partnership on Clean Development (2006–2011, including the US and China) and the International Energy and Climate Initiative – Energy+ (since 2010, International Energy and Climate Initiative – Energy+ 2015). The latter, led by Norway, has 16 national government members (from Africa, Asia and Europe), and multiple non-governmental partners, e.g. the World Bank and the World Business Council for Sustainable Development (WBCSD). It aims at promoting energy efficiency and renewables by incentivizing commercial investments. While some papers focus on the legitimacy of climate clubs (e.g. Karlsson-Vinkhuyzen and McGee 2013), others focus on their effectiveness (see Moncel and van Asselt 2012 for an overview).

Different arguments are put forward to underpin the potential of climate clubs. It might be easier to reach agreement in smaller clubs of countries that are more willing to push forward climate protection (based on the argument of Olson 1971). Falkner (2015) distinguishes three dominant rationales of climate clubs. First, club benefits are created for the members. Second, a re-legitimation of the climate regime by giving great powers a privileged position in the negotiations while acknowledging their greater responsibility at the same time. Third, the potential of climate clubs to enhance the bargaining efficiency of the international negotiations by facilitating agreement amongst smaller groups of players. Further pros and cons of climate clubs will be discussed below.

Another case for TEAs is contracts between cities from different countries. City networks on sustainability issues have some tradition. The International Council for Local Environmental Initiatives (since 1990) has more than 1,000 cities, towns and metropolises from all continents as members (ICLEI 2015). Over 1,700 cities and municipalities are members of the Climate

Alliance (since 1990, Climate Alliance 2015), and have voluntarily committed to reduce greenhouse gas emissions by 10 per cent every five years. The C40 Cities Climate Leadership Group (since 2005) pushed the Compact of Mayors (2015), which is currently signed by cities with more than 5 per cent of the global population. The Compact of Mayors has adopted a common monitoring, reporting and verification standard, the Greenhouse Gas Protocol for Cities (GHG Protocol 2015). The standard is built on experience with a private sector initiative, the Carbon Disclosure Project (CDP 2015), and has established a joint carbon registry.

As with climate clubs, there is also some research on city alliances. A special issue in Local Environment reviewed the early studies (Betsill and Bulkeley 2007). Interesting questions are the motivations for joining city alliances, and their environmental effectiveness. The early literature is mostly descriptive in nature and undertakes single or comparative case studies. For example, Betsill and Bulkeley (2004) show for six case studies of municipalities in the UK that membership in Cities for Climate Protection (CCP) is mostly motivated by the availability of additional financial and political resources, and not so much by transfer of technical and best practice knowledge. International recognition of the local engagement and the re-framing of existing measures in terms of climate change helps increase legitimacy and place those activities higher on the local agenda. Gustavsson *et al.* (2009) explore the potential of city networks for Swedish cities. Kern and Bulkeley (2009) analyse modes of cooperation in three transnational municipal networks (Climate Alliance, CCP and Energie-Cités). Members are active to quite different degrees in terms of information and communication, funding, recognition, benchmarking and certification.

Bulkeley and Broto (2013) collected an impressive database with more than 600 'urban climate change experiments' from 100 systematically selected global cities. All these experiments are explicitly targeted at reducing greenhouse gas emissions or at adapting to climate change. Most experiments are found in Europe, Latin America and Asia. Less of them relate to adaptation, but many to urban infrastructure, the built environment and energy. Half of the experiments involve partnerships, for example between local governments and the private sector. More recently, Hakelberg (2014) collected a sample of 274 European cities of which 41 per cent became members of city networks until 2009. The econometric analysis shows that membership in a city network increases the likelihood of adopting a local climate strategy. In contrast, there is no such effect on geographically neighbouring cities. Top-down governmental policies have a stronger effect on local climate strategies than city network membership.

Some studies explore the reasons why city alliances exist and might (not) be effective. Bulkeley (2010) generally stresses the changing role of cities and states in political systems, and highlights political economy reasons. Furthermore, urban areas are expected to be particularly vulnerable to climate change, though some more so than others (e.g. IPCC 2014; Corfee-Morlot *et al.* 2009; Gill *et al.* 2007; Campbell-Lendrum and Corvalan 2007). This might contribute to urgency in climate change adaptation and mitigation in some cities. Generally the local approach offers potentially easier stakeholder engagement, concrete action, resource mobilization and investment, mostly because actors are directly involved (e.g. Corfee-Morlot *et al.* 2009; Sippel and Jenssen 2009). On the other hand, urban action cannot be understood as being disconnected from national law. While the latter sets the context for the former, the former can help enforcing national action by contracts, building trust and through the political process. As a further reason, there might be local co-benefits due to investments, local pollution, or first-mover advantages if a city specializes in technological solutions (although e.g. Urpelainen (2009) shows that local co-benefits are not sufficient to motivate local front-runners). Further pros and cons of city alliances will be discussed below.

Approaches to study city alliances, climate clubs, and other modes of trans-national environmental agreements resonate with different literature streams. Some scholars study subnational climate policies from the multi-level perspective (e.g. Betsill and Bulkeley 2006; Monni and Raes 2008). Hooghe and Marks (2003) disentangle different modes that might be helpful to characterize different transnational governance patterns. Type I governance refers to hierarchically nested arrangements (like in a classic federal system), while Type II governance refers to arrangements that cross hierarchies or overlap between jurisdictions. The literature on fiscal federalism (Oates 1972, 2005) and environmental federalism (Shobe and Burtraw 2012) uses more economic concepts to study the allocation of policies between subsidiarity and centralization. This approach might be helpful to study TEAs.

The debate on transnational climate governance got further impetus from Elinor Ostrom after her Nobel laureate speech (Ostrom, 2010, 2012). She rooted the considerations on addressing climate change both down from the top and up from the bottom in the concept of polycentric governance. In such governance modes many centres of decision making, which are formally independent from each other, make mutual adjustments for ordering their relationships (Ostrom *et al.* 1961). This line of inquiry was taken up further by Cole (2011) and recently by Jordan *et al.* (2015).

3   Scope and limits of international environmental agreements

International environmental agreements with a focus on climate agreements have been analysed in the economic literature since the 1990s. This has led to the development of various models that serve as a starting point for the analysis of TEAs. This section gives an overview of this strand of research and its main assumptions and results.

The literature on IEAs started with the seminal work of Carraro and Siniscalco (1993) and Barrett (1994). The basic idea is to transfer concepts from the theory of economic cartels (D'Aspremont *et al.* 1983; Chander and Tulkens 1995) to the study of stable coalitions that contribute to a public good. A large set of publications that refined the first contributions followed suit, with further analytical and simulation studies up to date. Most of this research is based, inter alia, on the following propositions:

1. Global environmental problems are about provision of public goods.
2. Players are aspiring and achieving individually rational decisions in a game theoretic framework.
3. International environmental agreements need to be self-enforcing.
4. Players are nation states; their payoffs are determined by national welfare.
5. Full global cooperation (the grand coalition) would yield the first-best outcome.
6. The social optimum is ideally achieved, in principle, by a single global policy instrument (e.g. a uniform carbon tax or an emission trading scheme).

Based on these propositions, some standard insights have been consolidated over a broad range of settings. Some of them can be stated in a stylized way as follows: [i] The social optimum cannot be achieved due to freerider incentives. [ii] If some countries or coalitions undertake unilateral emission reductions, their effect is dissipated due to carbon leakage. [iii] Cooperation is either broad but shallow, or deep but small. Thus, if we assume that reducing carbon emissions is associated with high mitigation costs and small damage reductions, a stable coalition will not have many signatories.

Although scientifically robust, these results are politically mostly frustrating. They do a good job in explaining the long-lasting stalemate and questionable effectiveness of the climate negotiation process under the UNFCCC.

Taking on that, two questions remain. First, if these results are valid for the climate case, is there any chance of averting the greatest market failure ever (Stern 2007) or, more pathetically, loss of life and quality of life for billions of people? Is there no alternative to accepting the inevitable? Second, are these results indeed valid for the climate case?

Some sceptical remarks may deserve attention. For example, some studies have determined social costs of carbon of just a few dollars per ton (in particular for higher discount rates, IPCC 2014). Several other studies have shown that the costs of mitigating emissions to limit greenhouse gas concentrations below 430–480 ppm by 2100 lead to a reduction of consumption growth by 0.04 to 0.14 percentage points over the twenty-first century (IPCC 2014), i.e. these costs might be relatively low. If at least one of these kinds of conclusions is valid, it seems that the gains from cooperation are shallow. The theory would thus imply broad cooperation. This implication is falsified by over 20 years of slow progress in climate negotiations.

Furthermore, the empirical examples of TEAs outlined above cannot be explained by the standard insights. Why should multiple climate clubs on overlapping issued be formed? Why do some climate clubs engage, although probably on a low level, in unilateral action? Why do cities from different countries start cooperation on emissions reductions, although most of their national governments do not, although there is no (single) global policy instrument in place, and although there are still many cities that do not participate in city networks? Instead, theory would predict cities to be freeriders.

Solving such puzzles seems to be important both for climate protection and for scientific inquiry. One starting point for analysis could be to reconsider some of the six propositions outlined above. In the following, we want to explore how proposition (3), (4) or (5) might be relaxed, while keeping the remaining propositions.

4   Proposals for theoretical analysis

In this section we give two selected proposals for economic models that concentrate on transnational environmental agreements: climate clubs and city alliances. Both can be observed empirically. However, both have got little attention in the economic literature so far even though they offer interesting concepts. We give general outlines for these two approaches that can serve as seeds for further model development. In addition, we give a detailed outlook on promising lines of further research in these and related areas.

4.1   Climate clubs

One way to open up the classical approach of one single international environmental agreement is to allow heterogeneous countries to form climate clubs. As described in the global governance literature, climate clubs may have different effects and may improve over one monolithic agreement through different rationales (cf. Falkner 2015).

The aspect of club benefits for the members of a climate coalition is analysed by Nordhaus (2015). He finds that a climate club that imposes trade sanctions on non-participants can induce a larger stable coalition with more abatement than a coalition without sanctions. Asheim *et al.* (2006) model the case of symmetric countries and two coexisting agreements. The countries are partitioned in two regions and can choose whether they sign an agreement for that region or not. They conclude that a larger number of cooperating signatories can be sustained, compared to the standard case of a single IEA. The case of two coexisting TEAs is further analysed in a numerical study by Osmani and Tol (2010) who additionally consider two asymmetric country types in a three-stage sequence of play between the coalitions and the non-signatories. Their results show that the possibility of two coalitions could increase as well as decrease emission abatement in comparison to the standard case with one coalition.

Going beyond numerical examples, Hagen and Eisenack (2015) study the effect of multiple coexisting climate clubs in an analytical game theoretic setting. The paper allows for asymmetric countries and investigates if global cooperation for emissions abatement can be improved if countries can form coexisting TEAs. This very general analytical approach to climate clubs helps to get insights in the effects of negotiating coexisting climate clubs without being bound by specific assumptions on the concrete costs and benefits of countries emissions abatement. The rationale of this analysis will be introduced for the simplest version of this game theoretic climate clubs model. Its main results are derived and discussed.

The model is set up in the widely used two-stage game structure with countries first choosing to join a coalition or not (e.g. Carraro and Siniscalco 1993). In the second stage the members of a coalition decide cooperatively on the amount of emissions abatement that is undertaken by the coalition. The game is solved by backward induction. In contrast to the bulk of the existing literature, coexisting agreements are possible. Each stage of the model is set up as a simultaneous Nash game.

The simplest version of the model already allows for important insights to the idea of climate clubs. It considers two types of asymmetric countries and two possible TEAs. The number of abating countries of type i ($i = 1, 2$) is denoted by z_i. We assume linear benefits of global emissions abatement and a binary choice for countries between abatement, which is associated with abatement costs c, and pollution. An abating country of type i gets the payoff $\pi_i^a = -c + \alpha_i(z_1 + z_2)$. Asymmetric benefits of the countries are expressed by the parameter α_i where α_2 is normalized to $\alpha_2 = 1$ and $\alpha_1 \in [0,1]$. A type 1 country therefore benefits less or at most as much as a type 2 country from abatement. The net benefit of own abatement of each country is negative since $c > 1$. Thus, playing pollute is the dominant strategy if there is no TEA and all countries play pollute in the non-cooperative Nash equilibrium. In the first stage of the game countries decide about their TEA-participation. The case of one agreement is compared to that of two coexisting agreements. In the first case, countries of both types can choose to join or not to join the agreement. In the other case, each agreement consists of similar countries, representing e.g. regional agreements (cf. Asheim *et al.* 2006). Solving the second stage of the game first, the agreements cooperate internally in their decisions about their emissions abatement. In the two agreements case the agreements take their decisions independently and simultaneously. Maximization of the respective joint payoffs yields the second stage equilibrium with agreement i playing

$$z_i^* = k_i\,(abate)\,if\,\alpha_i k_1 + k_2 > c \tag{1}$$

$$z_i^* = 0\,(pollute)\,if\,\alpha_i k_1 + k_2 < c \tag{2}$$

with k_i denoting the number of type i signatories. This result already shows that the decision of each agreement depends on the number of its members, but not on the abatement decisions of the other countries. The application of the criteria of internal and external stability solves the first stage of the game. As playing pollute is a dominant strategy for non-signatories, internal stability is only given if the members of an agreement choose to abate and would change from abate to pollute if one country left the agreement so that $c > \alpha_1(k_1^* - 1) + k_2^* > \alpha_1 k_1^* + (k_2^* - 1)$. The stability conditions together with this linchpin condition indicate that a stable abating agreement may consist of countries of both types with the number of signatories satisfying

$$c + \alpha_1 > \alpha_1 k_1^* + k_2^* > c. \tag{3}$$

Setting either the number of type 1 or of type 2 members in the agreement to zero, we get the results for the size of the single agreement if it consists only of type 1 (4) or of type 2 (5) countries:

$$c + \alpha_1 > \alpha_1 k_1^* > c \tag{4}$$

$$c + 1 > k_2^* > c. \tag{5}$$

As the abatement decisions in the case of two agreements are mutually independent, the total number of abating countries in this case can be found by adding (4) and (5), and thus has to satisfy

$$2c + \alpha_1 + 1 > \alpha_1 k_1^{**} + k_2^{**} > 2c. \tag{6}$$

By comparing the equilibrium abating stable coalitions in the case of one single and two coexisting agreements, we find that two agreements lead to a greater number of agreement members as well as to a greater amount of global emissions abatement and welfare. This effect would be replicated for any larger number of admitted climate clubs. It is caused by the coalitions' and the outsiders' dominant abatement strategies that stem from the linear payoff-structure of the model.

As shown by Hagen and Eisenack (2015), linear benefits of abatement always lead to dominant abatement strategies, while other cost and benefit structures from emissions abatement may lead to non-dominant reaction functions. In the extreme case of linear costs and concave benefits from abatement, only one agreement would undertake emissions abatement while all other countries do not abate any emissions regardless of their potential membership in other agreements. The findings of Eisenack and Kähler (2015), who show that individual countries with convex benefits from abatement may have increasing reaction functions so that emissions abatement becomes a strategic complement, give rise to the question about the strategic behaviour of clubs that consist of such countries. In light of the previous analysis and the already existing economic literature, we may conclude that climate clubs improve the outcomes of climate negotiations in some cases. Even in the least desirable cases we find that the outcome of negotiations with climate clubs leads to the same amount of global emissions abatement as would be achieved with one single IEA.

4.2   *City alliances*

Cities are important actors regarding global climate change, both on the emitting and on the damage side. It might generally make sense that they organize an alliance among themselves in order to tackle these problems. In our proposed model we focus on the economic arguments of vulnerability, local co-benefits and enforceability.

The problem of enforcing an environmental agreement can be greatly diminished as cities are not 'above the law' like nation states in the international system. They can be bound to abide to contracts by national laws. This makes trust, compliance and enforcement less challenging problems. Generally, there are political, social and cultural links between rural and urban areas of one country. Additionally, a city alliance can introduce a voluntary and legal link between urban areas of multiple countries. The combination of these links might yield more cooperation than the usual economic approach of considering only a voluntary and self-enforcing agreement between countries.

Cities are potentially more vulnerable to climate change than other regions (Hallegatte and Corfee-Morlot 2011). Therefore they have stronger incentives to reduce climate change impacts. There can also be local co-benefits in mitigation, e.g. the removal of air pollution (Bollen *et al.* 2009; Harlan and Ruddell 2011) or a specialization on business opportunities from technological solutions like green energy (Jochem and Madlener 2003). Particularly early movers may have an advantage here.

For technical reasons, we characterize the actors in this section by their benefits and damages from emissions (in contrast the model specifications in section 4.1). In our model each country i consists of one *city* and one *rural* region. The payoff of each city $\pi^i_{city}(e^i_{city}, e) = B^i_{city}(e^i_{city}) - D^i_{city}(e)$ and each rural region $\pi^i_{rural}(e^i_{rural}, e) = B^i_{rural}(e^i_{rural}) - D^i_{rural}(e)$ depends on the benefits B^i_{city}/B^i_{rural} from its own emissions e_i, and, as usual, on the damage D^i_{city}/D^i_{rural} from global emissions $e = e^i_{city} + e^i_{rural} + e^{-i}$. The local emissions are an essential (but partly substitutable) factor of industrial production; they are linked to local benefits. Global emissions change the climate, which in turn creates local damages. In line with standard IEA literature (e.g. Hoel 1991), we assume for all regions positive but decreasing marginal benefits from local emissions $B^{i'} > 0, B^{i''} < 0$ and positive and increasing marginal damages from global emissions $D^{i'} > 0, D^{i''} > 0$.

We further assume the following properties of the benefit and damage functions:

$$D'_{city}(e) > D'_{rural}(e), \tag{7}$$

$$B'_{city}(e^i_{city}) < B'_{rural}(e^i_{rural}), \tag{8}$$

$$B''_{city}(e^i_{city}) > B''_{rural}(e^i_{rural}). \tag{9}$$

The first property corresponds to the comparatively higher vulnerability of cities. The second and third inequalities result from assuming local co-benefits from emissions reductions in cities (e.g. lower air pollution or a head start in green technology development). These co-benefits compensate for the loss of benefits from emissions reduction, and therefore, lead to a lower net loss of benefits from local greenhouse gas production.

The model comprises two stages: First, each city decides whether it wants to participate in the TEA by entering an alliance with all other willing cities. Second, each country decides on the emission level of its city and rural region. The entry decision ($c^i \in \{A, \neg A\}$) in the first stage is based only on the payoff of the city: Is π^i_{city} higher as an alliance member? The payoff of the rural regions or the other cities does not enter consideration here.

In the second stage of the game, countries choose the emissions that maximize their respective payoffs Π^i. If the city region of a country has entered an alliance, we assume that the country considers the damages to foreign cities of the alliance $D^{A \backslash i}_{city}$ to some degree. This works similar as in stable agreements between nation states that fully internalize all damages from the emissions to all other agreement members. The degree of internalization of foreign cities in an alliance where domestic cities are members is represented by a weight $x \in]0,1[$ because cities may not be able to force their national governments to fully integrate a city alliance into their emissions planning.

The optimization problem of each country i in the second stage is:

$$
\max_{e^i_{city}, e^i_{rural}} \Pi^i \left(e^i_{city}, e^i_{rural}, e^{-i}\right)
$$

$$
= \begin{cases} \text{if } c^i = \neg A : \pi^i_{city}\left(e^i_{city}, e\right) + \pi^i_{rural}\left(e^i_{rural}, e\right) \\ \text{if } c^i = A \quad : \pi^i_{city}\left(e^i_{city}, e\right) + \pi^i_{rural}\left(e^i_{rural}, e\right) - x \cdot D^{A \backslash i}_{city}(e). \end{cases} \quad (10)
$$

We assume that all countries simultaneously play a Nash game at this stage.

In the first stage all cities determine membership simultaneously in a Nash game

$$
\max_{c^i \in \{A, \neg A\}} \pi^i_{city}\left(e^i_{city}, e\right) = B^i_{city}\left(e^i_{city}\right) - D^i_{city}(e). \quad (11)
$$

It is obvious that an alliance between cities is easier to reach than an agreement between countries. Due to their high vulnerability, cities value emissions reductions more; at the same time, they are more likely to accept emission reductions because they have lower marginal benefits from emissions.

The largest part of the emissions reductions (in comparison to a status without any agreement) is borne by the cities in the alliance, because their benefits are reduced least if they lower emissions. They also have the largest reduction in damages. The rural areas (of the countries in which the cities are in the alliance) have to make some emission reduction effort as well, but their main contribution is not allowing any leakage. In a negotiation that only allows for nation states to form an agreement, even rural areas might want an agreement, but freerider incentives are much higher for them than for cities. Therefore they would prefer others to form an agreement and stay singletons themselves.

The national government is important in our model insofar as it ensures that no leakage of 'dirty' industry from cities to rural areas occurs. Of course, the willingness of governments to engage in local climate policy is important as well. However, in this model they don't have to enforce large emission reductions in (unwilling) rural areas, they only have to prevent them from increasing their emissions. Maintaining a *status quo* is more feasible in many political cases than enforcing unwanted change.

We conclude that if cities can form a mitigating alliance which national governments consider to some degree in their policy decision making, more cooperation and larger emission reductions can result. Cities have an incentive to enter a city alliance because they expect higher damages from climate change, and have lower costs of emission reduction than other regions (particularly taking into account co-benefits from greenhouse gas mitigation).

4.3   Outlook

There are many further approaches to transnational environmental agreements in addition to the analysis of those proposed above. We think that they offer promising extensions of the state of the art in research on international environmental agreements. We sketch some of them in the following.

Concerning climate clubs, one could think of overlapping clubs as an alternative to the proposed setting of coexisting disjoints clubs. If countries would be signatories of more than one climate club, this would change the strategic interaction of the clubs and possibly also the reaction functions in the game. Another way to include climate clubs as disjoint coalitions in the climate negotiations is to allow countries to form sub-coalitions in a first stage, followed by multilateral negotiations between the coalitions and remaining non-signatories. Possible effects of climate clubs in a broader sense include the generation of club-benefits as proposed, for instance, by Nordhaus (2015). By the creation of such benefits that only favour signatories of a climate agreement, the incentives to join are strengthened. This could be implemented through issue-linkage. Existing international agreements on other topics as, for example trade, would then be linked to climate agreements. Existing research on IEAs and trade (e.g. Eichner and Pethig 2015) could serve as a starting point here. Such multi issue clubs as well as climate clubs that do not negotiate on emission reductions but other issues like monitoring or technology sharing are a challenging but interesting modelling task. With regard to transaction costs we can say that, on the one hand, a shift towards smaller clubs of negotiating countries could possibly lower the transaction costs of forming a climate agreement, while possible interactions between clubs could impose additional transaction costs.

There are several economic arguments for an alliance between cities for emissions reductions. In our modelling approach we use vulnerability, local co-benefits and enforceability. In addition to these assumptions, we suggest three more possible reasons in favour of city alliances. First, transaction costs are potentially lower. The implementation of policy measures might be easier on a subnational than on a national level. Second, there is presumably less reason to behave opportunistically in moral hazard situations. The problem of individually rational but collectively harmful behaviour can be reduced if people directly observe each other. It might even be argued that urban areas are more likely to have a clientele that shares common norms, such as a collective commitment to behave responsibly and to abstain from opportunistic behaviour. Within such a group, information asymmetries are less problematic in a moral hazard configuration. Third, there can be learning effects. Transfer of policies between cities or even from a subnational to a national level could be modelled.

Our modelling proposal for city alliances can be combined with research on climate clubs. Cities within countries with low ambition could join climate clubs and exert their influence on the respective countries to join such agreements and take climate action. We actually observe that there are multiple city alliances in place, so these are, in our terminology, coexisting climate clubs of cities. What is the rationale and environmental effectiveness of cities forming coexisting TEAs, and how might cities strategically interact with national governments in heterogeneous TEAs where both cities and countries are members?

Apart from city alliances and climate clubs, there are many other actors that could participate in TEAs. Non-state actors play an important role for adaptation to climate change as well as for mitigation of emissions. Industry lobbies and transnational NGOs influence governments and groups of countries in different ways while subnational governments and internal politics also play an important role for the decisions national governments take. Involving these actors in transnational agreements might open up new possibilities for negotiations and climate action but also raise threats to effective agreements. Whether they are within an agreement between nation states or within a coalition only consisting of non-nation state actors, their interests differ substantially so that the effects of heterogeneity on their outcomes are not clear. These effects should not be neglected and deserve more attention in further research.

5 Conclusions

This chapter provides an exploration of some transnational initiatives for climate cooperation. The global governance literature finds ample empirical evidence for emerging TEAs. These can be only partially explained by the conventional economic literature that emphasizes the role of nation states with freerider incentives. We thus propose that more research is needed to understand and evaluate the role of TEAs in order to contribute to deal with climate change. We argue that this particularly requires to consider the strategic interaction of heterogeneous actors, not only nation state governments, and to consider coexisting and possibly overlapping contracts that stipulate emission reductions or other institutions that are conducive to this aim.

To illustrate and underpin this claim, we extend already existing game theoretic approaches to IEAs in order to analyse the strategic effects of TEAs. Our two examples show that both climate clubs and city alliances may be able to lead to an increase in emissions abatement and in global welfare. Climate clubs offer an opportunity to cooperate in more than one agreement at the same time. Cities can form alliances in which they agree to mitigate greenhouse gases; the effectiveness of such TEAs will depend on the political influence cities have on national governments.

We find that cooperation can be individually rational, even in the presence of freerider incentives. Depending on the characteristics of the actors, negotiation structures can facilitate cooperation. Multiple agreements, for example, can stimulate more countries to cooperate than a single IEA. National political and legal institutions can be used to avoid the problem of non-binding agreements if actors other than nation states cooperate. Cities, rural regions and other subnational actors can be compelled by law to enact an agreement. Both examples of TEAs have shown that such agreements may indeed be effective and improve over the standard single IEA consisting only of nation states. Depending on the structure of costs from mitigation efforts and damages from climate change, the example of climate clubs shows that it is not in any case clear if TEAs take climate action beyond lip service.

Beyond these two examples there are various other settings of heterogeneous actors that might be conducive to tackle climate change. Other forms, mechanisms and players in TEAs, like NGOs, issue linkage, policy learning, moral hazard and political economy warrant further attention. Also cooperative game theory may be used to model TEAs.

Although we have shown that game theoretic analysis might well be helpful to better understand the formation and effects of TEAs, it is clear that it also has its limitations. Some aspects like the re-legitimation of the climate regime (cf. Falkner 2015) or potentially irrational behaviour of agents are difficult to analyse in a game theoretic setting and might be better researched by other means. One can also question the legitimacy of TEAs with non-state actors in contrast to multilateral IEAs negotiated by national governments. Nevertheless, we argue that especially with regard to the slow progress of the international climate negotiations, and in light of the empirical development already going on, it is important to include non-state actors complementary to an IEA.

Non-cooperative game theory offers a conservative view on agreements, i.e. it tends to underrate cooperation incentives (Carbone *et al.* 2009). Therefore our positive findings carry a particularly heavy meaning; we expect a real potential for TEAs. Institutions and negotiation structures for climate governance can improve if they allow for transnational actors. A combination of different scientific approaches sharpens the view. The global governance literature widens the horizon for economic analysis and challenges the conventional theory of IEAs, as it offers observations that cannot easily be explained by existing models. This is both a provocation and great opportunity for further theory building. Economics offer rigorous methods for the analysis of incentives for cooperation, and model results can give new ideas for TEA structures and negotiation processes.

Understanding TEAs is of the highest importance, particularly in the light of the Paris agreement of 2015 which does not provide binding emission reduction targets for nation states. This challenges both the negotiating actors and research. Our study sketches several promising policy options and avenues for further research.

References

Andonova, L. B., Betsill, M. M. and Bulkeley, H. (2009), 'Transnational Climate Governance', *Global Environmental Politics*, 9 (2): 52–73.

Asheim, G. B., Froyn, C. B., Hovi, J. and Menz, F. C. (2006), 'Regional versus Global Cooperation for Climate Control', *Journal of Environmental Economics and Management*, 51 (1): 93–109.

Barrett, S. (1994), 'Self-enforcing International Environmental Agreements', *Oxford Economic Papers*, 46: 878–894.

Betsill, M. M. and Bulkeley, H. (2004), 'Transnational Networks and Global Environmental Governance: The Cities for Climate Protection Program', *International Studies Quarterly*, 48 (2): 471–493.

Betsill, M. M. and Bulkeley, H. (2006), 'Cities and the Multilevel Governance of Global Climate Change', *Global Governance*, 12 (2): 141–159.

Betsill, M. M. and Bulkeley, H. (2007), 'Looking Back and Thinking Ahead: A Decade of Cities and Climate Change Research', *Local Environment*, 12 (5): 447–456.

Biermann, F., Pattberg, P., van Asselt, H. and Zelli, F. (2009), 'The Fragmentation of Global Governance Architectures: A Framework for Analysis', *Global Environmental Politics*, 9 (4): 14–40.

Bollen, J., Guay, B., Jamet, S. and Corfee-Morlot, J. (2009), Co-Benefits of Climate Change Mitigation Policies, *OECD Economics Department Working Papers 693, OECD, Economics Department*.

Bulkeley, H. (2010), 'Cities and the Governing of Climate Change', *Annual Review of Environment and Resources*, 35: 229–253.

Bulkeley, H. and Broto, V. (2013), 'Government by Experiment? Global Cities and the Governing of Climate Change', *Transactions of the Institute of British Geographers*, 38 (3): 361–375.

C40 (2015), C40 Cities Climate Leadership Group, Retrieved from C40 Web site: www. c40.org/.

Campbell-Lendrum, D. and Corvalan, C. (2007), 'Climate Change and Developing-Country Cities: Implications for Environmental Health and Equity', *Journal of Urban Health*, 84: 109–117.

Carbone, J. C., Helm, C. and Rutherford, T. F. (2009), 'The Case for International Emission Trade in the Absence of Cooperative Climate Policy', *Journal of Environmental Economics and Management*, 58 (3): 266–280.

Carraro, C. and Siniscalco, D. (1993), 'Strategies for the International Protection of the Environment', *Journal of Public Economics*, 52 (3): 309–328.

CDP (2015), Carbon Disclosure Project, Retrieved from CDP Web site: www.cdp.net.

Chander, P. and Tulkens, H. (1995), 'A Core-theoretic Solution for the Design of Cooperative Agreements on Transfrontier Pollution', *International Tax and Public Finance*, 2 (2): 279–293.

Climate Alliance (2015), Celebrating 25 years of the Climate Alliance!, Retrieved from Climate Alliance Web site: www.climatealliance.org.

Cole, D. H. (2011), 'From Global to Polycentric Climate Governance', *Climate Law*, 2 (3): 395–413.

Compact of Mayors (2015), www.compactofmayors.org.

Corfee-Morlot, J., Kamal-Chaoui, L., Donovan, M., Cochran, I., Robert. A. and Teasdale, P.-J. (2009), Cities, Climate Change and Multilevel Governance, *OECD Environmental Working Papers*, 14, 2009.

D'Aspremont, C. A., Jacquemin, J., Gabszeweitz, J. and Weymark, J. A. (1983), 'On the Stability of Collusive Price Leadership', *Canadian Journal of Economics*, 16 (1): 17–25.

Eckersley, R. (2012), 'Moving Forward in the Climate Negotiations: Multilateralism or Minilateralism?', *Global Environmental Politics*, 12 (2): 24–42.

Eichner, T. and Pethig, R. (2015), 'Self-enforcing International Environmental Agreements and Trade: Taxes versus Caps', *Oxford Economic Papers*, 67 (4): 897–917.

Eisenack, K. and Kähler, L. (2015), 'Adaptation to Climate Change Can Support Unilateral Emission Reductions', *Oxford Economic Papers*, 68: 258–278.

Falkner, R. (2015), International negotiations: 'Towards Minilateralism', *Nature Climate Change*, 5: 805–806.

Finus, M. (2008), 'Game Theoretic Research on the Design of International Environmental Agreements: Insights, Critical Remarks, and Future Challenges', *International Review of Environmental and Resource Economics*, 2 (1): 29–67.

Gehring, T. and Oberthür, S. (2008), 'Interplay: Exploring Institutional Interaction', In O. Young, K. A. King and H. Schröder (eds), *Institutions and Environmental Change: Principal Findings, Applications, and Research Frontiers*, Cambridge, MA: MIT Press, 187–223.

GHG Protocol (2015), Greenhouse Gas Protocol for Cities, Global standard for measuring greenhouse gas emissions, Retrieved from GHG Web site: www.ghg protocol.org.

Gill, S., Handley, J., Ennos, A. and Pauleit, S. (2007), 'Adapting Cities for Climate Change: The Role of the Green Infrastructure', *Built Environment*, 33 (1): 115–133.

Gustavsson, E., Elander, I. and Lundmark, M. (2009), 'Multilevel Governance, Networking Cities, and the Geography of Climate-change Mitigation: Two Swedish Examples', *Environmental Planning*, 27: 59–74.

Habla, W. and Winkler, R. (2013), 'Political Influence on Non-cooperative International Climate Policy', *Journal of Environmental Economics and Management*, 66 (2): 219–234.

Hagen, A. and Eisenack, K. (2015), International Environmental Agreements with Asymmetric Countries: Climate Clubs vs. Global Cooperation, *FEEM Working Paper No. 58.2015*.

Hagen, A., Altamirano-Cabrera, J-C. and Weikard, H-P. (2016), The Influence of Political Pressure Groups on the Stability of International Environmental Agreements, *Oldenburg Discussion Papers in Economics V-391-16*.

Hakelberg, L. (2014), 'Governance by Diffusion: Transnational Municipal Networks and the Spread of Local Climate Strategies in Europe', *Global Environmental Politics*, 14 (1): 107–129.

Hale, T. and Roger, C. (2014), 'Orchestration and Transnational Climate Governance', *Review of International Organizations*, 9 (1): 59–82.

Hallegatte, S. and Corfee-Morlot, J. (2011), 'Understanding Climate Change Impacts, Vulnerability and Adaptation at City Scale: An Introduction', *Climatic Change*, 104 (1): 1–12.

Harlan, S. L. and Ruddell, D. M. (2011), 'Climate Change and Health in Cities: Impacts of Heat and Air Pollution and Potential Co-benefits From Mitigation and Adaptation', *Current Opinion in Environmental Sustainability*, 3 (3): 126–134.

Hoel, M. (1991), 'Global Environmental Problems: The Effects of Unilateral Actions Taken by One Country', *Journal of Environmental Economics and Management*, 20 (1): 55–70.

Hooghe, L. and Marks, G. (2003), 'Unraveling the Central State, but How? Types of Multilevel Governance', *American Political Science Review*, 97 (2): 233–243.

ICLEI (2015), ICLEI – the Global Cities Network, Retrieved from ICLEI Web site: www.iclei.org/iclei-members.html.

International Energy and Climate Initiative – Energy+ (2015), www.regjeringen.no/en/topics/foreign-affairs/development-cooperation/energy_plus/id672635/, accessed 11.12.2015.

IPCC (2014), *Climate Change 2014: Mitigation of Climate Change*, Cambridge: Cambridge University Press.

Isailovic, M., Widerberg, O. and Pattberg, P. (2013), Fragmentation of Global Environmental Governance Architectures. A Literature Review, *Report W-13/09, IVM Institute for Environmental Studies*, Amsterdam.

Jochem, E. and Madlener, R. (2003), The Forgotten Benefits of Climate Change Mitigation: Innovation, Technological Leapfrogging, Employment, and Sustainable Development, *Workshop on the Benefits of Climate Policy: Improving Information for Policy Makers*.

Jordan, A. J., Huitema, D., Hilden, M., van Asselt, H., Rayner, T. J., Schoenefeld, J. J., Tosun, J., Forster, J. and Boasson, E. L. (2015), 'Emergence of Polycentric Climate Governance and its Future Prospects', *Nature Climate Change*, 5: 977–982.

Karlsson-Vinkhuyzen, S. I. and McGee, J. (2013), 'Legitimacy in an Era of Fragmentation: The Case of Global Climate Governance', *Global Environmental Politics*, 13 (3): 56–78.

Keohane, R. O. and Victor, D. G. (2011), 'The Regime Complex for Climate Change', *Perspectives on Politics*, 9 (1): 7–23.

Kern, K. and Bulkeley, H. (2009), 'Cities, Europeanization and Multi-level Governance: Governing Climate Change through Transnational Municipal Networks', *Journal of Common Market Studies*, 47 (2): 309–332.

Marchiori, C., Dietz, S., and Tavoni, A., (2016), 'Domestic politics and the formation of International Environmental Agreements', *Journal of Environmental Economics and Management*, 81: 115–131.

Millard-Ball, A. (2012), 'Do City Climate Plans Reduce Emissions?', *Journal of Urban Economics*, 71 (3): 289–311.

Moncel, R. and van Asselt, H. (2012), 'All Hands on Deck! Mobilizing Climate Change Action beyond the UNFCCC', *Review of European Community and International Environmental Law*, 21 (3): 163–176.

Monni, S. and Raes, F. (2008), 'Multilevel Climate Policy: The Case of the European Union, Finland and Helsinki', *Environmental Science and Policy*, 11 (8): 743–755.

Nordhaus, W. (2015), 'Climate Clubs: Overcoming Free-riding in International Climate Policy', *American Economic Review*, 105 (4): 1339–1370.

Oates, W. E. (1972), *Fiscal Federalism*, New York: Harcourt Brace Jovanovich.

Oates, W. E. (2005), 'Toward a Second-Generation Theory of Fiscal Federalism', *International Tax and Public Finance*, 12 (4): 349–373.

Olson, M. (1971), *The Logic of Collective Action: Public Goods and the Theory of Groups*, Cambridge, Mass.: Harvard University Press.

Osmani, D. and Tol, R. (2010), 'The Case of Two Self-enforcing International Agreements for Environmental Protection with Asymmetric Countries', *Computational Economics*, 36 (2): 93–119.

Ostrom, E. (2010), 'Polycentric Systems for Coping with Collective Action and Global Environmental Change', *Global Environmental Change*, 20 (4): 550–557.

Ostrom, E. (2012), 'Nested Externalities and Polycentric Institutions: Must We Wait for Global Solutions to Climate Change Before Taking Actions at Other Scales?' *Economic Theory*, 49 (2): 353–369.

Ostrom, V., Tiebout, C. and Warren, R. (1961), 'The Organization of Government in Metropolitan Areas: A Theoretical Inquiry', *American Political Science Review*, 55 (4): 831–842.

Shobe, W. and Burtraw, D. (2012), Rethinking Environmental Federalism in a Warming World, *Climate Change Economics*, 03 (4): 1250018.

Sippel, M. (2010), Cities in Germany and their Climate Commitments: More Hype than Substance? *Discussion Paper MPRA Paper No. 23011, Institute of Energy Economics and Rational Energy Use, University Stuttgart*.

Sippel, M. and Jenssen, T. (2009), What About Local Climate Governance? A Review of Promise and Problems. *Discussion Paper MPRA Paper No. 20987, Institute of Energy Economics and Rational Energy Use, University Stuttgart*.

Stern, N. (2007), *The Economics of Climate Change: The Stern Review*, Cambridge: Cambridge University Press.

Stewart, R. B., Oppenheimer, M. and Rudyk, B. (2013), 'Building Blocks for Global Climate Protection', *Stanford Environmental Law*, 32: 341–392.

UNEP, United Nations Environment Programme (2015), Climate Commitments of Subnational Actors and Business: A Quantitative Assessment of their Emission Reduction Impact, *United Nations Environment Programme (UNEP)*, Nairobi.

Urpelainen, J. (2009), 'Explaining the Schwarzenegger Phenomenon: Local Frontrunners in Climate Policy', *Global Environmental Politics*, 9 (3): 82–105.

Wangler, L., Altamirano-Cabrera, J-C. and Weikard, H-P. (2013), 'The Political Economy of International Environmental Agreements: A Survey', *International Environmental Agreements: Politics, Law and Economics*, 13 (3): 387–403.

Weischer, L., Morgan, J. and Patel, M. (2012), 'Climate Clubs: Can Small Groups of Countries Make a Big Difference in Addressing Climate Change?' *Review of European, Comparative and International Environmental Law*, 21 (3): 177–192.

Widerberg, O. and Stenson, D. E. (2013), Climate Clubs and the UNFCCC-Complement, Bypass or Conflict? *FORES Study* 2013:3.

5 International trade and environmental cooperation among heterogeneous countries

Soham Baksi and Amrita Ray Chaudhuri

1 Introduction

We examine countries' incentives to cooperate in regulating emissions of a transboundary pollutant, when the countries differ in terms of the damage they face from pollution. Such heterogeneity may arise due to differential vulnerability to pollution induced damages across countries, or may reflect income differential across countries. As observed in the empirical literature on economic growth and the environment, citizens of richer countries typically demand better environmental quality and experience a greater disutility from pollution than citizens of poorer countries. The presence of such heterogeneity leads to differential environmental policies across countries, which in turn influence international trade, and raises a set of questions not adequately addressed in the existing literature on international environmental cooperation, which mainly focuses on models with symmetric countries under autarky. In this chapter, we address some of these issues involving international trade, transboundary pollution and environmental cooperation among heterogeneous countries. In particular, we analyse how the extent of heterogeneity and freer trade affect the sustainability of such cooperation. We also examine the role played by border tax adjustments (BTAs) in sustaining cooperation, where countries imposing a higher pollution tax on their domestic firms charge the BTA on imports of a polluting good from countries imposing a lower pollution tax.

These issues gain importance in light of the ongoing intergovernmental negotiations on climate change conducted under the aegis of the UNFCCC. Since the 1990s, while trade liberalization through regional and multilateral trade agreements has proliferated, intergovernmental negotiations to mitigate greenhouse gas emissions have floundered. Despite recognizing the need for more stringent environmental regulations, many developed countries have been reluctant to tighten their own regulations unless they are simultaneously matched by stricter regulations in developing countries. A main reason for this reluctance among developed countries has been the concern that their firms may lose international competitiveness if the stricter regulations are not matched by all other countries.[1] Moreover, if stricter regulations in developed countries lead to the shifting of polluting production to developing countries with laxer regulations (i.e. 'pollution leakage'), this would undermine the mitigation of transboundary pollutants at the global level.

One possible solution to these problems that has been recently proposed is the use of border tax adjustments based on differences in environmental regulations between a pair of trading countries (e.g. Eyland and Zaccour 2012, 2014; Ghosh *et al.* 2012; Böhringer *et al.* 2015, 2016).[2] It is unclear as to whether BTAs based on environmental regulations would be consistent with extant WTO rules. While some have argued that exemptions under Article XX of the WTO allow the use of such BTAs (e.g. Zhang 2010), others have suggested that this may not be the case and proposed a 'carbon footprint tax' as a WTO compliant alternative to BTAs (McAusland and Najjar 2015).[3]

In this chapter, we develop a theoretical framework which captures some of these issues underlying climate negotiations. Specifically, we consider an oligopoly model of trade in a polluting good between two countries, North and South, which differ in terms of their pollution damage parameter. The pollution damage parameter is assumed to be higher in the North. Production generates transboundary pollution, and each country imposes a pollution tax on its domestic firm, where the tax rate can be chosen either cooperatively or non-cooperatively. Since markets are imperfectly competitive, each country has an incentive to strategically distort its non-cooperative pollution tax in order to give its domestic firm a competitive advantage and capture rents from the other country (Barrett 1994; Kennedy 1994). We analyse the sustainability of environmental cooperation between the two countries within an infinitely repeated game framework, where cooperation is self-sustained through the use of trigger strategies.[4]

Unlike most of the literature on international environmental agreements (IEAs), our model allows for both international trade in a polluting good and heterogeneity among countries. Consequently, we are able to analyse how inter-jurisdictional pollution leakage, facilitated by international trade, affects the incentives of heterogeneous countries to cooperate with each other in terms of their environmental policies. We find that, when the two countries choose their pollution tax rates cooperatively, they set it at the same level. As a result, there is no pollution leakage in the cooperative equilibrium. By contrast, the non-cooperative tax rate is higher in the North, which leads to production shifting from the North to the South and an increase in net exports of the polluting good from the latter to the former. Our analysis shows that a greater degree of cross-country heterogeneity with respect to the pollution damage parameter reduces the likelihood of cooperation between the countries. Second, we find that trade liberalization increases both the global gains from cooperation as well as the likelihood of cooperation between the countries. Third, imposition of a border tax adjustment by the North on imports of the polluting good from the South weakens the North's incentive to cooperate. As well, the BTA strengthens the South's incentive to cooperate provided the countries are sufficiently heterogeneous. Whether the BTA ultimately facilitates cooperation between the two countries depends, in part, on the rules associated with the use of BTAs.

Our chapter contributes to a large literature on IEAs (reviewed in Marrouch and Ray Chaudhuri 2016). This literature mostly uses reduced form models, which abstract away from market structure, heterogeneity and trade flows between countries, by directly specifying the benefits and costs of identical countries as functions of their emission or abatement levels. To analyse the stability of self-enforcing IEAs, the dominant stream of the literature uses the internal and external stability criteria presented by d'Aspremont *et al.* (1983). Since they do not model international trade, the reduced form models cannot be used to analyse how trade liberalization, or the imposition of BTAs, affects the incentives of countries to cooperate in terms of their environmental policies. The few papers which examine the stability of IEAs with heterogeneous countries (e.g. McGinty 2007; Kolstad 2010; Pavlova and de Zeeuw 2013; Hagen and Eisenack 2015), do not address these issues since they abstract away from international trade.

A smaller literature explicitly models international trade while examining the stability of IEAs involving identical countries. Using an oligopoly model of trade with identical countries where firms face abatement standards, Barrett (1997) shows that a threat by IEA signatory countries to impose trade sanctions on non-signatory countries, accompanied by a minimum participation clause, may lead to a stable global IEA.[5] Using a similar setting where firms face emission taxes, Baksi and Ray Chaudhuri (2014) show that the global IEA is unstable under autarky, and that free trade may stabilize the global IEA. As markets become more competitive, it becomes more likely that the global IEA is stable. They further find that the imposition of a BTA destabilizes an otherwise stable global IEA. At the same time, if the global IEA is unstable under free trade, imposing a BTA may improve welfare. Eichner and Pethig (2013, 2014, 2015) use general equilibrium models of trade with perfect competition and identical countries, and inter alia find that large sub-coalitions are stable only when the gains from cooperation are small. Our chapter is closest to Benchekroun and Yildiz (2011), who use an oligopoly model of trade between two identical countries and a repeated game framework involving trigger strategies. They find that a move from autarky to free trade reduces the likelihood of cooperation between the countries. Unlike our paper, they consider emission standards, and do not analyse the impact of BTAs on cooperation.

We proceed further as follows. Section 2 presents our basic model without any BTA. Section 3 derives its equilibrium under full cooperation and non-cooperation in the one shot game. Section 4 presents the repeated game associated with the one shot game, and analyses the incentives of the countries to cooperate in the absence of a BTA. In Section 5, we analyse the impact of implementing a BTA on cooperation. The last section concludes.

2 The basic model

Consider two countries, 1 and 2, with one firm in each country. Both firms are identical and produce a homogeneous good at constant marginal cost, c. The two countries have segmented markets. In each market, the firms compete in quantities à la Cournot. The firm in country i sells x_{ij} units of the good in country j, with $i, j = 1, 2$. Inverse demand in each country is given by

$$p(Q_i) = p(0) - Q_i,$$

where $p(0) - c \equiv a > 0$, and $Q_i \equiv \sum_{j=1}^{2} x_{ji}$ is total quantity sold and consumed in country i.

A by-product of production in this industry is a perfectly transboundary pollutant such as carbon dioxide. With appropriate definition of units it is assumed that, for every unit of output they produce, the firms emit one unit of pollution.[6] The social cost of pollution is increasing and convex in the level of emissions affecting a country. Pollution damage in country i, D_i, is given by

$$D_i = \frac{1}{2}\beta_i\left[\sum_{i=1}^{2} X_i\right]^2,$$

(1)

where β_i denotes the pollution damage parameter in country $i = 1, 2$. Note that total production undertaken in country i is $X_i \equiv \sum_{j=1}^{2} x_{ij}$, and total global production is $\sum_{i=1}^{2} X_i = \sum_{i=1}^{2} Q_i$. We assume that $\beta_1 > \beta_2 > 0$, i.e. pollution damage is higher in country 1 than in country 2 for any given amount of global pollution. Henceforth, we refer to country 1 as the 'North' and country 2 as the 'South'. The environmental policy in country i is a tax imposed on the domestic firm at the rate t_i per unit of emission. Given our assumption of constant emission-output ratio, a tax per unit of emission is equivalent to a tax per unit of output produced of the polluting good. Moreover, each country imposes a tariff τ per unit of import from the other country.

Given the above setting, consumer surplus and producer surplus in country i are respectively given by $CS_i = \frac{1}{2}Q_i^2$ and $\pi_i = (p(Q_i) - c)x_{ii} + (p(Q_j) - c)x_{ij} - t_i X_i - \tau x_{ij}$. Country i's emission tax revenue is $ER_i = t_i X_i$, and its tariff revenue is $TR_i = \tau x_{ji}$, with $j \neq i$. In the basic model, welfare of country i is defined as

$$W_i = CS_i + \pi_i + ER_i + TR_i - D_i$$

(2)

While in the basic model there is no BTA, we extend this model in Section 5 by introducing a BTA. In the next two sections, we present a one shot game and the corresponding repeated game and derive the equilibriums in the absence of BTAs.

3   One shot game

In the one shot game, we consider two alternative scenarios – full cooperation and non-cooperation – which act as building blocks for our analysis. Superscripts *c* and *nc* are used to denote the fully cooperative and non-cooperative equilibriums, respectively. The one shot game consists of two stages. In the first stage, each country chooses its pollution tax rate either cooperatively or non-cooperatively depending on the scenario. In the second stage, each firm takes the policies set by the countries and the output decisions of the other firm as given, and chooses its own output. To obtain the subgame perfect Nash equilibrium, the model is solved using backward induction.

The second stage is common across the two scenarios, full cooperation and non-cooperation. The firm in country *i* chooses the output it sells at home and in the foreign market so as to maximize its own profit, i.e.

$$\underset{x_{ii},x_{ij}}{Max}\ \pi_i = \left(a - x_{ji} - x_{ii}\right)x_{ii} + \left(a - x_{jj} - x_{ij}\right)x_{ij} - t_i\left(x_{ii} + x_{ij}\right) - \tau x_{ij}$$

Simultaneously solving the first order conditions (FOCs) for the above profit maximization problem, the equilibrium quantities are obtained as

$$x_{ii} = \frac{a - 2t_i + t_j + \tau}{3} \tag{3}$$

$$x_{ij} = \frac{a - 2(t_i + \tau) + t_j}{3} \tag{4}$$

where $j \neq i$. The second order conditions (SOCs) are satisfied as we have

$$\frac{\partial^2 \pi_i}{\partial x_{ii}^2} < 0, \frac{\partial^2 \pi_i}{\partial x_{ij}^2} < 0 \text{ and } \frac{\partial^2 \pi_i}{\partial x_{ii}^2}\frac{\partial^2 \pi_i}{\partial x_{ij}^2} - \left(\frac{\partial^2 \pi_i}{\partial x_{ii}\partial x_{ij}}\right)^2 > 0.$$

The first stage of the game differs across the two scenarios, full cooperation and non-cooperation. Under full cooperation, the countries maximize their joint welfare. The optimization problem is then given by $Max(W_1 + W_2)$ with respect to t_i, where W_i is defined in (2). Simultaneously solving the two FOCs, we find that equilibrium tax rates in the cooperative equilibrium are equal in each country and given by $t_1^c = t_2^c = t^c$, where

$$t^c = \frac{a}{2\Omega}(4\beta_1 + 4\beta_2 - 1) - \frac{\tau}{2} \tag{5}$$

and $\Omega \equiv 2\beta_1 + 2\beta_2 + 1$. Moreover, the SOCs are satisfied since $\dfrac{\partial^2 (W_1 + W_2)}{\partial t_i^2} < 0$

for $i = 1, 2$. We note that $\dfrac{\partial t^c}{\partial \tau} = -\dfrac{1}{2} < 0$, implying that trade liberalization, in the form of bilateral tariff reductions, results in a higher cooperative emission tax rate. This is because trade liberalization increases global production for given t_i and t_j, which follows from (3) and (4), thereby increasing marginal damage from pollution. Further, $\dfrac{\partial t^c}{\partial \beta_1} = \dfrac{\partial t^c}{\partial \beta_2} = \dfrac{3a}{\Omega^2} > 0$, i.e. a higher pollution damage parameter in either country results in a higher cooperative emission tax rate.

Substituting (5) in (3) and (4), the equilibrium output levels under full cooperation are obtained as

$$x_{11}^c = x_{22}^c = \frac{a + \tau\Omega}{2\Omega} \tag{6}$$

$$x_{12}^c = x_{21}^c = \frac{a - \tau\Omega}{2\Omega} \tag{7}$$

Thus domestic sales increase, while exports decrease, in the tariff level. Note that exports are positive, i.e. $x_{12}^c = x_{21}^c > 0$, if and only if $\tau < \dfrac{a}{\Omega}$. Throughout the chapter, we assume that the tariff rate τ is sufficiently small (i.e. close to zero) and less than the prohibitive rate of tariff. Equations (6) and (7) imply that net export of each country is zero, as $Q_i^c = X_i^c$.[7] Using (2), the welfare level for country i under full cooperation is given by

$$W_i^c = \frac{a^2\left(1 + 4\beta_j\right)}{2\Omega^2},$$

with $W_2^c - W_1^c = \dfrac{2a^2}{\Omega^2}(\beta_1 - \beta_2) > 0$. The global production and welfare levels are respectively given by $X^c \equiv X_1^c + X_2^c = \dfrac{2a}{\Omega}$ and $W^c \equiv W_1^c + W_2^c = \dfrac{a^2}{\Omega}$, which are independent of the tariff rate. This is because, in the cooperative equilibrium, any decrease in tariff τ is offset by an increase in the tax rate t^c, such that global production and welfare remain unchanged at their efficient levels.

On the other hand, in the non-cooperative scenario, each country chooses its pollution tax rate to maximize its own welfare, taking as given the other country's tax rate. The optimization problem is now given by $\underset{t_i}{Max}\ W_i$, for $i = 1, 2$, where W_i is given by (2). The FOC for country i gives its reaction function $t_i(t_j)$, with $\dfrac{dt_i}{dt_j} = -\dfrac{4\beta_i + 1}{4\beta_i + 7} < 0$. Thus pollution taxes are strategic substitutes in the non-cooperative equilibrium. Simultaneously solving the two countries' FOCs, the non-cooperative equilibrium taxes are obtained as

$$t_i^{nc} = \frac{1}{4\Psi}\Big[4a\big(3\beta_i - \beta_j - 1\big) + \tau\big(5 - 8\beta_i + 4\beta_j\big)\Big], \tag{8}$$

where $\Psi \equiv \beta_1 + \beta_2 + 2$ and $i, j = 1, 2$ with $i \neq j$. The SOCs are satisfied since $\dfrac{\partial^2 W_i}{\partial t_i^2} < 0$. Moreover, the reaction functions of the two countries yield a stable equilibrium. Substituting (8) in (3) and (4), the output levels in the non-cooperative equilibrium are given by

$$x_{ii}^{nc} = \frac{1}{4\Psi}\left[a\left(4 - 8\beta_i + 8\beta_j\right) + \tau\left(1 + 8\beta_i - 4\beta_j\right)\right] \tag{9}$$

$$x_{ij}^{nc} = \frac{1}{4\Psi}\left[a\left(4 - 8\beta_i + 8\beta_j\right) - \tau\left(7 - 4\beta_i + 8\beta_j\right)\right] \tag{10}$$

We assume that parameter values are such that these quantities are positive. The global production level is given by $X^{nc} = \dfrac{4a - 3\tau}{\Psi}$, which is decreasing in the tariff level τ.[8] Thus, changes in the tariff level are not fully offset by adjustments of the non-cooperatively set tax rates, so that trade liberalization increases global production and pollution damage under non-cooperation, unlike under full cooperation. Moreover, we have

$$Q_1^{nc} - X_1^{nc} = X_2^{nc} - Q_2^{nc} = \frac{1}{\Psi}(4a - 3\tau)(\beta_1 - \beta_2) > 0 \tag{11}$$

which shows that the North – the country with the higher pollution damage parameter – is a net importer and the South a net exporter of the polluting good in the non-cooperative equilibrium.

Using (8), we have $\dfrac{\partial t_i^{nc}}{\partial \beta_i} = \dfrac{1}{4\Psi^2}(7 + 4\beta_j)(4a - 3\tau) > 0$ and $\dfrac{\partial t_i^{nc}}{\partial \beta_j} = -\dfrac{1}{4\Psi^2}(1 + 4\beta_i)$ $(4a - 3\tau) < 0$. In other words, the pollution tax rate in each country increases in its own pollution damage parameter, and decreases in the other country's pollution damage parameter, consistent with free-riding behaviour in the non-cooperative equilibrium. Moreover, we have $t_1^{nc} - t_2^{nc} = \dfrac{1}{\Psi}(4a - 3\tau)(\beta_1 - \beta_2) > 0$, i.e. the pollution tax rate is higher in the North, which explains the equilibrium pattern of trade given by (11). The welfare level for country i in the non-cooperative equilibrium is given by

$$W_i^{nc} = \frac{4a - 3\tau}{8\Psi^2}\left[4a\left(1 + \beta_j + 2\beta_j^2 - 3\beta_i - 2\beta_i^2\right) + \tau\left(3 - 4\beta_j - 8\beta_j^2 + 16\beta_i + 8\beta_i^2\right)\right]$$

In the neighbourhood of free trade, welfare is higher in the South as $\lim_{\tau \to 0}\left(W_2^{nc} - W_1^{nc}\right) = \dfrac{8a^2}{2\Psi^2}(\beta_1 - \beta_2)(\beta_1 + \beta_2 + 1) > 0$. Global welfare in the non-cooperative equilibrium is given by

$$W^{nc} \equiv W_1^{nc} + W_2^{nc} = \frac{4a - 3\tau}{4\Psi^2}\left[4a\left(1 - \beta_1 - \beta_2\right) + 3\tau\Omega\right],$$

which is concave in τ, with $\dfrac{\partial W^{nc}}{\partial \tau} = \dfrac{9}{2\Psi^2}\left(2a(\beta_1 + \beta_2) - \tau\Omega\right) \geq 0$ if and only if $\tau \leq \hat{\tau} \equiv \dfrac{2a}{\Omega}(\beta_1 + \beta_2)$.

Comparing the fully cooperative and the non-cooperative equilibria, we have

$$\lim_{\tau \to 0}\left(t_i^c - t_i^{nc}\right) = \dfrac{a}{2\Omega\Psi}\left[5\beta_i + 13\beta_j - 8\left(\beta_i^2 - \beta_j^2\right)\right] \tag{12}$$

$$\lim_{\tau \to 0}\left(W_i^c - W_i^{nc}\right) = \dfrac{a^2\left(\beta_i + \beta_j\right)}{2\Omega^2\Psi^2}\left[\begin{array}{c}41\beta_i - 23\beta_j + 4\left(\beta_i + \beta_j\right)\left(20\beta_i - 11\beta_j\right) \\ + 32\left(\beta_i - \beta_j\right)\left(\beta_i + \beta_j\right)^2\end{array}\right] \tag{13}$$

Since the markets are imperfectly competitive, each country has an incentive to inefficiently lower its non-cooperative pollution tax in order to give its domestic firm a competitive advantage and capture rents from the other country. Hence, in the interior equilibrium near free trade, we have $t_2^{nc} < t_1^{nc} < t^c$. While the North is always better off under cooperation, the same is true for the South provided the difference between β_1 and β_2 is not too large.[9] Global production and pollution are higher under non-cooperation than under cooperation if and only if $\tau \leq \hat{\tau}$, since

$$X^{nc} - X^c = \dfrac{3}{\Omega\Psi}\left[2a(\beta_1 + \beta_2) - \tau\Omega\right] \tag{14}$$

Moreover, global welfare is unambiguously higher under cooperation as

$$W^c - W^{nc} = \dfrac{9}{4\Omega\Psi^2}\left[2a(\beta_1 + \beta_2) - \tau\Omega\right]^2 > 0 \tag{15}$$

Next we determine the effect of trade liberalization on the gains from cooperation. The environmental gains from cooperation are defined as the reduction in global pollution achieved when moving from the non-cooperative to the cooperative equilibrium, i.e. $(X^{nc} - X^c)$. Similarly, the welfare gains from cooperation are defined as the difference $(W^c - W^{nc})$.

Proposition 1: *In the neighbourhood of free trade, bilateral tariff reductions increase the global environmental and welfare gains from cooperation.*

Proof: Using (14) and (15), we have $\dfrac{\partial\left(X^{nc} - X^c\right)}{\partial \tau} < 0$ and $\lim_{\tau \to 0} \dfrac{\partial\left(W^c - W^{nc}\right)}{\partial \tau} < 0$.

Proposition 1 follows from the fact that global production and pollution are independent of the tariff level under full cooperation, $\dfrac{\partial X^c}{\partial \tau} = 0$, and decreasing in the tariff level under non-cooperation, $\dfrac{\partial X^{nc}}{\partial \tau} < 0$. Moreover, global welfare is independent of the tariff level under full cooperation, $\dfrac{\partial W^c}{\partial \tau} = 0$, and

concave in τ under non-cooperation with $\lim_{\tau \to 0}\left(\dfrac{\partial W^{nc}}{\partial \tau}\right) > 0$. While trade liberalization makes cooperation more desirable from an environmental and global welfare standpoint, whether such cooperation can be sustained in the long run is what we turn to analyse next.

4 Repeated game

To examine the sustainability of cooperation between the heterogeneous countries, in this section we consider a supergame where the one shot game described in the previous section is repeated infinitely. According to the well known folk theorem, the cooperative equilibrium may be sustained by trigger strategies as long as the players' discount rates are sufficiently small, i.e. the players are sufficiently patient. A trigger strategy typically entails adopting the cooperative solution unless defection is observed. Defection by any one player in any period triggers a permanent breakdown of cooperation, and the players choose the non-cooperative solution in every period subsequent to the period when defection is observed. In every period, each player weighs the one period benefit of defecting against the present value of future losses from the breakdown of cooperation. If the latter is greater than the former for each player in every period, cooperation is self sustainable.

In the context of our model, the trigger strategy is applicable as follows. In every period, each country decides whether to set its tax at the cooperative level, t^c, or to defect from the cooperative outcome. In the case where one country unilaterally defects while the other plays the cooperative strategy, it is assumed that the cooperating country sets its tax rate at t^c in the period when defection happens. Thus, if country i defects, its optimization problem is given by $Max\ W_i\big|_{t_j = t^c}$ with respect to t_i. Solving the relevant FOC, the tax rate chosen by the defecting country, t_i^d, is obtained as

$$t_i^d = \frac{a\left(16\beta_i\beta_j - 20\beta_j + 16\beta_i^2 - 7\right) + \tau\Omega\left(11 - 4\beta_i\right)}{2\Omega\left(7 + 4\beta_i\right)}$$

The SOC is satisfied as $\dfrac{\partial^2 W_i\big|_{t_j = t^c}}{\partial t_i^2} < 0$.

If one of the countries defects in a given period, it is assumed that both countries play the non-cooperative strategy, t^{nc}, from the subsequent period onwards. When deciding whether to cooperate or defect in a given period, each country compares its one period gain from defecting against the present value of losses arising from the fact that both countries choose non-cooperation subsequent to a defection. The one period gain from defection for country i is given by

$$G_i \equiv W_i \big|_{t_i = t_i^d, t_j = t^c} - W_i^c$$

The loss in each future period is given by

$$L_i \equiv W_i^c - W_i^{nc}$$

Thus, country i has an incentive to defect if and only if $G_i > \dfrac{\theta_i}{1-\theta_i} L_i$, where $\theta_i \in [0,1]$ represents the discount factor of country i. Self-enforcing cooperation is sustainable if and only if the current gain from defection is less than the discounted lifetime cost of defection for each country, i.e. $G_i \leq \dfrac{\theta_i}{1-\theta_i} L_i$ for $i = 1,2$. Let $\hat{\theta}_i(\beta_1, \beta_2, \tau)$ represent the threshold value of the discount factor for country i such that

$$G_i = \frac{\hat{\theta}_i}{1-\hat{\theta}_i} L_i$$

Thus, for $\theta_i \geq \hat{\theta}_i$, country i chooses to implement the cooperative tax rate, and for $\theta_i < \hat{\theta}_i$, country i chooses to unilaterally defect. Note that if $\hat{\theta}_i > 1$, country i unilaterally defects for any value of its discount factor $\theta_i \in [0,1]$.

For analytical tractability, henceforth we assume $\beta_2 = 0.1$.[10] For $\beta_2 = 0.1$ and $\tau \to 0$, the quantities given by (6), (7), (9) and (10) are strictly positive in all cases (i.e. the fully cooperative equilibrium, non-cooperative equilibrium, and if either country defects) only if $\beta_1 < 0.41$.[11] Hence, for the remainder of this section, we restrict our attention to $\beta_1 \in (0.1, 0.41)$ and tariff rates that are close to zero. This ensures that production and trade takes place in equilibrium.

When $\beta_2 = 0.1$, the above mentioned threshold values of the discount factors for the two countries are given by

$$\hat{\theta}_1 \big|_{\tau \to 0} = \frac{16(10\beta_1 + 21)^2 (5\beta_1 + 1)^2}{(650\beta_1 + 400\beta_1^2 + 21)(1678\beta_1 + 2360\beta_1^2 + 800\beta_1^3 + 105)} \tag{16}$$

$$\hat{\theta}_2 \big|_{\tau \to 0} = \frac{20(10\beta_1 + 21)^2 (20\beta_1 + 1)^2}{(6430\beta_1 + 5400\beta_1^2 + 789)(250\beta_1 - 400\beta_1^2 + 69)} \tag{17}$$

For $\beta_1 \in (0.1, 0.41)$, we find that $\hat{\theta}_1 \big|_{\tau \to 0} < \hat{\theta}_2 \big|_{\tau \to 0}$.[12] Thus the North, which suffers more from pollution, is more likely to cooperate as it cooperates for a greater range of θ values than the South. Since it takes participation by both countries for self-enforcing cooperation between them, any factor that causes a decrease (respectively increase) in the higher of the two discount factor thresholds, i.e. $\max\{\hat{\theta}_1, \hat{\theta}_2\}$, is said to increase (respectively decrease) the likelihood of sustainable cooperation.

We begin by examining how the likelihood of cooperation is affected by the degree of asymmetry between the countries.

Proposition 2: *In the neighbourhood of free trade, a greater degree of asymmetry between the countries, as denoted by a higher β_1 given $\beta_2 = 0.1$, decreases the likelihood that cooperation is sustained between them.*

Proof: Using (16) and (17), for $\beta_1 \in (0.1, 0.41)$, we have $\hat{\theta}_1 |_{\tau \to 0} < \hat{\theta}_2 |_{\tau \to 0}$,

$$\frac{\partial \hat{\theta}_1}{\partial \beta_1} |_{\tau \to 0} < 0 \text{ and } \frac{\partial \hat{\theta}_2}{\partial \beta_1} |_{\tau \to 0} > 0.$$

Proposition 2 shows that the greater the heterogeneity between the North and the South in terms of their pollution damage parameter, the less (respectively, more) is the likelihood of cooperation by the South (respectively, North). An implication is that if asymmetry across the countries were reduced, for e.g. through economic growth or greater awareness of environmental damages in the South, which increases demand for environmental quality in that country, this would increase the likelihood of sustainable cooperation between them in terms of their pollution pricing policies.

Next, we examine the effect of trade liberalization on the likelihood of sustaining cooperation.

Proposition 3: *In the neighbourhood of free trade, bilateral tariff reductions increase the likelihood that cooperation is sustained between the heterogeneous countries.*

Proof: Using (16) and (17), for $\beta_1 \in (0.1, 0.41)$, we have $\hat{\theta}_1 |_{\tau \to 0} < \hat{\theta}_2 |_{\tau \to 0}$,

$$\frac{\partial \hat{\theta}_1}{\partial \tau} |_{\tau \to 0} < 0 \text{ and } \frac{\partial \hat{\theta}_2}{\partial \tau} |_{\tau \to 0} > 0.[13]$$

Thus, trade liberalization reduces (respectively, expands) the range of the discount factor for which the North (respectively, South) cooperates. Since $\hat{\theta}_1 |_{\tau \to 0} < \hat{\theta}_2 |_{\tau \to 0}$, it follows that bilateral tariff reductions in the neighbourhood of free trade increases the likelihood that environmental cooperation is sustained between the North and the South.[14] Propositions 1 and 3 highlight an optimistic result relative to the general conclusion in the IEA literature. Assuming symmetric countries, the literature finds that conditions under which larger coalitions become sustainable are typically associated with lower gains from cooperation. Propositions 1 and 3 together show that trade liberalization not only makes cooperation more likely between heterogeneous countries, but also increases the environmental and welfare gains from cooperation.

5 Border tax adjustment

The previous section showed that the South is less likely to cooperate than the North. In this section, we examine whether (the threat of) imposing a border tax adjustment by the North in the non-cooperative equilibrium can induce more cooperation from the South. To this end, we extend our basic model by allowing the countries to implement a BTA. The BTA takes the form of a 'carbon tariff' that is imposed by the country with the higher pollution (e.g. carbon) tax on imports of the polluting good from the other country. The carbon tariff rate is set proportional to the carbon tax differential across the two trading countries. In the fully cooperative equilibrium, both countries set the same tax rate, t^c, and the BTA plays no role. Within the repeated game framework, in the period where one of the countries defects from full cooperation, the BTA also plays no role since the cooperating country, setting the higher tax, does not observe the other country defecting within that period. Therefore, the fully cooperative equilibrium and the equilibrium where one country unilaterally defects remain as described in the previous sections.

The BTA does play a key role in the non-cooperative equilibrium, so we describe the non-cooperative equilibrium again, this time allowing for the BTA. Since $\beta_1 > \beta_2$, the non-cooperative pollution tax rate is higher in the North. Hence, the North imposes a BTA at the rate of $\delta(t_1 - t_2)$ per unit of import from the South, where δ is a parameter. We assume that $\delta = 1$, i.e. the carbon tariff rate accounts for the full differential in the carbon tax rates across the two countries.[15] Since the pollution tax rate is lower in the South, it does not impose any BTA on imports from the North in the non-cooperative equilibrium. For simplicity, in this section we assume that the general tariff rate, τ, is zero.

In the non-cooperative equilibrium with the BTA, producer surplus for the North remains the same as that specified in Section 2, i.e. $\Pi_1 = \pi_1$. The producer surplus for the South changes to $\Pi_2 = (p(Q_2) - c)x_{22} + (p(Q_1) - c)x_{21} - t_2 X_2 - \delta(t_1 - t_2)x_{21}$. North's revenue from the BTA is given by $BR_1 = \delta(t_1 - t_2)x_{21}$. Since $\tau = 0$, neither country collects any tariff revenue. Welfare of the North and the South is then given by

$$W_1^{BTA} = CS_1 + \Pi_1 + ER_1 + BR_1 - D_1$$

$$W_2^{BTA} = CS_2 + \Pi_2 + ER_2 - D_2$$

The sequence of moves in the game, as described previously, remains unchanged. Setting $\delta = 1$ and solving the two firms' profit maximization problems in the second stage, the non-cooperative equilibrium quantities are obtained as

$$x_{11}^{nc,BTA} = x_{21}^{nc,BTA} = \frac{a - t_1}{3}$$

$$x_{12}^{nc,BTA} = \frac{a - 2t_1 + t_2}{3}$$

$$x_{22}^{nc,BTA} = \frac{a + t_1 - 2t_2}{3}$$

The SOCs are satisfied as we have $\dfrac{\partial^2 \Pi_i}{\partial x_{ii}^2} < 0,\ \dfrac{\partial^2 \Pi_i}{\partial x_{ij}^2} < 0$ and $\dfrac{\partial^2 \Pi_i}{\partial x_{ii}^2}\dfrac{\partial^2 \Pi_i}{\partial x_{ij}^2} - \left(\dfrac{\partial^2 \Pi_i}{\partial x_{ii}\partial x_{ij}}\right)^2$

> 0 for $i, j = 1, 2$. Substituting the above quantities in W_i^{BTA} and then maximizing with respect to t_i gives the first stage reaction function of country i, $t_i(t_j)$.

From the North's reaction function we have $\dfrac{dt_1}{dt_2} = \dfrac{2 - 3\beta_1}{9\beta_1 + 10}$, which is positive

for sufficiently small values of β_1 that ensure the equilibrium quantities are positive. Moreover, the South's reaction function gives $\dfrac{dt_2}{dt_1} = -\dfrac{3(\beta_2 + 1)}{\beta_2 + 3} < 0$.

Simultaneously solving the two countries' FOCs, the non-cooperative equilibrium tax rates are obtained as

$$t_1^{nc,BTA} = \frac{a\left(-3 + 36\beta_1 + 7\beta_2\right)}{2\left(18 + 9\beta_1 + 8\beta_2\right)} \tag{18}$$

$$t_2^{nc,BTA} = \frac{a\left(3 - 36\beta_1 + 43\beta_2\right)}{2\left(18 + 9\beta_1 + 8\beta_2\right)} \tag{19}$$

The associated SOCs are satisfied, since $\dfrac{\partial^2 W_i^{BTA}}{\partial t_i^2} < 0$ for $i = 1, 2$. Moreover, the

reaction functions of the two countries yield a stable equilibrium.

For tractability and to facilitate comparison with the results in the previous sections, we again set $\beta_2 = 0.1$. Substituting the relevant tax rates, we find that the equilibrium quantities are strictly positive in all cases (i.e. the fully cooperative equilibrium, non-cooperative equilibrium with BTA, and if either country defects) for $\beta_1 \in (0.1, 0.41)$. Moreover, from (18) and (19) we have

$t_1^{nc,BTA} - t_2^{nc,BTA} = \dfrac{12a\left(15\beta_1 - 2\right)}{45\beta_1 + 94} > 0$ if and only if $\beta_1 > 0.13$. Accordingly, in this

section, we restrict attention to the range of β_1 values given by $\beta_1 \in (0.13, 0.41)$. This ensures that the North imposes a BTA on imports from the South in the non-cooperative equilibrium, as the pollution tax rate is higher in the former country.[16]

Comparing the cooperative equilibrium and the non-cooperative equilibrium with BTA, we find that $t_1^{nc,BTA} > t^c \mid_{\tau \to 0}$ for $\beta_1 \in (0.13, 0.41)$, while $t_2^{nc,BTA} \geq t^c \mid_{\tau \to 0}$ if and only if $\beta_1 \leq 0.17$. Thus the North raises its non-cooperative pollution tax above the efficient level, as this enables it to raise the BTA rate on imports from the South and earn more revenue from that source. The same consideration with respect to the BTA simultaneously dampens the South's rent capture motive to lower its tax in the non-cooperative equilibrium.[17] Global production and pollution are lower under full cooperation, i.e. $X^c \leq X^{nc,BTA}$, if and only if $\beta_1 \geq 0.24$. However, global welfare is higher under full cooperation, $W^c > W^{nc,BTA}$, for all $\beta_1 \in (0.13, 0.41)$. For individual countries, we have $W_1^c \geq W_1^{nc,BTA}$ if and only if $\beta_1 \geq 0.23$, and $W_2^c \geq W_2^{nc,BTA}$ if and only if $\beta_1 \leq 0.24$.

By changing their welfare levels in the non-cooperative equilibrium, imposition of the BTA by the North changes the loss functions, L_i, for both countries when cooperation breaks down. This, in turn, changes the discount factor thresholds that determine their decisions regarding cooperation. In the presence of the BTA, the modified thresholds for the North and the South are respectively given by

$$\hat{\theta}_1^{BTA} = \frac{16(1+5\beta_1)^2(94+45\beta_1)^2}{\left(\begin{array}{c}395091-877350\beta_1+6660500\beta_1^2\\+17897000\beta_1^3+14170000\beta_1^4+3600000\beta_1^5\end{array}\right)} \tag{20}$$

$$\hat{\theta}_2^{BTA} = \frac{20(1+20\beta_1)^2(94+45\beta_1)^2}{\left(\begin{array}{c}-320301+14919570\beta_1\\+63876800\beta_1^2+33891000\beta_1^3-10440000\beta_1^4\end{array}\right)} \tag{21}$$

Country i chooses to cooperate if and only if its discount factor θ_i exceeds the threshold value $\hat{\theta}_i^{BTA}$. Within the range of $\beta_1 \in (0.13, 0.41)$, we find that $\hat{\theta}_1^{BTA}$ is non-monotonic and concave in β_1, while $\hat{\theta}_2^{BTA}$ monotonically increases in β_1. Moreover, $\hat{\theta}_1^{BTA} \leq 1$ if and only if $\beta_1 \geq 0.23$, and $\hat{\theta}_2^{BTA} \leq 1$ if and only if $\beta_1 \leq 0.24$.

Comparison of each country's discount factor threshold with and without the BTA, allows us to infer how imposition of the BTA affects its incentive to cooperate with the other country over multiple periods. The following result holds.

Proposition 4: *Imposition of the BTA by the North on imports from the South makes it less likely that the North cooperates. As well, the BTA makes the South more likely to cooperate if and only if the countries are sufficiently heterogeneous in terms of their pollution damage parameter.*

Proof: Using (16), (17), (20) and (21), we have (i) $\hat{\theta}_1^{BTA} > \hat{\theta}_1 |_{\tau \to 0}$ for all $\beta_1 \in (0.13, 0.41)$, and (ii) $\hat{\theta}_2^{BTA} \leq \hat{\theta}_2 |_{\tau \to 0}$ if and only if $\beta_1 \geq 0.16$.

Imposition of the BTA in the non-cooperative equilibrium provides the North with additional revenue as well as levels the playing field for its firm in the domestic market. Consequently, the ability to impose a BTA makes the North less keen to cooperate with the South. For the South, the restriction imposed by the BTA on its ability to export to, and earn rents from, the North in the non-cooperative equilibrium weakens its incentive to defect from the cooperative equilibrium. At the same time, when β_1 is sufficiently small, i.e. $\beta_1 < 0.24$, global pollution is less in the non-cooperative equilibrium with BTA than in the cooperative equilibrium, which weakens the countries' incentives to cooperatively raise their tax. The net effect of these opposing tendencies is that the BTA makes the South more willing to cooperate only when β_1 is sufficiently large.

Overall, whether the BTA engenders more cooperation between the two countries depends on the rules governing its usage. These rules may permit the North to impose the BTA on imports from the South only if the South defects from the cooperative equilibrium ('regime 1'). Alternatively, the relevant rules may allow the North to unilaterally defect from the cooperative equilibrium and impose the BTA ('regime 2'). Which regime prevails in practice will depend on how the rules governing the use of BTAs are formulated at multilateral organizations such as the WTO.

The first regime involves the use of the BTA solely as a penalty for non-cooperation. The relevant multilateral trading rules, under this regime, would deny approval to a country to impose a BTA on imports from its trading partner if the former unilaterally defects while the latter is willing to set the cooperative pollution tax. In the context of our model, since the North cannot unilaterally defect from the cooperative equilibrium and impose the BTA under regime 1, and since the South would face a BTA if it defects unilaterally,[18] the relevant threshold values that determine cooperation between the two countries are $\hat{\theta}_1 \mid_{\tau \to 0}$ for the North and $\hat{\theta}_2^{BTA}$ for the South. If the countries are nearly symmetric, i.e. $\beta_1 \in (0.13, 0.16)$, we have $\hat{\theta}_1 \mid_{\tau \to 0} < \hat{\theta}_2 \mid_{\tau \to 0} < \hat{\theta}_2^{BTA} < 1$. Then, if the South does not cooperate in the absence of the BTA because its discount factor θ_2 is less than the threshold $\hat{\theta}_2 \mid_{\tau \to 0}$, the threat of the BTA cannot induce additional cooperation from the South as $\hat{\theta}_2 \mid_{\tau \to 0} < \hat{\theta}_2^{BTA}$. On the other hand, if the South's discount factor is $\theta_2 > \hat{\theta}_2 \mid_{\tau \to 0}$, the South cooperates in the absence of the BTA and hence the BTA cannot be imposed by the North under regime 1. Thus, the BTA does not affect the likelihood of cooperation between the countries when they are nearly symmetric. For intermediate levels of asymmetry, i.e. $\beta_1 \in (0.17, 0.24)$, we have $\hat{\theta}_1 \mid_{\tau \to 0} < \hat{\theta}_2^{BTA} < 1 < \hat{\theta}_2 \mid_{\tau \to 0}$, which indicates that the South defects in the absence of the BTA but may cooperate in its presence (specifically, the South cooperates if $\theta_2 > \hat{\theta}_2^{BTA}$). Hence, the threat of the BTA increases the likelihood of sustainable cooperation between the countries in this case. Finally, if the countries are too asymmetric i.e. $\beta_1 > 0.24$, sustainable cooperation between them is not possible with or without the BTA, as both $\hat{\theta}_2 \mid_{\tau \to 0}$ and $\hat{\theta}_2^{BTA}$ exceed 1 in such a case.

The second regime involves unrestricted use of BTAs – the relevant multilateral trading rules do not impose any restriction on the use of BTAs by countries. Under this regime, the BTA may be used as a disguised means of protection by the North, especially if trade agreements constrain the ability of countries to use more traditional trade policy instruments.[19] Under regime 2, the relevant threshold values that determine cooperation between the two countries are $\hat{\theta}_1^{BTA}$ for the North and $\hat{\theta}_2^{BTA}$ for the South. In the absence of a BTA, sustainable cooperation is possible between the countries if and only if $\beta_1 \in (0.1, 0.17)$, as we then have $\hat{\theta}_1 \mid_{\tau \to 0} < \hat{\theta}_2 \mid_{\tau \to 0} < 1$. However, when the North can unilaterally defect and impose a BTA, sustainable cooperation is possible if and only if $\beta_1 \in (0.23, 0.24)$, as we then have $\hat{\theta}_1^{BTA} < \hat{\theta}_2^{BTA} < 1$. Thus, the unrestricted use of BTAs makes cooperation less likely between nearly symmetric countries but can make cooperation more likely between more asymmetric countries.

Under regime 1, the BTA increases the likelihood of cooperation for $\beta_1 \in (0.17, 0.24)$, and does not affect the likelihood of cooperation for other values of β_1. By contrast, under regime 2, the BTA is detrimental for cooperation for $\beta_1 \in (0.13, 0.17)$, and increases the likelihood of cooperation for $\beta_1 \in (0.23, 0.24)$. Under either regime, when the threat of the BTA changes the sustainable equilibrium from non-cooperation to cooperation, this reduces global pollution and improves global welfare (welfare improves in the North, while it worsens in the South if $\beta_1 > 0.17$). Our results suggest that, in order to promote environmental cooperation between heterogeneous countries, the use of BTAs may need to be restricted so that they are used solely as a means of penalizing defection by a country from the cooperative outcome, and not as a disguised means of protection.

6   Conclusion

This chapter examines the role of trade liberalization and border tax adjustments on the incentives of heterogeneous countries to cooperate with each other in the pricing of a global pollutant. Using an oligopoly model of trade between two countries that differ in terms of their pollution damage parameter, we show that an increase in the degree of heterogeneity between the countries reduces the likelihood that cooperation is sustained between them. Moreover, freer trade in the form of bilateral tariff reductions increases both the gains from cooperation as well as the likelihood of cooperation. By contrast, trade restrictions in the form of border tax adjustments can foster or hinder cooperation, depending on the degree of heterogeneity between the countries and the rules governing the use of BTAs.

Our analysis shows that, when cooperation between countries is not possible (e.g. if the countries are very heterogeneous), global pollution is lower and global welfare is higher in the non-cooperative equilibrium with the BTA relative to their values in the non-cooperative equilibrium without the BTA. This suggests that a BTA may serve as a second best alternative to cooperation when cooperation cannot be sustained between countries. While the chapter has analysed one form of heterogeneity across countries, i.e. differences in pollution damage parameters, it would be interesting to consider other policy relevant differences between countries as well. Whether trade policy instruments such as tariffs and BTAs can be used to foster environmental cooperation between countries that differ in terms of size, market structure or emission intensity of output is left as work for the future.

Notes

1 For example, this was cited as an important factor to justify the US decision not to ratify the Kyoto Protocol and Canada's decision to withdraw from it.

2 The Waxman-Markey Bill (American Clean Energy and Security Act of 2009) proposed a cap-and-trade system for the US and required importers to purchase 'international reserve allowances' for goods from countries with laxer climate policies.

3 For environmental exemptions under the WTO, see https://www.wto.org/english/tratop_e/envir_e/envt_rules_exceptions_e.htm.

4 Other papers on international environmental agreements that use a repeated game framework include Barrett (1999), Asheim *et al.* (2006), Asheim and Holtsmark (2009) and Benchekroun and Yildiz (2011). Like them, we assume that the use of trigger strategies is credible.

5 Nordhaus (2015) also finds that trade sanctions by members on non-members can induce the latter to join a 'climate club' consisting of countries that set a common carbon price.

6 Thus we are assuming a constant emission intensity of output. Emissions can be reduced through a reduction in output, with forgone profit being the abatement cost for a firm. We do not model abatement as a separate choice variable for the firms.

7 Net export of the polluting good by country i is defined as its production minus consumption of that good, i.e. $X_i - Q_i$.

8 Note that $X^{nc} = \dfrac{4a - 3\tau}{\Psi} > 0$ implies $\tau < \dfrac{4}{3}a$, which is assumed to hold.

9 For example, when $\beta_2 = 0.1$, we find that $\lim_{\tau \to 0}(W_2^c - W_2^{nc}) \geq 0$ if and only if $\beta_1 \leq 0.17$.

10 Our results remain qualitatively unchanged for other values of β_2.

11 Fractions have been approximated to the second decimal place.

12 When $\beta_1 = \beta_2 = 0.1$, we have $\hat{\theta}_1 |_{\tau \to 0} = \hat{\theta}_2 |_{\tau \to 0} = 0.65$. As β_1 increases with β_2 remaining unchanged, $\hat{\theta}_1 |_{\tau \to 0}$ decreases while $\hat{\theta}_2 |_{\tau \to 0}$ increases. When $\beta_1 = 0.41$, we have $\hat{\theta}_1 |_{\tau \to 0} = 0.21$. Moreover, $\hat{\theta}_2 |_{\tau \to 0} \leq 1$ if and only if $\beta_1 \leq 0.17$. Thus, if $\beta_1 > 0.17$, using (13) and (17) we have $\lim_{\tau \to 0}(W_2^c - W_2^{nc}) < 0$ and $\hat{\theta}_2 |_{\tau \to 0} > 1$, and the South is unwilling to cooperate for any value of its discount factor.

13 To compute the effect of a marginal change in τ on $\hat{\theta}_i$ in the neighbourhood of free trade, i.e. $\dfrac{\partial \hat{\theta}_i}{\partial \tau} |_{\tau \to 0}$, we first take the derivative of $\hat{\theta}_i(\beta_1, \beta_2, \tau)$ with respect to τ and then evaluate the resulting expression, which is a function of β_1, β_2 and τ, at $\tau = 0$, $\beta_2 = 0.1$ and $\beta_1 \in (0.1, 0.41)$.

14 For the case of two identical countries, Benchekroun and Yildiz (2011) find that the increase in the benefit of defection due to trade liberalization dominates the increase in the lifetime cost of defection. Hence, trade liberalization raises the threshold discount factor, which is the same for identical countries, and makes cooperation between them less likely to be sustainable. In our model, trade liberalization raises (lowers) the threshold discount factor for the North (South).

15 When there is no BTA, as in the analysis in the previous sections, $\delta = 0$.

16 In the non-cooperative equilibrium with BTA, North's net import of the polluting good from South is given by $Q_1^{nc,BTA} - X_1^{nc,BTA} = X_2^{nc,BTA} - Q_2^{nc,BTA} = \dfrac{1}{3}\left(t_1^{nc,BTA} - t_2^{nc,BTA}\right)$.

17 Recall that, in the absence of the BTA, the non-cooperative tax rate is lower than its efficient level in both the countries. From (12), we have $\lim_{\tau \to 0}(t^c - t_i^{nc}) > 0$ for $\beta_2 = 0.1$ and $\beta_1 \in (0.1, 0.41)$.

18 Note that in the non-cooperative equilibrium we have $W_1^{nc,BTA} > W_1^{nc}$, i.e. the North gets a higher level of welfare by imposing the BTA than by not imposing it.

19 For $\tau = 0$ and $\beta_1 \in (0.13, 0.41)$, we have $X_2^{nc} - Q_2^{nc} > X_2^{nc,BTA} - Q_2^{nc,BTA}$, i.e. imposition of the BTA reduces the South's net exports to the North in the non-cooperative

equilibrium. Recall that the BTA motivates the North to inefficiently raise its non-cooperative pollution tax above the cooperative level, so that it can charge a higher BTA rate.

References

Asheim, G. B. and Holtsmark, B. (2009), 'Renegotiation-proof Climate Agreements with Full Participation: Conditions for Pareto-efficiency', *Environmental and Resource Economics*, 43(4): 519–533.

Asheim, G. B., Froyn, C. B., Hovi, J. and Menz, F. C. (2006), 'Regional versus Global Cooperation for Climate Control', *Journal of Environmental Economics and Management*, 51(1): 93–109.

d'Aspremont, C. A., Jacquemin, J., Gabszeweiz, J. and Weymark, J. A. (1983), 'On the Stability of Collusive Price Leadership', *Canadian Journal of Economics*, 16: 17–25.

Baksi, S. and Ray Chaudhuri, A. (2014), 'Trade, Border Tax Adjustments, and the Stability of International Environmental Agreements'. Presented at the Fifth World Congress of Environmental and Resource Economists, Istanbul.

Barrett, S. (1994), 'Strategic Environmental Policy and International Trade', *Journal of Public Economics*, 54: 325–338.

Barrett, S. (1997), 'The Strategy of Trade Sanctions in International Environmental Agreements', *Resource and Energy Economics*, 19(4): 345–361.

Barrett, S. (1999), 'A Theory of Full International Cooperation', *Journal of Theoretical Politics*, 11(4): 519–541.

Benchekroun, H. and Yildiz, H. M. (2011), 'Free Trade, Autarky and the Sustainability of an International Environmental Agreement', *The BE Journal of Economic Analysis & Policy*, 11(1).

Böhringer, C., Müller, A. and Schneider, J. (2015), 'Carbon Tariffs Revisited', *Journal of the Association of Environmental and Resource Economists*, 2(4): 629–672.

Böhringer, C., Carbone, J. C. and Rutherford, T. F. (2016), 'The Strategic Value of Carbon Tariffs', *American Economic Journal: Economic Policy*, 8(1): 28–51.

Eichner, T. and Pethig, R. (2013), 'Self-enforcing Environmental Agreements and International Trade', *Journal of Public Economics*, 102: 37–50.

Eichner, T. and Pethig, R. (2014), 'Self-enforcing Environmental Agreements, Trade, and Demand and Supply-side Mitigation Policy', *Journal of the Association of Environmental and Resource Economists*, 1(3): 419–450.

Eichner, T. and Pethig, R. (2015), 'Is Trade Liberalization Conducive to the Formation of Climate Coalitions?', *International Tax and Public Finance*, 22(6): 932–955.

Eyland, T. and Zaccour, G. (2012), 'Strategic Effects of a Border Tax Adjustment', *International Game Theory Review*, 14(3).

Eyland, T. and Zaccour, G. (2014), 'Carbon Tariffs and Cooperative Outcomes', *Energy Policy*, 65: 718–728.

Ghosh, M., Luo, D., Siddiqui, M. S. and Zhu, Y. (2012), 'Border Tax Adjustments in the Climate Policy Context: CO_2 versus Broad-based GHG Emission Targeting', *Energy Economics*, 34: 154–167.

Hagen, A. and Eisenack, K. (2015), 'International Environmental Agreements with Asymmetric Countries: Climate Clubs vs. Global Cooperation', Nota di Lavoro 58.2015, Fondazione Eni Enrico Mattei, Milan.

Kennedy, P. (1994), 'Equilibrium Pollution Taxes in Open Economies with Imperfect Competition', *Journal of Environmental Economics and Management*, 27: 49–63.

Kolstad, C. D. (2010), 'Equity, Heterogeneity and International Environmental Agreements', *The BE Journal of Economic Analysis & Policy*, 10(2).

McAusland, C. and Najjar, N. (2015), 'Carbon Footprint Taxes', *Environmental and Resource Economics*, 61: 37–70.

McGinty, M. (2007), 'International Environmental Agreements among Asymmetric Nations', *Oxford Economic Papers*, 59: 45–62.

Marrouch, W. and Ray Chaudhuri, A. (2016), 'International Environmental Agreements: Doomed to Fail or Destined to Succeed? A Review of the Literature', *International Review of Environmental and Resource Economics*, 9: 245–319.

Nordhaus, W. (2015), 'Climate Clubs: Overcoming Free-riding in International Climate Policy', *American Economic Review*, 105(4): 1339–1370.

Pavlova, Y. and de Zeeuw, A. (2013), 'Asymmetries in International Environmental Agreements', *Environment and Development Economics*, 18(1): 51–68.

Zhang, Z. (2010), 'The US Proposed Carbon Tariffs, WTO Scrutiny and China's Responses', *International Economics and Economic Policy*, 7(2–3): 203–225.

6 The effects of labour intensity and pollution damage on government policies and location choice

Benan Zeki Orbay[1] and Narod Erkol

1 Introduction

Developing countries try to attract foreign direct investment (FDI) for a faster economic growth and lower unemployment. Realizing the effect of FDI on development, researchers put more effort to determine which state attributes are more effective on location choice decisions. Most of these studies showed that market size, infrastructure, local policies (including environmental policies), input costs are closely related to location choice decisions. It is not uncommon to see firms from developed countries with strict environmental standards locate their production facilities abroad, especially when their production has severe environmental impact. There are a considerable number of studies analysing the relationship between environmental policy and location choice both empirically and theoretically. List and Co (2000), Xing and Kolstad (2002), Dean *et al.* (2009) and Chung (2014) are among the empirical studies finding significant negative relationship between environmental stringency and attractiveness of location. Manderson and Kneller's (2012) results do not support this negative relationship. On the theoretical side, supporting the mixed results in empirical literature, Elliot and Zhou (2013) show that greater stringency in environmental standards can also increase FDI. There are many other papers analysing the issue of location choice and environmental policies. Markusen *et al.* (1993) investigated the firms' location choice under international oligopoly and demonstrated that environmental policies are effective on firms' location choices and market structure and can alter pollution and welfare levels in the concerned countries. Markusen (1997) looks at the issue from the viewpoint of trade liberalization and shows that production sensitivity of multinational firms to environmental policies increases with liberalization. Ulph and Valentini (1997) analyse a similar issue by allowing inter-sectoral linkages between industries and demonstrated that in certain cases firms reallocate between countries due to the environmental regulations. More recently, Abe and Zhao (2005) analysed the relationship between environmental policies and the type of abatement technology of the local firm for the case where the choice of investment type for the foreign firm is endogenously determined. They have showed that if South owns a poor abatement technology, it should impose a high pollution tax to attract FDI; conversely, if it owns a good abatement technology, then attracting joint ventures with a low pollution tax is a better alternative. Kayalica and Lahiri (2005) examined the effects of FDI on the environmental policies of a host country competing with another country for a third country market. They show that free entry motivates less severe policies for the host country. Çelik and Orbay (2011) analysed the interaction between environmental and trade policies and location choice in a two-country model. They showed that FDI is preferred by the host country only for sufficiently low levels of marginal damage of pollution. Excluding the location choice, Barrett (1994) and Kennedy (1994) focus on the optimal environmental policies under oligopolistic settings and demonstrated that depending on the mode of competition optimal pollution taxes differ from the traditional Pigouvian tax. A more recent study by Ferrara *et al.* (2015) determine the FDI preventing and attracting environmental standards.

Here, our focus is on how location choice of a firm from a developed country directly and indirectly depends on exogenous factors, such as labour intensity and marginal damage of pollution in an environment where government policies are chosen observing the location choice. In order to understand these direct and indirect effects, one should note that, when labour intensity is high, the employment effect of production is more substantial, thus, the host country's policies change accordingly and thus, labour intensity indirectly affects location choice. Besides, labour intensity directly affects location decision because with lower wage rate in the host country, production becomes cheaper with more labour intensity. We construct a two-country theoretical model with two firms located in each of these countries. We indicate the developed country as 'North' and the developing country as 'South'; we further assume that the firm located in South has a less efficient production technology than the firm located in North. Each of these firms pollutes the local environment and there is no cross-border pollution. The environmental damages caused by the firms are assumed to be publicly known. Both firms use two types of inputs, labour and other local inputs in fixed proportions. Labour is assumed to be cheaper in South. In the first stage of the game, North Firm decides where to locate. Its choices are to produce at home or to move the production facility to the South country. In the second stage, South and North Countries reveal the level of government policy. Firms decide their country specific production levels à la Cournot in the third stage. Our results show that subsidization is the optimal policy choice for the case where North Firm produces at home. Equilibrium subsidies of both countries increase as the employment effect of production increases; and decrease as marginal damage of pollution increases. An increase in foreign firm's marginal production cost level also results in an increase in equilibrium subsidies. Besides, higher marginal production cost of the local firms can create a subsidy increase only if the employment effect of production is sufficiently high. On the other hand, taxing is the South Government's optimal choice when North Firm locates in South. Equilibrium tax of the South Country decreases as the employment effect of production of both firms increases. Interestingly, regardless of how high the employment effect of the North Firm is, equilibrium tax level always decreases with an increase in the foreign firm's production cost. However, equilibrium tax increases with its own firm's production cost only for sufficiently low levels of employment effect. If there is sufficiently high employment effect, South prefers to lower the taxes despite the cost disadvantage of its own firm. Depending on these policies, producing at home is always the best location choice for the North Firm. Producing at home becomes even more attractive with higher (lower) employment effect of the North (South) Firm and lower marginal pollution damage. In the last part of this study, we aim to analyse how the social welfare levels of the countries and environmental pollution levels change when the countries determine a uniform cooperative government policy through an environmental pollution agreement. Results show that total environmental pollution is lower at the uniform cooperative equilibrium, but it is not welfare improving.

This chapter is organized as follows. In Section 2, the basic model and the solutions of the output choice and government policy choice stages are given. Section 3 discusses the solution of the location choice stage. Section 4 compares the equilibrium of this game with the case where governments determine their uniform policy with an environmental pollution agreement cooperatively. Finally, Section 5 provides a summary and some concluding remarks.

2   The model

In this section, we constructed a two-country model with a domestic developing country (the South) and a foreign developed country (the North). Each country has one firm producing a homogenous good and generating local pollution during the production process. South Firm's production and abatement technology is less efficient compared to the North Firm. The environmental damage caused by the firms is publicly known. Marginal damages of pollution are constant and the North Firm's marginal damage is lower than the South Firm ($\theta_S > \theta_N$). In the first stage of the game, the North Firm decides on its location for production. The options are producing the total output in the South (FDI) and producing the total output at home. In the second stage, both South and North Countries determine the tax levels. In the last stage, firms choose their output levels observing the tax levels imposed by South and North governments. Figure 6.1 represents this game.

For simplicity, we assume that there are no fixed costs in our model. The marginal costs of both North and South Firms are assumed to be composed of fixed proportion amount of labour (L_N and L_S) and other local inputs (X_N and X_S). Thus, marginal costs can be written as follows:

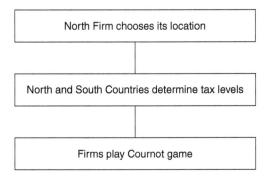

Figure 6.1 Stages of the game

$$c_N = w_N L_N + p_N X_N \qquad (1a)$$

$$c_S = w_S L_S + p_S X_S \qquad (1b)$$

where w_N and w_S are wage rates in two countries ($w_S < w_N$), p_N and p_S are the prices of other inputs. With this definition, c_N and c_S represent marginal costs.

Suppose that γ represents wages paid by companies as a fraction of marginal costs. Using above, γs are defined to be,

$$\gamma_N = \frac{w_N L_N}{c_N} \qquad (2a)$$

$$\gamma_S = \frac{w_S L_S}{c_S} \qquad (2b)$$

If we consider the case where the North Firm produces in South, the North Firm's marginal cost c_N^s can be written as

$$c_N^s = w_S L_N + p_N X_N \qquad (3)$$

Defining $\kappa = \dfrac{w_S}{w_N}$, (3) can be written as $c_N^s = \kappa \gamma_N c_N + (1 - \gamma_N) c_N$ and wages paid by North Firm in South is $\kappa \gamma_N c_N$. Finally, marginal cost of North Firm for production in South can be expressed as

$$c_N^s = \rho c_N \qquad (4)$$

where $\rho = \kappa \gamma_N + (1 - \gamma_N)$. Here ρ represents the extent of the production cost advantage of North Firm when it produces in South.

Consumption takes place in both South and North and inverse demand functions are:

$$P_i = a_i - b_i Q_i, i = N, S \tag{5}$$

where $Q_i = q_{ii} + q_{ji}$ $\{i, j\} = \{N, S\}$, $i \neq j$, the total output and q_S and q_N are the amounts produced by the South Firm and North Firm and P_i is the price in each country. South Firm faces the following profit maximization problem:

$$\max{}_{q_{SS} q_{NS}} \pi_S = \begin{bmatrix} (a_S - b_S (q_{SS} + q_{SN}) q_{SS} \\ + ((a_N - b_N (q_{NS} + q_{NN})) q_{NS} - C_{SS} q_{SS} - C_{NS} q_{NS} \end{bmatrix} \tag{6a}$$

where $C_{SS} = c_S + \tau_S$ is the total unit cost of selling at home which is the sum of tax rate τ_S imposed by the South per unit of production and the marginal cost of production, similarly, $C_{NS} = c_S + \tau_S + t$ is the total unit cost of selling in North which is the sum of marginal cost of production, tax and the transportation cost t. The profit maximization problem of the North Firm can be formulated as:

$$\max{}_{q_{NN} q_{SN}} \pi_N = \begin{bmatrix} (a_N - b_N (q_{NS} + q_{NN}) q_{NN} \\ + ((a_S - b_S (q_{SS} + q_{SN})) q_{SN} - C_{NN} q_{NN} - C_{SN} q_{SN} \end{bmatrix} \tag{6b}$$

where C_{NN} is the total unit cost of selling in North and C_{SN} is the total unit cost of selling in South for the North Firm. Clearly, these unit costs will differ depending on the production location choice of the North Firm later in the following sections. Solving the reaction functions obtained from equations (6a) and (6b) simultaneously yields the market stage equilibrium outputs as follows:

$$\bar{q}_{SS} = \frac{1}{3b_S} (a_S + C_{SN} - 2C_{SS}) \tag{7a}$$

$$\bar{q}_{NS} = \frac{1}{3b_N} (a_N + C_{NN} - 2C_{NS}) \tag{7b}$$

$$\bar{q}_{NN} = \frac{1}{3b_N} (a_N + C_{NS} - 2C_{NN}) \tag{7c}$$

$$\bar{q}_{SN} = \frac{1}{3b_S} (a_S + C_{SS} - 2C_{SN}) \tag{7d}$$

Substituting these equilibrium outputs, we obtain the following Cournot-Nash equilibrium profit levels as follows:

$$\pi_S = \frac{b_S(a_N + C_{NN} - 2C_{NS})^2 + b_N(a_S + C_{SN} - 2C_{SS})^2}{9b_N b_S} \qquad (8a)$$

$$\pi_N = \frac{b_S(a_N - 2C_{NN} + C_{NS})^2 + b_N(a_S - 2C_{SN} + C_{SS})^2}{9b_N b_S} \qquad (8b)$$

2.1   Market stage game 1: North Firm produce in its country of origin

In this section, we consider the case where the North Firm stays at home and exports to the South. North Firm's total unit cost when it sells in North is

$$C_{NN}^h = c_N + \tau_N \qquad (9a)$$

and when it sells in South is

$$C_{SN}^h = c_N + \tau_N + t \qquad (9b)$$

Here τ_N represents the tax imposed by the North government. Substituting these cost levels into the above equilibrium output and profit levels (given in equation (7) and (8)) and denoting them as q_{ii}^h, q_{ij}^h and π_i^h $(\{i, j\} = \{N, S\}, i \neq j)$, we can derive the following social welfare functions for South and North respectively:

$$SW_S^h = CS_S^h + \pi_S^h - (\theta_S - \tau_S - \gamma_S c_S)(q_{SS}^h + q_{NS}^h) \qquad (10a)$$

$$SW_N^h = CS_N^h + \pi_N^h - (\theta_N - \tau_N - \gamma_N c_N)(q_{NN}^h + q_{SN}^h) \qquad (10b)$$

CS_i^h is the consumer surplus in each country for the market stage game 1.

The optimal taxes for the South and North Countries under the market stage game 1 can be computed by solving the first order conditions, $\dfrac{dSW_S^h}{d\tau_S} = 0$ and $\dfrac{dSW_N^h}{d\tau_N} = 0$ simultaneously. Algebraic analysis of the sign of these equilibrium taxes, τ_S^h, τ_N^h, are quite complex, but numerical analysis is represented in the following figures. As can easily be seen from Figure 6.2, despite the pollution, both countries prefer to subsidize their firms instead of taxing. This result can be explained by the incentives to support domestic firms in the international competition environment and to increase employment effect of production.

The following propositions represent the results on how these subsidies (taxes) change with some critical parameters of the model.

Proposition 1: When North Firm produces in its country of origin, equilibrium subsidies (taxes) of both countries increase (decrease) as the employment effect of production increases.

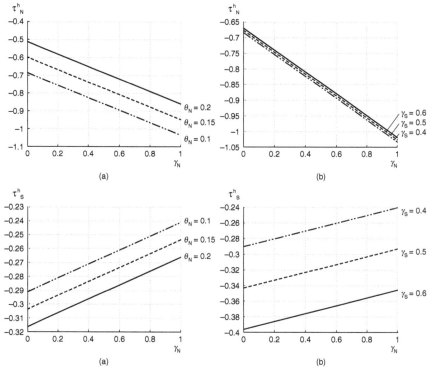

Figure 6.2 Equilibrium taxes of North and South Countries when North produces at home. ($K = 0.8$, $t = 0.01$, $\theta_S = 0.2$, $\theta_N = 0.1$ (*fig.* (*b*)), $\gamma_S = 0.4$ (*fig.* (*a*)), $c_S = 0.3$, $c_N = 0.2$, $b_S = 1$, $a_S = 1$, $b_N = 1$, $a_N = 2$)

Proof: $\dfrac{d\tau_N^h}{d\gamma_N} = \dfrac{-c_N(3b_N + 4b_S)}{2(b_N + b_S)}$ Clearly $\dfrac{d\tau_N^h}{d\gamma_N} < 0$. Similarly, $\dfrac{d\tau_S^h}{d\gamma_S} = $

$\dfrac{-c_S(3b_S + 4b_N)}{2(b_N + b_S)} < 0$. □

From this result we can say that when the employment effect of production becomes more substantial, countries increases (decrease) their subsidies (taxes) regardless of marginal damage of pollution.

We also analyse how optimal taxes change with marginal production costs of the firms. The following Proposition summarizes the results.

Proposition 2: When North Firm produces in its country of origin, equilibrium subsidies (taxes) of both countries

i)   increase (decrease) with the foreign firm's marginal production cost level,
ii) decrease (increase) with their own firms' marginal production cost level if the employment effect of production is sufficiently low.

Proof: i) $\dfrac{d\tau_N^h}{dc_S} = \dfrac{b_N(\gamma_S - 1)}{2(b_N + b_S)}$. Since, $\gamma_S \leq 1$, $\dfrac{d\tau_N^h}{dc_S} < 0$. Similarly, $\dfrac{d\tau_S^h}{dc_N} = \dfrac{b_S(\gamma_N - 1)}{2(b_N + b_S)}$.

Since, $\gamma_N \leq 1$, $\dfrac{d\tau_S^h}{dc_N} < 0$.

ii) $\dfrac{d\tau_N^h}{dc_N} = \dfrac{b_N + 2b_S - \gamma_N(3b_N + 4b_S)}{2(b_N + b_S)}$. Clearly, $\dfrac{d\tau_N^h}{dc_N} > 0$ iff $\dfrac{b_N + 2b_S}{3b_N + 4b_S} > \gamma_N$.

Similarly, $\dfrac{d\tau_S^h}{dc_S} = \dfrac{b_S + 2b_N - \gamma_S(3b_S + 4b_N)}{2(b_N + b_S)}$ and $\dfrac{d\tau_S^h}{dc_S} > 0$ iff $\dfrac{b_S + 2b_N}{3b_S + 4b_N} > \gamma_S$. □

For the low levels of γ_i, this result is in accordance with the conventional result of strategic trade literature, which states that governments should subsidize the winners more. However, when the employment effect of production becomes sufficiently high, then we observe a reverse effect. It is possible to say that for high levels of γ_i, the employment effect dominates disadvantage of the decreasing relative efficiency of the domestic firm, thus, governments prefer to support their firms more by increasing (lowering) subsidies (taxes).

Finally, as stated in the following proposition, when local marginal damage of pollution is higher the local subsidy (tax) becomes lower (higher) for both countries.

Proposition 3: When North Firm produces in its country of origin, equilibrium subsidies (taxes) of both countries decrease (increase) with the local firm's marginal damage of pollution.

Proof: $\dfrac{d\tau_N^h}{d\theta_N} = \dfrac{3b_N + 4b_S}{2(b_N + b_S)} > 0$ and $\dfrac{d\tau_S^h}{d\theta_S} = \dfrac{3b_S + 4b_S}{2(b_N + b_S)} > 0$. □

Barrett (1994) and Kennedy (1994) showed that under imperfect competition the governments may have an incentive to impose environmental policies weaker than the Pigouvian tax[2] to support their own firms in international competition environment. More specifically, Barrett (1994) demonstrated that the mode of competition is important: when firms compete à la Cournot governments prefer weaker environmental policies, however, when the competition is à la Bertrand governments choose stronger environmental policies. In our model, clearly, the Barrett (1994) result still holds under Cournot competition. Moreover, together with the additional employment effect of production, weaker environmental policies extend even up to subsidies.

2.2 *Market stage game 2: both firms produce in South*

In this section, we consider the case where the North Firm engages in an FDI and produces total output in South playing a Cournot-Nash game with the South Firm. In this case, the total unit cost of the North Firm when it sells in South is

$$C_{SN}^f = \rho c_N + \tau_S \tag{11a}$$

which is the sum of tax rate τ_S and marginal cost of production. Similarly, total unit cost of North Firm when it sells in North is

$$C_{NN}^f = \rho c_N + \tau_S + t \tag{11b}$$

Denoting q_{ii}^f, q_{ij}^f and π_i^f ($\{i,j\} = \{N,S\}$, $i \neq j$) as the Cournot equilibrium output and profit levels computed at C_{SN}^f and C_{NN}^f, we can write down the social welfare function for North and South Countries, respectively, as follows:

$$SW_S^f = CS_S^f + \pi_S^f - (\theta_N - \tau_S - \kappa\gamma_N c_N)(q_{SN}^f + q_{NN}^f)$$
$$- (\theta_S - \tau_S - \gamma_S c_S)(q_{SS}^f + q_{NS}^f) \tag{12a}$$

$$SW_N^f = CS_N^f + \pi_N^f \tag{12b}$$

CS_i^f is again the consumer surplus in each country for the market stage game 2, θ_i is the marginal damage of pollution for each firm. The terms $\kappa\gamma_N c_N(q_{SN}^f + q_{NN}^f)$ and $\gamma_S c_S(q_{SS}^f + q_{NS}^f)$ in equation (12a) represent the employment effect of the production by South and North Firms respectively.

By solving the f.o.c., $\dfrac{dSW_S^f}{d\tau_S} = 0$, we obtain the optimal tax for the South Country. For this case, we denote equilibrium tax for South as τ_S^f. As in the previous section, algebraic analysis of the sign of this tax is quite complicated but Figure 6.3 shows that in contrast with the case where both firms produce in their country of origin, South Country prefers to tax both firms.

Moreover, in contrast with the Barrett (1994) result, for all our feasible parameter values, taxes are higher than the marginal damage of pollution (stricter than the Pigouvian tax) even though the competition mode is Cournot (see Figure 6.4). Obviously, when both firms are producing in South and the North Firm's profits go to the North Country, South cannot tolerate pollution by subsidizing or lowering taxes below the marginal damage of pollution.

The following propositions analyse how the equilibrium tax changes with the critical parameters of our model.

Proposition 4: When both firms produce in South, equilibrium tax of the South country decreases as the employment effect of production of both firms increase.

Proof: $\dfrac{d\tau_S^f}{d\gamma_S} = -\dfrac{3c_S(b_N + b_S)}{6b_N + 10b_S} < 0$. Similarly, $\dfrac{d\tau_S^f}{d\gamma_N} = -\dfrac{3c_N(b_S + b_N)\kappa}{6b_N + 10b_S} < 0$. $\quad\square$

Similar to the market stage game 1, when the employment effects of production are higher, South government prefers to impose a lower tax. The difference in the extent of these effects is related to the ratio of $c_S / \kappa c_N$.

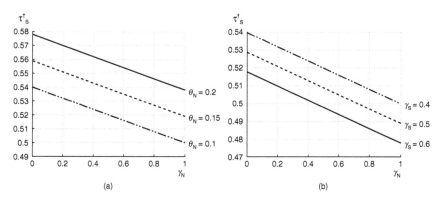

Figure 6.3 Equilibrium Tax of South Country when both firms produce in South. ($K = 0.8$, $t = 0.01$, $\theta_S = 0.2$, $\theta_N = 0.1$ (*fig. (b)*), $\gamma_S = 0.4$ (*fig. (a)*), $c_S = 0.3$, $c_N = 0.2$, $b_S = 1$, $a_S = 1$, $b_N = 1$, $a_N = 2$)

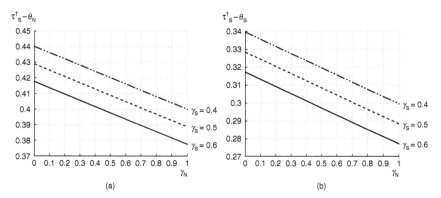

Figure 6.4 The difference between Equilibrium tax of South Country and marginal damage of pollutions when both firms produce in South. ($K = 0.8$, $t = 0.01$, $\theta_S = 0.2$, $\theta_N = 0.1$, $c_S = 0.3$, $c_N = 0.2$, $b_S = 1$, $a_S = 1$, $b_N = 1$, $a_N = 2$)

Proposition 5: When both firms produce in South, equilibrium tax of the South country

i)   decreases with c_N,
ii) increases with c_S iff the employment effect is sufficiently low.

Proof: $\dfrac{d\tau_S^f}{dc_N} = -\dfrac{3(b_N + b_S)\gamma_N \kappa}{6b_N + 10b_S} - \dfrac{\rho}{2} < 0.$ $\dfrac{d\tau_S^f}{dc_S} = \dfrac{3b_N + b_S - 3(b_N + b_S)\gamma_S}{6b_N + 10b_S} > 0$

iff $\dfrac{3b_N + b_S}{3(b_N + b_S)} > \gamma_S.\square$

Interestingly, regardless of how high is the employment effect of the North Firm, tax of South always decreases with increasing c_N, however, tax increases with c_S only for sufficiently low levels of employment effect. If there is sufficiently high employment effect, South prefers to lower the taxes despite the cost disadvantage of its own firm. Obviously, increasing c_N, creates a competition advantage for the local firm in terms of rent shifting, thus, local government supports this advantage by lowering the tax, besides, since there is an additional positive employment effect from the foreign firm, this tax reduction becomes more reasonable.

As in the previous case, when marginal damage of pollution is higher the South Country's tax (subsidy) becomes higher (lower). The following proposition states this result.

Proposition 6: When North Firm produces in South, equilibrium tax of South Country increases with both firms' marginal damage of pollution.

Proof: $\dfrac{d\tau_S^f}{d\theta_N} = \dfrac{d\tau_S^f}{d\theta_S} = \dfrac{3(b_N + b_S)}{6b_N + 10b_S} > 0.$ $\square$

3   The location choice

In this section, we analyse the first stage game where North Firm decides where to locate. For this purpose, we substitute equilibrium taxes and costs for each location choice into the profit function given in equation (8b) and compare for different location choice. Unfortunately, algebraic comparison of these profits is also quite complex, thus, we prefer to perform some numerical analysis to present the results. The following figures show the profit difference of the North Firm as a function of employment effect, at different parameter values of marginal damage of pollution and employment effect of the South Firm.

As can easily be seen from Figure 6.5, North Firm prefers to locate in its country of origin for all our parameter values. This can be explained by drastically different government policies. We know from above that countries prefer to subsidize their firms in the case where North Firm locates in its country of origin, however, South Country prefers to tax when North Firm locates there. Although producing at home is always preferred by the North Firm, it becomes even more attractive with increasing employment effect, γ_N. However, when employment effect of the South Firm increases, North Country is still preferred, but profit difference becomes less pronounced because taxes in South decrease with increasing γ_S. On the other hand, when θ_N increases, again profit difference reduces due to the lower subsidies in North. When North Firm locates in South, clearly, taxes will increase with increasing θ_N, but this increase is relatively less compared to the reduction in subsidies in North. Thus, we observe a lower profit difference with increasing θ_N.

In summary, South Country is not an attractive location choice for the North Firm due to the government policy choices. With lower employment effect of the South Firm and lower marginal pollution damage of the North Firm, South Country's policies become stricter whereas North Country's

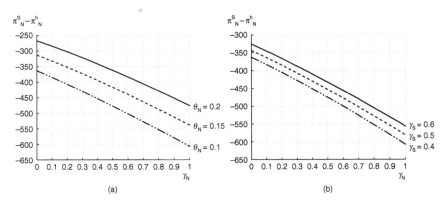

Figure 6.5 The profit difference of North Firm at different location choices. ($K = 0.8$, $t = 0.01$, $\theta_S = 0.2$, $\theta_N = 0.1$ (*fig.* (*b*)), $\gamma_S = 0.4$ (*fig.* (*a*)), $c_S = 0.3$, $c_N = 0.2$, $b_S = 1$, $a_S = 1$, $b_N = 1$, $a_N = 2$)

policies become more supportive, thus, producing at home becomes even more attractive for the North Firm.

4 Cooperative environmental policies

After observing that producing in its country of origin is a more attractive location choice for the North Firm, it will be interesting to analyse how the social welfare levels of the countries and environmental pollution levels change if a unique cooperative government policy is determined by the countries with an environmental pollution agreement.

In order to determine optimal level of such a policy, the total social welfare level of North and South Countries should be maximized. The total social welfare level can be written as follows.

$$SW^T = SW_S^h + SW_S^h \qquad (13)$$

By solving the f.o.c., $\dfrac{dSW^T}{d\tau} = 0$, we obtain equilibrium cooperative tax level as follows:

$$\tau^c = \frac{\begin{array}{c} -2(a_S b_N + a_N b_S + (b_N + b_S)(c_S + c_N + t - 3(c_N \gamma_N + c_S \gamma_S) \\ + 3(\theta_N + \theta_S)) \end{array}}{4(b_N + b_S)} \qquad (14)$$

As can easily be seen from the following figures, this tax is also negative, thus, optimal uniform cooperative policy for the countries is subsidization.

When we compare total social welfare levels, we observe that both countries are better off at the non-cooperative case. Although this result seems to

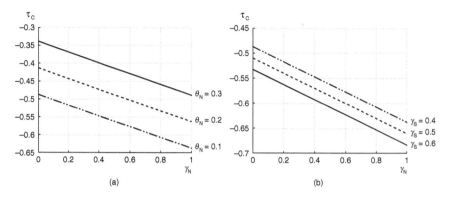

Figure 6.6 Equilibrium uniform cooperative government policies. ($K = 0.8$, $t = 0.01$, $\theta_S = 0.2$, $\theta_N = 0.1$ (*fig. (b)*), $\gamma_S = 0.4$ (*fig. (a)*), $c_S = 0.3$, $c_N = 0.2$, $b_S = 1$, $a_S = 1$, $b_N = 1$, $a_N = 2$)

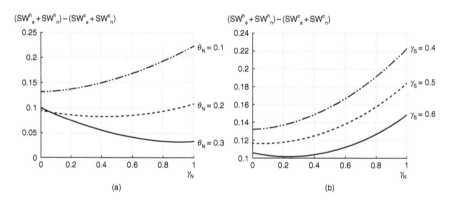

Figure 6.7 Equilibrium total social welfare levels between non-cooperative and coopera-tive cases. ($K = 0.8$, $t = 0.01$, $\theta_S = 0.2$, $\theta_N = 0.1$ (*fig. (b)*), $\gamma_S = 0.4$ (*fig. (a)*), $c_S = 0.3$, $c_N = 0.2$, $b_S = 1$, $a_S = 1$, $b_N = 1$, $a_N = 2$)

be surprising at a first glance, considering the fact that we are restricting our-selves to a uniform cooperative policy, it is possible to observe a lower total welfare level at the cooperative case.[3] The following figures show that the dif-ference between total social welfare levels at non-cooperative and coopera-tive equilibrium change with variables of the model but it is always positive.

On the other hand, as it is intuitively expected, total pollution level is higher at the non-cooperative equilibrium (see Figure 6.8).

In our model government policies are in fact in the form of excise tax, i.e. it is paid per unit production in each country. It is observed that in such a set-up, despite the pollution, subsidization is a better policy option for the governments at both non-cooperative and uniform cooperative equilibrium. In both the cooperative and non-cooperative case, subsidization has positive

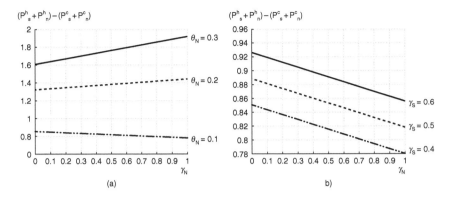

Figure 6.8 The difference of pollution between non-cooperative and cooperative cases. ($K = 0.8$, $t = 0.01$, $\theta_S = 0.2$, $\theta_N = 0.1$ (*fig.* (*b*)), $\gamma_S = 0.4$ (*fig.* (*a*)), $c_S = 0.3$, $c_N = 0.2$, $b_S = 1$, $a_S = 1$, $b_N = 1$, $a_N = 2$)

effects on profits, consumer surplus and employment effect of production and clearly these positive effects are dominating. Although the total environmental pollution is lower, unfortunately, the uniform cooperative equilibrium is not welfare improving.

5   Conclusion

This study focused on how government policies and location choice of the firms are related with labour intensity and marginal damage of pollution of production. In a simple two-country intra-industry trade model, there is a single firm in each of the developed country 'North' and the developing country 'South' and each of these firms pollutes the local environment. We assume that in the first stage of the game, North Firm decides where to locate. Its choices are to stay at home or move the production facility to the South. In the second stage South and North Countries reveal the level of their policies. Depending on the location choice of the North Firm, the firms decide their country specific production levels à la Cournot in the third stage; according to the results, subsidization is the optimal policy choice for the case where North Firm produces at home. With higher employment effect of production, both countries choose more supportive policies. An increase in foreign firms' marginal production cost also results in an increase in equilibrium subsidies. In contrast with the traditional result, which states that governments should support the winners more, higher marginal production cost of the local firms can create a subsidy increase if the employment effect of production is sufficiently high. Equilibrium subsidy levels become lower with an increase in marginal damage of pollution. On the other hand, when North Firm locates in South, taxing is the South government's optimal choice. Equilibrium tax becomes lower as the employment effect of production of both firms increases. Interestingly, regardless of how high is the employment effect of the North Firm, tax level always decreases with an increase in the foreign firm's production cost, however, it increases with its own firm's production cost for sufficiently low levels of employment effect. Producing at home is the best location choice for the North Firm under these policy choices. Finally, we showed that uniform policy choice of governments, determined by an environmental pollution agreement cooperatively, is not welfare improving, but it reduces total environmental pollution.

This study is the first attempt to examine the effects of labour intensity and marginal damage of pollution on government policies and location choice. A possible extension of this analysis is to look at how the results change if the governments declare their policies before North Firm chooses its location. In another extension, robustness of the results can be checked using a model where government policies are altered to environmental policies controlling the maximum quantity of pollution that the firms are allowed to emit into the atmosphere.

Notes

1 The first version of this chapter was a joint work with Hakan Orbay who passed away on 15 September 2011. This version is dedicated to the memory of my beloved husband, Hakan Orbay.
2 The Pigouvian tax is known as the optimal environmental tax policy in perfectly competitive markets and is equal to the marginal damage of pollution.
3 In the case of the non-uniform cooperative solution, equilibrium does not exist. The non-cooperative solution is Pareto optimal.

References

Abe, K. and Zhao, L. (2005), 'Endogenous International Joint Ventures and the Environment', *Journal of International Economics*, 67: 221–240.

Barrett, S. (1994), 'Strategic Environmental Policy and International Trade', *Journal of Public Economics*, 54: 325–338.

Chung, S. (2014), 'Environmental Regulation and Foreign Direct Investment: Evidence from South Korea', *Journal of Development Economics*, 108: 222–236.

Çelik, S. and Orbay, B.Z. (2011), 'Location Choice under Trade and Environmental Policies', *Economic Modelling*, 28: 1710–1715.

Dean, J.M., Lovely, M.E. and Wang, H. (2009), 'Are Foreign Investors Attracted to Weak Environmental Regulations? Evaluating the Evidence from China', *Journal of Development Economics*, 90: 1–13.

Elliott, R.J.R. and Zhou, Y. (2013), 'Environmental Regulation Induced Foreign Direct Investment', *Environmental and Resource Economics*, 55: 141–158.

Ferrara, I., Missios, P. and Yildiz, H.M. (2015), 'Pollution Havens, Endogenous Environmental Policy and Foreign Direct Investment', *Southern Economic Journal*, 82: 257–284.

Kayalica, M.O. and Lahiri, S. (2005), 'Strategic Environmental Policies in the Presence of Foreign Direct Investment', *Environmental and Resource Economics*, 30: 1–21.

Kennedy, P.W. (1994), 'Equilibrium Pollution Taxes in Open Economies with Imperfect Competition', *Journal of Environmental Economics and Management*, 27: 49–63.

List, A.J. and Co, C.Y. (2000), 'The Effects of Environmental Regulations on Foreign Direct Investment', *Journal of Environmental Economics and Management*, 40: 1–20.

Manderson, E. and Kneller, R. (2012), 'Environmental Regulations, Outward FDI and Heterogeneous Firms: Are Countries Used as Pollution Havens?', *Environmental and Resource Economics*, 51: 317–352.

Markusen, J.R. (1997), 'Costly Pollution Abatement, Competitiveness and Plant Location Decisions', *Resource and Energy Economics*, 19: 299–320.

Markusen, J.R., Morey, E.R. and Olewiler, N. (1993), 'Environmental Policy when Market Structure and Plant Locations are Endogenous', *Journal of Environmental Economics and Management*, 24: 69–86.

Ulph, A. and Valentini, V. (1997), 'Plant Location and Strategic Environmental Policy with Inter-Sectoral Linkages', *Resource and Energy Economics*, 19: 363–383.

Xing, Y. and Kolstad, C.D. (2002), 'Do Lax Environmental Regulations Attract Foreign Investment?', *Environmental and Resource Economics*, 21: 1–22.

Part III

Firm heterogeneity

7 Foreign penetration and environmental policies

Sajal Lahiri and Yingyi Tsai

1 Introduction

Much has been written on the flow of foreign direct investment (FDI) toward countries with limited restrictions on pollution emission. Low and Yeats (1992) found that many polluting industries migrated to countries with less strict environmental restrictions in the 1970s and 1980s. Lucas *et al.* (1992) put forward evidence for the fact that the stricter regulation of pollution in the OECD countries led to significant displacement of polluting activities from those countries.

On the demand side of FDI, there is strong evidence to suggest that the major developing countries are competing for FDI from the developed countries. In 1990–91, total inflow FDI into China was $2.7 billion, and the figure for India was $0.1 billion. These figures rose steadily to $55.02 billion and $5.50 billion for China and India respectively in 2004–05 (Panagariya, 2006). This huge flow of FDI into countries with low controls on emissions has alleged to have created pollution havens. The empirical evidence in this respect is however mixed.[1]

The pollution haven hypothesis identifies lower emission standards as the cause of FDI inflow. Could FDI inflow also cause lower emission standards? In other words, could there be reverse causality as well. For a given amount of FDI, a country weighs the marginal benefits and costs of environmental restrictions, and then decides on the optimal level of policy. An inflow of FDI can alter these benefits and/or costs and thus the level of optimal policy. In this chapter we shall examine this latter causality. We consider a Cournot oligopolistic market for a non-tradeable commodity. A number of domestic and foreign firms serve the market. We shall assume the number of foreign firms to be exogenous, but we shall consider two scenarios depending on whether there is free entry and exit of domestic firms or not, i.e. whether the number of domestic firms is endogenous or exogenous.[2] All firms emit pollution when producing commodities and have access to abatement technology when the pollution emission is restricted. Under the above specification, we consider as an instrument a uniform emission standards for both sets of firms.[3] We then characterize the optimal environmental policy under the two scenarios and examine how an increase in the number of foreign firms affects the optimal policy.

In the literature many have considered environmental policies in oligopolistic models (see, Carraro *et al.* (1996)). Barrett (1994) demonstrates that governments may impose weak environmental standards in oligopolistic markets. Katsoulacos and Xepapadeas (1995) examine emission taxes and find that it can over-internalize the externality under free entry and exit. Spulber (1985) considers emission standards and shows that they lead to excessive industry pollution under free entry and exit, but not under a fixed number of firms. Ebert (1992) and Ulph (1992, 1996) compare different environmental policies under different types of oligopolistic competitions. Ebert (1998) examines relative emission standards under symmetric Cournot oligopoly. Maloney and McCormick (1982) and Levin (1985) allow for asymmetries between firms like we do here. Spulber (1985), Conrad and Wang (1993), Katsoulacos and Xepapadeas (1995) and Farzin (2003) examine the effects of different environmental policies on market structure. Lahiri and Symeonidis (2007) consider welfare and pollution implications for multilateral piecemeal reforms of environmental policies in an international oligopolistic model with and without free entry and exit of firms.

There is also a small literature on the relationship between FDI and the environment (see, for example, Markusen *et al.*, 1993, 1995). Lahiri and Ono (2007) analyse the different effects of a tax and a quantity restriction on pollution control when the country is small in the market of FDI, i.e. the number of foreign firms is endogenous. Finally, Lahiri and Ono (2015), like here, consider two sets of firms, but they allow for different emission standards for the two sets of firms and they also consider an additional instrument of lump-sum taxes.

The next section sets up the basic framework of analysis. Then in section 3 we analyse optimal emission standards: in section 3.1 the number of domestic firms is fixed, and in section 3.2 it is endogenous. Finally, section 4 makes some concluding remarks.

2   The model

We consider a partial equilibrium model in which n number of identical foreign firms and m number of identical domestic firms compete in the market for a non-tradeable commodity in a host country. The inverse demand function for this commodity is given by:

$$p = \alpha - \beta X, \tag{1}$$

where p and X are respectively the price and the domestic demand for the commodity. Since the commodity is non-tradeable, total domestic demand X is equal to total production by domestic and foreign firms. That is,

$$X = nx_f + mx_d, \tag{2}$$

where x_d and x_f are production by each domestic and each foreign firm respectively.

The size of total production creates effluent emissions that represent pollution for the society. In the absence of abatement, each domestic and foreign firm would emit pollution in the amount θ_d and θ_f respectively per unit of output. Therefore the total gross amount of pollution would be $\theta_d m x_d + \theta_f n x_f$. The government is assumed to have a pollution control policy, which allows only z units of pollution per unit of output produced. Accordingly, total net emissions of pollution Z are given by:

$$Z = zX. \tag{3}$$

The damage function associated with emissions in the industry is an increasing function of total net emissions, $D = D(Z)$, as assumed in most applications of environmental economics.

For the sake of simplicity we will assume this to be linear:

$$D(Z) = \rho Z$$

where ρ is the constant marginal disutility of pollution.

In order to abate pollution beyond the allowance each firm is assumed to incur the cost of γ per unit of pollution and thus the total cost on account of pollution abatement for each domestic and foreign firm is $t_d x_d$ and $t_f x_f$ respectively, where:

$$t_i = \gamma(\theta_i - z), i = d, f. \tag{4}$$

Each domestic and each foreign firm has a marginal cost of production c_d and c_f respectively, and cost of abatement of pollution t_d and t_f respectively per unit of production, therefore its profits are

$$\pi_i = \left(p - c_i - t_i\right) x_i - F_i, i = d, f, \tag{5}$$

where F_d and F_f are respectively the level of fixed costs faced by each domestic and foreign firm.

Assuming Cournot-Nash behaviour of the foreign firms, the first-order profit-maximizing condition in the symmetric equilibrium is given by:

$$p - c_i - t_i = \beta x_i, i = d, f. \tag{6}$$

We shall consider two scenarios. In the first the number of domestic firms is fixed, and in the second there is free entry and exit of domestic firms so that

$$\pi_d = 0. \tag{7}$$

The welfare function becomes:

$$W(z,n) = CS + m\pi_d - \rho Z, \tag{8}$$

where $d\,CS = -X dp$.

3   Optimal emission standard

3.1   *The case of fixed number of domestic firms*

We first consider both the number of domestic firms, m, and the number of foreign firms, n, as exogenously given.

Using (1), (2) and (6), we get

$$\beta(m+1)x_d + \beta n x_f = a - c_d - t_d, \tag{9}$$

$$\beta m x_d + \beta(n+1)x_f = a - c_f - t_f, \tag{10}$$

which are solved to give

$$x_d^* = \frac{a - (n+1)(c_d + \gamma\theta_d) + n(c_f + \gamma\theta_f) + \gamma z}{\beta(m+n+1)}, \tag{11}$$

$$x_f^* = \frac{a - (m+1)(c_f + \gamma\theta_f) + m(c_d + \gamma\theta_d) + \gamma z}{\beta(m+n+1)}, \tag{12}$$

and totally differentiating (9) and (10), and using (4), we obtain

$$dx_d = dx_f = \frac{\gamma dz}{\beta(m+n+1)}. \tag{13}$$

Then substituting (1) and (4) into (6), and then differentiating it and using (13), we get

$$dX = \frac{\gamma(m+n)dz}{\beta(m+n+1)}, \tag{14}$$

$$dp = -\beta dX. \tag{15}$$

Since an increase in z is a relaxation of the environmental policy and it applies to all firms, it reduces total unit cost of production and hence it increases production of each firm and total production and reduces price.

Turning to welfare, changes in its individual components are:

$$\frac{dCS}{dz} = \frac{\gamma(m+n)(mx_d^* + nx_f^*)}{(m+n+1)}, \tag{16}$$

$$\frac{d\pi_d}{dz} = \frac{2\gamma x_d}{(m+n+1)}, \tag{17}$$

$$\frac{dZ}{dz} = z\left(m \cdot \frac{dx_d^*}{dz} + n \cdot \frac{dx_f^*}{dz}\right) + (mx_d^* + nx_f^*). \tag{18}$$

That is, a relaxation of the environmental standards increases consumers' surplus, increases profits and increases pollution emission. Substituting these expression in the welfare equation, we get:

$$\frac{dW}{dz} \equiv f(z,m) = \frac{\beta(mx_d^* + nx_f^*)[(m+n)\gamma - (m+n+1)\rho] + 2m\beta\gamma x_d^* - \rho\gamma(m+n)z}{\beta(m+n+1)}, \tag{19}$$

and thus the expression for optimal emission standards is obtained by setting $dW/dz = 0$, giving:[4]

$$z^* = \frac{\beta(mx_d^* + nx_f^*)[(m+n)\gamma - (m+n+1)\rho] + 2m\beta\gamma x_d^*}{\rho\gamma(m+n)}. \tag{20}$$

From (20), we observe that the optimal level of emission standards will not be the strictest, i.e. it will be positive, if and only if the domestic firms' share of the market is sufficiently large, i.e.

$$z^* > 0 \quad \Leftrightarrow \quad \frac{mx_d^*}{mx_d^* + nx_f^*} > \frac{(m+n+1)\rho - (m+n)\gamma}{2\gamma}.$$

Note that the above condition will be satisfied if $(m+n)\gamma > (m+n+1)\rho$. That is, for the optimal emission standards to be strictest the marginal disutility of pollution ρ has to be sufficiently large. The parameter ρ represents the marginal disutility of pollution and γ the marginal private cost of reducing pollution. Since the government has to balance costs to the producers and consumers, it has to compare these two parameters when deciding on the optimal level of emission standards.

Turning to the effect of an increase in the number of foreign firms on the optimal emission standards, from (19) and (20), we find

$$\frac{dz^*}{dn} = -\frac{f_n}{f_z},$$

where $f_z < 0$ from the second-order condition. This equation can be expressed as

$$(m+n)(m+n+1)^2(-f_z)\cdot\frac{dz*}{dn} = x_d m(m+n+1)(\rho-2\gamma)$$

$$+x_f[(m+n+1)(m+2n)\rho-(m+n)\{(m+n)^2+2m\}\gamma].$$

From the above equation it follows that an increase in the number of foreign firms will lead to less (more) stricter emission standards if ρ (γ) is sufficiently larger than γ (ρ).

Formally,

Proposition 1. When the number of domestic firms is exogenously given, the optimal emission standards satisfies:

1.   the optimal emission standards is not the strictest if and only if the domestic firms' market share is sufficiently large, and
2.   an increase in the number of foreign firms will lead to less (more) stricter emission standards if ρ (γ) is sufficiently larger than γ (ρ).

3.2   *The case of free entry and exit of domestic firms*

In this section the number foreign firms n will continue to be treated as an exogenous variable. However, we shall assume free entry and exit of domestic firms via (7) and so m will be an endogenous variable in this section.

Substituting (6) in (5) and then using (7), we solve for x_d as

$$\hat{x}_d = \sqrt{\frac{F_d}{\beta}}, \tag{21}$$

which gives

$$\frac{\partial\hat{x}_d}{\partial z} = \frac{\partial\hat{x}_d}{\partial n} = 0. \tag{22}$$

That is, environmental policy here has no effect on the level of output of each domestic firm. For a given level of emission standards, an increase in the number of foreign firms also does not affect the output of each domestic firm. But they will have effects on the number of domestic firms and the output of each foreign firm. For a given level of emission standards, an increase in the number of foreign firms also does not affect the output of each domestic firm. Substituting (21) in (9) and (10), we solve for $\hat{m}$ and $\hat{x}_f$ as

$$\hat{m}, = \frac{a-(n+1)c_d + nc_f - (n+1)\beta\hat{x}_d - \gamma(\theta_d - z)+n\gamma(\theta_f - \theta_d)}{\beta\hat{x}_d} \tag{23}$$

$$\hat{x}_f = \frac{c_d - c_f + \beta \hat{x}_d + \gamma(\theta_d - \theta_f)}{\beta},$$ (24)

which gives us

$$\frac{\partial \hat{m}}{\partial z} = \frac{\gamma}{\beta \hat{x}_d} \cdot \frac{\partial \hat{x}_f}{\partial z} = 0,$$ (25)

$$\frac{\partial \hat{m}}{\partial n} = \frac{c_f - c_d - \beta \hat{x}_d + \gamma(\theta_f - \theta_d)}{\beta \hat{x}_d}, \frac{\partial \hat{x}_f}{\partial n} = 0.$$ (26)

Thus, a relaxation of the environmental policy does not affect total output produced by foreign firms, but increases that by domestic firms by increasing the number of domestic firms. For a given level of emission standards, an increase in the number of foreign firms does not affect the output of each foreign firm but it may or may not increase the number of domestic firms. If the domestic firms are less efficient than the domestic firms, i.e. if $c_f + \gamma \theta_f < c_d + \gamma \theta_d$, an increase in the number of foreign firms will crowd out domestic firms.

Since profits of domestic firms is zero because of the free entry and exit, welfare here is given by $W = CS - \rho Z$, and thus using the above derivations, it can be shown that

$$\frac{dW}{dz} = (\gamma - \rho)(\hat{m} \hat{x}_d + n \hat{x}_f) - \frac{\rho \gamma z}{\beta},$$

and therefore[5]

$$\hat{z} = \frac{\beta(\gamma - \rho)(\hat{m} \hat{x}_d + n \hat{x}_f)}{\rho \gamma}.$$ (27)

From (27) it follows that when $\rho > \gamma$ the country will impose the strictest possible emission standards, i.e. $\hat{z} = 0$. However, some pollution will be allowed if $\gamma > \rho$. From (22), (24), (26) and (27), it can be easily verified that $d\hat{z} / dn = 0$. Formally,

Proposition 2. When there is free entry and exit of foreign firms, the optimal emission standards which is applied uniformly to all firms, satisfies:

1. When $\rho > \gamma$, the optimal emission standards will take the value zero,
2. $\hat{z} > 0$ if and only if $2\rho > \gamma > \rho$, and
3. an increase in the number of foreign firms has no effect on the optimal emission standards.

As mentioned before, the parameter ρ represents the marginal disutility of pollution and γ the marginal private cost of reducing pollution. The latter is important because a stricter emission standard affects profits and consumers' surplus negatively more when γ is higher. it raises costs of production and thus price. Therefore, the government has to compare these two parameters when deciding on the optimal level of emission standards. An increase in the number of foreign firms increases the total production by foreign firms, but reduces that by the domestic firms by the same amount. Thus it has no effect on the optimal emission standards.

4 Conclusion

Foreign direct investment (FDI) is often viewed sceptically by environmentalists who are concerned about the environmental consequence of strategic mobility of foreign capital: foreign capital moving to countries with low environmental restrictions on production. Here the direction of causation is from environmental policy to FDI. In this chapter, we consider the other direction of causality. That is, we examine the effect of FDI on environmental policies, and we find that FDI does not necessarily lead to lower environmental standards.

We conduct our analysis in an oligopolistic framework where a number of domestic firms compete with a number of foreign firms in the host-country market. Both sets of firms create pollution while producing and possess an abatement technology. We consider two scenarios depending on whether there is free entry and exit of domestic firms or not. Our results depend crucially on whether there is free entry and exit of domestic firms. For example, under free entry and exit of domestic firms, FDI does not affect the level of optimal emission standards, but it does when the number of domestic firms is exogenous. Even under the latter scenario, FDI may not make environmental policies less stringent.

Notes

1 Jeppesen *et al.* (2002) provide an excellent survey on this subject. Becker and Henderson (2000) and Gray (1997), for example, find evidences in favour of the pollution hypothesis. However, there are others who do not (see, for example, Duffy-Deno (1992), Levinson (1996) and McConnell and Schwab (1990)).
2 Even though in a different context, Lahiri and Ono (2011), Bagwell and Staiger (2015) and Koska and Stahler (2015) also consider Cournot oligopolistic models with endogenous number of domestic and/or foreign firms.
3 According to Helfand (1991), emission standards can take a variety of forms: an emission restriction per unit of output, an emission restriction per unit of certain input, restrictions on the use of a particular input, or mandated use of a particular emission-control technology. A restriction on emission in the form of a restriction on emission *per unit of output* is sometimes called a relative emission standard (Ebert (1998)).
4 It can be verified that the second-order condition is satisfied if and only if $\gamma[(m+n)^2 + 2m] < 2\rho[(m+n)^2 + m + n]$.
5 It can be verified that the second-order condition is satisfied if and only if $\gamma < 2\rho$.

References

Bagwell, Kyle and Robert Staiger, 2015, Delocation and trade agreements in imperfectly competitive markets, *Research in Economics*, 69(2), 132–156.

Barrett, S., 1994, Strategic environmental policy and international trade, *Journal of Public Economics*, 54, 325–338.

Becker, R. and J. Henderson, 2000, Effects of air quality regulations on polluting industries, *Journal of Political Economy*, 108, 379–421.

Carraro, C., Y. Katsoulacos and A. Xepapadeas, 1996, *Environmental Policy and Market Structure*, Dordrecht: Kluwer Academic Publishers.

Conrad, K. and J. Wang, 1993, The effect of emission taxes and abatement subsidies on market structure, *International Journal of Industrial Organization*, 11, 499–518.

Duffy-Deno, K., 1992, Pollution abatement expenditures and regional manufacturing activity, *Journal of Regional Science*, 32: 419–436.

Ebert, U., 1992, Pigouvian taxes and market structure: the case of oligopoly and different abatement technologies, *Finanzarchiv*, 49, 154–166.

Ebert, U., 1998, Relative standards: a positive and normative analysis, *Journal of Economics*, 67, 17–38.

Farzin, Y.H., 2003, The effects of emission standards on industry, *Journal of Regulatory Economics*, 24, 315–327.

Gray, W. B., 1997, Manufacturing plant location: does state pollution regulation matter?, NBER Working Papers 5880, National Bureau of Economic Research, Inc.

Helfand, G., 1991, Standards versus standards: the effect of different pollution restrictions, *American Economic Review*, 81, 622–634.

Jeppesen, T., J.A. List and H. Folmer, 2002, Environmental regulations and new plant location decisions: evidence from a meta-analysis, *Journal of Regional Science*, 42(1), 19–49.

Katsoulacos, Y. and A. Xepapadeas, 1995, Environmental policy under oligopoly with endogenous market structure, *Scandinavian Journal of Economics*, 97, 411–420.

Koska, Onur and Frank Stahler, 2015, Factor price differences in a general equilibrium model of trade and imperfect competition, *Research in Economics*, 69(2), 248–259.

Lahiri, S. and Y. Ono, 2007, Relative emission standard versus tax under oligopoly: the role of free entry, *Journal of Economics*, 91(2), 107–128.

Lahiri, S. and Y. Ono, 2011, An oligopolistic Heckscher-Ohlin model of foreign direct investment, *The Japanese Economic Review*, 62(3), 331–347.

Lahiri, S. and Y. Ono, 2015, Pollution, foreign direct investment, and welfare, *Research in Economics*, 69(2), 238–247.

Lahiri, S. and G. Symeonidis, 2007, Piecemeal multilateral environmental policy reforms under asymmetric oligopoly, *Journal of Public Economic Theory*, 9, 885–899.

Levin, D., 1985, Taxation within Cournot oligopoly, *Journal of Public Economics*, 27, 281–290.

Levinson, A., 1996, Environmental regulation and industrial location: international and domestic evidence, in J. Bhagwati and R. Hudec (eds), *Harmonization and Fair Trade*, Cambridge, Mass.: MIT Press.

Low, P. and A. Yeats, 1992, Do dirty industries migrate?, in P. Low (ed.), *International Trade and the Environment*, Washington, DC: The World Bank, 89–103.

Lucas, R.E.B., D. Wheeler and H. Hettige, 1992, Economic development, environmental regulation and the international migration of toxic industrial pollution: 1960–1988, in P. Low (ed.), *International Trade and the Environment*, Washington, DC: The World Bank, 67–86.

McConnell, V.D. and Schwab, R.M., 1990, The impact of environmental regulation on industry location decisions: the motor vehicle industry, *Land Economics,* 66: 67–81.

Maloney, M. and R.E. McCormick, 1982, A positive theory of environmental quality regulation, *Journal of Law and Economics*, 25, 99–123.

Markusen, J.R., E.R. Morey and N. Olewiler, 1993, Environmental policy when market structure and plant locations are endogenous, *Journal of Environmental Economics and Management*, 24, 69–86.

Markusen, J.R., E.R. Morey and N. Olewiler, 1995, Competition in regional environmental policies when plant locations are endogenous, *Journal of Public Economics*, 56, 55–57.

Panagariya, A., 2006, India and China: trade and foreign investment, paper presented at the conference 'Challenges of Economic Policy Reform in Asia', Stanford Center for International Development, 1–3 June 2006.

Spulber, D.F., 1985, Effluent regulation and long run optimality, *Journal of Environmental Economics and Management*, 12, 103–116.

Ulph, A., 1992, The choice of environmental instruments and strategic international trade, in R. Pethig (ed.), *Conflicts and Cooperation in Managing Environmental Resources*, Berlin: Springer, ch. 5, 111–132.

Ulph, A., 1996, Environmental policy instruments and imperfectly competitive international trade, *Environmental and Resource Economics*, 7, 333–355.

8 Abatement level in environmental agreements when firms are heterogeneous in abatement costs

Luis Gautier

1 Introduction

There is an important number of regional and international environmental agreements which countries have agreed upon in order to tackle environmental degradation (e.g. reduce greenhouse gases). In addition, member countries exhibit varying pollution abatement technologies and degrees of pollution intensities as well as different cost structures. As new agreements take place (e.g. COP21 Paris) and existing ones evolve as climate and economic conditions change, the analysis of policy reform of environmental policy becomes timely and relevant. With these in mind, this chapter builds a two-country model where firms compete in a Cournot fashion, face an emission tax and exhibit heterogeneous abatement costs. In this context, the analysis of policy reform is presented, particularly its impact on global emissions. It is shown that asymmetries in abatement and production costs play a crucial role in the extent to which global emissions fall via unilateral and multilateral policy reform.

Over the last several decades a number of multilateral environmental agreements have been established which exemplify efforts of policy reform, e.g. see Barrett (2003) and the IEA Database Project[1] for examples of environmental agreements. For instance, the Convention on Long-range Transboundary Air Pollution (LRTAP) illustrates how LRTAP member countries identify ways to reduce emissions of air pollutants via unilateral and multilateral policy reform, and the UNECE Committee on Environmental Policy provides support to member countries to enhance cooperation and reduce transboundary pollution. The Basel Convention[2] also illustrates multilateral efforts to address the disposal of hazardous waste including technology transfer to manage waste, and the Clean Technology Fund exemplifies efforts to provide funds to promote low-carbon technologies across countries.[3] More recently, the COP21 2015 meeting in Paris brought countries together in the sense of putting forward independent, nationally determined contributions (INDCs) along with policies, including market-based mechanisms and standards. The Paris agreement may not necessarily achieve the desired level of pollution abatement of greenhouse gases (e.g. Barrett *et al.* 2015; Kahn 2016) and, therefore, countries may need to adjust INDCs and policies accordingly. Even if national emission targets are achieved, economic conditions are likely to change thereby prompting countries to adjust policy.

Concerns about losing competitiveness to foreign competition has been used as an argument by less-developed and developed countries to avoid implementing carbon pricing policies as well as other environmental policies. Indeed, the literature has studied aspects of strategic environmental policy and the characterization of optimal policy (e.g. Ulph 1996; Ulph and Ulph 1996, 2007; Bayındır-Upmann 2003; Turunen-Red and Woodland 2004; Silva and Zhu 2009; Bhattacharya and Pal 2010; Elliott and Zhou 2013; Ambec and Coria 2013; Caplan and Silva 2005) and the pollution haven hypothesis (e.g. Zarsky 1999; Neumayer 2001; Grether and de Melo 2004). The idea here is that countries may engage in laxer (less stringent) environmental policy (e.g. lower emission taxes or lower costs in the form of laxer environmental regulation) in order to avoid losing to foreign competition and attract profits. The contribution of the present work to this literature is that here I look at elements of strategic environmental policy, but with particular attention to policy reform and its impact on global emissions in the presence of heterogeneous abatement costs across countries; I do not delve into the characterization of optimal policy since this has been examined in the aforementioned literature. For instance, as countries set laxer environmental policies to become more cost competitive (e.g. set cost-reducing policies) optimal taxation may be adjusted which may, consequently, have an impact on global emissions. I explore changes in both production costs and pollution abatement costs via policy reform and how these may alter optimal emission taxes, with particular attention to the effects on global emissions. Aspects of strategic environmental policy are captured via the combination of policy reforms such as lower taxation and at the same cost-reducing (or alternatively cost-increasing) reforms. The aforementioned literature does not focus on the analysis of policy reforms and does not delve into the role of asymmetries in pollution intensity coefficients, both key contributions of this chapter.

The present analysis also contributes to a second important branch of the literature which examines the policy reform of reducing emissions under imperfect competition (e.g. Hoel 1991), particularly the role of environmental standards (e.g. Kayalica and Lahiri 2005; Bhattacharya and Pal 2010) and emission taxes (e.g. Hatzipanayotou *et al.* 2005; Lahiri and Symeonidis 2007; Gautier 2013, 2014). The contribution to this line of research is on the policy reform of emission taxes. Lahiri and Symeonidis (2007) examine the effects of policy reform of emission taxes on global emissions, but do not look at the implications of welfare which is an aspect I examine in section 4. Furthermore, Gautier (2013, 2014) examines aspects of policy reform of taxes on welfare, but the present analysis adds to these works by incorporating changes in costs (both abatement and production costs) into the policy reform of emission taxes. This is important because as cost structures change governments may adjust optimal taxation, thus having an impact on the extent to which policy reform may reduce global emissions. Additionally, part of the literature has assumed linear demand or specific cost functions to derive some of the results about policy reform. This chapter, in contrast, presents a model with asymmetries in pollution abatement and production costs, and demand functions in a general setting thus providing a unified framework of analysis.

The model set-up consists of two countries where firms behave à la Cournot, face an emission tax and exhibit heterogeneity in the cost functions across countries. The heterogeneity in costs is captured through two channels. First, marginal abatement costs may differ across countries. This captures differences in pollution abatement technologies across countries as well as differences in pollution intensities. Different costs structures also capture different levels of production efficiencies in terms of marginal production costs. These two aspects are important in the analysis of policy reform since in the context of environmental agreements countries are likely to exhibit these types of asymmetries. Second, there is heterogeneity in costs through a cost parameter, assumed to be exogenous, which changes the *level* of the cost functions for any level of output and emissions, i.e. shifts costs for any level of output and emissions. This is an important channel through which cost heterogeneity is captured because it allows to examine potential policy reform on costs (whether cost-reducing or cost-increasing policies) within each country. For instance, exogenous changes in this parameter not only may be interpreted as cost-reducing policies in both pollution abatement and production costs (e.g. cost-reducing R&D), but also the exogenous nature of the parameter allows to see how cost-reducing (or alternatively cost-increasing) policies may affect the effectiveness of policy reforms of emission taxes on reducing emissions, e.g. cost-reducing policy affects optimal taxation and consequently policy reform of taxes.

The analysis indicates that differences in pollution intensities across countries as well as asymmetries in production and abatement costs affect the effectiveness of policy reform to lower global emissions. Additionally, policy reforms consisting of cost-reducing policies (to increase firms' cost competitiveness in one country, say) may reduce global emissions as long as these are coupled with an emission tax. But also cost-increasing policy reforms are presented, and conditions derived, such that global emissions fall. This type of analysis is pertinent in the context of environmental agreements where countries may put forward stricter environmental policies on the one hand (e.g. higher emission taxes), but at the same time cost-reducing policies which may induce higher emissions.

The chapter is structured as follows. Section 2 presents the building blocks of the model. Section 3 presents the comparative statics analysis with implications for policy reform. Section 4 then looks at the welfare implications of policy reform. In section 5, I conclude by discussing some of the limitations of the analysis and suggesting questions for future research.

2   The model

This section presents the main building blocks of the model. Consider a home and foreign country where only one firm operates in each country.[4] Firms compete for the production of an imperfect substitute, which is exported to a third market exclusively.

Demand faced by each firm is given by a function $P^k = P^k(q^h, q^f)$, where q^k denotes output in country $k = h, f$; and where (subscripts denote partial derivatives) $P_{q^k} < 0$, $2P_{q^k} + q^k P_{q^k q^k} < 0$, for $k = h, f$. Moreover, as in Dixit (1986) and Lahiri and Symeonidis (2007) I shall assume that the 'own effect' is greater than the cross-effect, i.e. $2P_{q^h}^h + q^h P_{q^h q^h}^h < P_{q^f}^h + q^h P_{q^h q^f}^h < 0$ and $2P_{q^f}^f + q^f P_{q^f q^f}^f < P_{q^h}^f + q^f P_{q^f q^h}^f$ for $k = h, f$. These will aid to ensure stability in the global equilibrium.

Each firm pollutes the environment and without any loss of generality let e^k denote the pollutant in country $k = h, f$. I follow Requate (2006) in the structure of the cost function for each firm operating in each country $k = h, f$. In particular, consider a cost function $C^k = C^k(q^k, e^k)$ where (subscripts denote partial derivatives) $C_{q^k}^k > 0$, $C_{e^k}^k < 0$, $C_{q^k e^k}^k = C_{e^k q^k}^k < 0$, $C_{q^k q^k}^k > 0$, $C_{e^k e^k}^k > 0$, $C_{e^k e^k}^k C_{q^k q^k}^k - C_{q^k e^k}^{k2} > 0$, and as in Lahiri and Symeonidis (2007) the pollution intensity is defined as the ratio $-C_{e^k q^k}^k / C_{e^k e^k}^k > 0$ for $k = h, f$.[5]

Each firm faces an emission tax for each unit of pollution it fails to abate. Specifically, the home-country firm faces a per-unit emission tax, t^h, for the level of pollution, e^h, it fails to abate, and analogously the foreign-country firm faces a tax, t^f, which targets e^f.

Firms and governments play a two-stage non-cooperative game. Each country chooses the tax simultaneously taking the other country's tax as given. Firms (home and foreign) then take policy as given and maximize profits by choosing the level of emissions and output in a Cournot-Nash fashion. The assumption of simultaneous decision on output and emissions assumes away issues of the strategic choice of abatement; these have been analysed elsewhere (e.g. Carlsson 2000; Montero 2002a, 2002b; Gautier 2014). I assume interior solutions throughout the analysis and the model is solved by backward induction.

In particular, the home-country's firm solves

$$\max_{q^h e^h} \pi^h = P^h q^h - z^h C^h(q^h, e^h) - e^h t^h \tag{1}$$

where z^h is a positive constant. Larger (smaller) values of z^h capture higher (lower) costs for any q^h and e^h.[6] For example, the firm may face new regulation which in turn reflects on higher production and abatement pollution costs; alternatively, the firm may enjoy lower costs (i.e. a smaller z^h) as a result of cost-reducing technology. The role of z^h is analogous to the role of $R \& D$ in e.g. Montero (2002a), but in the present model this is exogenous.

Maximization of (1) yields the following first-order conditions (subscripts denote partial derivatives)

$$P^h + q^h P^h_{q^h} - z^h C^h_{q^h} = 0 \tag{2}$$

$$-z^h C^h_{e^h} - t^h = 0 \tag{3}$$

Analogously, the foreign country's firm profits are given by

$$\max_{q^f, e^f} \pi^f = P^f q^f - z^f C^f (q^f, e^f) - e^f t^f \tag{4}$$

where z^f is a positive constant and its interpretation is analogous to z^h. From (4), first-order conditions are given by

$$P^f + q^f P^f_{q^f} - z^f C^f_{q^f} = 0 \tag{5}$$

$$-z^f C^f_{e^f} - t^f = 0 \tag{6}$$

Equations (2), (3), (5), (6) implicitly determine the equilibrium level of output and emissions, q^h, q^f, e^h, e^f. Stability for the local and global equilibrium require $\pi^h_{q^h q^h} \pi^f_{q^f q^f} - \pi^h_{q^h q^f} \pi^f_{q^f q^h} > 0$, and $\pi^k_{q^k q^k} \pi^k_{e^k e^k} - \pi^k_{q^k e^k} \pi^k_{e^k q^k} > 0$ for $k = h, f$.

3 Comparative statics

The comparative static effects of the tax, t^h and t^f, and the cost parameters z^h and z^f, on output on emissions are examined. The analysis of policy reform is then presented.

Total differentiation of (2), (3), (5), (6) yields the following system:

$$\begin{bmatrix} 2P^h_{q^h} + q^h P^h_{q^h q^h} - z^h C^h_{q^h q^h} & P^h_{q^f} + q^h P^h_{q^h q^f} & -z^h C^h_{q^h e^h} & 0 \\ -z^h C^h_{e^h q^h} & 0 & -z^h C^h_{e^h e^h} & 0 \\ P^f_{q^h} + q^f P^f_{q^f q^h} & 2P^f_{q^f} + q^f P^f_{q^f q^f} - z^f C^f_{q^f q^f} & 0 & -z^f C^f_{q^f e^f} \\ 0 & -z^f C^f_{e^f q^f} & 0 & -z^f C^f_{e^f e^f} \end{bmatrix}$$

$$\begin{bmatrix} dq^h \\ dq^f \\ de^h \\ de^f \end{bmatrix} = \begin{bmatrix} C^h_{q^h} dz^h \\ C^h_{e^h} dz^h + dt^h \\ C^f_{q^f} dz^f \\ C^f_{e^f} dz^f + dt^f \end{bmatrix}$$

where the determinant of the coefficient matrix is $\mu < 0$. I shall follow Lahiri and Symeonidis (2007: 890) in the definition of pollution intensity, $-C^k_{q^k e^k} / C^k_{e^k e^k} > 0$, for $k = h, f$. Using the above system the effect of the tax and cost parameter z^k (for given tax) on output and emissions is given by

$$\Delta dq^h = \frac{-C_{q^h e^h}^h}{C_{e^h e^h}^h}\left[-\left(2P_{q^f}^f + q^f P_{q^f q^f}^f\right) + z^f \frac{C_{e^f e^f}^f C_{q^f q^f}^f - C_{e^f q^f}^{f2}}{C_{e^f e^f}^f}\right]dt^h - \frac{C_{q^f e^f}^f}{C_{e^f e^f}^f}\left[P_{q^f}^h + q^h P_{q^h q^f}^h\right]dt^f$$

$$+ \left(C_{q^h}^h - C_{e^h}^h \frac{C_{q^h e^h}^h}{C_{e^h e^h}^h}\right)\left[-\left(2P_{q^f} + q^f P_{q^f q^f}\right) + z^f \frac{C_{e^f e^f}^f C_{q^f q^f}^f - C_{e^f q^f}^{f2}}{C_{e^f e^f}^f}\right]dz^h$$

$$+ \left(C_{q^f}^f - C_{e^f}^f \frac{C_{q^f e^f}^f}{C_{e^f e^f}^f}\right)\left(P_{q^f}^h + q^h P_{q^h q^f}^h\right)dz^f$$

(7)

$$\Delta dq^f = \frac{-C_{q^f e^f}^f}{C_{e^f e^f}^f}\left[-\left(2P_{q^h}^h + q^h P_{q^h q^h}^h\right) + z^h \frac{C_{e^h e^h}^h C_{q^h q^h}^h - C_{e^h q^h}^{h2}}{C_{e^h e^h}^h}\right]dt^f - \frac{C_{q^h e^h}^h}{C_{e^h e^h}^h}\left[P_{q^h}^f + q^f P_{q^f q^h}^f\right]dt^h$$

$$+ \left(C_{q^f}^f - C_{e^f}^f \frac{C_{q^f e^f}^f}{C_{e^f e^f}^f}\right)\left[-\left(2P_{q^h}^h + q^h P_{q^h q^h}^h\right) + z^h \frac{C_{e^h e^h}^h C_{q^h q^h}^h - C_{e^h q^h}^{h2}}{C_{e^h e^h}^h}\right]dz^f$$

$$+ \left(C_{q^h}^h - C_{e^h}^h \frac{C_{q^h e^h}^h}{C_{e^h e^h}^h}\right)\left(P_{q^h}^f + q^f P_{q^f q^h}^f\right)dz^h$$

(8)

where $\Delta := \mu / C_{e^h e^h}^h C_{e^f e^f}^f z^h z^f < 0$. In this type of analytical framework the effect of taxes has been examined in the literature (e.g. Lahiri and Symeonidis 2007; Gautier 2014, 2016) so here I just make a few remarks. First, an increase in the emission tax in one country renders the firm in that country relatively less cost competitive and, as a result, output in that country falls; the firm in the other country reacts strategically by raising output. Moreover, global output, $q^h + q^f$, falls from a tax increase since by assumption the own effect dominates the cross effect.

The effect of the tax on emissions works through changes in output and the abatement induced by the tax. Results on the effects of the tax on emissions are analogous to those in the literature: an increase in the tax in the home country reduces output and thus emissions in that country, but raises output and emissions in the foreign country since the tax renders the home firm relatively less cost competitive. As a result, global emissions, $e^h + e^f$, fall with a tax-increase at home if the home country is pollution intensive vis-à-vis the foreign country; global emissions rise otherwise if the foreign country exhibits a sufficiently large pollution intensity. The notion of a relative (and sufficient) pollution-intensive country is clearly defined later on.

It is noteworthy that an increase in the tax in the home country raises abatement in that country exclusively (i.e. the term $\Delta / z^h C_{q^h e^h}^h$ in equation 9), thereby lowering emissions in that country. As a result, a change in the tax in one country impacts emissions in that country via changes in output and abatement, whereas the impact on emissions in the other country works exclusively via changes in output.

In particular, the effect of taxes on foreign and home emissions is given by

$$\Delta de^h = \frac{-C^h_{q^h e^h}}{C^h_{e^h e^h}} \left[\frac{-C^h_{q^h e^h}}{C^h_{e^h e^h}} \left(\frac{-\left(2P^f_{q^f} + q^f P^f_{q^f q^f}\right)}{+z^f \dfrac{C^f_{e^f e^f} C^f_{q^f q^f} - C^{f2}_{e^f q^f}}{C^f_{e^f e^f}}} \right) + \Delta/z^h C^h_{q^h e^h} \right] dt^h$$

$$+ \frac{C^h_{q^h e^h}}{C^h_{e^h e^h}} \frac{C^f_{q^f e^f}}{C^f_{e^f e^f}} \left(P^h_{q^f} + q^h P^h_{q^h q^f} \right) dt^f \tag{9}$$

$$\Delta de^f = \frac{-C^f_{q^f e^f}}{C^f_{e^f e^f}} \left[\frac{-C^f_{q^f e^f}}{C^f_{e^f e^f}} \left(\frac{-\left(2P^h_{q^h} + q^h P^h_{q^h q^h}\right)}{+z^h \dfrac{C^h_{e^h e^h} C^h_{q^h q^h} - C^{h2}_{e^h q^h}}{C^h_{e^h e^h}}} \right) + \Delta/z^f C^f_{q^f e^f} \right] dt^f$$

$$+ \frac{C^f_{q^f e^f}}{C^f_{e^f e^f}} \frac{C^h_{q^h e^h}}{C^h_{e^h e^h}} \left(P^f_{q^h} + q^f P^f_{q^f q^h} \right) dt^h \tag{10}$$

where $\mu < 0$, $\Delta := \mu / C^h_{e^h e^h} C^f_{e^f e^f} z^h z^f$, the term $\Delta / z^k C^k_{q^k e^k}$ denotes the abatement induced by the emission tax, and the term $-(2P^k_{q^k} + q^k P^k_{q^k q^k}) + z^k (C^k_{e^k e^k} C^k_{q^k q^k} - C^{k2}_{e^k q^k}) / C^k_{e^k e^k}$ captures changes in emissions via changes in output for $k = h, f$.

Next, I look into the effects of the cost parameters z^h and z^f on home/foreign emissions and output.

The effect on home-country output from a change in z^h (for given tax) is given by the second line in (7). There are two opposing effects at play. On the one hand, an increase in z^h raises the cost of an extra unit of output in the home country, $C^h_{q^h}$, thereby lowering output in that country. Since the home country becomes relatively less cost competitive, output rises in the foreign country. On the other hand, an increase in z^h raises the cost of abating an extra unit of pollution in the home country, $-C^h_{e^h} C^h_{e^h q^h} / C^h_{e^h e^h}$, which in turn results in higher output, less abatement and higher emissions in that country; emissions will increase up to the point where marginal abatement costs equal the tax. Since the home country raises output as a result of higher marginal abatement costs, the foreign country reacts strategically by reducing production. Therefore, home (foreign)-country output rises (falls) *if and only if* the effect via the increase in marginal abatement costs is sufficiently large. And global output, $q^h + q^f$, increases under the aforementioned necessary and sufficient condition since the effect of z^h on home output (i.e. the own effect) completely offsets the effect on foreign output.

It is noteworthy that the channel whereby z^h affects the cost of reducing an extra unit of pollution (and thus output and emissions in the home country) depends crucially upon the presence of an emission tax: the upward shift in the marginal abatement cost of the home firm, resulting from an increase in z^h, induces the home firm to increase output and emissions up to the point where the new marginal abatement cost curve meets the emission tax in that country. Without the emission tax this effect vanishes and therefore the term $-C^h_{e^h}C^h_{e^hq^h}/C^h_{e^he^h}$ becomes negligible. An analogous analysis applies to the emission tax in the foreign country and changes in z^f.

Next, I analyse the effects on home and foreign emissions resulting from changes in z^k (for given tax). An increase in z^k exhibits the two opposing effects on output aforementioned with the corresponding effects on emissions. For instance, an increase in z^h raises costs for each extra unit of output, $C^h_{q^h}$, which lowers output and consequently emissions in the home country; as a result, emissions in the foreign country rise as the foreign firm reacts by increasing output. Additionally, an increase in z^h raises the costs of abating an extra unit of pollution which results in an increase in output and thus emissions in the home country; as a result, foreign emissions fall as the foreign firm reacts by lowering output.

It is noteworthy that the term $\Delta C^h_{e^h}/z^h C^h_{q^he^h}$ in equation (11) captures the effect of z^h on emissions, e^h, via abatement: higher abatement costs result in less abatement which in turn reflects on higher emissions; this effect compensates changes in emissions via changes in output as long as the effect via marginal abatement costs in the home country is sufficiently large (i.e. $C^h_{q^h} < C^h_{e^h}C^h_{q^he^h}/C^h_{e^he^h}$).

In particular, the change in home and foreign emissions arising from a change in z^k, $k = h, f$, is given by

$$
\begin{aligned}
\Delta de^h = &-\frac{C^h_{q^he^h}}{C^h_{e^he^h}}\left[\left(C^h_{q^h} - C^h_{e^h}\frac{C^h_{q^he^h}}{C^h_{e^he^h}}\right)\left(-\left(2P^f_{q^f} + q^f P^f_{q^fq^f}\right)+z^f\frac{C^f_{e^fe^f}C^f_{q^fq^f}-C^{f2}_{e^fq^f}}{C^f_{e^fe^f}}\right)\right.\\
&\left.+C^h_{e^h}\Delta/z^h C^h_{q^he^h}\right]dz^h \\
&-\frac{C^h_{q^he^h}}{C^h_{e^he^h}}\left(C^f_{q^f} - C^f_{e^f}\frac{C^f_{q^fe^f}}{C^f_{e^fe^f}}\right)\left(P^h_{q^f} + q^h P^h_{q^hq^f}\right)dz^f
\end{aligned}
\tag{11}
$$

$$
\begin{aligned}
\Delta de^f = &-\frac{C^f_{q^fe^f}}{C^f_{e^fe^f}}\left[\left(C^f_{q^f} - C^f_{e^f}\frac{C^f_{q^fe^f}}{C^f_{e^fe^f}}\right)\left(-\left(2P^h_{q^h} + q^h P^h_{q^hq^h}\right)+z^h\frac{C^h_{e^he^h}C^h_{q^hq^h}-C^{h2}_{e^hq^h}}{C^h_{e^he^h}}\right)\right.\\
&\left.+C^f_{e^f}\Delta/z^f C^f_{q^fe^f}\right]dz^f \\
&-\frac{C^f_{q^fe^f}}{C^f_{e^fe^f}}\left(C^h_{q^h} - C^h_{e^h}\frac{C^h_{q^he^h}}{C^h_{e^he^h}}\right)\left(P^f_{q^h} + q^f P^f_{q^fq^h}\right)dz^h
\end{aligned}
\tag{12}
$$

The net effect on global emissions, $e^h + e^f$, resulting from a change in z^k depends upon the relative pollution intensities as well as the effects via marginal abatement and production costs. If, for instance, the home country is the more pollution-intensive country (i.e. $-C^h_{q^h e^h} / C^h_{e^h e^h} > -C^f_{q^f e^f} / C^f_{e^f e^f}$), then global emissions rise as long as marginal abatement costs in the home country are sufficiently large. This is because with a sufficiently large effect via marginal abatement costs emissions rise at home, which completely offsets the reduction in emissions in the foreign country because the home country is relatively more pollution intensive. But if the foreign country is sufficiently more pollution intensive (i.e.

$$-C^h_{q^h e^h} / C^h_{e^h e^h} (-(2P^f_{q^f} + q^f P^f_{q^f q^f}) + C^f_{e^f e^f} C^f_{q^f q^f} - C^{f2}_{e^f q^f} / C^f_{e^f e^f}) + \Delta / z^h C^h_{q^h e^h} < C^f_{q^f e^f} / C^f_{e^f e^f}$$

$(P^f_{q^h} + q^f P^f_{q^f q^h}))$, then global emissions may fall.

Proposition 3.1 *An increase in costs in the home country, z^h (for given tax): (i) raises output in the home country, (ii) lowers output in the foreign country, and (iii) raises global output if and only if the effect via the increase in marginal abatement costs is sufficiently large (i.e. $C^h_{q^h} < C^h_{e^h} C^h_{q^h e^h} / C^h_{e^h e^h}$).*

Proposition 3.2 *Let marginal abatement costs be sufficiently large in the home country as defined in proposition 3.1. Then, an increase in costs in the home country (i.e. increase in z^h) increases global emissions, if the home country is at least as pollution intensive as the foreign country (i.e. $-C^h_{q^h e^h} / C^h_{e^h e^h} \geq -C^f_{q^f e^f} / C^f_{e^f e^f}$). Global emissions fall otherwise if the foreign country is sufficiently pollution intensive, i.e. $-C^h_{q^h e^h} / C^h_{e^h e^h} (-(2P^f_{q^f} + q^f P^f_{q^f q^f}) + C^f_{e^f e^f} C^f_{q^f q^f} - C^{f2}_{e^f q^f} / C^f_{e^f e^f}) + \Delta / z^h C^h_{q^h e^h} < C^f_{q^f e^f} / C^f_{e^f e^f} (P^f_{q^h} + q^f P^f_{q^f q^h})$.*

One implication of proposition 3.2 is that a sufficiently less pollution-intensive country can set regulation resulting in higher costs (e.g. marginal abatement costs) and still yield a reduction in global emissions as long as the role of the emission tax is part of the policy mix.

Next, I analyse the effect of policy reform of the cost parameter z in more detail. The change in global emissions, $E = e^h + e^f$, from a change in the cost parameter z^h and z^f (for given tax), using (11) and (12) yields

$$\Delta dE = \left[\left(C^h_{q^h} - C^h_{e^h} \frac{C^h_{q^h e^h}}{C^h_{e^h e^h}} \right) \left[-\frac{C^h_{q^h e^h}}{C^h_{e^h e^h}} \left(-(2P^f_{q^f} + q^f P^f_{q^f q^f}) + z^f \frac{C^f_{e^f e^f} C^f_{q^f q^f} - C^{f2}_{e^f q^f}}{C^f_{e^f e^f}} \right) \right. \right.$$
$$\left. \left. -\frac{C^f_{q^f e^f}}{C^f_{e^f e^f}} \left(P^f_{q^h} + q^f P^f_{q^f q^h} \right) \right] - \frac{C^h_{q^h e^h}}{C^h_{e^h e^h}} C^h_{e^h} \Delta / z^h C^h_{q^h e^h} \right] dz^h$$
$$+ \left[\left(C^f_{q^f} - C^f_{e^f} \frac{C^f_{q^f e^f}}{C^f_{e^f e^f}} \right) \left[-\frac{C^f_{q^f e^f}}{C^f_{e^f e^f}} \left(-(2P^h_{q^h} + q^h P^h_{q^h q^h}) + z^h \frac{C^h_{e^h e^h} C^h_{q^h q^h} - C^{h2}_{e^h q^h}}{C^h_{e^h e^h}} \right) \right. \right.$$

$$-\frac{C^h_{q^h e^h}}{C^h_{e^h e^h}}\left(P^h_{q^f}+q^h P^h_{q^h q^f}\right)\right]-\frac{C^f_{q^f e^f}}{C^f_{e^f e^f}}C^f_{e^f}\Delta/z^f C^f_{q^f e^f}\bigg]dz^f \tag{13}$$

Consider a policy reform consisting of $dz^h = dz^f = d\tilde{z} < 0$ (i.e. an equal decrease in the cost parameter z across countries) and let $C^h_{q^h}-C^h_{e^h}C^h_{e^h q^h}/C^h_{e^h e^h} = C^f_{q^f}-C^f_{e^f}C^f_{e^f q^f}/C^f_{e^f e^f} \leq 0$ (i.e. cost effects via z are symmetric across countries where the effect via marginal abatement costs is relatively large). Then, (13) yields $dE < 0$. i.e. global emissions fall as a result of lower costs as long as the cross effects in demand are relatively small (e.g. $|P^h_{q^f}+q^h P^h_{q^h q^f}|\leq|2P^h_{q^h}+q^h P^h_{q^h q^h}|$) or equal across countries, i.e. $P^h_{q^f}+q^h P^h_{q^h q^f} = P^f_{q^h}+q^f P^f_{q^f q^h}$. This is because equally lower costs (i.e. $d\tilde{z} < 0$) results in lower emissions since the effect via lower marginal costs in each country induces less output, more abatement and therefore lower emissions. It is noteworthy that this result holds even as pollution intensities differ across countries, i.e. $-C^f_{e^f q^f}/C^f_{e^f e^f} \neq -C^h_{e^h q^h}/C^h_{e^h e^h}$. In contrast, if the effect via emission taxes on marginal abatement costs is small in each country so that the term $C^k_{e^k} \approx 0$ becomes negligible (and so $C^h_{q^h} \approx C^f_{q^f}$), and still under the assumption of relatively small cross effects in demand, then $dE > 0$ and so global emissions rise with policy reform $d\tilde{z} < 0$. This result underscores the importance of coupling cost reduction policies with emission taxes if global emissions are to be tackled.

To further illustrate the role of pollution intensities suppose that the foreign country is sufficiently large as defined in proposition 3.2 and that there is asymmetry in the extent to which the cost parameter, z, affects output in each country, i.e. assume $C^h_{q^h}-C^h_{e^h}C^h_{e^h q^h}/C^h_{e^h e^h} > 0$ and $C^f_{q^f}-C^f_{e^f}C^f_{e^f q^f}/C^f_{e^f e^f} < 0$. Then, a policy reform consisting of $dz^h > 0$ and $dz^f > 0$ results in higher global emissions. This is because, on the one hand, higher costs in the foreign country, the relatively more pollution-intensive country, increase emissions in that country because the effect via higher marginal abatement cost is sufficiently large. On the other hand, higher costs in the home country lowers output and emissions in that country (since the effect via higher marginal abatement cost is sufficiently small in the home country), but this is completely offset by the increase in foreign, sufficiently more pollution-intensive output.

Now consider the policy reform $dz^h < 0$ and $dz^f > 0$, and suppose that the foreign country is sufficiently pollution intensive. Further, suppose that in the foreign country only the effect of the tax on marginal abatement costs is negligible (i.e. $C^f_{e^f} \approx 0$), and in the home country the cost of producing an extra unit of output is large (i.e. $C^h_{q^h} > C^h_{e^h}C^h_{e^h q^h}/C^h_{e^h e^h}$).[7] As a result, global emissions fall in the case where the pollution-intensive country, with no real presence of emission taxes in marginal abatement costs, raises costs; while the relatively less pollution-intensive country, with relatively high costs of producing an extra unit of output, reduces costs.

As a final policy reform consider $dz^h > 0$ and $dz^f < 0$. Suppose pollution-intensity coefficients and asymmetry in the effects of the cost parameter are as follows: (i) the foreign country is sufficiently pollution intensive, and (ii) the tax-effect, $C^k_{e^k}$, is small in the sense that $C^k_{e^k} \Delta / z^k C^k_{e^k e^k}$ for $k = h, f$ in (13) becomes negligible, but at the same time the inequality $C^f_{q^f} - C^f_{e^f} C^f_{e^f q^f} / C^f_{e^f e^f} < 0$ still holds because the pollution intensity $-C^f_{e^f q^f} / C^f_{e^f e^f}$ is assumed to be sufficiently large and the inequality $C^h_{q^h} - C^h_{e^h} C^h_{e^h q^h} / C^h_{e^h e^h} > 0$ still holds because $-C^h_{e^h q^h} / C^h_{e^h e^h}$ is assumed to be sufficiently small. Thus, in this case global emissions fall, on the one hand, via the reduction in costs in the foreign country, z^f, but on the other global emissions increase via an increase in z^h. Global emissions can fall if the foreign country, the pollution-intensive country, sets a sufficiently aggressive cost-reducing policy, i.e. $dz^f < 0$ and large.

Proposition 3.3 *Suppose there is symmetry across countries in the cost effects via z (i.e. $C^h_{q^h} - C^h_{e^h} C^h_{e^h q^h} / C^h_{e^h e^h} = C^f_{q^f} - C^f_{e^f} C^f_{e^f q^f} / C^f_{e^f e^f}$). Then, in the case where the effects on marginal abatement costs via the tax are negligible (large) in both countries, global emissions rise (fall) with a multilateral cost-reducing policy reform (i.e. $dz^h = dz^f < 0$) as long as the cross effects via demand are relatively small.*

Proposition 3.4 *Let the foreign country be sufficiently pollution intensive as defined in proposition 3.2 and, additionally, let the effects on marginal abatement costs via the tax be negligible in the foreign country (i.e. $C^f_{e^f} \approx 0$), and the cost of producing an extra unit of output relatively large in the home country (i.e. $C^h_{q^h} > C^h_{e^h} C^h_{e^h q^h} / C^h_{e^h e^h}$). Then a policy reform of lower costs in the home country ($dz^h < 0$) but higher costs in the foreign country ($dz^f > 0$) results in lower global emissions.*

Next, I analyse the effects of policy reform of taxes, t^h and t^f, on global emissions, but since the analysis of taxes has been studied in the literature (e.g. Lahiri and Symeonidis 2007; Gautier 2016) here I just make two remarks. Using (10) and (12), the effect of the tax on global emissions, $E = e^h + e^f$, is given by

$$\Delta dE = \frac{-C^h_{q^h e^h}}{C^h_{e^h e^h}} \left[\frac{-C^h_{q^h e^h}}{C^h_{e^h e^h}} \left(-\left(2P^f_{q^f} + q^f P^f_{q^f q^f}\right) + z^f \frac{C^f_{e^f e^f} C^f_{q^f q^f} - C^{f2}_{e^f q^f}}{C^f_{e^f e^f}} \right) + \Delta / z^h C^h_{q^h e^h} \right.$$
$$\left. - \frac{C^f_{q^f e^f}}{C^f_{e^f e^f}} \left(P^f_{q^h} + q^f P^f_{q^f q^h} \right) \right] dt^h$$

$$\frac{-C^f_{q^f e^f}}{C^f_{e^f e^f}} \left[\frac{-C^f_{q^f e^f}}{C^f_{e^f e^f}} \left(-\left(2P^h_{q^h} + q^h P^h_{q^h q^h}\right) + z^h \frac{C^h_{e^h e^h} C^h_{q^h q^h} - C^{h2}_{e^h q^h}}{C^h_{e^h e^h}} \right) + \Delta / z^f C^f_{q^f e^f} \right.$$

$$-\frac{C^h_{q^h e^h}}{C^h_{e^h e^h}}\left(P^h_{q^f}+q^h P^h_{q^h q^f}\right)\bigg]dt^f$$

(14)

where the first term captures changes in global emissions from changes in output and the term $\Delta/z^k C^k_{q^k e^k}$ captures changes in global emissions arising from the abatement induced by the tax.

Remark 3.5 *Global emissions fall with an increase in the emission tax in the home country, if the home country exhibits a relatively large intensity coefficient or if pollution intensities across countries are equal (i.e.* $-C^h_{q^h e^h}/C^h_{e^h e^h} \ge -C^f_{q^f e^f}/C^f_{e^f e^f}$). *Alternatively, global emissions rise if the foreign country exhibits a sufficiently large pollution-intensity coefficient as stated in proposition 3.2.*

Remark 3.6 *Let (i) the foreign country be sufficiently pollution intensive as defined in proposition 3.2 and (ii) the cross effect on demand in both countries is either small or equal across countries. Then, a proportional increase in the emission tax in the home and foreign country (i.e.* $dt^h = dt^f > 0$) *reduces global emissions.*

Up to this point the analysis has looked at policy reform consisting of changes in either taxes or the cost parameters z^k. In order to combine policy reforms it is important to note that policy reform of the cost parameter, z^k, may induce changes in taxes since taxes in equilibrium are a function of the cost parameter, i.e. $t^{h*}(z^h, z^f)$, $t^{f*}(z^h, z^f)$. I delve into the characterization of policy in section 4. With this in mind, consider the policy reform of $dz^h < 0$ which gives the possibility of $dt^h > 0$, if $t^h_{z_h} < 0$, or $dt^h < 0$, if $t^h_{z_h} > 0$, where for given z^f, $dt^h = t^h_{z_h} dz^h$. The case where $t^h_{z_h} < 0$ may denote that, with a higher z^h, the government offsets damages from transboundary pollution and losses in welfare via the profit-shifting effect as home firms lose market share as a result of higher cost. Using (13) and (14), in the case where $t^h_{z_h} < 0$ global emissions fall as long as (i) the home country is at least as pollution intensive as the foreign country (i.e. $-C^h_{q^h e^h}/C^h_{e^h e^h} \ge -C^f_{q^f e^f}/C^f_{e^f e^f}$) and (ii) the increase in emissions via lower marginal costs, due to a reduction in z^h, is small (i.e. $C^h_{q^h} < C^h_{q^h} C^h_{q^h e^h}/C^h_{e^h eh}$). This is because global emissions fall via the reduction in z^h and at the same time via a higher tax, t^h. Global emissions rise otherwise under the same conditions if $dz^h > 0$ and $t^h_{z_h} < 0$, where higher costs, z^h, result in higher global emissions since $C^h_{q^h} < C^h_{e^h} C^h_{q^h e^h}/C^h_{e^h e^h}$, and concomitantly, because the government lowers the emission tax.

As a second policy reform, consider an equal increase in the tax and cost parameter in the home country (i.e. $dt^h = dz^h > 0$). It is noteworthy that this policy reform requires $t^h_{z_h} = 1$. With this in mind it can be shown that global emissions fall as long as the home country is at least as pollution intensive as the foreign country and the increase in emissions via higher marginal abatement costs, resulting from an increase in z^h, is sufficiently small, i.e. the role of the emission tax in the home country is small, $C_{e^h}^h + 1 > 0$. This result is important because it suggests that a pollution-intensive country, with a relatively small role of its emission tax, may reduce global emissions via taxation and higher costs.

In particular, combining (13) and (14) yields

$$\Delta dE = \left[\left(C_{q^h}^h - \frac{C_{e^h q^h}^h}{C_{e^h e^h}^h} (C_{e^h}^h + 1) \right) \eta - \frac{C_{e^h q^h}^h}{C_{e^h e^h}^h} (C_{e^h}^h + 1) \Delta / z^h C_{e^h e^h}^h \right] d\alpha \tag{15}$$

where $dt^h = dz^h = d\alpha$ and

$$\eta := \frac{-C_{q^h e^h}^h}{C_{e^h e^h}^h} \left(-\left(2 P_{q^f}^f + q^f P_{q^f q^f}^f \right) + z^f \frac{C_{e^f e^f}^f C_{q^f q^f}^f - C_{e^f q^f}^{f2}}{C_{e^f e^f}^f} \right) - \frac{C_{q^f e^f}^f}{C_{e^f e^f}^f} \left(P_{q^h}^f + q^f P_{q^f q^h}^f \right)$$

whence $\eta > 0$, if $-C_{q^h e^h}^h / C_{e^h e^h}^h \geq -C_{e^f e^f}^f / C_{e^f e^f}^f$.

Proposition 3.7 *Let the home country be relatively pollution intensive and suppose that the change in emissions via the cost of an extra unit of output is small. Then, a policy reform consisting of a tax increase ($dt^h > 0$) and reduction in costs ($dz^h < 0$) lowers global emissions.*

Proposition 3.8 *Let the home country be relatively pollution intensive and assume $t_{z^h}^h = 1$. Then, a policy reform consisting of higher costs and taxation ($dt^h = dz^h > 0$) lowers global emissions as long as the role of the emission tax in the home country is small, i.e. $C_{e^h}^h + 1 > 0$.*

4 Welfare and policy reform

In this section, I examine the impact of policy reform on welfare, i.e. how policy reform in one country affects welfare in the other country. The analysis can be thought of as efforts by countries to coordinate multilateral policy. As presented in the literature (e.g. Kayalica and Lahiri 2005; Hatzipanayotou et al. 2005; Gautier 2014) this type of analysis captures the externalities and inefficiencies of the non-cooperative equilibrium.

I shall follow Ulph and Ulph (2007) and Gautier (2014) in the set-up of the welfare function where consumer surplus effects are assumed away. In this way issues of strategic environmental policy, as it pertains to profit-shifting effects, and transboundary pollution can be the focus of the analysis.

Define welfare in the home country as follows

$$W^h = \pi^h + e^h t^h - \varphi^h(E) \tag{16}$$

where φ^h denotes damages from pollution in the home country, which satisfies $\varphi^{h'} > 0$, $\varphi^{h''} > 0$ and $E = e^h + e^f$ denotes global emissions. Since the function $\varphi^h(\cdot)$ depends on global emissions, damage from pollution in the home country captures also effects via transboundary pollution. An analogous expression applies to W^f, the welfare function of the foreign country. The home and foreign country simultaneously choose the emission tax taking the other country's policy as given. This yields a non-cooperative policy vector $t^{h*}(z^h, z^f)$, $t^{f*}(z^h, z^f)$. I shall assume interior solutions in order to account for the interaction between taxes and the cost parameters in policy reform.

Differentiation of the welfare function for each country yields (subscripts denote partial derivatives)

$$dW^h = \left[q^h P_{q^f}^h \frac{\partial q^f}{\partial t^h} - z^h C_{e^h}^h \frac{\partial e^h}{\partial t^h} - \varphi^{h'} \frac{\partial E}{\partial t^h} \right] dt^h$$
$$+ \left[q^h P_{q^f}^h \frac{\partial q^f}{\partial t^f} - z^h C_{e^h}^h \frac{\partial e^h}{\partial t^f} - \varphi^{h'} \frac{\partial E}{\partial t^f} \right] dt^f \tag{17}$$

$$dW^f = \left[q^f P_{q^h}^f \frac{\partial q^h}{\partial t^f} - z^f C_{e^f}^f \frac{\partial e^f}{\partial t^f} - \varphi^{f'} \frac{\partial E}{\partial t^f} \right] dt^f$$
$$+ \left[q^f P_{q^h}^f \frac{\partial q^h}{\partial t^h} - z^f C_{e^f}^f \frac{\partial e^f}{\partial t^h} - \varphi^{f'} \frac{\partial E}{\partial t^h} \right] dt^h \tag{18}$$

where at the Nash equilibrium the first term in (22) and (23) are equal to zero.

I want to see how taxes and the cost parameter in one country affect the other country's welfare, starting at the Nash equilibrium. This is to have a sense of how policy reform affects welfare across countries. To achieve this, I look at the foreign country's welfare, where differentiation of W^f, starting at the Nash equilibrium while keeping in mind that $t^{h*}(z^h, z^f)$, $t^{f*}(z^h, z^f)$, gives (subscripts denote partial derivatives and dropping the "*" superscript for notational simplicity)

$$dW^f = \left[W_{t^h}^f t_{z^h}^h + W_{z^h}^f \right] dz^h + \left[W_{t^h}^f t_{z^f}^h + W_{z^f}^f \right] dz^f \tag{19}$$

where the term $W_{z^h}^f$ is given by the last term in (18), $W_{z^h}^f = q^f P_{q^h}^f q_{z^h}^h + t^f e_{z^h}^f - \varphi^{f'} E_{z^h}$, and $W_{z^f}^f = q^f P_{q^h}^f q_{z^f}^h + t^f e_{z^f}^f - \varphi^{f'} E_{z^f}$.

To delve into the analysis of (19), I first characterize optimal policy and then find the expression for $t_{z^h}^h$. In particular, using (17) optimal taxation in the home country satisfies (subscripts denote partial derivatives)

$$t^{h*} = -\frac{q^h P_{q^f}^h q_{t^h}^f}{e_{t^h}^h} + \varphi^{h'} \frac{e_{t^h}^f}{e_{t^h}^h} + \varphi^{h'} \tag{20}$$

where $P_{q_{rh}^h}^h < 0$, $q_{t^h}^f > 0$, $e_{t^h}^f > 0$. An analogous expression applies to t^{f*}. The term $e_{t^h}^h$ could be positive or negative as discussed in previous sections, but for now consider the case where $e_{t^h}^h < 0$. The first term denotes the incentives to set a lower tax to offset the profit-shifting effect arising from the foreign country, the second term also puts a downward pressure on the optimal tax in order to address transboundary pollution coming from the foreign country (a lower tax at home lowers output in the foreign country thereby lowering pollution coming from that country); and the third term addresses damages from pollution arising from emissions in the home country. An analogous analysis applies to t^{f*}.

There are a number of opposing effects on the optimal tax in the home country arising from changes in z^h. First, an increase in z^h may lower output at home which prompts the home country to lower the tax; and second, an increase in z^h may result in an increase in emissions in the foreign country thereby exacerbating damages from transboundary pollution. Third, an increase in global emissions creates additional damages from pollution, and thus adjustments in the tax in the home country, resulting from non-linearities in the damage function in both countries.

To explore these effects further consider a cost function of the end-of-pipe $C(q,e) = \tilde{c}q + (\delta q - e)^2 / 2$ where the first (second) term denotes production (abatement) costs, abatement is given by $a = \delta q - e$, where δ is a positive constant which denotes pollution intensity, and $C_{qe} = C_{eq} = -\delta < 0$, $C_{qq} = \delta^2 > 0$, $C_{ee} = 1 > 0$, $C_{ee}C_{qq} - C_{qe}^2 = 0$. In this case $C_q - C_e C_{eq} / C_{ee} = \tilde{c} > 0$, $e_{t^h}^h < 0$, $e_{t^f}^f < 0$, $q_{t^f}^f < 0$, $q_{t^h}^h < 0$, $e_{t^f}^h > 0$, $q_{t^f}^h > 0$, $e_{t^h}^f > 0$, $q_{t^h}^f > 0$, $q_{z^f}^f < 0$, $q_{z^h}^h < 0$, $e_{z^f}^h > 0$, $q_{z^f}^h > 0$, $e_{z^h}^f > 0$, $q_{z^h}^f > 0$. Moreover, consider the case of linear demand where $P_{q^h}^h = P_{q^f}^f = -\beta$, $P_h^h = P_h^f = -\gamma$, $\beta > \gamma > 0$, where γ denotes the degree of product differentiation: $\beta = \gamma$ captures the case of homogeneous goods, whereas $0 = \gamma$ the case of completely differentiated products. In what follows I shall assume this demand and cost structure to derive results.

Differentiation of (20) and an analogous expression for t^{f*}, with respect to z^h, and using (7)–(12) yields[8]

$$\omega t_{z^h}^h = P_{q^f}^h q_{t^h}^f q^h / z^h - \varphi^h{}' e_{t^h}^f / (z^h)^2 + \varphi^{h''} e_{t^h}^h E_{t^h} E_{z^h} - \varphi^{f''} e_{t^h}^h E_{t^f} E_{z^h} \frac{P_{q^f}^h q_{t^h}^h}{e_{t^f}^f P_{q^h}^f q_{t^f}^h} \quad (21)$$

where $e_{t^h}^h < 0$, $e_{t^f}^f < 0$, $q_{t^h}^h < 0$, $q_{t^h}^f > 0$, $\omega = (e_{t^h}^h)^2 - e_{t^h}^h (E_{t^h})^2 \varphi^{h''} > 0$. The first and second terms capture, respectively, reductions in the tax to offset profit-shifting and transboundary pollution. The last two terms could be positive or negative under a number of assumptions about global emission. But if, for example, the last two terms arising from non-linearities in the damage function are negligible (e.g. marginal damage functions are not too convex), then $t_{z^h}^h < 0$. Alternatively, suppose that conditions are such that $E_{t^k} < 0$ for

$k = h, f$ and $E_{z^h} > 0$. Then, the third term is positive thus indicating that the tax at home is adjusted upwards with an increase in z^h in order to tackle higher damages at home resulting from higher global emissions. The fourth term is negative thus indicating that the tax at home is lowered with an increase in z^h in order to reduce damages in the foreign country resulting from higher global emissions: specifically, an increase in z^h induces an increase in t^h which lowers damages to the foreign country via transboundary pollution, but this is completely offset by a reduction in t^h in order to reduce emissions in the foreign country and thus damages in that country.

To complete the set-up necessary to analyse policy reform, I make a few remarks about the terms $W_{t^h}^f$ and $W_{z^h}^f$ in (19) assuming a cost function of the end-of-pipe as defined earlier. First, in $W_{t^h}^f = q^f P_{q^h}^f q_{t^h}^h + (t^f - \varphi^{f'})e_{t^h}^f - \varphi^{f'}e_{t^h}^h$ an increase in the tax in the home country raises welfare in the foreign country via the profit-shifting term, $q^f P_{q^h}^f q_{t^h}^h > 0$, the reduction in transboundary pollution, $-\varphi^{f'}e_{t^h}^h > 0$, and lower abatement costs, $t^f e_{t^h}^f > 0$; but welfare in the foreign country falls as a result of higher emissions in the foreign country and thus higher damages from pollution, $-\varphi^{f'}e_{t^h}^f < 0$. Second, from the term $W_{z^h}^f = q^f P_{q^h}^f q_{z^h}^h + t^f e_{z^h}^f - \varphi^{f'}E_{z^h}$ an increase in z^h raises welfare in the foreign country via profit-shifting, lower abatement costs and lower transboundary pollution as long as higher costs reduce emissions at home; but welfare in the foreign country falls via higher emissions in the foreign country as a result of an increase in z^h i.e. $-\varphi^{f'}e_{z^h}^f < 0$.

With the above results in mind and under the assumption of a cost function of the end-of-pipe as defined earlier, the following results are stated. An increase in costs in the home country, z^h, for given tax, raises welfare in the foreign country if global emissions fall with z^h (i.e. $E_{z^h} < 0$) and thus damages from global pollution do not lower welfare in the foreign country, i.e. $-\varphi^{f'}E_{z^h} > 0$. Alternatively, if $E_{z^h} > 0$ welfare in the foreign country rises if the home country reduces costs (i.e. z^h falls) and the reduction in damages from global pollution is sufficiently large, i.e. $-\varphi^{f'}E_{z^h} < 0$ and large so that $W_{z^h}^f > 0$. Moreover, an increase in the tax in the home country lowers (raises) welfare in the foreign country if global emissions rise (fall) with the tax, i.e. $E_{t^h} > (<)0$. Therefore, a policy reform consisting of lower costs in the home country raises welfare in the foreign country as long as (i) the reduction in global emissions lowers damages in the foreign country sufficiently (i.e. $E_{z^h} > 0$, $-\varphi^{f'}E_{z^h} < 0$ and large), and (ii) the tax in the home country rises as a result (i.e. $t_{z^h}^h < 0$) with a corresponding reduction in global emissions via the tax (i.e. $E_{t^h} < 0$).

Proposition 4.1 *Suppose the cost function is of the end-of-pipe, i.e. $C(q,e) = cq + (\delta q - e)^2 / 2$. And let global emissions fall with an increase in the tax in the home country $(E_{t^h} < 0)$ and with a reduction in costs in the home country $(E_{z^h} > 0)$. Then, a policy reform consisting of lower costs in the home country $(dz^h < 0)$ with a subsequent increase in taxation $(t_{z^h}^h < 0)$ increases* welfare in the foreign country as long as the reduction in damages from global emissions in the foreign country resulting from the cost reduction is large, i.e. $q^f P^f_{q^h} q^h_{z_h} + t^f e^f_{z_h} < \varphi^f E_{z_h}$.

It is important to note that the conditions $E_{z_h} > 0$ and $E_{t_h} < 0$ in proposition 4.1 hold in the case where the pollution intensity coefficient in the home country is large $-C^h_{e^h q^h} / C^h_{e^h e^h} > -C^f_{e^f q^f} / C^f_{e^f e^f}$ and the abatement resulting from lower costs is large, i.e. the term $-C^h_{e^h} \Delta / C^h_{e^h e^h} z^h$ in (13) is sufficiently large. Additionally, for $E_{z_h} > 0$ and $E_{t_h} < 0$ to be consistent with $t^h_{z_h} < 0$, non-linearities ought be relatively small (i.e. $\varphi^{h"}$ and $\varphi^{f"}$ small).

5 Conclusion

The analysis of policy reform is timely and relevant. Recent developments in the kind and number of international/regional agreements suggest that regulatory and environmental policies are likely to be adjusted to new environmental challenges, thereby prompting policy reform across countries. This chapter considers a two-country model where firms behave in a Cournot fashion and face an emission tax, and countries undertake policy reform of emissions taxes and cost-related regulations associated to production costs and pollution abatement costs. The model allows for asymmetries in abatement cost functions, thereby capturing differences in pollution intensities (i.e. emissions per unit of output) and marginal abatement costs. The analysis indicates, *inter alia*, that the ability of countries to reduce local and global emissions via policy reform depends crucially on these asymmetries. For example, unilateral policy consisting of higher taxes and lower costs by the pollution-intensive country may reduce global emissions. Other multilateral policies are analysed where the presence of an emission tax to reduce emissions, via the incentives created by the marginal abatement cost function, is crucial in reducing emissions.

Inevitably, the analysis and policy implications depend crucially on the model assumptions, but at the same time the chapter presents several important potential lines for future research. First, the analysis can be easily extended to the *n*-firm case in order to capture aspects of industry size and free entry and exit of firms. Even though the factors driving the results do not change, incorporating more firms into the analysis can add interesting aspects of firm competition and how this may alter the effectiveness of policy reform. Second, in many cases international agreements force countries to face policy choices to tackle local and global pollutants, while facing pressure to be more competitive in the global market. In this context adding more pollutants to the analysis in the spirit of Ambec and Coria (2013), while keeping asymmetries in abatement cost functions, would render the analysis richer and perhaps more pertinent to current environmental agreements. Third, in the current chapter the parameter z, which captures exogenous changes in production and pollution abatement costs, can be endogenized. Even though the literature has endogenized this type of cost parameter, the focus has been to think about it in terms of environmental R&D affecting pollution abatement costs (e.g. Montero 2002a, 2002b) or a subsidy to R&D (e.g. Gautier 2014). Fourth, an additional line of research would be to incorporate aspects of political economy in the decision-making process determining policy reform, which in the present chapter are assumed away but which play an important role in regional/international agreements.

Notes

1 Ronald B. Mitchell. 2002–2016. International Environmental Agreements Database Project (Version 2014.3). Available at: http://iea.uoregon.edu/ Date accessed: 25 March 2016.
2 The Basel Convention on the Control of Transboundary Movements of Hazardous Wastes and their Disposal of 1989. See www.basel.int/TheConvention/Overview/tabid/1271/Default.aspx.
3 www.climatefundsupdate.org/listing/clean-technology-fund.
4 By assuming one firm in each country I can focus on the role of asymmetries in abatement costs. The *n* firm case does not change the key results.
5 For examples of industry/countries with asymmetries in pollution intensities within the US see DOC (2010), and across countries see Sterner and Köhlink (2015: 254).
6 Gautier (2015) considers a similar type of cost parameter, but specifically on abatement costs and in a closed-economy Cournot setting; here the cost parameter affects not only abatement costs and is presented in an international setting.
7 One cost function which satisfies this latter condition is a cost function of the end-of-pipe $C(q,e) = c(q) + g(a)$, where the first (second) term denotes production (abatement) costs, $a = \delta(q) - e$, $\delta > 0$, $\delta'' > 0$; and $C_{qe} = C_{eq} < 0, C_{qq} > 0, C_{ee} > 0$, $C_{ee}C_{qq} - C_{qe}^2 > 0$.
8 The goal here is to analyse unilateral policy by the home country and its impact on welfare of the foreign country without a policy change in the foreign country. This exemplifies cases where countries act unilaterally without any policy response by other countries. Consistent with this goal I assume that the foreign country does not change policy as a result of a unilateral policy change by the home country.

References

Ambec, S. and Coria, J. (2013), 'Price vs quantities with multiple pollutants', *Journal of Environmental Economics and Management*, 66: 123–140.
Barrett, S. (2003), *Environment and Statecraft: The Strategy of Environmental Treaty-making*, Oxford: Oxford University Press.
Barrett, S., Carraro, C. and de Melo, J. (2015), *Towards a Workable and Effective Climate Regime*, VOX CEPR's Policy Portal. Available at: www.voxeu.org/content/towards-workable-and-effective-climate-regime.
Bayındır-Upmann, T. (2003), 'Strategic environmental policy under free entry of firms', *Review of International Economics*, 11: 379–396.
Bhattacharya, R.N. and Pal, R. (2010), 'Environmental standards as strategic outcomes: A simple model', *Resource and Energy Economics*, 32(3): 408–420.

Carlsson, F. (2000), 'Environmental taxation and strategic commitment in duopoly models', *Environmental & Resource Economics*, 15(3): 243–256.

Caplan, A.J. and Silva, E.C.D. (2005), 'An efficient mechanism to control correlated externalities: Redistributive transfers and the coexistence of regional and global permit markets', *Journal of Environmental Economics and Management*, 49: 68–82.

Dixit, A. (1986), 'Comparative statics for oligopoly', *International Economic Review*, 27(1): 107–122.

DOC (2010), 'U.S. carbon dioxide emissions intensities over time: A detailed accounting of industries, government and households', *Department of Commerce Economics and Statistics Administration*, U.S. Department of Commerce, April.

Elliott, R.J.R. and Zhou, Y. (2013), 'Environmental regulation induced foreign direct investment', *Environmental & Resource Economics*, 55: 141–158.

Gautier, L. (2013), 'Multilateral policy reform of emission taxes and abatement subsidies in a two-country model with oligopolistic interdependence', *Environmental Economics and Policy Studies*, 15(1): 59–71.

Gautier, L. (2014), 'Policy reform of emission taxes and environmental research and development incentives in an international Cournot model with product differentiation', *Environment and Development Economics*, 19(4): 440–465.

Gautier, L. (2015), 'Horizontal product differentiation, pollution abatement and emission taxes under oligopoly', in M.G. Fikru and M. Install (eds), *Economics of Environmental Policy in Oligopolistic Markets*, New York: Nova Science Publishers, 1–20.

Gautier, L. (2016), 'Emission taxes and product differentiation in the presence of foreign firms', *Journal of Public Economic Theory*, doi: 10.1111/jpet.12204.

Grether, J.M. and de Melo, J. (2004), 'Globalization and dirty industries: Do pollution havens matter?', in R.E. Baldwing and A. Winters (eds), *Challenges to Globalisation: Analyzing the Economics*, Chicago: University of Chicago Press.

Hatzipanayotou, P., Lahiri, S. and Michael, M.S. (2005), 'Reforms of environmental policies in the presence of cross-border pollution and public private clean-up', *Scandinavian Journal of Economics*, 107(2): 315–333.

Hoel, M. (1991), 'Global environmental problems: The effects of unilateral actions taken by one country', *Journal of Environmental Economics and Management*, 20(1): 55–70.

Kahn, M.W. (2016), 'The climate change adaptation literature', *Journal of Environmental Economics and Policy*, 10(1): 166–178.

Kayalica, M.Ö. and Lahiri, S. (2005), 'Strategic environmental policies in the presence of foreign direct investment', *Environmental & Resource Economics*, 30(1): 1–21.

Lahiri, S. and Symeonidis, G. (2007), 'Piecemeal multilateral environmental policy reforms under asymmetric oligopoly', *Journal of Public Economic Theory*, 9(5): 885–899.

Montero, P. (2002a), 'Permits, standards, and technology innovation', *Journal of Environmental Economics and Management*, 44(1): 23–44.

Montero, P. (2002b), 'Market structure and environmental innovation', *Journal of Applied Economics*, 5(2): 293–325.

Neumayer, E. (2001), 'Pollution havens: An analysis of policy options for dealing with an elusive phenomenon', *Environment and Development Economics*, 10(2): 147–177.

Requate, T. (2006), 'Environmental policy under imperfect competition', in T. Tietenberg and H. Folmer (eds), *The International Yearbook of Environmental and Resource Economics 2006/2007*, Cheltenham: Edward Elgar Publishing Limited, 120–207.

Silva, E.C.D. and Zhu, X. (2009), 'Emissions trading of global and local pollutants, pollution havens and free riding', *Journal of Environmental Economics and Management*, 58(2): 169–182.

Sterner, T. and Köhlink, G. (2015), 'Pricing carbon: The challenges', in S. Barrett, C. Carraro and J. de Melo (eds), *Towards a Workable and Effective Climate Regime*, VOX CEPR's Policy Portal. Available at: www.voxeu.org/content/towards-workable-and-effective-climate-regime.

Turunen-Red, A. and Woodland, A.D. (2004), 'Multilateral reforms on trade and environmental policy', *Review of International Economics*, 12(3): 321–336.

Ulph, A. (1996), 'Environmental policy and international trade when governments and producers act strategically', *Journal of Environmental Economics and Management*, 30: 265–281.

Ulph, A. and Ulph, D. (1996), 'Trade, strategic innovation and strategic environmental policy: A general analysis', in C. Carraro, Y. Katsoulacos and A. Xepapadeas (eds), *Environmental Policy and Market Structure*, Netherlands: Kluwer Academic Publishers, 181–208.

Ulph, A. and Ulph, D. (2007), 'Climate change: Environmental and technology policies in a strategic context', *Environmental & Resource Economics*, 37(1): 159–180.

Zarsky, L. (1999), 'Havens, halos and spaghetti: Untangling the evidence about foreign direct investment and the environment', *OECD Conference on Foreign Direct Investment and the Environment*, 47–73.

9 Environmental quota in an asymmetric trade competition with heterogeneous firms

*Rafael Salvador Espinosa Ramírez and
M. Özgür Kayalıca*

1 Introduction

The consequences derived from pollution could be numerous. The greenhouse effect, urban pollution, change in oceans, catastrophic snowfalls, meteorological disturbances such as the El Niño are just a few examples of a much larger set of challenges arising from pollution. The cost of these challenges is huge and pollution is a key contributing factor. According to the Extreme Weather Sourcebook 2008 (National Center for Atmospheric Research, US), the increase in costs caused by natural disasters like hurricanes, twisters and floods – just in the US – reached a yearly average of $16,972 million (1999 constant prices) between 1955 and 2006. In addition, the effect of pollution on human health has reached alarming levels mainly in metropolitan areas where the number of respiratory illnesses has increased 200 per cent, intestinal illnesses 110 per cent and additive illnesses 75 per cent in the last ten years according to the 2007 Report of the World Health Organization.

Many efforts have been made in order to reduce these devastating effects of global pollution. However, these efforts have to be coordinated among governments all over the world. Some unsuccessful examples of these efforts are the Rio Conference in Brazil in 1992 and the Johannesburg Summit in 2002. The debates behind these meetings lie on one fact: the intensive use of natural resources and intensity production process is blamed as the main cause of pollution.

However, it seems that the governments are not necessarily willing to apply environmental policies because these policies may increase production costs and undermine the international competitiveness of domestic industries. On the other hand, the pollution regulation negotiations are not only affected by the cost-benefit analysis of setting a pollution control, but also by the difference among the firms located in each country as well as by the differences in the country size. The relative difference among firms, and consequently in their performance, may affect not only the negotiation process, but also the impact of pollution on the health of the people and on the benefits of production and trade. In a globalized context pollution policies may affect trade and hence, the benefits granted by trading. In this sense, pollution control represents a trade distortion.

Certainly the literature on environmental regulations is vast,[1] but the existing literature on environmental regulations and trade competition has not been explored enough.[2] This is our main motivation in this chapter as we try to analyse the welfare effects of pollution regulation when heterogeneous firms and countries with different sizes trade. The main contribution of this chapter on the literature is to set a theoretical model in which country size is relevant in the setting of environmental regulation in the presence of trade. Symmetry in countries and homogenous firms are common features of most of the literature that studies trade competition and environmental regulations.

Trade between similar products as the reciprocal exports of one product from one country to another is an assumption we will consider in this chapter. This two-way trade in similar (but not strictly identical) products is called intra-industry trade.[3] It has also been referred to as cross-hauling and has been discussed in the point-pricing literature of perfect competition. However, many attempts have been made at imperfect competitive framework and especially in a Cournot oligopolistic setting.[4]

Brander and Krugman (1983) prove that the rivalry of oligopolistic firms serves as an independent cause of international trade, where the rivalry gives rise to 'dumping' of output in foreign markets or a two-way trade in the same product.[5] They also show that reciprocal dumping is rather striking in that there is pure waste in the form of unnecessary transportation costs. Without free entry and low transportation costs, welfare may improve as trade opens up and reciprocal dumping occurs, but welfare may decline with high transportation costs.

We assume that there is one firm in each country and they are heterogeneous because they have different cost structures. Environmental degradation comes as a by-product of production. We shall use a reciprocal dumping model with pollution quota to determine the effect of the environmental policies on the welfare of each country under non-cooperative and cooperative settings. Although there is no cross-border pollution, each country has to take into account the effect of the environmental policies on the producer surplus of firm, consumer surplus and pollution disutility on local welfare.

The model is spelt out in detail in the following section. In section 3, we derive the properties of the optimal pollution quota in a non-cooperative equilibrium. In section 4, we solve the model for cooperative equilibrium, which represents an international effort. Finally, some concluding remarks are made in section 5.

2 The model

In this model we assume that there are two countries having a two-way trade, country A and country B, producing a homogeneous good. We consider a partial equilibrium model of an oligopolistic industry in which there are n identical firms in A, and m identical firms in B. Each firm has a Cournot perception: each firm takes the output of other firms as given while maximizing its products.

Labour is the only factor of production in each country. We are assuming, without loss of generality, that the labour endowment in country B (l^B) is larger than that in country A (l^A), so we can define country B as the larger country and country A as the smaller country. Total amount of labour in the world is normalized as $l^A + l^B = 1$. According to Markusen and Venables (1988), labour is offered inelastically under perfect competition and constant returns to scale, such that the price of labour is *numeraire*. The productivity is homogeneous between countries.

The homogeneous output produced by heterogeneous firms located in A and B are X and Y respectively where $X = X^A + X^B$ and $Y = Y^A + Y^B$, such that X^A is consumed in country A and X^B is exported to country B. Similarly, Y^B is for local consumption in B and Y^A is exported to A.

The marginal costs of firms in A and B are K_X and K_Y respectively. These costs are taken to be constant, and therefore equal to average variable costs.[6] A part of K_j ($j = X, Y$) is given by technology and factor market conditions, and another part is policy induced, and this will be spelt out later on. There is transportation cost t incurred in exporting goods from one country to the other, which is borne by the producers. The markets are segmented and we assume quasi-linear inverse utility functions as:

$$U(P_A, \mu_A) = \frac{\beta l^A P_A^2}{2} - \lambda_A l^A P_A + \mu_A \tag{1}$$

$$U(P_B, \mu_B) = \frac{\beta l^B P_B^2}{2} - \lambda_B l^B P_B + \mu_B \tag{2}$$

where P^A and P^B are the price in both countries, and μ_A and μ_B are the consumption in the numeraire goods, and β, λ_A, and λ_B are the usual positive parameters determining the preferences and the impact on consumption by a price change. Using Roy's identity we get the linear demands in both countries which are linear in prices and no income effect:

$$D_A = l^A(\lambda_A - \beta P^A), \tag{3}$$

$$D_B = l^B(\lambda_B - \beta P^B). \tag{4}$$

where

$$D_A = nX^A + mY^A, \tag{5}$$

$$D_B = nX^B + mY^B. \tag{6}$$

(5) and (6) are the demand of country A and B respectively. Rewriting (3) and (4) we get the demand functions to work with

$$P_A = a_A - \frac{b}{l^A} D_A, \tag{7}$$

$$P_B = a_B - \frac{b}{l^B} D_B, \tag{8}$$

Such that $b = 1/\beta$, $a_A = \lambda_A / \beta$ and $a_B = \lambda_B / \beta$.

The profits of each firm located in A and B are given by

$$\Pi_A = (P_A - K_X) X^A + (P_B - K_X - t) X^B \tag{9}$$

$$\Pi_B = (P_B - K_Y) Y^B + (P_A - K_Y - t) Y^A \tag{10}$$

Each firm decides what proportion of the commodity it produces is for domestic consumption and how much for export. Under Cournot-Nash assumptions the first order maximization conditions are:[7]

$$a_A - K_X = b(n+1) X^A - bm Y^A, \tag{11}$$

$$a_B - K_X - t = b(n+1) X^B - bm Y^B, \tag{12}$$

$$a_B - K_Y = b(m+1) Y^B - bn X^B, \tag{13}$$

$$a_A - K_Y - t = b(m+1) Y^A - bn X^A, \tag{14}$$

such that we have a separable system where (11) is solved with (14) and (12) with (13). This system yields the equilibria where two-way trade arises and, given the linearity of demand functions, the second order conditions are satisfied. The closed form solutions for the following variables are obtained as:

$$\Pi_A = b(X^A)^2 + b(X^B)^2 \tag{15}$$

$$\Pi_B = b(Y^B)^2 + b(Y^A)^2 \tag{16}$$

$$Y^A = l^A \frac{(n+1)(a_A - K_Y - t) - n(a_A - K_X)}{b(m+n+1)} \tag{17}$$

$$X^A = l^A \frac{(m+1)(a_A - K_X) - m(a_A - K_Y - t)}{b(m+n+1)} \tag{18}$$

$$X^B = l^B \frac{(m+1)(a_B - K_X - t) - m(a_B - K_Y)}{b(m+n+1)} \tag{19}$$

$$Y^B = l^B \frac{(n+1)(a_B - K_Y) - n(a_B - K_X - t)}{b(m+n+1)} \tag{20}$$

Equations (5)–(10) and (15)–(20) form the backbone for the following analysis.

Next we set the welfare of each country taking into account the use of the pollution policy. The welfare W_i ($i = A, B$) can be written as,

$$W_A = n\Pi_A + CS_A - \psi_A Z_A \tag{21}$$

$$W_B = m\Pi_B + CS_B - \psi_B Z_B \tag{22}$$

$n\Pi_A$ y $m\Pi_B$ are the producer surplus of firms located in A and B respectively. CS_i is the consumer surplus and it is well known that

$$CS_A = bD_A^2 / 2, \tag{23}$$

$$CS_B = bD_B^2 / 2. \tag{24}$$

Furthermore $\psi_i Z_i$ is the pollution-policy impact on welfare given by the government-induced policy. In both countries Z_i is the total amount of harmful pollution in country i defined as $Z_A = nz_A X$ and $Z_B = mz_B Y$ for country A and B respectively,[8] where z_i is the amount of pollution per unit of output, ψ_i is the marginal disutility of pollution which we assume, as do Lahiri and Ono (1998) and Markusen *et al.* (1993 and 1995), is constant.[9] In order to keep the analysis at a tractable level, we assume that the marginal disutility of pollution in both countries is the same so that $\psi_A = \psi_B = \psi$.[10]

The government determines the level of allowed pollution emitted by firms per unit of output (z_i), and consequently the amount of disutility for pollution. In the next section, we determine the optimal pollution tax.

3 Optimal non-cooperative pollution quota

Using the above setting we determine the optimal pollution policy. In this sense this policy is a restriction on the amount of pollution allowed to the firms as a result of the production process. To do that, we define K_j as

$$K_j = C_j + T_j \tag{25}$$

where C_j is the part of the unit cost that is determined by technological and factor market conditions (i.e. marginal cost), and is taken to be constant. As the production of X and Y implies emission of pollution, T_j is the unit policy-induced cost of pollution abatement. This policy-induced cost is defined following Lahiri and Ono (1998) as[11]

$$T_j = \gamma(\theta - z_i) \tag{26}$$

where θ is the amount of pollution per-unit of output produced so that θX and θY are the total amount of pollution produced per firm (before any abatement) located in country A and B respectively,[12] z_i is the maximum quantity of pollution per unit of output produced that the firms in country i are allowed to emit into the atmosphere.[13]

We assume that the abatement technology is such that it costs each firm a constant amount γ to abate one unit of pollution and it is identical in both countries. The parameter γ and θ together with the policy instrument used by the government will determine the policy-induced part of the unit cost $K_j's$.

Total differentiation of demands (17)–(20) and (25)–(26) gives:

$$dX^A = l^A \frac{(m+1)\gamma}{b\alpha} dz_A - l^A \frac{m\gamma}{b\alpha} dz_B \qquad (27)$$

$$dX^B = l^B \frac{(m+1)\gamma}{b\alpha} dz_A - l^B \frac{m\gamma}{b\alpha} dz_B \qquad (28)$$

$$dY^A = l^A \frac{(n+1)\gamma}{b\alpha} dz_B - l^A \frac{n\gamma}{b\alpha} dz_A \qquad (29)$$

$$dY^B = l^B \frac{(n+1)\gamma}{b\alpha} dz_B - l^B \frac{n\gamma}{b\alpha} dz_A \qquad (30)$$

where $\alpha = m+n+1$.

From (27) to (30) we get the total differentiation of (5) and (6) as

$$dD_A = l^A \frac{n\gamma}{b\alpha} dz_A + l^A \frac{m\gamma}{b\alpha} dz_B \qquad (31)$$

$$dD_B = l^B \frac{n\gamma}{b\alpha} dz_A + l^B \frac{m\gamma}{b\alpha} dz_B \qquad (32)$$

An increase in the local allowed pollution increases the output produced locally for local consumption in a greater proportion than the fall in the production of the imported good. Thus, the local demand increases. An increase in the foreign allowed pollution reduces the output produced locally for local consumption in a smaller proportion than the increase in the production of the imported good. Thus the local demand increases. From (31) and (32) we can define the effect of pollution quota on consumer surplus in (23) and (24) as:

$$dCS_A = l^A \frac{D_A n\gamma}{\alpha} dz_A + l^A \frac{D_A m\gamma}{\alpha} dz_B \qquad (33)$$

$$dCS_B = l^B \frac{D_B n\gamma}{\alpha} dz_A + l^B \frac{D_B m\gamma}{\alpha} dz_B \qquad (34)$$

An increase in the pollution quota imposed by any country increases unequivocally the consumer surplus in both countries. More allowed pollution encourages the production and reduces the price of the goods.

On the other hand, using (27)–(30) we can define the effect of pollution quota on producer surplus in (15) and (16) as:

$$
d\Pi_A = \frac{2(m+1)\gamma}{\alpha}\left[X^A l^A + X^B l^B\right]dz_A - \frac{2m\gamma}{\alpha}\left[X^A l^A + X^B l^B\right]dz_B \tag{35}
$$

$$
d\Pi_B = \frac{2(n+1)\gamma}{\alpha}\left[Y^A l^A + Y^B l^B\right]dz_B - \frac{2n\gamma}{\alpha}\left[Y^A l^A + Y^B l^B\right]dz_A \tag{36}
$$

An increase in the amount of allowed pollution set by a local government will encourage the local production because local producers have a competitive advantage over foreign producers. The producer surplus of local producers increases and the producer surplus of foreign producers declines.

Next, we determine the effect of pollution quota over the amount of harmful pollution affecting the health of the people. Considering $Z_A = nz_A X$ and $Z_B = mz_B Y$ for country A and B respectively, we differentiate these expressions taking into account (27)–(30) such that

$$
dZ_A = \left(nX + \frac{n(m+1)\gamma z_A}{b\alpha}\right)dz_A - z_A\frac{mn\gamma}{b\alpha}dz_B \tag{37}
$$

$$
dZ_B = \left(mY + \frac{m(n+1)\gamma z_B}{b\alpha}\right)dz_B - z_B\frac{mn\gamma}{b\alpha}dz_A \tag{38}
$$

It is easy to see that the increase in the allowed amount of pollution in any local country increases the amount of harmful pollution in this country by the increase in the pollution quota itself and by the increase in production. On the other hand, this increase in the allowed pollution quota reduces the competitive advantage of the foreign firms reducing the harmful pollution in the foreign country.

From (33) to (38) total differentiation of (21) and (22) with respect to the pollution quota policies yields the following expressions:

$$
dW_A = \frac{n}{b\alpha}\left[2b(m+1)\gamma\left(l^A X^A + l^B X^B\right) + bl^A D_A\gamma - b\alpha X\psi - z_A(m+1)\gamma\psi\right]dz_A
$$
$$
- \frac{m\gamma}{b\alpha}\left[2nb\left(l^A X^A + l^B X^B\right) - bl^A D_A - z_A n\right]dz_B, \tag{39}
$$

$$
dW_B = \frac{m}{b\alpha}\left[2b(n+1)\gamma\left(l^A Y^A + l^B Y^B\right) + bl^B D_B\gamma - b\alpha Y\psi - z_B(n+1)\gamma\psi\right]dz_B
$$
$$
- \frac{n\gamma}{b\alpha}\left[2mb\left(l^A Y^A + l^B Y^B\right) - bl^B D_B - z_B m\right]dz_A. \tag{40}
$$

The first term inside the square brackets in (39) and (40) is the producer surplus effect. With an increase in the pollution quota in a local country, the cost for local firms is reduced and the producer surplus increases. The local firms' cost advantage give them a competitive advantage over the foreign competitors and the producer surplus of the foreign firms is reduced.

The second term inside the square brackets in (39) and (40) is the consumers' surplus effect. It is unambiguously positive to any pollution quota in both countries since an increase in the allowed quota reduces the cost for abatement pollution and consequently increases the amount of output produced, reducing the price for consumers.

Finally, the remaining terms in the square brackets in (39) and (40) represent the harmful pollution effect. When more pollution is allowed in a local country the cost of the firm located in this country is reduced and the production increases. As a result, local welfare is reduced by a larger negative impact on human health. On the other hand, this allowed quota would reduce the output produced by the foreign firm and consequently the amount of harmful pollution in the foreign country.

Taking into account the concavity assumptions about the welfare functions, we must have

$$\frac{d^2 W_A}{dz_A^2} = \frac{n\gamma}{b\alpha^2}\left[2(m+1)^2 \gamma\left(l^{A^2} + l^{B^2}\right) + l^{A^2} n\gamma - 2\alpha(m+1)\psi\right] < 0$$

$$\frac{d^2 W_B}{dz_B^2} = \frac{m\gamma}{b\alpha^2}\left[2(n+1)^2 \gamma\left(l^{A^2} + l^{B^2}\right) + l^{B^2} m\gamma - 2\alpha(n+1)\psi\right] < 0$$

Clearly, the above conditions are satisfied if and only if

$$\psi > \gamma\Delta_A$$

$$\psi > \gamma\Delta_B$$

where

$$\Delta_A = \frac{2(m+1)^2 \left(l^{A^2} + l^{B^2}\right) + l^{A^2} n}{2(m+1)\alpha} < 1$$

$$\Delta_B = \frac{2(n+1)^2 \left(l^{A^2} + l^{B^2}\right) + l^{B^2} m}{2(n+1)\alpha} < 1$$

We consider the case where the governments behave in a non-cooperative fashion to obtain the non-cooperative Nash pollution levels of emission standards, z_A^N and z_B^N. Setting the coefficients of dz_A and dz_B from (39) and (40) respectively equal to zero we get

$$z_A^N A_1 = X^A\left[\alpha\left(\gamma l^A - \psi\right) + (m+1)\gamma l^A\right] + X^B\left[2(m+1)\gamma l^B - \alpha\psi\right] + l^A \gamma m Y^A$$

(41)

$$z_B^N A_2 = Y^B \left[\alpha \left(\gamma l^B - \psi \right) + (n+1) \gamma l^B \right] + Y^A \left[2(n+1) \gamma l^A - \alpha \psi \right] + l^B \gamma n X^B$$

$$(42)$$

Such that

$$A_1 = \frac{b}{\gamma \psi (m+1)} > 0$$

$$A_2 = \frac{b}{\gamma \psi (n+1)} > 0$$

The optimal values of z_A^N and z_B^N have not been fully characterized yet. Apart from the size of the countries given by l^A and l^B, other parameters affecting the values of z_A^N and z_B^N are the marginal disutility level, ψ, and the marginal cost of abatement, γ.

From now on, we assume a monopoly in each country, it means $m = n = 1$. This assumption will simplify the analysis. In the case the size of the countries are quite different such that $l^A \ll l^B$, $l^A \to 0$, and $l^B \to 1$ we get from (41) and (42) that

$$z_A^N A_1 = X^B \left[4\gamma - 3\psi \right] \tag{43}$$

$$z_B^N A_2 = Y^B \left[5\gamma - 3\psi \right] + \gamma X^B \tag{44}$$

When γ is very small or the marginal pollution disutility is sufficiently large, imposing pollution control has no costs to firms and only benefits on the health of the people. Therefore, the optimal policy in both countries is to impose the severest pollution restrictions because the pollution quota in (43) and (44) is negative, i.e. $z_A^N = 0$ and $z_B^N = 0$.

On the other hand, when γ is greater than or equal to ψ, the optimal pollution policy in both countries are positive holding the second order concavity condition.[14] The optimal quota in both countries would depend on the marginal pollution disutility and on the unit cost for abating pollution. Formally, we can write the following proposition.

Proposition 1. *In a reciprocal dumping model of trade with a large difference between the size of the countries such that $l^A \ll l^B$, $l^A \to 0$, and $l^B \to 1$, at the non-cooperative equilibrium, the optimal pollution quotas are given by the following:*

1. *if $\gamma \ll \psi$, then $z_A^N = 0$ and $z_B^N = 0$*
2. *if $\gamma \geq \psi$, then $z_A^N > 0$ and $z_B^N > 0$*

This proposition can be explained intuitively as follows, when the marginal disutility from pollution is sufficiently bigger than the marginal cost for abating pollution ($\psi \gg \gamma$), the harmful effect of pollution outweighs the benefit obtained by the producer and consumer surplus. The governments set the severest pollution policy as it reduces the optimal output and consequently the pollution level.

On the other hand, a higher or equal marginal cost of abatement means that pollution control ($\gamma \geq \psi$) has significant negative impact on production and price. A reduction in output reduces the producer and consumer surplus, in this sense this reduction in output increases prices and reduces consumer surplus. Therefore, the governments are forced to allow positive amount of pollution. All the results mentioned above are independent of the heterogeneity of the firms. The relative efficiency of each firm is not relevant in the case in which the countries are quite different in size.

Alternatively, in the case where both countries are similar size such that $l^A \approx l^B \approx 0.5$ the optimal policies are:

$$z_A^N A_1 = X^A \left[\frac{5}{2} \gamma - 3\psi \right] + X^B \left[2\gamma - 3\psi \right] + \frac{\gamma}{2} Y^A \tag{45}$$

$$z_B^N A_2 = Y^B \left[\frac{5}{2} \gamma - 3\psi \right] + Y^A \left[2\gamma - 3\psi \right] + \frac{\gamma}{2} X^B \tag{46}$$

When the marginal pollution disutility ψ is sufficiently larger than the unit cost for abating pollution γ, imposing pollution control has no costs but only benefits. Therefore the optimal policy in both countries is to impose the severest pollution restrictions, i.e. $z_A^N = 0$ and $z_B^N = 0$. In the other case, when γ is sufficiently larger than ψ both policy instruments are positive.[15] Finally, when the marginal pollution disutility is equal to the marginal cost of abatement, the optimal pollution policies will depend on the efficiency of the competing firms. Formally, we can write the following proposition:

Proposition 2. *In a reciprocal dumping model of trade with a similar size between the countries such that $l^A \approx l^B \approx 0.5$, at the non-cooperative equilibrium, the optimal pollution quotas are given by the following:*

1. *if $\psi \gg \gamma$, then $z_A^N = z_B^N = 0$*
2. *if $\gamma \gg \psi$, then $z_A^N, z_B^N > 0$*
3. *if $\gamma = \psi$, and $C_X \gg C_Y$ then $z_A^N > 0, z_B^N = 0$*
4. *if $\gamma = \psi$, and $C_X \ll C_Y$ then $z_A^N = 0, z_B^N > 0$*

This proposition can be explained intuitively as follows. When the marginal disutility for pollution is sufficiently larger than the marginal cost for abating pollution ($\psi \gg \gamma$), the harmful effect of pollution outweighs the benefit obtained by the producer and consumer surplus. Once again, the governments in both countries set the severest pollution policy as it reduces the optimal output and consequently the pollution level.

On the other hand, a sufficiently larger marginal cost for abatement pollution than marginal disutility for pollution ($\gamma \gg \psi$) means that pollution control has a negative impact on production and price. A reduction in output reduces the producer surplus, increases the prices and reduces the consumers' surplus. Therefore, in this case ($\gamma \gg \psi$), the governments are forced to allow positive amount of pollution.

When both countries are similar in size and the cost for abating pollution is equal to the marginal pollution disutility, the optimal pollution policies depend on the firms' relative efficiency. The country with the most efficient firm will set the strictest pollution policy since the sum of benefit in consumer and producer surplus is smaller than the harm on people's health by the amount of emitted pollution despite the loss in competiveness of the efficient firm.

On the other hand, the country where the inefficient firm is located, sets a positive pollution policy since the benefit in producer and consumer surplus is larger than the loss in the emitted amount of harmful pollution. The government encourages the competitiveness of the inefficient firm.

4 Cooperative pollution quota

After determining the optimal non-cooperative policies above, we shall now analyse the cooperative policies. In other words, we will consider that country A sets the optimal policy, z_A, considering not only the impact of this policy on her own welfare but also on the welfare of the country B as well. Country B sets z_B in the same sense. Formally, following from (39) and (40) we have

$$dW_A = (T_1 + T_4)dz_A \tag{47}$$

$$dW_B = (T_2 + T_3)dz_B \tag{48}$$

where

$$T_5 = (T_1 + T_4) = \frac{1}{3b}\left[4b\gamma H_1 + bl^A D_A \gamma - 3bX\psi - z_A 2\gamma\psi - 2b\gamma H_2 + b\gamma l^B D_B + z_B \gamma\right]$$

$$T_6 = (T_2 + T_3) = \frac{1}{3b}\left[4b\gamma H_2 + bl^B D_B \gamma - 3bY\psi - z_B 2\gamma\psi - 2b\gamma H_1 + b\gamma l^A D_A + z_A \gamma\right]$$

Such that $H_1 = l^A X^A + l^B X^B > 0$ and $H_2 = l^A Y^A + l^B Y^B > 0$.

Setting the coefficients in (47) and (48) equal to zero and solving simultaneously both expressions for z_A and z_B we have the optimal policies such that:

$$z_A^c A_3 = \gamma\left[H_2(5-2\psi) + H_1(10\psi-1)\right] - 3\psi[Y + 2X\psi] \tag{49}$$

$$z_B^c A_3 = \gamma\left[H_1(5-2\psi) + H_2(10\psi-1)\right] - 3\psi[X + 2Y\psi] \tag{50}$$

where

$$A_3 = \frac{\gamma(4\psi^2 - 1)}{b}$$

and the second order condition holds in both cases when

$$\gamma < H_3 \psi$$

such that $l^A l^B 1.09 < H_3 < 2.18$

$$H_3 = \frac{12}{11(1^{A^2} + 1^{B^2})} > 1$$

Both expressions above are ambiguous. The optimal policies depend first on the marginal disutility of pollution and on the marginal cost of pollution abatement in both countries. Besides, the differences in the relative size of the countries could produce some interesting results.

As a first result, it is straightforward to see that when the marginal cost for abating pollution is relatively smaller than the marginal disutility of pollution, the best policy would be to set a strict pollution policy since the benefit obtained on the health of the people is larger than the cost for abating pollution of each firm. Given the second order condition is satisfied and considering that the marginal cost of abating pollution is sufficiently small ($\gamma \to 0$), we can rewrite (49) and (50) as

$$z_A^c A_3 = -3\psi [Y + 2X\psi] < 0 \tag{51}$$

$$z_B^c A_3 = -3\psi [X + 2Y\psi] < 0 \tag{52}$$

Clearly both governments are willing to set the strictest pollution policy independently of the size of the countries and the pollution marginal disutility. When γ is very small (or the marginal pollution disutility is sufficiently large), imposing pollution control has no costs but only benefits on the health of the people. Therefore, the optimal policy in both countries is to impose the severest pollution restrictions because the pollution quota in (49) and (50) is negative, i.e. $z_A^c = 0$ and $z_B^c = 0$. Formally we can say:

Proposition 3. *In a reciprocal dumping model of trade, at a cooperative equilibrium, where the marginal cost for abatement pollution is sufficiently smaller than the marginal pollution disutility, the optimal pollution quotas are each zero.*

Intuitively, the explanation is simple. When no cost is attached to the abatement of pollution, the firms are not affected by this cost and the setting of a strict pollution quota does not affect the consumer and producer surplus. The only impact is on the amount of emitted pollution. A strict pollution quota is set by both countries in order to benefit the health of the people. This result is independent of the size of each country and of the firm heterogeneity.

On the other hand, when the cost for abating pollution is larger than the marginal pollution disutility, the impact of a strict pollution policy may affect the consumer and producer surplus. The negative impact on consumer and producer surplus comes from the reduction in the production made by the firms when the cost increases. Even when there is a benefit given by the pollution reduction, the total effect on welfare is determined by reduction in the amount of consumer surplus and producer surplus.

However, the size of each country is important because in a cooperative equilibrium the maximizer country may be tempted to play in favour of her interest if the other market is not sufficiently large. The larger country may not be interested in taking care of her small partner because the impact of a policy on the consumer surplus, producer surplus and health of the people in the small country may be negligible. If so, the larger country may find setting a pollution policy could be a waste of policy effort.

In the case marginal cost of abating pollution is sufficiently larger than the marginal disutility of pollution ($\gamma \gg \psi$), we have to take into account the second order condition ($\gamma < H_3 \psi$). How much bigger can the marginal abatement cost be than the marginal disutility of pollution? Let us assume that the marginal pollution disutility is close to the limit of the second order condition such that

$$\psi = \frac{\gamma}{H_3} + \varepsilon \tag{53}$$

where $\varepsilon > 0$ is an infinitesimal number close to zero, which can be omitted. Substituting (53) into (49) and (50) we have

$$z_A^c A_3 = \gamma \left[5H_2 - H_1 - \frac{3Y}{H_3} \right] + \gamma^2 \left[10\frac{H_1}{H_3} - 2\frac{H_2}{H_3} - 6\frac{X}{H_3^2} \right] \tag{54}$$

$$z_B^c A_3 = \gamma \left[5H_1 - H_2 - \frac{3X}{H_3} \right] + \gamma^2 \left[10\frac{H_2}{H_3} - 2\frac{H_1}{H_3} - 6\frac{Y}{H_3^2} \right] \tag{55}$$

We shall consider first the case in which both countries have similar size. In the case in which both countries are similar such that $l^A \approx l^B \approx 0.5$ we have that

$$H_1 = 0.5X$$

$$H_2 = 0.5Y$$

$$H_3 = 2.18$$

Substituting these three expressions into (54) and (55) we have

$$z_A^c A_3 = \gamma [1.12Y - 0.5X] + \gamma^2 [1.03X - 0.46Y] \tag{56}$$

$$z_B^c A_3 = \gamma [1.12X - 0.5Y] + \gamma^2 [1.03Y - 0.46X] \tag{57}$$

In the case in which the marginal cost of pollution abatement is sufficiently large ($\gamma \gg 0$) holding the second order condition, the weight attached to the second term in the right hand side of (56) and (57) is larger than the weight attached to the first term, and the value of the optimal policy depends on the difference between the output of each firm. If the firm located in country A is much more efficient than the firm located in country B ($C_X \ll C_Y$), the optimal output of the firm located in A is much larger than the output produced by the firm located in country B ($X \gg Y$). In this case, the optimal pollution cooperative policy is positive for the country A and is the strictest one for the country B. The contrary result is obtained with the heterogeneity of the firms. Formally, we can write the following proposition:

Proposition 4. *In a reciprocal dumping model of trade with a similar size between the countries such that $l^A \approx l^B \approx 0.5$, and assuming that the marginal cost of abatement pollution is sufficiently large ($\gamma \gg 0$), at the cooperative equilibrium, the optimal pollution quotas are the following:*

1.   if $C_X \gg C_Y$, then $z_A^c = 0$ and $z_B^c > 0$
2.   if $C_X \ll C_Y$, then $z_A^c > 0$ and $z_B^c = 0$

Intuitively speaking, the country where the most inefficient firm is located, sets the strictest pollution policy since the impact of her own production on consumer surplus and producer surplus in that country and on the other country is negligible. With a large marginal cost of abating pollution the cost of the inefficient firm is larger and consequently the best policy is to benefit the health of the society by setting the strictest policy. Setting a strict pollution policy there is a reduction in the competitiveness of the firm in that country but increase in the competitiveness of the other firm, which benefits from consumer surplus.

On the other hand, the country where the most efficient firm is located sets a positive pollution policy since the benefit on consumer surplus in both countries, and on producer surplus in this country is larger than the damage through pollution disutility. With a large marginal cost for abating pollution the setting of a lax pollution policy helps the efficiency of the efficient firm located in the country.

Now, let us consider the case that both countries differ in size. In particular in the case where $l^A \to 0$, $l^B \to 1$, we have

$$H_1 = X^B$$

$$H_2 = Y^B$$

$$H_3 = 1.09$$

Substituting these three expressions into (54) and (55) we have

$$z_A^c A_3 = \gamma\left[5Y^B - X^B - 2.75Y\right] + \gamma^2\left[4.12X^B - 1.83Y^B - 5.05X^A\right] \tag{58}$$

$$z_B^c A_3 = \gamma\left[5X^B - Y^B - 2.75X\right] + \gamma^2\left[4.12Y^B - 1.83X^B - 5.05Y^A\right] \tag{59}$$

Again, in the case in which the marginal cost of abatement pollution is sufficiently larger ($\gamma \gg 0$) given the second order condition holds, the weight attached to the second term in the right hand of (58) and (59) is bigger than the weight attached to the first term. In this case, the second term in (58) is negative by definition since the output produced by the firm located in the small country for local market is always larger than the output for foreign market due to transportation cost ($X^A > X^B$). The optimal pollution policy set by the small country is always the strictest one ($z_A^c A_3 = 0$).

In the case where ($Y^A < Y^B$), the optimal policy set by the larger country is pretty ambiguous. The only result we can get is when the firm located in the small country is sufficiently more inefficient than the firm located in the large country ($C_Y \ll C_X$), the optimal policy would be the strictest one. Formally, we can write the following proposition:

Proposition 5. *In a reciprocal dumping model of trade where countries differ sufficiently in size such that* $l^A \to 0$, $l^B \to 1$, *and assuming that the marginal cost of abatement pollution is sufficiently large (³ $\gg 0$), at the cooperative equilibrium, the optimal pollution quotas are given by the following:*

1. if $C_X \gg C_Y$, then $z_B^c = 0$
2. $z_A^c = 0$

Intuitively, the weight of the small country in the total market is too small, such that the benefit in consumer surplus and producer surplus in both countries is negligible. The small country's best policy is to set the strictest pollution policy in order to benefit from improving the health of his people.

On the other hand, the large country sets the strictest policy only if the firm located in the large country is sufficiently more efficient than the firm located in the small country. The main proportion of the production in the world is by the firms located in the large country. The amount of pollution produced by this firm is huge and the large country is urged to take some measures to reduce the harm on people by pollution. The benefit in consumer surplus in both countries and the producer surplus in the large country is reduced to a lesser extent relative to the benefit produced by the reduction in pollution.

5   Conclusion

Even when the economic progress implies the creation of competitive conditions in which the amount of production and the efficiency of its process should be maximized in order to have successful business in a competitive world, nations should recognize that the way these conditions have been set is far from environmental concerns. There is an unequivocal and close relation between productivity and environment. Moreover, in an even more integrated economy, environmental concerns are deeply related with the commercial activity. Strategic trade, production and environment are part of the equation governments should solve in order to get the optimal policies for a better welfare.

Environmental disturbances arise as a major concern for the governments nowadays. Some regulatory policies are required urgently. However, these policies should maximize the welfare of producers and consumers, preserving at the same time the environmental balance.

Even when some environmental policies may affect positively the productivity, the assumption of this chapter, and according to the most of the literature, is that the pollution control policies may affect the competitiveness negatively. Governments are very careful to establish firm control for environmental protection as this involves increasing production costs undermining the competitiveness, and as a consequence, discourages creation and survival of domestic firms.

In this sense environmental regulations are considered as trade barriers. They are debated in international forums and are part of the routine on the negotiation of international trade agreements, mainly those that concern developing countries, because they are the ones that are most exposed to the establishment of polluting firms. On the other hand, industrial activity is one of the most important promoters of development, so these countries and their governments must consider their economic performances, with the preservation of natural resources and the cleanliness of their environment in the short, medium and long term.

We develop here a model of Cournot oligopoly, of partial equilibrium under conditions of reciprocal dumping between two asymmetric countries. We consider one firm located in each country producing for local consumption and to export. Companies generate pollution in their production processes, but in turn, they have appropriate technology to bring it down. We use one of the most used environmental policy instrument: quotas (quantitative limits on the emission of pollutants).

We calculate the optimal quota of pollution that maximizes the welfare in each country under two scenarios: non-cooperative and cooperative setting. In addition, such quantities determine the optimal strategic policies under specific conditions that relate to the cost structure of firms, particularly the amount of the abatement cost per unit of pollution and its relationship with the marginal disutility for contaminating. Such policy has important involvement on the social welfare function in both countries, which involves the consumer surplus, the firm benefits and the social cost for polluting.

In the non-cooperative setting the optimal pollution quota depends first on the asymmetry between the countries. When countries are sufficiently different in size, the optimal pollution quota in both countries depends on the marginal costs for abating pollution and on the marginal disutility for polluting. With a marginal pollution disutility sufficiently larger than the cost for abatement pollution, the impact of pollution control on people's health of the small country is larger than the loss in producer and consumer surplus, then the government in the small country will set the strictest pollution policy. On the other hand, with pollution disutility sufficiently smaller than the cost for abatement pollution, the impact of encouraging production on people's health is negligible and the governments in both countries will set a positive pollution quota.

In the case in which both countries are similar in size, the optimal pollution quota set by each country, under a non-cooperative context, is expected to be the same. The optimal pollution policy will depend on the level of marginal cost of abatement pollution and on the marginal pollution disutility. As mentioned before, with a marginal pollution disutility sufficiently larger than the cost for abatement pollution, the impact of pollution control on people's health in both countries is larger than the loss in producer and consumer surplus, then the government in both countries will set the strictest pollution policies. On the other hand, with pollution disutility sufficiently smaller than the cost of abatement pollution, encouraging production on people's health is negligible and the government in both countries will set positive pollution quotas. However, when the cost of abating pollution and the marginal pollution disutility are equal, the policy set by each country will depend on the efficiency of the firms located in each country. The country where the most efficient firm is located will set a strict pollution policy because of the significant cost of harmful pollution. On the other hand, the country where the inefficient firm is located will set a positive pollution policy in order to benefit from consumer and producer surplus.

Under the cooperative setting, both countries agree to set a cooperative pollution quota taking into account the effect of this optimal quota on the other country's welfare. In other words, both governments are going to decide the optimal pollution policy, which affects not only the local damage of pollution on people's health, consumer and producer surplus, but also the consumer and producer surplus in the other country. If each country is concerned with the welfare of the other country the optimal pollution quota will be determined primarily by the marginal pollution disutility and the marginal cost for abatement pollution. However, when both countries set cooperative policy, they have to take into account the efficiency of their firms in order to compensate the benefit and losses of a cooperative policy.

At first, when the marginal cost for abatement pollution is sufficiently smaller than the marginal pollution disutility, imposing pollution control has no costs but only benefit in the health of the people independent of the size of the markets. Neither government will be willing to allow any pollution quota. The health of the people is so important that consumer and producer surplus losses are not relevant for the policy setting. This result is similar to the non-cooperative case and its intuition is quite straightforward.

On the other hand, when the marginal cost for abatement pollution is sufficiently larger than the marginal pollution disutility the optimal cooperative policy should take into account the size of the countries and the efficiency of the firms since the benefit in consumer and producer surplus is going to depend on the market possibilities of trading. In the case in which both countries are similar in size, the optimal pollution quota will depend on the efficiency between firms. If the firm located in a local country is sufficiently less efficient than the firm located abroad, the local government will set a strict pollution policy in order to benefit from the reduction in the harming pollution and the benefit given by the most efficient foreign firm in the consumer surplus by trade in the imported good. The local firm is sufficiently inefficient and the impact on local consumer and producer surplus is negligible. Therefore, it is better to take care of pollution damage. In this sense the foreign country will set a positive pollution quota because the benefit of the foreign producer surplus (and producing and trading for the local country) and consumer surplus is larger than the harm of pollution on people's health.

Finally, in the case in which both countries are sufficiently different in size and the marginal cost of pollution abatement is sufficiently larger than the marginal pollution disutility, the optimal cooperative policy will be the strictest one for the small country since the benefit in consumer surplus given by trading with the large country is larger than the loss in producer surplus. This policy will reduce the producer surplus but will reduce the harming pollution. On the other hand, in the large country it is not a clear policy and the only possible result is when the firm in the large country is sufficiently more efficient than the firm located in the small country. In this case the pollution damage is large and the government in the large country will set the strictest pollution policy.

Notes

1   An extensive survey is given by Cropper and Oates (1992), and recently by Requate (2005).
2   An outstanding reference on trade and the environment is given by Copeland and Taylor (2003).
3   Seminal papers on intra-industry trade are Balassa (1966), Krugman (1979) and Lancaster (1980).
4   Some clear examples are Brander (1981) and Brander and Krugman (1983).
5   Normally, the phenomenon of dumping in international trade can be explained by the standard theory of monopolistic price discrimination. A good survey is provided by Caves and Jones (1977).
6   Implicitly, there is a numeraire good in the background which is produced under competitive conditions. As mentioned before, there is also just one factor of production in each country whose price is determined in the competitive sector.
7   They can be considered separately given the assumption of constant marginal costs.

8 As we are considering a small economy, we ignore cross-border pollution. For an analysis of cross-border pollution, see for example, Copeland (1996).
9 Other authors, like Asako (1979), consider that marginal disutility is an increasing function of the output. However, this alternative assumption will not contradict our results and a constant marginal disutility is a more convenient assumption. On the other hand, it is easier to get some close form solutions.
10 The damage for pollution is the same in both countries. Apart from some particular exceptions, the damage on any human being is generally identical.
11 For simplicity θ and γ are the same in both countries. The policy-induced cost function is also used in Kayalica and Lahiri (2005). Although there seem to be similarities with that paper (in which an export-oriented trade model is used) here, the study is based on a reciprocal-trade model.
12 Implicitly, this unit pollution parameter is taken to be over and above the level that the World Health Organization (WHO) considers to be harmless. On the other hand, $n\theta X$ and $m\theta Y$ are the countries' total pollution produced by A and B respectively before any abatement.
13 Like in the case of θ, these instruments are taken to be over and above the level that the WHO considers as harmless.
14 Under these assumptions, the second order concavity conditions may be written as $\psi > \gamma\frac{2}{3}$ and $\psi > \gamma\frac{3}{4}$. In both cases the optimal pollution policy in country B is negative, therefore the optimal quota will be zero.
15 Here the concavity conditions hold.

References

Asako, K. (1979), 'Environmental Pollution in an Open Economy', *Economic Record,* 55 (151): 359–367.

Balassa, B. (1966), 'Tariff Reductions and Trade in Manufactures', *American Economic Review*, 56: 466–473.

Brander, J. A. (1981), 'Intra-industry Trade in Identical Commodities', *Journal of International Economics*, 11: 1–14.

Brander, J. A. and Krugman, P. (1983), 'A "Reciprocal Dumping" Model of International Trade', *Journal of International Economics*, 15: 313–321.

Caves, R. E. and Jones, R. W. (1977), *World Trade and Payments: An Introduction* (2nd ed.). Boston: Little, Brown and Company.

Copeland, B. R. (1996), 'Pollution Content Tariffs, Environmental Rent Shifting, and the Control of Cross-border Pollution', *Journal of International Economics*, 40: 459–476.

Copeland, B. R. and Taylor, M. S. (2003), *Trade and the Environment: Theory and Evidence*, Princeton, NJ: Princeton University Press.

Cropper, M. L. and Oates, W. E. (1992), 'Environmental Economics: A Survey', *Journal of Economic Literature*, 30: 675–740.

Kayalica, M. O. and Lahiri, S. (2005), 'Strategic Environmental Policies in the Presence of Foreign Direct Investment', *Environmental and Resource Economics*, 30: 1–21.

Krugman, P. (1979), 'Increasing Returns, Monopolistic Competition and International Trade', *Journal of International Economics*, 9: 469–479.

Lahiri, S. and Ono, Y. (1998), Protecting Environment in the Presence of Foreign Direct Investment: Tax versus Quantity Restriction. *mimeo* Department of Economics, University of Essex.

Lancaster, K. (1980), 'Intra-industry Trade Under Perfect Monopolistic Competition', *Journal of International Economics*, 10: 151–175.

Markusen, J. and Venables, A. (1988), 'Trade Policy with Increasing Returns and Imperfect Competition: Contradictory Results from Competing Assumptions', *Journal of International Economics*, 24 (3): 299–316.

Markusen, J. R., Morey, E. R. and Olewiler, N. (1993), 'Environmental Policy when Market Structure and Plant Locations are Endogenous', *Journal of Environmental Economics and Management*, 24: 69–86.

Markusen, J. R., Morey, E. R. and Olewiler, N. (1995), 'Competition in Regional Environmental Policies when Plant Locations are Endogenous', *Journal of Public Economics*, 56: 55–57.

Requate, T. (2005), Environmental Policy under Imperfect Competition: A Survey, Economics Working Papers No. 2005,12, Christian-Albrechts-University of Kiel, Department of Economics.

Part IV
Environmental technology

10 The effectiveness of international technology agreements for environmental issues

The impacts of R&D costs

Chisa Kajita and Toshiyuki Fujita

1 Introduction

Technologies are expected to play an integral role in climate change mitigation (e.g. Hoffer *et al.* 2002; Barrett 2003, 2009). However, these technologies tend to require high costs in the phase of research and development (R&D) (e.g. Carbon dioxide Capture and Storage (CCS)). Moreover, knowledge acquired through R&D in one country spills over into others, causing a free-rider problem (e.g. de Coninck *et al.* 2008; Lessmann and Edenhofer 2011; El-Sayed and Rubio 2014). For the above reasons, each country may not individually and voluntarily conduct a sufficient level of R&D. To resolve this problem, a mechanism that promotes multilateral technological collaboration in the R&D phase is considered necessary. We will hereafter use the term International Technology Agreement (ITA) to refer to this mechanism. An ITA is a joint-research project that is carried out by the group of countries who are voluntary participants. Through knowledge sharing and collaboration, countries may be able to develop technologies more effectively and at lower costs than when they work independently.

Barrett (2006) first proposed a basic theoretical framework for technological cooperation in the context of global environmental issues. He shows that the mechanism, in which the signatories collectively decide whether to adopt the technologies, can be effective only when the technologies exhibit the characteristics of increasing returns to adoption. Hoel and de Zeeuw (2010) modify the above model based on the assumption that the cost of adoption can be reduced as a result of R&D activities. Moreover, they insist that a technology agreement can be effective even if the technology does not exhibit the characteristic of increasing returns. Recent studies have examined such technology-based agreements. Hong and Karp (2012) show that the values of the three elements (R&D level, the number of signatories and social welfare) can be greater when mixed as opposed to pure strategies are applied. El-Sayed and Rubio (2014) reveal that the number of signatories is negatively related to the degree of R&D spillover. Urpelainen (2014) further identifies the conditions under which technology agreements have a positive effect on climate agreements such as the Kyoto Protocol.

The aim of this chapter is to investigate the impacts of R&D costs on the effectiveness of an ITA. We consider a game in which players are countries and their strategies include technology-related R&D and its adoption. ITA members collectively decide whether to conduct R&D under exogenously determined R&D costs, denoted as p. We assume that, once a country invests p, the cost of technology adoption can be reduced by $\dfrac{1}{N+1}$, where N denotes the number of countries that share the resource. We solve the following game by focusing on R&D costs p: in the first stage, each country decides whether to join an ITA; in the second stage, signatories collectively decide whether to conduct R&D; in the third stage, each country independently decides whether to adopt the technology. By solving the above game, four conclusions are obtained.

First, the number of signatories has a U-shaped relationship with R&D costs: when R&D costs are either sufficiently low or high, many countries rationally join an ITA.

Second, there is a threshold regarding R&D costs that determines an ITA's effectiveness: when R&D costs are below the threshold, the ITA is functional; else, it is not. Moreover, the threshold is an increasing function of the number of countries that share the resource: the value of the threshold is higher in the context of global environmental issues compared with local environmental issues.

Third, when an ITA functions, it can always induce technology adoption in all countries (full adoption). In this study, full adoption refers to full participation in pollution reduction activities, because the benefit of adopting the technology is improvement of the environment. Full participation is the main objective of the Paris Agreement adopted at the 21st Conference of Parties in 2015. Therefore, our third result implies that there is a possibility that an ITA may help the success of the Paris Agreement by promoting diffusion of environmental technologies.

Fourth, when an ITA functions, the ITA can improve all non-cooperative situations, except for the case in which the first-best is achieved in a non-cooperative situation. Only when R&D costs are quite low, could the first-best be achieved in a non-cooperative situation.

The remainder of this chapter is organized as follows. We present the basic model settings and game procedures in Section 2, and derive the agreement size in equilibrium as a game solution in Section 3. In Section 4, we summarize our discussions, offering our conclusions in Section 5.

2   The model

There are $N(\geq 3)$ identical countries sharing a resource, indexed $i = 1, \ldots, N$. The R&D decision of country i is denoted as $M_i \in \{0,1\}$: $M_i = 0$ (not conducting R&D) or $M_i = 1$ (conducting R&D). $M(= \sum_j M_j)$ denotes the total number of countries conducting R&D ($0 \leq M \leq N$).[1] The cost of the R&D effort is defined as pM_i, where p is determined exogenously. In addition, each country decides whether to adopt the technology. The adoption decision of country i is denoted as $x_i \in \{0,1\}$: $x_i = 0$ (not adopting the technology) or $x_i = 1$ (adopting the technology). $X(= \sum_j x_j)$ denotes the total number of countries that adopt the technology ($0 \leq X \leq N$). We establish the technology adoption cost of each country as $\dfrac{N+1-M}{N+1}$. The cost of adoption for an individual country depends on the total number of countries conducting R&D. This reflects that knowledge acquired through R&D in one country fully spills over into others. If none of the countries conduct R&D, then the adoption cost will be 1. When only one country conducts R&D, this cost will be reduced to $1 - \dfrac{1}{N+1}$. From the above, it is evident that $\dfrac{1}{N+1}$ signifies the R&D benefit. The adoption cost evidently has two characteristics. First, it is a decreasing function of the total number of countries conducting R&D.[2] Second, it is an increasing function of the total number of countries.[3] In addition, we set the adoption benefit as b. The net benefit function of country i can be expressed as follows:

$$\pi_i = bX - \frac{N+1-M}{N+1} x_i - pM_i. \tag{1}$$

The first term on the right-hand side of equation (1) denotes the benefit of adopting the technology. It indicates that the adoption benefit for one country spills over to other countries. The second term indicates the adoption cost, which reflects the characteristics of R&D spillover. From the above, we can assume that there are two positive externalities. The third term shows the R&D costs. In this study, we introduce the following assumption:

$$\frac{1}{N+1} < b < \frac{N}{N+1},$$

where $\dfrac{1}{N+1} < b$ means that it will be rational for each country to adopt the technology if all of the countries conducted R&D. $b < \dfrac{N}{N+1}$ means that each country will not individually conduct R&D and adopt the technology.

If all countries make decisions to cooperatively conduct R&D and adopt technologies, they will choose an R&D level that minimizes $\dfrac{N+1-M}{N+1} N + pM$. When the cost of adoption is low enough for all countries to adopt these technologies, each country will receive a net benefit, which is each country's benefit in a first-best situation (see Appendix A), as expressed below.

$$Nb - \min_{M} \left[\frac{N+1-M}{N+1} + \frac{M}{N} p \right] \qquad (2)$$

Let us consider the non-cooperative solution, which is a sub-game perfect equilibrium for the following two-stage coalition formation game. In the first stage, each country decides whether to conduct R&D, and in the second stage, they independently make a decision regarding adoption of the technology. The following two situations can be considered in light of symmetric non-cooperative equilibria (NCEs) (see Appendix B).

NCE (i): None of the countries conduct R&D or adopt technologies.
NCE (ii): All countries conduct R&D as well as adopt the technologies.

In some cases, a first-best outcome may be achieved in relation to NCE (ii). However, in other cases, NCE (ii) cannot achieve a first-best outcome. There is, however, a possibility of improving NCE (ii) in such cases. Moreover, NCE (i) can evidently be improved. We consider ITAs as a mechanism for improving the situations described above.

The number of ITA signatories is defined as k ($1 \leq k \leq N$). The signatories will attempt to persuade many countries to adopt the technologies by collectively conducting R&D to reduce the adoption cost. By considering these procedures, we can develop the following three-stage coalition formation game:

Stage 1: Each country chooses whether to join an agreement (determination of k).
Stage 2: The signatories collectively determine whether to conduct R&D (determination of M).
Stage 3: Each country independently decides whether to adopt the technology (determination of X).

3   Solution of the game

3.1   Third stage

Each country decides whether to adopt a technology by choosing the value of x_i. Country i will only choose to adopt the technology if $\dfrac{\partial \pi_i}{\partial x_i} \geq 0$, and not otherwise. The equilibrium in the third stage is expressed as

$$x_i^* = \begin{cases} 0 \ if \ M < (N+1)(1-b) \\ 1 \ if \ M \geq (N+1)(1-b) \end{cases}.$$

From the above, it is evident that if the number of countries conducting R&D is greater than $(N+1)(1-b)$, it would be rational for each country to adopt the technology.

3.2 Second stage

In the second stage, the signatories collectively decide whether to conduct R&D. Based on our assumption, when signatories conduct R&D, the number of countries conducting R&D coincides with the number of signatories. From the previous discussion, it is clear that the number of signatories must be greater than $(N+1)(1-b)$ to induce countries to adopt the technologies. Here, we define $\bar{k} = (N+1)(1-b)$. We can easily conjecture that the net benefit for each signatory will be different between the case of $1 \le k < \bar{k}$ and $\bar{k} \le k \le N$.[4]

When $1 \le k < \bar{k}$, even if the signatories conduct R&D, they will fail to persuade countries to adopt the technologies.[5] In this case, R&D cannot benefit the signatories. Therefore, it would be rational for signatories not to conduct R&D.

$$M_i^* = 0 \left(1 \le k < \bar{k}\right)$$

If $\bar{k} \le k \le N$, then the signatories may be able to achieve full adoption by conducting R&D. In this case, the net benefit for each signatory, π_i^s, can be expressed as

$$\pi_i^s = Nb - \frac{N+1-k}{N+1} - p. \tag{3}$$

If $\pi_i^s \ge 0$, namely $k \ge \tilde{k} = (N+1)(1-Nb+p)$, it would be rational for the signatories to conduct R&D. The condition under which $\bar{k} < \tilde{k} \le N$ holds is

$$(N-1)b < p \le Nb - \frac{1}{N+1}.$$

From the above condition, we observe that the shape of π_i^s may change depending on the range of p. Figures 10.1, 10.2, and 10.3 depict the relationship between the number of the signatories and the net benefit for each signatory in three cases. There are: case 1: $0 < p \le (N-1)b$, case 2: $(N-1)b < p \le Nb - \frac{1}{N+1}$, and case 3: $Nb - \frac{1}{N+1} < p$. By applying these figures, we can identify the optimal R&D decision for the signatories as shown below.

Case1: $0 < p \le (N-1)b$ $M_i^* = 1$ *if* $\bar{k} \le k \le N$.

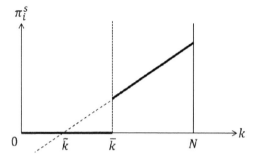

Figure 10.1 The net benefit for each signatory as a function of the agreement size in case 1

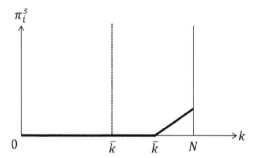

Figure 10.2 The net benefit for each signatory as a function of the agreement size in case 2

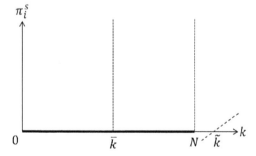

Figure 10.3 The net benefit for each signatory as a function of the agreement size in case 3

$$\text{Case 2}: (N-1)b < p \le Nb - \frac{1}{N+1} \quad M_i^* = \begin{cases} 0 \text{ if } \overline{k} \le k < \tilde{k} \\ 1 \text{ if } \tilde{k} \le k \le N \end{cases}.$$

$$\text{Case 3}: Nb - \frac{1}{N+1} < p \quad M_i^* = 0 \text{ if } \overline{k} \le k \le N.$$

If the number of the signatories is less than $\overline{k}$, it would always be rational for signatories not to conduct R&D. Otherwise; the optimal R&D decision for each signatory depends on R&D costs. This means that to achieve full adoption, at least the agreement size should be greater than $\overline{k}$. In case 1, we can observe a leap in the net benefit for each signatory at point $\overline{k}$. Because R&D costs are sufficiently low, it is always rational for the signatories to the agreement greater than $\overline{k}$, to conduct R&D. In case 2, if the agreement size is greater than $\tilde{k}$, each signatory will rationally decide to conduct R&D. Even if the number of the signatories lies between $\overline{k}$ and $\tilde{k}$, the signatories can induce full adoption by conducting R&D. However, in this case, because the net benefit for each signatory will be negative, they will choose not to conduct R&D. In case 3, the cost of conducting R&D is too high for the signatories. Even if all countries join an agreement, it will not be effective.

3.3 First stage

We investigate the number of signatories in equilibrium k^* by comparing the net benefit for each signatory and non-signatory. Each signatory's net benefit is denoted as $\pi_i^s(k)$ and that of each non-signatory's is denoted as $\pi_i^n(k)$. To derive k^*, the internal and external stabilities of the agreement should be considered. Internal stability indicates that signatories do not have an incentive to withdraw from the agreement: $\pi_i^s(k) \ge \pi_i^n(k-1)$. External stability shows that non-signatories do not have an incentive to join the agreement: $\pi_i^n(k) > \pi_i^s(k+1)$. When both internal and external stability are satisfied simultaneously, this agreement is defined as being self-enforcing.[6] Now, we consider the size of the self-enforcing agreement in each case.

We set $0 < p \le \frac{1}{N+1}$ in case 1.1 and $\frac{1}{N+1} < p \le (N-1)b$ in case 1.2, since the discussion of coalition stability in case 1.1 is not the same as in case 1.2.[7] We derive the size of the self-enforcing agreement in four cases separately: case 1.1, 1.2, 2 and 3.

First, we focus on case 1.1, $0 < p \le \frac{1}{N+1}$. When $k = \overline{k}$, we have

$$\pi_i^s(\overline{k}) = Nb - \frac{N+1-\overline{k}}{N+1} - p \ge 0, \tag{4}$$

$$\pi_i^n\left(\bar{k}-1\right)=0. \tag{5}$$

Since $\pi_i^s\left(\bar{k}\right)\geq\pi_i^n\left(\bar{k}-1\right)$ holds, the agreement of size $\bar{k}$ has internal stability. In addition, we have

$$\pi_i^n\left(\bar{k}\right)=Nb-\frac{N+1-\bar{k}}{N+1}, \tag{6}$$

$$\pi_i^s\left(\bar{k}+1\right)=Nb-\frac{N+1-\left(\bar{k}+1\right)}{N+1}-p. \tag{7}$$

Since $\pi_i^n(\bar{k})\leq\pi_i^s(\bar{k}+1)$ holds, an agreement of size $\bar{k}$ does not have external stability. In an agreement of size greater than $\bar{k}$, we can get

$$\pi_i^s(k)=Nb-\frac{N+1-k}{N+1}-p, \tag{8}$$

$$\pi_i^n(k-1)=Nb-\frac{N+1-(k-1)}{N+1}. \tag{9}$$

Since $\pi_i^s(k)\geq\pi_i^n(k-1)$ always holds, an agreement of size $k(>\bar{k})$ is internally stable. This means that an agreement of size $k(>\bar{k})$, except for the case of $k=N$, is externally unstable. The agreement of size N has external stability, since N is the total number of countries. Thus, there are no non-signatories. Therefore, the agreement of size N is self-enforcing. Further, in an agreement of size smaller than $\bar{k}$, since $\pi_i^n(k)=\pi_i^s(k+1)=0$, it is not self-enforcing. From the above discussion, the agreement size of N is the only stable agreement in case 1.1.

Second, we consider case 1.2, $\dfrac{1}{N+1}<p\leq(N-1)b$. When $k=\bar{k}$, we have equations (4) and (5). Since $\pi_i^s(\bar{k})\geq\pi_i^n(\bar{k}-1)$ holds, the agreement of size $\bar{k}$ has internal stability. Moreover, we have equations (6) and (7). Since $\pi_i^n(\bar{k})>\pi_i^s(\bar{k}+1)$ holds, the agreement of size $\bar{k}$ has external stability. From the above, it is revealed that the agreement of size $\bar{k}$ is self-enforcing. Now, we investigate whether the agreement of size $\bar{k}$ is the only stable agreement. In an agreement of size greater than $\bar{k}$, we get the equations (8) and (9). Since $\pi_i^s(k)<\pi_i^n(k-1)$ always holds, an agreement of size $k(>\bar{k})$ is internally unstable: it is not self-enforcing. Further, in an agreement of size smaller than $\bar{k}$, since $\pi_i^n(k)=\pi_i^s(k+1)=0$, it is not self-enforcing. From the above discussion, an agreement size of $\bar{k}$ is the only stable agreement in case 1.2.

Third, we see case 2, $(N-1)b<p\leq Nb-\dfrac{1}{N+1}$. When $k=\tilde{k}$, we have

$$\pi_i^s\left(\tilde{k}\right)=Nb-\frac{N+1-\tilde{k}}{N+1}-p\geq0, \tag{10}$$

$$\pi_i^n\left(\tilde{k}-1\right)=0. \tag{11}$$

Since $\pi_i^s\left(\tilde{k}\right)\geq\pi_i^n\left(\tilde{k}-1\right)$ holds, the agreement of size $\tilde{k}$ has internal stability. In addition, we have

$$\pi_i^n\left(\tilde{k}\right)=Nb-\frac{N+1-\tilde{k}}{N+1}, \tag{12}$$

$$\pi_i^s\left(\tilde{k}+1\right)=Nb-\frac{N+1-\left(\tilde{k}+1\right)}{N+1}-p. \tag{13}$$

If $\dfrac{1}{N+1}<p$, $\pi_i^n(\tilde{k})>\pi_i^s(\tilde{k}+1)$ will hold.[8] In case 2, since the agreement of size always has external stability, the agreement of size $\tilde{k}$ is self-enforcing. In an agreement of size larger than $\tilde{k}$, we get the equations (8) and (9). Since $\pi_i^s(k)<\pi_i^n(k-1)$ always holds, an agreement of size $k(>\tilde{k})$ is internally unstable. Thus, it cannot be self-enforcing. Moreover, an agreement of size smaller than $\tilde{k}$, since $\pi_i^n(k)=\pi_i^s(k+1)=0$, is not self-enforcing. From the above discussion, the agreement size of $\tilde{k}$ is the only stable agreement in case 2.

Finally, we show case 3, $Nb-\dfrac{1}{N+1}<p$. Since $\pi_i^s(k)=\pi_i^n(k-1)=0$ and $\pi_i^n(k)=\pi_i^s(k+1)=0$ hold for all k, only the agreement of size N has internal and external stabilities.[9] However, even if all countries join the agreement, they will not be able to obtain a positive net benefit by conducting R&D. Although the agreement size of N may be the only stable agreement in case 3, the effect of this agreement is equal to nothing.

4   Outcomes with international technology agreements

From the above discussion, we summarize the game solutions in Lemma 1.

Lemma 1 *For the coalition game of an international technology agreement with N symmetric countries, the solutions of the game are characterized by four types of R&D costs:*

$$\left(k^*,M^*,X^*\right)=\begin{cases}(N,N,N)\,if\,Case\,1.1:0<p\leq\dfrac{1}{N+1}\\[2mm]\left(\overline{k},\overline{k},N\right)\,if\,Case\,1.2:\dfrac{1}{N+1}<p\leq(N-1)b\\[2mm]\left(\tilde{k},\tilde{k},N\right)\,if\,Case\,2:(N-1)b<p\leq Nb-\dfrac{1}{N+1}\\[2mm](N,0,0)\,if\,Case\,3:Nb-\dfrac{1}{N+1}<p\end{cases}.$$

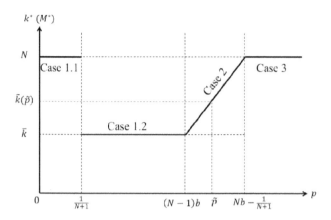

Figure 10.4 The agreement size (the number of countries that conduct R&D) in equilibrium as a function of R&D costs

Lemma 1 is summarized in Figure 10.4 which shows the stable agreement size k^* (= the stable number of countries that conduct R&D M^*) for a given N. Since $\tilde{k} = (N+1)(1 - Nb + p)$, $\tilde{k}$ is denoted as a function of p: $\tilde{k}(p)$.

From Figure 10.4, we can see that the number of signatories has a U-shaped relationship with R&D costs. In case 1.1, R&D costs are lower than the R&D benefit, $\dfrac{1}{N+1}$. In this case, no countries deviate from the situation in which all countries conduct R&D and adopt technologies: there are no free-riders. In case 1.2, there are some free-riders. If the number of signatories is smaller than $\overline{k}$, signatories cannot reduce the cost of adoption enough to induce technology adoption. Therefore, the signatories in the agreement of size $\overline{k}$ do not have incentive to free-ride. In case 2, signatories in an agreement of size $\overline{k}$ cannot get a positive benefit from conducting R&D, since R&D costs are relatively high. If the agreement size becomes greater than $\overline{k}$, the cost of adoption is decreased. In this case, the signatories may get a positive benefit only when the decrease in adoption costs offsets the increase in R&D costs.

Moreover, it is obvious that, when $p \leq \overline{p}(N) = Nb - \dfrac{1}{N+1}$, an ITA bring a positive social welfare. From this fact, $\overline{p}(N)$ is considered to be the threshold that determines the effectiveness of an ITA: if R&D costs p is lower than $\overline{p}(N)$, an ITA is functional, otherwise it is not. For better understanding, we introduce Figure 10.5.

Figure 10.5 has three lines and each line is the boundary line of each case, $\dfrac{1}{N+1}$ (the long dashed line), $(N-1)b$ (the short dashed line) and $\overline{p}(N)$ (the solid line). An ITA is functional in the lower area of the solid line. Moreover, the slope of the solid line is positive: $\overline{p}(N)$ is an increasing function of the number of countries that share the resource N. This means that the value of the threshold under global environmental issues is higher than under local

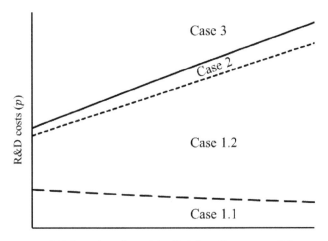

Figure 10.5 Image of the region where ITA functions

ones. In addition, from Lemma 1, it is revealed that, when $p \leq \bar{p}(N)$, an ITA induces all countries to adopt technologies in equilibrium, otherwise, the situation under no countries adopt technologies is achieved. From the above discussion, we can get Propositions 1 and 2.

Proposition 1 *For the coalition game of an international technology agreement with N symmetric countries, there are three types of equilibrium in which full adoption is achieved by an ITA.*

Proposition 2 *For the coalition game of an international technology agreement with N symmetric countries, there is the threshold regarding R&D costs that determines the effectiveness of an ITA: if R&D costs are lower than the certain level, an ITA is functional, otherwise, it is not. The threshold is an increasing function of the number of countries that share the resource.*

Moreover, the purpose of an ITA is to improve the NCEs. From the discussion so far, it is obvious that an ITA can improve NCE (i).[10] Can an ITA improve NCE (ii)? We show the answer to this question in Proposition 3.

Proposition 3 *When the first-best is not achieved in NCE (ii), which is the non-cooperative state where all countries conduct R&D and adopt technologies, an ITA can always improve NCE (ii).*

The proof of Proposition 3 is shown in Appendix C. In our chapter, NCE (ii) may achieve the first-best. If NCE (ii) coincides with the first-best, an ITA is not needed. In this case, if an ITA is introduced by accident, it may bring the same or even worse social welfare than NCE (ii). However, under some conditions, NCE (ii) does not coincide with the first-best. In this case, an ITA can always improve NCE (ii).

5   Conclusion

We have considered the effectiveness of an ITA, in which the signatories collectively decide whether to conduct R&D, by focusing on R&D costs. The role of R&D is to reduce the cost of technology adoption. When an ITA is not introduced, there are two non-cooperative equilibria, NCE (i) and (ii): All countries neither conduct R&D nor adopt technologies in NCE (i), while all countries both conduct R&D and adopt technologies in NCE (ii). Under some conditions, the first-best may be achieved in NCE (ii). However, in most cases, we have the chance to improve NCE (i) and (ii) by introducing an ITA. We investigate whether an ITA can improve NCE (i) and (ii) and find that three types of situations can be achieved in equilibrium when an ITA can bring positive effects. In all situations, an ITA induces technology adoption in all countries. In addition, an ITA always improves non-cooperative equilibria except the case in which the first-best is achieved in NCE (ii). When the first-best is achieved in NCE (ii), an ITA is likely to decrease the social welfare.

Moreover, we find that there is a threshold regarding R&D costs that determines the effectiveness of an ITA: if R&D costs are lower than the threshold, an ITA is functional, otherwise it is not. The threshold has a positive relationship with the number of countries that share the resource: the value of the threshold is high (low) when the number of countries that share the resource is large (small). In general, high R&D costs tend to be required to develop and deploy an environmental technology for global warming such as CCS. Our findings insist the effectiveness of an ITA in the real world.

For simplicity, this chapter used a linear function of the cost of adoption. However, to reflect the real situation more closely, it would be necessary to use a more complicated function. In addition, in our chapter, R&D always succeeds. However, this situation will not happen in the reality. Thus, we should consider the risk of R&D. These concerns are our future studies.

Appendix A: Derivation of the first-best

We treat M as a continuous value. When we differentiate equation (2) with respect to M, $\dfrac{1}{N+1} - \dfrac{p}{N}$ can be obtained. If $\dfrac{N}{N+1} \geq p$, equation (2) will be an increasing function of M. Otherwise, it will be a decreasing function of M. Since $0 \leq M \leq N$, the net benefit for each country in the first-best can be shown as the following:

$$\begin{cases} Nb - \dfrac{1}{N+1} - p \ if \ \ 0 < p \leq \dfrac{N}{N+1} \\ \qquad Nb - 1 \ if \ \ \dfrac{N}{N+1} < p \end{cases}.$$

In the first-best, if R&D costs are relatively low, all countries conduct R&D as well as adopt the technologies. If the R&D costs are relatively high, the situation in which no countries conduct R&D and adopt technologies can be the first-best.

Appendix B: Derivation of non-cooperative equilibria

We focus on symmetric sub-game perfect Nash equilibria in a non-cooperative game. In the second stage, each country decides whether to adopt technology. When $\frac{\partial \pi_i}{\partial x_i} = b - \frac{N+1-M}{N+1} \geq 0$, each country adopts technology. If the adoption benefit b is greater than the cost of adoption $\frac{N+1-M}{N+1}$, it becomes rational for each country to adopt the technology.

In the first stage, each country decides on an R&D level. If each country decides not to conduct R&D, the cost of adoption 1 becomes lower than the adoption benefit b, and so no countries will adopt technologies and the net benefit for each country will be zero. It is not rational for country i to deviate from this state and conduct R&D. When country i individually conducts R&D, the cost of adoption will be $\frac{N}{N+1}$. However, since $b < \frac{N}{N+1}$, no country will adopt the technologies. In this case, the net benefit for country i will be $-\frac{N}{N+1} - p < 0$. It is obvious that country i cannot increase the net benefit by deviating. Therefore, the situation in which no countries conduct R&D is the non-cooperative equilibrium.

There is another non-cooperative equilibrium. When each country conducts R&D, the cost of adoption $\frac{1}{N+1}$ becomes greater than the adoption benefit b, and so it will be rational for all countries to adopt technologies. In this case, the net benefit for each country will be $Nb - \frac{1}{N+1} - p$. When only country i deviates from this state and individually chooses not to conduct R&D, the cost of adoption will be $\frac{2}{N+1}$. If the adoption benefit is greater than $\frac{2}{N+1}$, all countries will adopt the technologies. In this case, the net benefit which country i can get by deviating can be shown as:

$$\begin{cases} 0 & if \ \dfrac{1}{N+1} < b < \dfrac{2}{N+1} \\ Nb - \dfrac{2}{N+1} & if \ \dfrac{2}{N+1} \leq b < \dfrac{N}{N+1} \end{cases}.$$

Table 10B.1 Non-cooperative equilibrium

	$\dfrac{1}{N+1} < b < \dfrac{2}{N+1}$	$\dfrac{2}{N+1} \le b < \dfrac{N}{N+1}$
$0 < p \le \dfrac{1}{N+1}$	NCE (i), NCE (ii)	
$\dfrac{1}{N+1} < p \le Nb - \dfrac{1}{N+1}$	NCE (i), NCE (ii)	NCE (i)
$Nb - \dfrac{1}{N+1} < p$	NCE (i)	

If the above net benefit is greater than $Nb - \dfrac{1}{N+1} - p$, country i will choose to deviate.[11] When the country i rationally choose not to deviate, the situation in which all countries conduct R&D will be a non-cooperative equilibrium.

From the above discussion, we can notice that there may be the following two non-cooperative equilibria.

NCE (i): None of the countries conduct R&D or adopt technologies.
NCE (ii): All countries conduct R&D as well as adopt the technologies.

NCE (ii) may coincide with the first-best. From Appendix A, we know that when R&D costs are lower than $\dfrac{N}{N+1}$, NCE (ii) can achieve the first-best. We summarize the non-cooperative equilibria by using Table B.1.

From Table B.1, it is revealed that the non-cooperative equilibrium may change depending on R&D costs and the adoption benefit. We notice that NCE (i) and (ii) may exist at the same time when R&D costs and the adoption benefits are relatively low. In this case, the social optimum may be achieved without introducing ITAs.

Appendix C: Proof of proposition 3

NCE (ii) is the situation in which all countries conduct R&D and adopt technologies. Therefore, social welfare will be shown as the following:

$$N\left(Nb - \frac{1}{N+1} - p \right) = N^2 b - \frac{N}{N+1} - Np. \tag{C.1}$$

From now on, we consider social welfare, which is obtained by introducing the ITAs. In case 1.1, since $\left(k^*, M^*, X^*\right) = \left(N, N, N\right)$ is achieved, social welfare will be the same as (C.1). In case 1.2, since $\left(k^*, M^*, X^*\right) = \left(\bar{k}, \bar{k}, N\right)$ is achieved, social welfare will be

$$\bar{k}\left(Nb-\frac{N+1-\bar{k}}{N+1}-p\right)+\left(N-\bar{k}\right)\left(Nb-\frac{N+1-\bar{k}}{N+1}\right)=N^2b-\frac{N+1-\bar{k}}{N+1}N-\bar{k}p.$$

$$(C.2)$$

In case 2, since $\left(k^*,M^*,X^*\right)=\left(\tilde{k},\tilde{k},N\right)$ is achieved, social welfare will be

$$\tilde{k}\left(Nb-\frac{N+1-\tilde{k}}{N+1}-p\right)+\left(N-\tilde{k}\right)\left(Nb-\frac{N+1-\tilde{k}}{N+1}\right)=N^2b-\frac{N+1-\tilde{k}}{N+1}N-\tilde{k}p.$$

$$(C.3)$$

From now on, we investigate whether the social welfare in NCE (ii) is increased by introducing ITAs. First, we focus on the case of $\frac{1}{N+1}<b\le\frac{1}{N}$. When $0<p\le Nb-\frac{1}{N+1}$, NCE (ii) exists and always achieves the first-best. When $0<p\le\frac{1}{N+1}$, the social welfare with ITAs is shown by (C.1). Hence, the social welfare with ITAs is same as that in NCE (ii). When $\frac{1}{N+1}<p\le Nb-\frac{1}{N+1}$, the social welfare with ITAs may be shown by (C.2) or (C.3). In this case, the value of (C.2) and (C.3) will be lower than (C.1). Hence, ITAs may bring lower social welfare than NCE (ii).

Next, we consider the case of $\frac{1}{N}<b<\frac{2}{N+1}$. When $0<p\le Nb-\frac{1}{N+1}$, NCE (ii) exists. Moreover, especially only when $0<p\le\frac{N}{N+1}$, NCE (ii) coincides with the first-best. When $0<p\le\frac{1}{N+1}$, the social welfare with ITAs is the same as that in NCE (ii). When $\frac{1}{N+1}<p\le\frac{N}{N+1}$, the social welfare with ITAs may be shown by (C.2) or (C.3). In this case, the value of (C.2) and (C.3) will be lower than (C.1). Hence, ITAs may bring lower social welfare than in NCE (ii). When $\frac{N}{N+1}<p\le Nb-\frac{1}{N+1}$, the social welfare with ITAs may be also shown by (C.2) or (C.3). In this case, the value of (C.2) and (C.3) will be higher than (C.1). Hence, ITAs can improve the social welfare in NCE (ii).

Lastly, we consider the case of $\frac{2}{N+1}\le b<\frac{N}{N+1}$. Only when $0<p\le\frac{1}{N+1}$, does NCE (ii) exist and achieves the first-best. In this case, the social welfare with ITAs is the same as that in NCE (ii).

From the above discussion, we notice that ITAs can improve NCE (ii) only when both $\frac{1}{N}<b<\frac{2}{N+1}$ and $\frac{N}{N+1}<p\le Nb-\frac{1}{N+1}$ simultaneously hold.

This condition is the only case in which the first-best cannot be achieved in NCE (ii).

Acknowledgements

We are grateful for comments on earlier versions of this chapter given by Tetsushi Murao and participants of the 5th WCERE. Japan Society financially supports this research for the Promotion of Science (KAKENHI No. 15K03438 and 15H06466).

Notes

1 It is possible that M is assumed to be a continuous variable. However, we presume that, even if we use a continuous variable, the characteristics of the results will not be changed apparently. In addition, to simplify our discussion, we use a discrete variable function. The same setting is used in Cabral (2000). In his chapter, only the case of $p = 1$ is considered. He, also, uses a discrete-variable function.

2 Hoel and de Zeeuw (2010) and El-Sayed and Rubio (2014) introduce the same assumption.

3 Barrett (2006) introduces the same assumption.

4 In line with our assumption, $(N+1)(1-b) < N$ holds for all b.

5 Because the number of countries conducting R&D is lower than $(N+1)(1-b)$.

6 Here, the number of the signatories in the equilibrium corresponds to the size of a self-enforcing agreement.

7 In line with our assumption, $(N-1)b$ is always greater than $\dfrac{1}{N+1}$ for all b.

8 Since $\pi_i^n(\bar{k}) - \pi_i^s(\bar{k}+1) = -\dfrac{1}{N+1} + p$, we can notice that $\dfrac{1}{N+1} < p$ is the condition under which $\pi_i^n(\bar{k}) > \pi_i^s(\bar{k}+1)$ holds.

9 If we adopt that $\pi_i^s(k) > \pi_i^n(k-1)$ and $\pi_i^n(k) \geq \pi_i^s(k+1)$, which have different equal positions in our definition as the internal and external stabilities, the agreement of size 1 becomes the only stable agreement. Although the stable size of agreement may be changed depending on equal position, the characteristics of equilibrium, namely no countries conduct R&D and adopt technologies, will be never changed.

10 In the outcome NCE (i), none of the countries conduct R&D or adopt technologies, so the social welfare will be zero.

11 When $0 < p \leq \dfrac{1}{N+1}$, country i does not have incentive to deviate. When $\dfrac{1}{N+1} < p \leq Nb - \dfrac{1}{N+1}$, if $\dfrac{1}{N+1} < b < \dfrac{2}{N+1}$, country i will not deviate. Otherwise, namely in the case of $\dfrac{2}{N+1} < b \leq \dfrac{N}{N+1}$, country i will. When $Nb - \dfrac{1}{N+1} < p$, country i always deviates.

References

Barrett, S. (2003), 'Global Climate Change and the Kyoto Protocol', in *Environment and Statecraft: The Strategy of Environmental Treaty-making*. New York: Oxford University Press, 359–398.

Barrett, S. (2006), 'Climate Treaties and "Breakthrough" Technologies', *The American Economic Review*, 96 (2): 22–25.

Barrett, S. (2009), 'The Coming Global Climate-Technology Revolution', *The Journal of Economic Perspectives*, 23 (2): 53–75.

Cabral, L. (2000), 'R&D Cooperation and Product Market Competition', *International Journal of Industrial Organization*, 18: 1033–1047.

de Coninck, H., Fischer, C., Newell, R. G. and Ueno, T. (2008), 'International Technology-Oriented Agreements to Address Climate Change', *Energy Policy*, 36: 335–356.

El-Sayed, A. and Rubio, S. J. (2014), 'Sharing R&D Investments in Cleaner Technologies to Mitigate Climate Change', *Resource and Energy Economics*, 38: 168–180.

Hoel, M. and de Zeeuw, A. (2010), 'Can a Focus on Breakthrough Technologies Improve the Performance of International Environmental Agreements?', *Environmental and Resource Economics*, 47: 395–406.

Hoffer, M. I., Caldeira, K. and Benford, G. (2002), 'Advanced Technology Paths to Global Climate Stability: Energy for a Greenhouse Planet', *Science*, 298: 981–987.

Hong, F. and Karp, L. (2012), 'International Environmental Agreement with Mixed Strategies and Investment', *Journal of Public Economics*, 96: 685–697.

Lessmann, K. and Edenhofer, O. (2011), 'Research Cooperation and International Standards in a Model of Coalition Stability', *Resource and Energy Economics*, 33: 36–54.

Urpelainen, J. (2014), 'Sinking Costs to Increase Participation: Technology Deployment Agreements Enhance Climate Cooperation', *Environmental Economics and Policy Studies*, 16: 229–240.

11 Adaptation technology and free-riding incentives in international environmental agreements[1]

Hassan Benchekroun, Walid Marrouch and Amrita Ray Chaudhuri

1 Introduction

The purpose of this chapter is to investigate how increasing the efficiency of adaptation technology to avoid the damage from a transboundary pollutant affects individual countries' incentives to participate in international environmental agreements (IEAs) that mitigate emissions.

This question gains importance in light of the current policy debate surrounding climate change. Persistent failure plagues international negotiations at the UN Climate Conferences (for example, at recent UNFCCC COP Meetings at Copenhagen, 2009, Cancun, 2010 and Doha, 2012) such that binding commitments on emission targets remain elusive. At the same time, policy-makers are setting aside substantial funds for developing more efficient adaptive measures to safeguard against imminent damage from climate change.[2] Since 1980, the World Bank has approved more than 500 operations related to disaster management including those caused by climate change, amounting to more than US$40 billion. There exist several adaptation funds run by the UNFCCC, World Bank and European Commission that have already contributed millions of dollars towards adaptation (see, for example, Le Goulven 2008).

Our chapter contributes to the vast literature on IEAs (for a survey, see Barrett 2005 and Jørgensen *et al.* 2010). This chapter sets up a game theoretic framework, which incorporates both adaptation and participation in a global agreement on emission reduction as policies available to individual countries dealing with a global pollutant. We consider a fixed cost of not participating in an IEA borne by each non-signatory. If this fixed cost is sufficiently large, it is possible to construct a stable coalition of any size. We are interested in the comparative statics with respect to the adaptation cost parameter, and we use the fixed cost parameter to move around the baseline that the comparative static analysis is applied to. We show that the existence of a more efficient adaptation technology reduces the incentive of a coalition member to free-ride and leave the grand coalition, that is, the coalition that includes all countries. Moreover, we show that this positive impact of increased efficiency of adaptation technology can be accompanied by an increase in the gains from cooperation over the control of emissions, and a reduction in global emissions. Thus, more efficient adaptation, rather than merely being a substitute for the failed attempts at negotiating an IEA, as suggested, for example, in *The Econ*omist (November 2010) and other media outlets, may actually foster international cooperation on mitigating emissions of GHGs.[3]

We note that a recent strand in the literature focuses on international cooperation on R&D and/or development and adoption of 'breakthrough technologies' (e.g. Barrett 2006; El-Sayed and Rubio 2011; Hoel and de Zeeuw 2010). In this chapter, we abstract from the development and the adoption phase of the technology and focus on international cooperation on emissions.

In order to model adaptation, we follow closely the recent theoretical models of adaptation. The existing literature on adaptation can be broadly categorized into two streams. The first provides a description of the trade-off facing countries when deciding how to allocate resources between mitigation of emissions and adaptation (see for example Ingham *et al.* 2005; Tol 2005; Tulkens and van Steenberghe 2009). The second stream explicitly incorporates adaptation in integrated assessment models to analyse the interaction between mitigation and adaptation (see for example Bosello *et al.* 2011; De Bruin *et al.* 2009). Other integrated assessment models such as RICE (Nordhaus and Yang 1996) implicitly capture adaptation by incorporating the costs of adaptation in the regional damage function. For a survey of the literature on the economics of adaptation, please refer to Agrawala *et al.* (2011).

This chapter is more closely related to a set of recent studies that model adaptation within a two-country framework and compare the non-cooperative and cooperative equilibria (Ebert and Welsch 2012; Eisenack and Kähler 2012; Zehaie 2009). Whilst these papers examine how the presence of adaptation affects emission and welfare levels at the non-cooperative and cooperative equilibria, they do not examine how adaptation affects the incentives of an individual country to participate in a global effort to curb emissions. In this chapter we investigate the relationship between adaptation technology and the likelihood of sustaining a self-enforcing international environmental agreement over emissions. We model an increase in the efficiency of adaptation technology as a reduction in the marginal cost of providing adaptive measures. We show that the existence of more efficient adaptation technologies reduces an individual country's incentive to free-ride on an international environmental agreement over pollution emissions.

We follow Ebert and Welsch (2012) and assume that countries undertake adaptation and emission decisions simultaneously, as, for example, in the case of liming of lakes to avoid acidification. As shown by Zehaie (2009), this model is equivalent to one in which adaptation occurs after emission decisions are undertaken, as, for example, in the case of flood evacuation programmes. Thus, our results are applicable to those types of adaptive measures that are undertaken either simultaneously with emissions or ex-post.[4]

Ebert and Welsch (2012) find that when countries undertake adaptation and emissions simultaneously, adaptation alters the effective damage function such that the emission strategies of countries may be either strategic substitutes or strategic complements depending on the shape of the effective damage function. Eisenack and Kähler (2012) build on this result and show that, when one country acts as a Stackelberg leader and the follower has a positively sloped best response function, the leader has an incentive to unilaterally mitigate emissions leading to higher global welfare. By contrast, we study the free-riding incentives of individual countries from a given coalition where all coalition members jointly mitigate emissions. Moreover, to ensure that our results are not driven by specific non-standard assumptions about the properties of the effective damage function, we use the standard framework used in this literature where pollution damage is quadratic in emissions. We obtain emission strategies that are strategic substitutes, in line with the standard result in the literature on transboundary pollution games. This facilitates comparison of our results to the existing literature examining free-riding incentives from international environmental agreements.

A related paper by de Bruin *et al.* (2011) explicitly models coalition formation in the presence of adaptation. They present a calibrated model of climate change which provides numerical results about the stability of coalitions for two different levels of adaptation (the levels pertaining to the non-cooperative equilibrium and the cooperative equilibrium), assuming sequential decisions about adaptation and mitigation, and a damage function that is linear in emissions. By contrast, our aim is to determine the impact of a change in the equilibrium adaptation level following a change in adaptation technology. Furthermore, in our framework, decisions about adaptation and mitigation are simultaneous, the damage from pollution is strictly convex and the results are derived analytically.

In our analysis, we consider an exogenous decrease in the marginal cost of adaptation. This allows us to focus on the impact of the arrival of a new technology and abstract from the game of investment in R&D to invent the new technology. The game we consider can be viewed as a second stage of a two stage game, similar to Athanassoglou and Xepapadeas (2012), where in an initial phase countries invest in their technologies. Such a change in technology choice can be, for example, the result of an international agreement to increase investment in technologies, as discussed in Barrett (2006) and Hoel and de Zeeuw (2010). The policy relevance of such a scenario is broadened in light of 'technology transfer' programmes funded by international organizations such as the UNFCCC to ensure that innovative adaptation technologies become accessible globally (see, for example, Biagini *et al.* 2014).[5]

We proceed as follows. Section 2 presents the model. Section 3 characterizes the equilibrium of the model. Section 4 presents the effects of increasing the efficiency of adaptation technology on countries' free-riding incentives. Section 5 provides a numerical example. Section 6 provides concluding remarks.

2 The model

Let $N = \{1,...,n\}$ denote the set of all countries, with $n \geq 3$. Countries are assumed to be identical. The transboundary pollution problem has two stages.

Stage 1

Each country decides whether to be a member of a given coalition structure within which members set their emission levels cooperatively. Our objective is to examine how the free-riding incentive of an individual country is affected by increasing the efficiency of adaptation. We define the free-riding incentive to be the negative of the internal stability criterion, as used in d'Aspremont *et al.* (1983). The internal stability criterion is denoted by the difference between the welfare of an individual country from being a member of a given coalition and the welfare of the country if it were to unilaterally leave the coalition. This concept is extensively used in the IEA literature (see, for example, Barrett 1994; Rubio and Ulph 2006, and others). We use it in this chapter to facilitate comparison of our results to the existing literature.[6]

Stage 2

In stage 2, each country implements its emission and adaptation strategies simultaneously. We assume that a by-product of production activities of each country is the emission of a global pollutant. Country i emits $e_i \geq 0$ units of the pollutant with the aggregate emissions denoted by $E = \sum_{i=1}^{n} e_i$. Let $B(e_i)$ represent the benefit to country i from its own emissions as follows:

$$B(e_i) \equiv e_i \left(\alpha - \beta \frac{e_i}{2} \right) \tag{1}$$

with $\alpha > 0$ and $\beta > 0$. We have $B''(e_i) < 0$ and $B'(e_i) > 0$ for all $e_i < \bar{e} \equiv \dfrac{\alpha}{\beta}$.

Each country can spend resources on adaptation to avoid the damage from pollution. The level of adaptation chosen by country i is denoted by a_i.

Let $D(E, a_i)$ represent the damage to country i from pollution as follows:

$$D(E, a_i) \equiv Max \left\{ 0, \frac{\omega}{2} E^2 - a_i E \right\} \tag{2}$$

with $\omega > 0$.[7]

The damage may be nil even when the emissions are positive.[8] This happens when adaptation is large enough. Throughout the chapter we shall focus on the case where the damage is positive, that is, the equilibrium level of adaptation undertaken is not large enough to fully eliminate the negative impact of emissions. Assumption 1, given below, provides the exact condition regarding parameter values under which damage is positive in equilibrium.

The damage function, as given by (2), when positive, captures two features pertaining to climate change. First, the damage is strictly convex in global emissions. Second, the marginal damage from emissions, $\dfrac{\partial D(E,a_i)}{\partial E} = \omega E - a_i$,

is decreasing in the level of adaptation.[9] We also have that $\dfrac{\partial D(E,a_i)}{\partial a_i} = -E < 0$

for all $E > 0$, that is, pollution damage faced by country i is decreasing in the level of country i's adaptation. Adaptation is, thus, modelled as a private good to each country while mitigation is a global public good. Therefore, a_i reduces the damage of country i only. This is in line with real examples of adaptive measures currently being undertaken by different countries, as mentioned earlier, such as flood evacuation schemes and construction of levees.

From (2), it also follows that $\dfrac{\partial^2 D(E,a_i)}{\partial E \partial a_i} = \dfrac{\partial^2 D(E,a_i)}{\partial a_i \partial E} = -1$. This implies that

the marginal benefit of adaptation is increasing in the global emission level, E.

Let $C(a_i)$ represent the cost of adaptation of country i as follows:

$$C(a_i) \equiv \frac{c}{2}a_i^2 \tag{3}$$

where $c > 0$. Our modelling of adaptation in (2) and (3) is in line with Tulkens and van Steenberghe (2009) who consider the full cost minimization problem faced by countries in the presence of both mitigation and adaptation. The cost function, (3), reflects the fact that undertaking adaptive measures is indeed costly in reality (see Le Goulven 2008).[10] We also assume that the cost of adaptation is strictly convex and increasing in a_i, in line with de Bruin *et al.* (2011) and Zehaie (2009). This reflects that some types of adaptation are associated with an increasing marginal cost. For example, starting with those stretches of the coast that are easiest to protect, elongating levees implies incurring increasing physical difficulties of protecting more irregularly shaped coastlines and opportunity costs of protection, such as destruction of landscape/beaches or economic costs of uprooting fishing villages.[11]

Social welfare of each country is assumed to be given by the following:

$$W(E,a_i) \equiv B(e_i) - D(E,a_i) - C(a_i) \tag{4}$$

where $B(e_i)$, $D(E,a_i)$ and $C(a_i)$ are given by (1), (2), and (3) respectively.

In the non-cooperative case, the objective of country i's government, with $i = 1,...,n$, is to simultaneously choose e_i and a_i that maximize its own welfare, taking as given the emission and adaptation strategies of the other countries. That is,

$$\max_{e_i,a_i} W(E,a_i) \tag{5}$$

where $W(E,a_i)$ is given by (4).[12]
In the fully cooperative case, the countries simultaneously choose e_i and a_i that maximize joint welfare. That is,

$$\max_{e_i,a_i} \sum_{i=1}^{n} W(E,a_i). \tag{6}$$

The (cooperative and non-cooperative) equilibrium level of adaptation is given by

$$a_i = \frac{E}{c}. \tag{7}$$

From (2), it follows that

$$D(E,a_i) = Max\left\{0, \frac{\omega}{2}E^2 - \frac{E^2}{c}\right\} \tag{8}$$

Clearly when the cost of adaptation c is small enough, the full damage from emissions, as given by (2), can be neutralized (brought to zero). Since we are interested in cases where the damage from emissions is positive we add the following assumption.

Assumption 1: *We have that* $\omega > \underline{\omega} \equiv \dfrac{2}{c}$.

Assumption 1 also ensures that, in the non-cooperative equilibrium and the fully cooperative equilibrium, the marginal benefit to each country from its own emissions is non-negative, that is, $e_i < \bar{e}$ such that $B'(e_i) \geq 0$.

It can be shown that the non-cooperative equilibrium emission and welfare of each country are given by $e_{nc} \equiv \dfrac{\alpha}{\beta + n\left(\omega - \dfrac{1}{c}\right)}$ and

$$W_{nc} \equiv \frac{\left(2cn\omega - 2n + c\beta + n^2 - cn^2\omega\right)c\alpha^2}{2\left(c\beta - n + cn\omega\right)^2}$$

respectively and that the fully coopera-

tive equilibrium emission and welfare of each country are respectively given

by $e_c \equiv \dfrac{\alpha}{\beta + n^2\left(\omega - \dfrac{1}{c}\right)}$ and $W_c \equiv \dfrac{c\alpha^2}{2\left(c\beta - n^2 + cn^2\omega\right)}$. Assumption 1 ensures that

$e_{nc} \in (0,\bar{e})$, $e_c \in (0,\bar{e})$ and $\dfrac{\partial D}{\partial E} \geq 0$, as mentioned in footnote 7[13]. We note that $e_{nc} > e_c$ and $W_c > W_{nc}$ as long as Assumption 1 is satisfied.

3   The international environmental agreement

Consider the scenario where some of the countries decide to form an international environmental agreement. More specifically, let $S \subset N$ denote the coalition of countries that sign an agreement over emissions and $N \setminus S$ denote the set of countries that do not. We denote the size of coalition S by s.

We assume that the non-signatories and signatories simultaneously choose their emissions levels.[14] The coalition members jointly play as a singleton in the game, taking as given the emission strategies of the $(n-s)$ other players. Thus, the coalition maximizes the joint welfare of all its members. If we regard the coalition members jointly as a single player, the total number of players in the game is $(n-s+1)$. Each of the non-signatories plays as a singleton in the game, taking as given the strategies of the $(n-s)$ other players. Thus, each non-signatory maximizes its own welfare when choosing its emission level.

The objective of each non-signatory country i's government, with $i \in N \setminus S$, is to simultaneously choose e_i and a_i that maximize its own welfare, taking as given the emissions and adaptation strategies of the coalition S and the other non-signatories. That is,

$$\max_{e_i, a_i} W\left(\left(e_i + \sum_{j \in N \setminus (S \cup \{i\})} e_j + \sum_{k \in S} e_k\right), a_i\right) - F(s), i \in N \setminus S. \tag{9}$$

In (9), $F(s)$ represents a fixed cost of not signing the IEA that is not related to environmental costs, and is borne by each non-signatory. For example, a non-signatory may face retaliation from the signatories in the form of trade penalties such as border tax adjustments (see Carraro and Marchiori 2003, for a discussion of the literature on issue linkage in the context of IEAs) or a loss of reputation in the international political and economic forum (see Hoel and Schneider 1997; Rose and Spiegel 2009).[15] We will assume that $F(s) = F > 0$ for $s \geq 2$ and $F(s) = 0$ when $s \in \{0,1\}$. In the absence of a coalition, $s \in \{0,1\}$, the cost of not being in a coalition is nil. When a coalition exists, $s \geq 2$, the cost F is assumed to be independent of the coalition size s. This is done only for simplicity and is not crucial for the results of the chapter.

The equilibrium adaptation levels are given by:

$$a_s^* = a_{ns}^* = \frac{1}{c} E^* \tag{10}$$

where E^* is given by (18). Notice that in equilibrium, the non-signatory and signatory countries each choose the same level of adaptation. This is due to the fact that the effect of adaptation is purely local. Thus, the equilibrium level is the same for each country, regardless of whether the country is maximizing its individual welfare or the joint welfare of all signatories.

From (9), we have the following best response function of each non-signatory country:

$$
e_i = \frac{\alpha - \left(\omega - \frac{1}{c}\right)\left(\sum_{j \in N \setminus (S \cup \{i\})} e_j + \sum_{k \in S} e_k\right)}{\beta + \omega - \frac{1}{c}}, i \in N \setminus S.
\tag{11}
$$

The signatories' maximization problem is given by:

$$
\max_{\{e_i\}_{i \in S}, \{a_i\}_{i \in S}} \sum_{i \in S} W\left(\left(e_i + \sum_{k \in S \setminus \{i\}} e_k + \sum_{j \in N \setminus S} e_j\right), a_i\right)
\tag{12}
$$

This results in the following best response function of each signatory country:

$$
e_i = \frac{\alpha - s\left(\omega - \frac{1}{c}\right)\left(\sum_{j \in N \setminus S} e_j + \sum_{k \in S \setminus \{i\}} e_k\right)}{\beta + s\left(\omega - \frac{1}{c}\right)}, i \in S.
\tag{13}
$$

For all countries, non-signatories and signatories, the adaptation strategies are as given by (7).

By symmetry, let e_s denote the emissions of a representative signatory, and e_{ns} denote the emissions generated by a representative non-signatory. The sum of the emissions of the signatory and non-signatory countries, that is global emissions, is given by $E = se_s + (n-s)e_{ns}$.

The best response functions of each non-signatory and signatory country respectively can be written as:

$$
e_{ns}(e_s) = \frac{\alpha - \left(\omega - \frac{1}{c}\right)se_s}{\beta + (n-s)\left(\omega - \frac{1}{c}\right)}
\tag{14}
$$

$$
e_s(e_{ns}) = \frac{\alpha - s\left(\omega - \frac{1}{c}\right)(n-s)e_{ns}}{\beta + s^2\left(\omega - \frac{1}{c}\right)}
\tag{15}
$$

The equilibrium emission levels of each non-signatory and signatory country respectively are given by:

$$e_{ns}^* = \frac{\beta + s(s-1)\left(\omega - \dfrac{1}{c}\right)}{\beta + \left(n + s(s-1)\right)\left(\omega - \dfrac{1}{c}\right)} \frac{\alpha}{\beta} < \bar{e} \tag{16}$$

$$e_s^* = \frac{\beta - (n-s)(s-1)\left(\omega - \dfrac{1}{c}\right)}{\beta + \left(n + s(s-1)\right)\left(\omega - \dfrac{1}{c}\right)} \frac{\alpha}{\beta} < \bar{e} \tag{17}$$

We note that $e_{ns}^* > 0$, under Assumption 1.

Assumption 2: *We have that* $\omega < \bar{\omega} \equiv \dfrac{1}{2}\omega + \dfrac{\beta}{(n-s)(s-1)}$.

Assumption 2 ensures that $e_s^* > 0$, as shown by (17).

The equilibrium level of total emissions is given by:

$$E^* = \frac{n\alpha}{\beta + \left(n + s(s-1)\right)\left(\omega - \dfrac{1}{c}\right)} \tag{18}$$

We note that, under Assumption 1, E^* is always positive.

The welfare of each signatory country, at the equilibrium, is given by:

$$W_s^*(s) \equiv e_s^*\left(\alpha - \beta\frac{e_s^*}{2}\right) - \left(\frac{\omega}{2}(E^*)^2 - a_s^* E^*\right) - \frac{c}{2}a_s^{*2} \tag{19}$$

$$= \frac{\alpha^2}{2} \frac{\left(\omega - \dfrac{1}{c}\right)^2 (s-1)(n-s)\left(s(1-s-n)-n\right) + \beta^2 - \beta\left(n(n-2) - 2s(s-1)\right)\left(\omega - \dfrac{1}{c}\right)}{\beta\left(\beta + (n-s+s^2)\left(\omega - \dfrac{1}{c}\right)\right)^2}$$

The welfare of each non-signatory country, at the equilibrium, is given by:

$$W_{ns}^*(s) \equiv e_{ns}^*\left(\alpha - \beta\frac{e_{ns}^*}{2}\right) - \left(\frac{\omega}{2}(E^*)^2 - a_{ns}^* E^*\right) - \frac{c}{2}a_{ns}^{*2} - F(s) \tag{20}$$

$$= \frac{\alpha^2}{2} \frac{\left(\omega-\frac{1}{c}\right)^2 s(s-1)(2n-s+s^2)+\beta^2-\beta(n(n-2)-2s(s-1))\left(\omega-\frac{1}{c}\right)}{\beta\left(\beta+(n-s+s^2)\left(\omega-\frac{1}{c}\right)\right)^2} - F(s)$$

4 Free-riding and more efficient adaptation technologies

An increase in the efficiency of adaptation technology is equivalent to a decrease in the marginal cost of adaptation, c. In the following analysis, it is useful to define the following:

$$\Phi(s) \equiv W_s^*(s) - W_{ns}^*(s-1) - F(s-1) \tag{21}$$

where $W_s^*(s)$ represents the welfare of an individual country from participating in a coalition of size s and $W_{ns}^*(s-1)$ represents the welfare of an individual country from leaving a coalition of size s.

Within our context, the incentive of a country to participate in a coalition of size $s \geq 3$ is given by:[16]

$$W_s^*(s) - W_{ns}^*(s-1) = \Phi(s) + F \tag{22}$$

$$= \frac{n^2\alpha^2\left(\omega-\frac{1}{c}\right)^2(s-1)\Psi}{2\beta\left(\left(\beta+(n-s+s^2)\left(\omega-\frac{1}{c}\right)\right)\left(\beta+\left(\omega-\frac{1}{c}\right)(-3s+n+s^2+2)\right)\right)^2} + F$$

where

$$\Psi \equiv -(n-3s+s^2)(n+s+ns-2s^2+s^3)\left(\omega-\frac{1}{c}\right)^2 \tag{23}$$

$$-\beta^2(s-3)-2\beta\left(\omega-\frac{1}{c}\right)(-n+3s+ns-4s^2+s^3-2)$$

Let

$$\hat{F}(s) \equiv -\Phi(s) \text{ for all } s = 3,...,n. \tag{24}$$

Clearly if F is large enough, that is, $F > \hat{F}(s)$, then none of the members of a coalition of size s has an incentive to free-ride. Thus the interval $[-\Phi(s), \infty)$ represents the range of fixed cost such that no coalition member finds it profitable to leave the coalition. We say that an increase in adaptation efficiency (that is, a decrease of c) reduces the incentive of a coalition member to leave a coalition of size s if $\dfrac{\partial \Phi(s)}{\partial c} < 0$. This implies that the interval $[-\Phi(s), \infty)$ expands. This holds also for the case where $s = n$, that is, the grand coalition. When $F = \hat{F}(s)$, a coalition member is just indifferent between staying in the coalition of size s or leaving the coalition. If $\dfrac{\partial \hat{F}(s)}{\partial c} > 0$ and $F = \hat{F}(s)$, then a marginal decrease in c, will result in the coalition member being strictly better off by staying in the coalition of size s than by leaving it.

In our model the signatories and non-signatories are assumed to choose their emission levels simultaneously. In this case, it has been established that the maximum size of the stable coalition is small, typically either two or three, regardless of the gains from cooperation (see, for example, Carraro and Siniscalco 1993).[17] In line with these findings, in our model, as long as $F = 0$, the largest stable coalition is of size two, regardless of the efficiency of adaptation. In order to illustrate the full effect of changes in the cost of adaptation, we, therefore, include cases with $F > 0$. With $F > 0$, it is possible to generate larger stable coalitions within this framework. In the following analysis, we first analytically show the effect of more efficient adaptation on the range of F for which the grand coalition is stable. In Section 5, we use Example 1, to further illustrate that the size of a stable IEA increases with an increase in efficiency of adaptation measures at a given value of F.

Note that Assumption 2 is satisfied for all finite values of ω when $s = n$. We postpone the analysis of cases where $s < n$, to later in the section.

4.1 The grand coalition

We now study the impact of a change in c on $\Phi(n)$, for a given ω. Recall that the larger is Φ, the smaller the incentive of a coalition member to free-ride and leave the coalition. Let $X \equiv \left(\omega - \dfrac{1}{c}\right)$. Note that from Assumption 1 we have $X > \dfrac{\omega}{2} > 0$.

Proposition 1: *The incentive of a coalition member to free-ride and leave the grand coalition, that is, the IEA that includes all countries, decreases when adaptation efficiency increases (that is, when c decreases):* $\dfrac{\partial \Phi(n)}{\partial c} < 0$.

Proof: From (22) and (23), it follows that

$$\frac{\partial\left(\Phi(n)\right)}{\partial X} = \frac{\left(z_0 + z_1 X + z_2 X^2\right)(n-1)Xn^2\alpha^2}{\left(\beta + Xn^2\right)^2\left(X\left(n^2 - 2n + 2\right) + \beta\right)^3}$$

with

$$z_0 \equiv \beta^2\left(3 - n\right) \tag{25}$$

$$z_1 \equiv 2\beta\left(n^2\left(3 - n\right) - 3(n-1)\right) \tag{26}$$

$$z_2 \equiv n^4\left(3 - n\right) - 2(n-1)\left(-2n + 3n^2 + 2\right) \tag{27}$$

From $(25)-(27)$, we have $z_0 \leq 0, z_1 < 0$ and $z_2 < 0$ for $n \geq 3$ and therefore

$$\frac{\partial\left(\Phi(n)\right)}{\partial X} < 0.$$

This, together with the fact that X is increasing in c, yields Proposition 1   ■

Given (24), a direct implication of Proposition 1 is that a decrease in c causes a decrease in $F(n)$. That is, a more efficient adaptation technology enlarges the set of the fixed cost F under which the grand coalition is stable. Consider a decrease of c from some level c' to $c'' < c'$ (resulting from an increase in efficiency of the adaptation technology). There exists a range of F, such that the decrease in c stabilizes an otherwise unstable grand coalition.

Why does more efficient adaptation technology reduce free-riding incentives? From (11) and (13), it follows that the more efficient is adaptation at reducing marginal damage from emissions, the flatter the best response function of each country in terms of emissions. That is, the lower is c, the less aggressive each country is in its emission strategy and, therefore, the lower the gap between the global emission levels under non-cooperation and under full cooperation, making it less costly to cooperate on emission strategies.

The best response functions are flatter the lower is c for the following reason. In the absence of adaptation, in response to an increase in other countries' emissions, the only option available to a given country is to decrease its own emissions. In the presence of adaptation, however, when other countries increase emissions, the given country may, instead of reducing its own emissions, decrease its own damage by increasing adaptation. The greater the efficiency of the adaptation technology, the greater the substitutability between mitigation and adaptation in response to changes in the level of others' emissions. This explains why the higher the efficiency of adaptation technology, the lower the free-riding incentives of individual countries in this transboundary pollution game.

Next, we study how the aggregate gains from cooperation change with c. Let G denote the gains from forming a coalition of size s as compared to the non-cooperative equilibrium. That is,

$$G \equiv sW_s^* + (n-s)W_{ns}^* - n\left(W_{ns}^*\big|_{s=0}\right) \tag{28}$$

$$= \frac{\Gamma(s-1)X^2n^2s\alpha^2}{2\left(\beta + (n-s+s^2)X\right)^2(\beta+nX)^2\beta} - (n-s)F$$

with $\Gamma = n(s-1)(s-n)X^2 + \beta n\left(2n-3s+s^2\right)X - \beta^2(s-2n+1)$.

In the case of the grand coalition $s = n$ we have the following.

Proposition 2: *There exists $\bar{n} > 0$ such that when $n > \bar{n}$, a marginal increase of adaptation efficiency results in an increase of the welfare gains from forming the grand coalition (that is, of size $s = n$) as compared to the non-cooperative equilibrium.*

Proof: See Appendix A.

The value of $\bar{n}$ depends on β, ω and c and may well be smaller than 3 in which case an increase in adaptation efficiency always results in an increase in welfare gains from a coalition. This happens, for example, when β is small enough. More precisely, we have the following corollary.

Corollary: *Assume $\beta \in \left(0, \bar{\beta}\right)$ where $\bar{\beta} \equiv \dfrac{6\left(\omega - \dfrac{1}{c}\right)}{\left(\sqrt{\dfrac{11}{3}} + 1\right)}$, then for all $n \geq 3$, a marginal increase in adaptation efficiency results in an increase in the gains from the formation of the grand coalition.*

Proof: See Appendix B.

Why do the gains from cooperation increase with the efficiency of adaptation? Since the cost of adaptation is convex in the level of adaptation, failing to reach a cooperative equilibrium on emissions increases the cost to each individual country through this channel. This explains why the gains from cooperation may increase as more adaptation is undertaken. This, together with the fact that more adaptation is undertaken in equilibrium the more efficient is adaptation, explains Proposition 2.

Propositions 1 and 2 give a rather optimistic message. An increase in the efficiency of adaptation technology can result in a decrease of individual countries' incentives to free-ride on a global agreement and an increase of the gains from a global agreement. Within the subset of IEA models that allow the coalition to move as a Stackelberg leader, it is well established that incentives to free-ride are small only when the gains from cooperation are negligible. See, for example, Barrett (1994) and Rubio and Ulph (2006) who show that large coalitions are stable only when the coalition-induced global welfare improvements relative to the non-cooperative outcome are small. This raises the concern that if more efficient adaptation moves the world to the region of parameters where the grand coalition becomes stable it may also simultaneously result in a decrease in the gains from cooperation. We there-fore examine if this is the case within our setting, where we use a Cournot-Nash framework, rather than a Stackelberg approach. Indeed, an increase in adaptation efficiency results in an increase in the non-cooperative equilibrium welfare as well as the cooperative equilibrium welfare. The increase of the lat-ter may well be smaller than the increase of the former, in which case we would have a decrease in the gains in welfare. We find that, in our model, as shown by Proposition 2 and the Corollary, the resulting decrease in free-riding incen-tives is not necessarily accompanied by a decrease in the gains from coopera-tion. Moreover, in the following section we present a numerical example to illustrate that when more efficient adaptation measures increase the size of a stable coalition, this may be accompanied by an increase in global welfare.

We also note that our optimistic result relies on our assumption that coun-tries undertake adaptation and emissions simultaneously. This is because, under this assumption, countries cannot use adaptation strategically to reduce their own mitigation effort at the expense of others', as they do when adaptation decisions are undertaken prior to mitigation (see Zehaie 2009). In those cases where adaptation decisions are undertaken prior to mitigation, more efficient abatement technologies may have a more pessimistic impact. As shown by Zehaie (2009) for the case of two countries, cooperation on abatement, after adaptation decisions are undertaken, reduces environmental quality thereby reducing the gains from cooperation.

4.2 Subcoalitions

The main results of this chapter, as given by Propositions 1 and 2, were shown for the grand coalition. Next, we examine the case of a coalition of countries of size $s < n$. We show that Proposition 1 extends to the case where $s \in \{3,..,n\}$. That is,

$$\frac{\partial\big(\Phi(s)\big)}{\partial c} < 0 \text{ for all } n \geq 3 \text{ and } s \in \{3,..,n\}.$$

The proof is available in Appendix D. The case where $s = 2$ needs a special treatment which is provided later. For now, we proceed with analysing the gains from cooperation for $n \geq 3$ and $s \in \{3,..,n\}$.

The algebraic expressions for the impact of a change in adaptation effi-ciency on the gains from cooperation are too cumbersome to derive analytical results. We, therefore, proceed by fixing the number of countries n to 10 and consider coalitions of size $s \in \{3,..,9\}$.

For notational convenience, let us define $P(s,X)$ as given by:

$$P(s,X) \equiv \frac{80X^3}{\beta^3}\left(s^4 - 2s^3 + 31s^2 - 5s + 200\right)$$
$$- \frac{10X^2}{\beta^2}\left(s^4 - 2s^3 + 7s^2 - 66s + 60\right)$$
$$- \frac{30X}{\beta}\left(s^2 - 3s + 20\right) - 2(19 - s).$$

For $n = 10$, it can be shown that the sign of $\dfrac{\partial G}{\partial c}$ is the opposite of the sign of $P(s,X)$. Moreover, for Assumption 2 to hold, we must have $X < \bar{X} \equiv \dfrac{\beta}{(n-s)(s-1)}$ which in the case of $n = 10$ becomes $X < \dfrac{\beta}{(10-s)(s-1)}$.

Table 11.1 provides the value of the upper bound of $\dfrac{X}{\beta}, \dfrac{\bar{X}}{\beta}$, for different values of s between 3 and 9.

In Figure 11.1, we plot $P(s,.)$ for $s \in \{3,..9\}$ with $\dfrac{X}{\beta} < \dfrac{\bar{X}}{\beta}$.

The curve with the highest maximum corresponds to the plot of $P\left(9, \dfrac{X}{\beta}\right)$ over $\left[0, \dfrac{1}{8}\right]$. The dashed curve corresponds to the plot of $P\left(3, \dfrac{X}{\beta}\right)$ over its domain $\left[0, \dfrac{1}{14}\right]$. The other curves correspond to the cases of $s = 4,..,8$.

The range of X which satisfies Assumptions 1 and 2 depends on the values of ω and β. For example, for $\beta = 1$ and $\omega = \dfrac{1}{25}$, the relevant range of X is $\dfrac{1}{50} < \dfrac{X}{\beta} < \dfrac{\bar{X}}{\beta}$. Within this range, we can observe that for all $s \in \{3,..,8\}$ we have

Table 11.1 Upper bound of $\dfrac{X}{\beta}$ as s varies

s	3	4	5	6	7	8	9
$\dfrac{X}{\beta}$	$\dfrac{1}{14}$	$\dfrac{1}{18}$	$\dfrac{1}{20}$	$\dfrac{1}{20}$	$\dfrac{1}{18}$	$\dfrac{1}{14}$	$\dfrac{1}{8}$

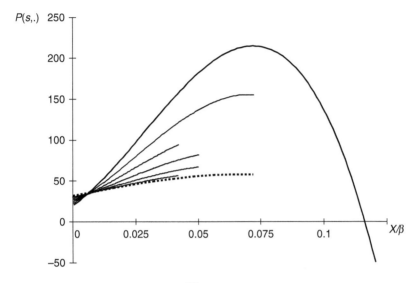

Figure 11.1 P(s,.) as a function of $\dfrac{X}{\beta}$

$P(s,X) > 0$ and therefore, $\dfrac{\partial G}{\partial c} < 0$, that is, an increase in adaptation efficiency increases the gains from the formation of a coalition. This is also true for $s = 9$ when X does not exceed a certain threshold. A similar conclusion can be reached if we use other values of n, β and ω.

For completeness, we examine the case where $s = 2$ and determine how the incentive of a coalition member to leave the coalition evolves as c changes: $\dfrac{\partial \Phi(2)}{\partial c}$.

Proposition 3: *The incentive of a coalition member to free-ride and leave a coalition of size 2, that is, the IEA that consists of two countries,*

(i) *increases when adaptation efficiency increases (that is, $\dfrac{\partial \Phi(2)}{\partial c} > 0$) if either*

   $n > 3$, *or* $n = 3$ *and* $\dfrac{1}{c} > \omega - \dfrac{1}{4}\beta\left(\sqrt{5} + 1\right)$.

(ii) *decreases when adaptation efficiency increases if $n = 3$ and*

   $\dfrac{1}{c} < \omega - \dfrac{1}{4}\beta\left(\sqrt{5} + 1\right)$.

Proof: See Appendix C.

For $n > 3$, or when $n = 3$ and c is small enough, the impact of an increase in adaptation efficiency contrasts in the case of a coalition of size 2 with the case of larger coalitions. While this may appear to be a pessimistic outcome, its relevance is mitigated by the fact that the sign of $W_s^*(2) - W_{ns}^*(1) = \Phi(2)$ is always positive. Even if the incentive to stay in a size 2 coalition diminishes when c decreases, it is always in the best interest of a coalition member to stay in the coalition.

The approach to determine the sign of $\dfrac{\partial G}{\partial c}$ for the case $s \in \{3,..,9\}$ can be repeated for $s = 2$ and it yields $\dfrac{\partial G}{\partial c} < 0$ for $s = 2$.

5   Numerical example

Thus far we have focused on the free-riding incentives of individual countries from an existing IEA. In this section, we derive the internally and externally[18] stable coalition size, s^*, for different values of c. As mentioned earlier, it can be shown analytically that for $F = 0$, the largest stable coalition is of size 2 regardless of the value of c. For $F > 0$, it is possible to have larger stable coalitions. In order to illustrate the main result, we use Example 1: $\alpha = 2$, $\beta = 20$, $n = 10$, $\omega = 1$ and $F = 0.05$. We note that Assumptions 1 and 2 are satisfied for these parameter values.

Table 11.2 shows that as the adaptation technology becomes more efficient, as denoted by lower values of c, larger coalitions become internally and externally stable. This is in line with our main finding that more effective adaptation technologies decrease the free-riding incentives of countries, as reported in the previous section. Table 11.2 also shows that when a more effective adaptation technology does stabilize a larger coalition the gains from cooperation, G, increase and total emissions, E^*, decrease.

6   Concluding remarks

According to *The Economist* (27 November 2010),

> the green pressure groups and politicians who have driven the debate on climate change have often been loth to see attention paid to adaptation, on the ground that the more people thought about it, the less motivated they would be to push ahead with emissions reduction.

Table 11.2 Stable coalition size as c varies

c	2:3	2:37	2:5	3	4	7
S^*	10	8	7	6	5	4
G	1:028	0:84	0:745	0:676	0:572	0:414
E^*	0:261	0:344	0:391	0:428	0:471	0:515

We show that an increase in the efficiency of adaptation technology may result in a reduction of individual countries' incentives to free-ride on an IEA and an increase in the gains from forming the IEA. Therefore, the concern of environmentalists with adaptation is partially mitigated.

The incentives to free-ride on an IEA may decrease in the presence of adaptation. We show that the more efficient is adaptation at reducing marginal damage from emissions, the flatter the best response functions of each country in terms of emissions. This reduces the levels of global emissions in the non-cooperative equilibrium, making it less costly to cooperate on emission strategies. This is because, when other countries increase emissions, each individual country may, instead of reducing its own emissions, decrease its own damage by increasing adaptation. However, since the cost of adaptation is convex in the level of adaptation, failing to reach a cooperative equilibrium on emissions increases the cost to each individual country through this channel. This explains why the gains from cooperation increase as more adaptation is undertaken.

In the current chapter, we have made a few simplifying assumptions in order to illustrate the main insights as clearly as possible. Relaxing these may generate further insights, which is left for future work. For example, in this chapter, we have analysed the case of identical countries. In reality, different regions are vulnerable to different degrees to the effects of climate change and will therefore undertake different amounts/types of adaptation. For example, Southern Europe is expected to be affected more than Northern Europe by climate change. Therefore, allowing for asymmetries across countries would be a relevant extension. Also, this chapter assumes that the benefits and costs of adaptation and mitigation are contemporaneous, which may not be representative of certain adaptive measures. It would be useful to set up a dynamic model to understand the intertemporal tradeoffs arising from a relaxation of this assumption. For example, Zehaie (2009) has shown that when investment in adaptation occurs before the level of emissions is decided, adaptation has strategic effects. It would be interesting to investigate how these strategic effects influence participation in IEAs. Another interesting and policy relevant extension of the model would be to investigate how local investments to reduce the local (not global) value of c can be used strategically, and whether this induces participation in IEAs.

Appendices

Appendix A: Proof of Proposition 2

For $s = n$, we have:

$$G = \frac{(n-1)^2 n^3 \alpha^2 X^2}{2(\beta + n^2 X)(\beta + nX)^2}$$

We have that

$$\frac{\partial G}{\partial X} = \frac{1}{2} \frac{Xn^3\alpha^2(n-1)^2 n^3}{(Xn^2+\beta)^2(\beta+Xn)^3}(X-X_1)(X_2-X)$$

where $X_1 = -\frac{1}{2n}\beta\left(\sqrt{\frac{n+8}{n}}-1\right) < 0$ and $X_2 = \frac{1}{2n}\beta\left(\sqrt{\frac{n+8}{n}}+1\right) > 0$. Therefore, we have the following:

$$\frac{\partial G}{\partial X} > 0 \text{ iff } X < X_2$$

Since $X \equiv \left(\omega - \frac{1}{c}\right)$ we have $\dfrac{\partial G}{\partial c} = \dfrac{\partial G}{\partial X}\dfrac{\partial X}{\partial c} = \dfrac{1}{c^2}\dfrac{\partial G}{\partial X}$ and therefore:

$$\frac{\partial G}{\partial c} < 0 \text{ iff } \frac{\omega - \dfrac{1}{c}}{\beta} > \frac{1}{2n}\left(\sqrt{\frac{n+8}{n}}+1\right)$$

This along with the fact that $L(n) \equiv \dfrac{1}{2n}\left(\sqrt{\dfrac{n+8}{n}}+1\right)$ is monotonically decreasing in n and $\lim\limits_{n\to\infty} L(n) = 0$ implies that there exists $\bar{n}$ such that for any $n > \bar{n}$ we have $\dfrac{\omega - \dfrac{1}{c}}{\beta} > L(n)$ and therefore $\dfrac{\partial G}{\partial c} < 0$. ∎

Appendix B: Proof of corollary

This follows from the fact that $L(n) \equiv \dfrac{1}{2n}\left(\sqrt{\dfrac{n+8}{n}}+1\right)$ is monotonically decreasing in n and therefore if $\dfrac{\left(\omega - \dfrac{1}{c}\right)}{\beta} > L(3) = \dfrac{1}{6}\left(\sqrt{\dfrac{11}{3}}+1\right)$ (or $\beta < \bar{\beta}$) we necessarily have $\dfrac{\left(\omega - \dfrac{1}{c}\right)}{\beta} > L(n) = \dfrac{1}{2n}\left(\sqrt{\dfrac{n+8}{n}}+1\right)$ for all $n \geq 3$. This, along with the fact that $\dfrac{\partial G}{\partial c} = \dfrac{\partial G}{\partial X}\dfrac{\partial X}{\partial c} = \dfrac{1}{c^2}\dfrac{\partial G}{\partial X}$ gives $\dfrac{\partial G}{\partial c} < 0$ for all $n \geq 3$. ∎

Appendix C: Proof of Proposition 3

We have

$$\frac{\partial \Phi(2)}{\partial X} = \frac{\Omega X n^2 \alpha^2}{(2X + Xn + \beta)^3 (Xn + \beta)^3}$$

where

$$\Omega \equiv X^3\left(-5n^3 + 8n + 8\right) + X^2\beta\left(-9n^2 + 12n + 16\right) + X\beta^2\left(12 - 3n\right) + \beta^3$$

The sign of $\frac{\partial \Phi(2)}{\partial X}$ is the same as that of Ω. For convenience we use the notation $\Omega(n)$ to specifically analyse Ω as a function of n. We first note that

$$\Omega'(n) = X\left(12X\beta - 18Xn\beta + 8X^2 - 3\beta^2 - 15X^2n^2\right)$$

is strictly decreasing in n, implying the following:

$$\Omega'(n) < \Omega'(2) = -\left(24X\beta + 52X^2 + 3\beta^2\right)X < 0 \text{ for } n > 2$$

Therefore, the function $\Omega(n)$ is a strictly decreasing function of n. The evaluation of $\Omega(2)$ gives the following:

$$\Omega(2) = (4X + \beta)\left(2X\beta - 4X^2 + \beta^2\right)$$

or

$$\Omega(2) = 4(4X + \beta)\left(\frac{1}{4}\beta\left(\sqrt{5} + 1\right) - X\right)\left(X + \frac{1}{4}\beta\left(\sqrt{5} - 1\right)\right)$$

Therefore,

$$\Omega(2) > 0 \text{ iff } X < \hat{X} \equiv \frac{1}{4}\beta\left(\sqrt{5} + 1\right).$$

From Assumption 2, we have $X < \dfrac{\beta}{n-2}$. Moreover, for $n > 3$, we have $\dfrac{\beta}{n-2} < \hat{X}$.

This implies that, for $n > 3$, $X < \hat{X}$ and therefore, $\dfrac{\partial \Phi(2)}{\partial X} > 0$. For $n = 3$, from Assumption 2, we have $X < \hat{X} < \beta$. Thus, for $X \in (0, X)$, we have $\Omega(2) > 0$, and for $X \in \left(\hat{X}, \beta\right)$, we have $\Omega(2) < 0$. That is, as long as $\omega - \dfrac{1}{c} < \dfrac{1}{4}\beta\left(\sqrt{5}+1\right)$, we have $\Omega(2) > 0$, and for $\omega - \dfrac{1}{c} > \dfrac{1}{4}\beta\left(\sqrt{5}+1\right)$, we have $\Omega(2) < 0$. ∎

Appendix D: Generalizing Proposition 1 to any $s < n$

From (22) and (23), we have that

$$\frac{\partial(\Phi(s))}{\partial X} = -Xn^2\alpha^2\left(s-1\right)\frac{z_3 X^3 + z_2\beta X^2 + z_1 3\beta^2 X + z_0}{\left(\left(n+(s-1)(s-2)\right)\left(n-s+s^2\right)X^2 + 2\beta\left(n+(s-1)^2\right)X + \beta^2\right)^3}$$

(29)

with

$$z_0 \equiv \beta^3\left(s-3\right)$$

(30)

$$z_1 \equiv \left(n(s-1)+s(s-1)(s-3)-2\right)$$

(31)

$$z_2 \equiv \left(3(s+1)n^2 + 6s\left(s^2 - 2s - 1\right)n + \left(3s^3 - 9s^2 - 4\right)(s-1)^2\right)$$

(32)

$$z_3 \equiv \left(\begin{array}{c} n\left(n\left(n(s+3)+3(s-2)\left(s(s+2)-1\right)\right)+\left(3s\left(s(s-1)-4\right)+4\right)(s-1)^2\right) \\ +s\left(s(s-2)\left(s(s-2)-1\right)-4\right)(s-1)^2 \end{array}\right)$$

(33)

From $(30)-(3)$, it follows that $z_0 \geq 0, z_1 \geq 0$, $z_2 \geq 0$, and $z_3 \geq 0$ for $s \geq 3$. The denominator in (29) is positive for $s \geq 3$. Therefore, we have that

$$\frac{\partial(\Phi(s))}{\partial X} < 0.$$

This, together with the fact that X is increasing in c, generalizes Proposition 1 for any $s < n$.

Notes

1 Acknowledgements: Hassan Benchekroun would like to acknowledge the financial support of the Canadian Social Sciences and Humanities Research Council (SSHRC) and Fonds de Recherche du Quebec – Societe et Culture (FRQSC).

Amrita Ray Chaudhuri would like to thank the Board of Regents of The University of Winnipeg for financial support.

2 A recent article (27 November 2010) in *The Economist*, entitled 'How to live with climate change: It won't be stopped, but its effects can be made less bad', captures the ongoing developments as follows:

> in the wake of the Copenhagen summit, there is a growing acceptance that the effort to avert serious climate change has run out of steam... Acceptance, however, does not mean inaction. Since the beginning of time, creatures have adapted to changes in their environment.

3 Indeed, it seems that countries are realizing the importance of including adaptation in international negotiations, given the 'Cancun Adaptation Fund' that was established at the COP16 Meetings held at Cancun in December 2010. (UNFCCC Press Release, 11 December 2011, http://unfccc.int/.les/press/news_room/press_releases_and_advisories/application/pdf/pr_20101211_cop16_closing.pdf).

4 Given the wide variety of adaptive measures, the existing literature is divided on the issue of the timing of adaptation in relation to mitigation. Zehaie (2009) shows that if adaptation is undertaken before mitigation, adaptation can be used strategically by each country to reduce its own mitigation efforts and increase those of others. Zehaie (2009) also shows that this strategic effect of adaptation disappears if either adaptation and mitigation are undertaken simultaneously or if adaptation occurs after mitigation.

5 According to the UNFCCC, and part of the Cancun Adaptation Fund, 'the developed country Parties and other developed Parties included in Annex II shall take all practicable steps to promote, facilitate and finance, as appropriate, the transfer of, or access to, environmentally sound technologies and know-how to other Parties'. http://unfccc.int/cooperation_and_support/technology/items/1126.php.

6 We note that there exist other approaches to analysing coalition stability. For example, Breton *et al.* (2010) model the dynamic aspect of coalition formation using an evolutionary process to determine which countries join and/or leave the coalition over time. Another approach examines the 'farsighted' stability criterion that allows for a more sophisticated behaviour of players. In deciding whether to join or leave a coalition, a player considers the implication of her decision on other players' decision to leave or stay in a coalition (see, for example, Diamantoudi and Sartzetakis 2002; Osmani and Tol 2009; de Zeeuw 2008).

7 Other papers in the game-theoretic literature on IEAs to use a damage function that is quadratic in emissions include Diamantoudi and Sartzetakis (2006), Biancardi and Villani (2010) and Rubio and Ulph (2006).

8 We thank an anonymous referee for pointing this out.

9 For the interior solution levels of emissions and adaptation derived below, we have $\frac{\partial D}{\partial E} \leq 0$. Please refer to Assumption 1, as specified at the end of this section. As long as Assumption 1 is satisfied, it can be shown that $\frac{\partial D}{\partial E} \leq 0$

10 According to Le Goulven (2008), existing adaptation funds include the following. The UNFCCC pledged $50 million through the SPA (Strategic Priority: Piloting an Operational Approach to Adaptation) in 2001. The UNFCCC pledged $165 million through the LDCF (Least Developed Countries Fund) in 2001. The UNFCCC pledged $65 million through the SCCF (Special Climate Change Fund) in 2001. Also in 2001, the Kyoto Protocol set up an Adaptation Fund which pledged $160–950 million by 2012. In 2008, the World Bank's Pilot Program for Climate Resilience under the Strategic Climate Fund pledged $500 million. In 2007, the European Commission pledged EUR

50 million under the Global Climate Change Alliance and the German Ministry of the Environment pledged EUR 60 million.

11 An alternative justification provided by Zehaie (2009) is the following: 'Since self-protection decreases exposure to pollution but does not solve the problem of pollution, it is reasonable to assume that the opportunities to substitute self-protection for abatement gradually deteriorate when the level of self-protection increases.'

12 Given (2), the tradeoff facing each country when choosing its levels of emission, e_i, and adaptation, a_i, draws a parallel with the literature on multiple pollutants in the context of climate change, where some pollutants such as CO_2 increase global warming and others such as SO_2 have a cooling effect (see, for example, Legras and Zaccour 2011).

13 In fact, we have $e_{nc} \in (0, \bar{e})$, $e_c \in (0, \bar{e})$ and $\dfrac{\partial D}{\partial E} \geq 0$ as long as $\omega > \dfrac{1}{c}$, which is a less restrictive condition than Assumption 1.

14 Therefore, adaptation cannot be used strategically to induce countries to reduce emissions or participate in the agreement.

15 Rose and Speigel (2009) apply the idea of reputation spillovers to the relationship between environmental interaction and international exchange. In a model of international asset exchange, they show that countries that participate more in IEAs also experience better economic outcomes, in both theory and practice.

16 For $s = 2$ we have $\Phi(2) = W_s^*(2) - W_{ns}^*(1)$ since $F(1) = 0$. The analysis of this case is postponed to section 4.2.

17 As noted by Diamantoudi and Sartzetakis (2006), when coalition members and non-members decide on their emission strategies simultaneously, that is, under the Nash-Cournot setup, and costs and benefits from emissions are quadratic, the stable coalition size cannot exceed two (see, for example, De Cara and Rotillon 2001; Finus and Rundshagen 2001; and Rubio and Casino 2001).

References

Agrawala, S., Bosello, F., Carraro, C., de Cian, E. and Lanzi, E. (2011), 'Adapting to climate change: costs, benefits, and modelling approaches', *International Review of Environmental and Resource Economics*, 5: 245–284.

d'Aspremont, C. A., Jacquemin, J., Gabszeweiz, J. and Weymark, J. A. (1983), 'On the stability of collusive price leadership', *Canadian Journal of Economics*, 16: 17–25.

Athanassoglou, S. and Xepapadeas, A. (2012), 'Pollution control with uncertain stock dynamics: when, and how, to be precautious', *Journal of Environmental Economics and Management*, 63(3): 304–320.

Barrett, S. (1994), 'Self-enforcing international environmental agreements', *Oxford Economic Papers*, 46: 878–894.

Barrett, S. (2005), 'The theory of international environmental agreements', in K.-G. Mäler and J. Vincent (eds), *Handbook of Environmental Economics*, Vol. 3, Amsterdam: Elsevier, 1457–1516.

Barrett, S. (2006), 'Climate treaties and "breakthrough" technologies', *American Economic Review*, 96: 22–25.

Biagini, B., Kuhl, L., Gallagher, K. S. and Ortiz, C. (2014), 'Technology transfer for adaptation', *Nature Climate Change*, 4: 828–834.

Biancardi, M. and Villani, G. (2010), 'International environmental agreements with asymmetric countries', *Computational Economics*, 36(1): 69–92.

Bosello, F., Carraro, C. and de Cian, E. (2011), 'Adaptation can help mitigation: an integrated approach to post-2012 climate policy', *Working Papers 2011.69, Fondazione Eni Enrico Mattei*.

Breton, M., Sbragia, L. and Zaccour, G. (2010), 'A dynamic model for international environmental agreements', *Environmental and Resource Economics*, 45: 25–48.

de Bruin, K., Dellink, R. and Tol, R. (2009), 'AD-DICE: an implementation of adaptation in the DICE model', *Climate Change*, 95: 63–81.

de Bruin, K., Weikard, H.-P. and Dellink, R. (2011), 'The role of proactive adaptation in international climate change mitigation agreements', *CERE Working Paper 2011:9*, Centre for Environmental and Resource Economics (CERE), Umeå University, Sweden.

de Cara, S. and Rotillon, G. (2001), 'Multi greenhouse gas international agreements', Mimeo.

Carraro, C. and Marchiori, C. (2003), 'Endogenous strategic issue linkage in international negotiations', *Working Papers 2003.40, Fondazione Eni Enrico Mattei*.

Carraro, C. and Siniscalco, D. (1993), 'Strategies for the international protection of the environment', *Journal of Public Economics*, 52: 309–328.

Diamantoudi, E. and Sartzetakis, E. S. (2002), 'International environmental agreements: the role of foresight', *CORE Discussion Papers 2002061*.

Diamantoudi, E. and Sartzetakis, E. S. (2006), 'Stable international environmental agreements: an analytical approach', *Journal of Public Economic Theory*, 8(2): 247–263.

Ebert, U. and Welsch, H. (2012), 'Adaptation and mitigation in global pollution problems: economic impacts of productivity, sensitivity, and adaptive capacity', *Environmental and Resource Economics*, 52: 49–64.

The Economist (2010), 'How to live with climate change', 27 November. www.economist.com/node/17575027.

Eisenack, K. and Kähler, L. (2012), 'Unilateral emission reductions can lead to Pareto improvements when adaptation to damages is possible', *Oldenburg Discussion Papers in Economics V-344-12*.

El-Sayed, A. and Rubio, S. J. (2011), 'Self-enforcing international environmental agreements with R&D spillovers', Mimeo, University of Valencia.

Finus, M. and Rundshagen, B. (2001), 'Endogenous coalition formation in a global pollution control', *Working Paper, FEEM, Nota di Lavoro 43.2001*.

Hoel, M. and Schneider, K. (1997), 'Incentives to participate in an international environmental agreement', *Environmental and Resource Economics*, 9: 153–170.

Hoel, M. and de Zeeuw, A. (2010), 'Can a focus on breakthrough technologies improve the performance of international environmental agreements?' *Environmental and Resource Economics*, 47: 395–406.

Ingham, A., Ma, J. and Ulph, A. (2005), 'Can adaptation and mitigation be complements?', *Discussion Paper 79, Tyndall Centre for Climate Change Research*.

Jørgensen, S., Martín-Herrán, G. and Zaccour, G. (2010), 'Dynamic games in the economics and management of pollution', *Environmental Modeling and Assessment*, 15: 433–467.

Le Goulven, K. (2008), 'Financing mechanisms for adaptation', *Commission on Climate Change and Development*.

Legras, S. and Zaccour, G. (2011), 'Temporal flexibility of permit trading when pollutants are correlated', *Automatica*, 47: 909–919.

Nordhaus, W. and Yang, Z. (1996), 'A regional dynamic general-equilibrium model of alternative climate-change strategies', *American Economic Review*, 86: 741–765.

Osmani, D. and Tol, R. (2009), 'Toward farsightedly stable international environmental agreements', *Journal of Public Economic Theory*, 11: 455–492.

Rose, A. K. and Spiegel, M. M. (2009), 'Noneconomic engagement and international exchange: the case of environmental treaties', *Journal of Money, Credit and Banking*, 41: 337–363.

Rubio, J. S. and Casino, B. (2001), 'International cooperation in pollution control', *Working Paper, Instituto Valenciano de Investigaciones Económicas.*

Rubio, S. J. and Ulph, A. (2006), 'Self-enforcing international environmental agreements revisited', *Oxford Economic Papers*, 58: 233–263.

Tol, R. (2005), 'Adaptation and mitigation: trade-offs in substance and methods', *Environmental Science and Policy*, 8: 572–578.

Tulkens, H. and van Steenberghe, V. (2009), 'Mitigation, adaptation, suffering: in search of the right mix in the face of climate change', *Working Papers 2009.79, Fondazione Eni Enrico Mattei.*

de Zeeuw, A. (2008), 'Dynamic effects on the stability of international environmental agreements', *Journal of Environmental Economics and Management*, 55(2): 163–174.

Zehaie, F. (2009), 'The timing and strategic role of self-protection', *Environmental and Resource Economics*, 44: 337–350.

12 Cooperation in environmental standards when abatement technology differs

Merve Kumaş, M. Özgür Kayalıca and Gülgün Kayakutlu

1 Introduction

As stated by the European Union (EU), most environmental problems have a transboundary nature and often a global scope, and they can only be addressed effectively through international cooperation. That is why local or global environmental problems should be overcome at international level. There are over two hundred and fifty international environmental agreements today (Mathur and Dang 2009). While multilateral environmental agreements (MEAs) try to solve environmental issues, the World Trade Organization (WTO) has been trying to liberalize international trade. The relationship between MEAs and WTO and, hence, between environment and trade has attracted many politicians and scholars worldwide.

The literature on trade and environment is vast. The pollution generated in one region can be carried to other regions through international trade and it may have global effect by creating transboundary externalities. Copeland and Taylor (1995) analyse the effect of free trade on environmental policies, pollution level and welfare by considering transboundary pollution. They find that if the income-induced differences between countries are sufficiently high, then trade worsens the global pollution level. Hatzipanayotou *et al.* (2008) show that an increase in one country's pollution spillover effect increases the pollution level and decreases the welfare level in this country but leads the opposite situation in the rival country. Therefore, an equal increase in spillover effects in both countries can result in less pollution and better welfare for both countries. Kayalica and Kayalica (2005) also investigate the transboundary pollution externalities under the consumption tax and the import tariff. They find that higher marginal disutility of pollution or less efficient firms make governments apply higher consumption tax and lower tariff rates. On the other hand, higher demand leads lower consumption tax and higher tariff rates.

Both the local and transboundary pollutions lead governments to apply environmental regulations to decrease the negative environmental effect on welfare. Facing strict environmental policies may make firms adapt new solutions in their production activities (e.g. shifting the production into more green products, improving the production technology to generate less pollution, changing the plant location). The literature on environmental regulations and technology has very important studies, most of which take the technology level as endogenous and thus see the impact of regulations on the change of technology level. Environmental regulations can affect the market structure by changing the cost of production. Since the cost of productions are associated with the profits of firms, they can affect incentives for the entry and exit of firms. Therefore, when they have a new abatement technology, incumbent firms may have a request for increasing environmental regulation to make their rivals more costly. In this way, they can reduce their own costs and have a competitive advantage while their rivals have a barrier to entry (Millimet *et al.* 2009). In their study, Mendez and Trelles (2000) assert that cooperation between countries increases global welfare and decreases global pollution level. In addition, they show that in an abatement market in which one country offers to pay another country for abatement, global welfare and abatement increase if the technologically superior country acts as a buyer and the difference in technological efficiencies of countries is high.

There are also other studies that focus on the effect of government incentives, such as tax and subsidies on R&D. For example, Carraro and Soubeyran (1993), Carraro and Siniscalco (1992) and Ulph and Ulph (2007) are some of them. Montero (2002) develops a two-country model to search the R&D incentives under four policy instruments; emission standards, performance standards, tradable permits and auctioned permits. The results show that standards can lead to higher incentives than permits. Moreover, Poyago-Theotoky (2007) compares independent environmental R&D and R&D cartel under emission tax. He finds that if there is large environmental damage and efficient R&D, R&D cartel is superior to the independent R&D in terms of emission reduction and welfare. Similarly, Stenbacka and Tombak (1998) show that under the subsidy policy, R&D cooperation leads to higher social welfare than R&D competition.

Millimet (2003) finds that if the pollution abatement intensity is low, the number of small establishments increases in industries with high state environmental abatement cost and decreases in industries with low state environmental abatement cost. This situation is opposite in the case of high pollution abatement intensity. The number of large establishments rises if there is high state environmental abatement cost and falls if there is low state environmental abatement cost. He states that the optimal size of establishments increases in industries with the high pollution abatement intensity because the large establishments may choose to invest in abatement technology to deal with the pollution restriction. On the other hand, when there is low state environmental abatement cost, small firms may not find it profitable to invest in any abatement technology because they can benefit from their smaller size in the face of pollution restriction.

In this chapter, we develop a model in which there are two countries, labelled A and B, and each country has one local firm. The local firm in each country produces a homogeneous product and it serves both domestic and foreign markets. It is assumed that production activities generate pollution and there is transboundary (cross-border) pollution between the countries. It is also assumed that the firms differ from each other in terms of their abatement technology level (i.e. one of the firms has inferior environmental technology). Considering intra-industry trade and allowing transboundary pollution, we aim to observe the impact of asymmetric technology levels on the optimal environmental policies and welfare for non-cooperative and cooperative solutions.

The chapter is organized as follows. Section 2 introduces the model, and section 3 presents optimal pollution quotas under non-cooperative, cooperative and uniform scenarios. Section 4 introduces comparative statistics for specific parameters. Finally, section 5 discusses the results and makes some concluding remarks.

2   The model

In our model, there are two countries, labelled A and B. Each country has one domestic firm. The domestic firms produce a homogeneous product and they serve both domestic markets and foreign markets. It is assumed that there is an intra-industry trade between the countries. There is a two-stage game in which governments impose environmental policy then firms determine their production level simultaneously based on the given policies. The inverse demand functions for the good are given by[1]

$$pa = \alpha - b.Da \qquad (1)$$

$$pb = \alpha - b.Db \qquad (2)$$

where pa and pb are the prices in each country. The firm in country A produces qa for the consumption of local market and qax for export to country B. Similarly, the firm in country B produces qb for the consumption of local market and qbx for export to country A. Hence, the total demands of countries consist of the demand for local production and the demand for exported product. These are given by

$$Da = qa + qbx \qquad (3)$$

$$Db = qb + qax \qquad (4)$$

Profit of each firm is given by π

$$\pi a = (pa - \kappa a).qa + (pb - \kappa a).qax \qquad (5)$$

$$\pi b = (pb - \kappa b).qb + (pa - \kappa b).qbx \qquad (6)$$

where *pa* and *pb* are the constant marginal (average) cost of the domestic firms in country A and B. These are given by

$$\kappa a = c + \mu a (\theta a - za) \tag{7}$$

$$\kappa b = c + \mu b (\theta b - zb) \tag{8}$$

where, c is the constant per unit cost determined by technological and factor market conditions and it is assumed to be equal for both firms. θa and θb are the gross pollution before abatement; *za* and *zb* are the maximum quantity of pollution per unit of output that the firms are allowed to emit into the atmosphere. μa and μb is the constant unit abatement cost. It implies that the higher (lower) the μ the less (more) efficient the firm and generates more (less) pollution.

The firms are assumed to behave in a Cournot–Nash fashion. The first order profit maximizing conditions are found as

$$b.qa = pa - \kappa a \quad b.qax = pb - \kappa a \tag{9}$$

$$b.qb = pb - \kappa b \quad b.qbx = pa - \kappa b \tag{10}$$

Using (1) (2) and (9) (10) and when the closed form solutions are solved, we find the output and price as

$$qa = qax = \frac{\alpha - 2\kappa a + \kappa b}{3b} \tag{11}$$

$$qb = qbx = \frac{\alpha - 2\kappa b + \kappa a}{3b} \tag{12}$$

$$pa = pb = \frac{\alpha + \kappa a + \kappa b}{3} \tag{13}$$

Differentiating equation (11) and (12) we obtain

$$dqa = dqax = \frac{2\mu a}{3b} dza - \frac{\mu b}{3b} dzb \tag{14}$$

$$dqb = dqbx = -\frac{\mu a}{3b} dza + \frac{2\mu b}{3b} dzb \tag{15}$$

Each firm will increase (decrease) its production for both local market and foreign market when it is allowed to emit more (less) pollution; or its rival in other country is allowed to emit less (more) pollution. As expected, the firms are more sensitive to their own country's policy than the rival country's policy.

Countries can benefit from the profits generated by the domestic firm, however, they both dislike pollution. It is assumed that pollution occurs during production and there is cross border pollution between the two countries. It is also assumed that the countries are more sensitive to the pollution caused by local production than the pollution caused by foreign production.

The welfare functions of country A and B are given by Wa and Wb, respectively, as:

$$Wa = \frac{(\alpha - pa)^2}{2b} + \pi a - \phi 1.(qa + qax).za - \phi 2.(qb + qbx).zb \tag{16}$$

$$Wb = \frac{(\alpha - pb)^2}{2b} + \pi b - \phi 1.(qb + qbx).zb - \phi 2.(qa + qax).za \tag{17}$$

The welfare function of each country consists of four terms. The first term is the consumer surplus, the second term is the profit gain generated by the domestic firms, and the last two terms are the disutility of pollution generated by local production and foreign production, respectively. $\phi 1$ and $\phi 2$ are the marginal disutility of pollution caused by local and foreign production and both are assumed to be constant. Pollution caused by the foreign production is the transboundary pollution. It is assumed that local pollution is more harmful than the transboundary pollution (i.e. $\phi 1 > \phi 2$).

Totally differentiating the welfare functions we get

$$9b\,dWa = A1.dza + A2.dzb \tag{18}$$

$$9b\,dWb = A3.dza + A4.dzb \tag{19}$$

where

$$A1 = (\alpha - c).(10\mu a - 6\phi 1) - 17\mu a^2.(\theta a - za) + 12\mu a.\phi 1.(\theta a - 2za) \\ + 6\mu a.\phi 2.zb + \mu b.(\theta b - zb).(7\mu a - 6\phi 1) \tag{20}$$

$$A2 = -(\alpha - c).(2\mu b + 6\phi 2) - 5\mu b^2.(\theta b - zb) + 12\mu b.\phi 2.(\theta b - 2zb) \\ + 6\mu b.\phi 1.za + \mu a.(\theta a - za).(7\mu b - 6\phi 2) \tag{21}$$

$$A3 = -(\alpha - c).(2\mu a + 6\phi 2) - 5\mu a^2.(\theta a - za) + 12\mu a.\phi 2.(\theta a - 2za) \\ + 6\mu a.\phi 1.zb + \mu b.(\theta b - zb).(7\mu a - 6\phi 2) \tag{22}$$

$$A4 = (\alpha - c)(10\mu b - 6\phi 1) - 17\mu b^2.(\theta b - zb) + 12\mu b.\phi 1.(\theta b - 2zb) \\ + 6\mu b.\phi 2.za + \mu a.(\theta a - za).(7\mu b - 6\phi 1) \tag{23}$$

A1 and A4 represent the effect of each government's environmental policy on its own welfare. A2 and A3 represent the externalities, which show the effect of one government's environmental policy on the other country's welfare.

3 The optimal environmental policies

Using the above framework we shall find the optimal policies under three different scenarios: (i) non-cooperative behaviour; (ii) cooperative behaviour; and finally (iii) uniform policy. Once we find the optimal values, we discuss and compare the differences in the optimal policies under different scenarios; and their effect on welfare for each country.

3.1 Non-cooperative environmental policies

In the first case, we consider that governments act in a non-cooperative behaviour. There is a two-stage game in which first the governments determine the pollution quota and then the domestic firms determine their output levels based on the pollution quotas taken from the first stage of the game.

To assure the concavity conditions are held, we need to show that the welfare functions of countries are concave in za and zb. In addition, we have to assure the stability condition. The condition is given by[2]

$$Wza(za).Wzb(zb) - Wza(zb).Wzb(za) > 0 \tag{24}$$

Setting A1 and A4 equal to zero, we find the countries' non-cooperative policy instruments as[3]

$$
\begin{aligned}
\mathrm{M}\, za^{N} = {} & \mu b.(24\phi 1 - 17 \mu b).[(\alpha - c).(10 \mu a - 6\phi 1) - \mu a.\theta a.(17 \mu a - 12\phi 1) \\
& - \mu b.\theta b.(7 \mu a - 6\phi 1)] + (7 \mu a \mu b - 6 \mu a \phi 2 - 6 \mu b \phi 1).[(\alpha - c).(10 \mu b - 6\phi 1) \\
& + \mu a.\theta a.(7 \mu b - 6\phi 1) - \mu b.\theta b.(17 \mu b - 12\phi 1)]
\end{aligned}
\tag{25}
$$

$$
\begin{aligned}
\mathrm{M}\, zb^{N} = {} & \mu a.(24\phi 1 - 17 \mu b).[(\alpha - c).(10 \mu b - 6\phi 1) - \mu b.\theta b.(17 \mu b - 12\phi 1) \\
& - \mu a.\theta a.(7 \mu b - 6\phi 1)] + (7 \mu a \mu b - 6 \mu a \phi 1 - 6 \mu b \phi 2).[(\alpha - c).(10 \mu a - 6\phi 1) \\
& + \mu b.\theta b.(7 \mu a - 6\phi 1) - \mu a.\theta a.(17 \mu a - 12\phi 1)]
\end{aligned}
\tag{26}
$$

Due to the excessive number of parameters and the size of equations, we need to determine appropriate simulation values for the variables given our constraints (such as positive values of price and output) and assumptions. The values should also satisfy second order conditions and stability conditions. The firm in country A is assumed to be less efficient in terms of abatement technology compared to the firm in country B. Based on this assumption, the firm in country A produces more pollution than the firm in country B does. The maximum values of the abatement cost and the level of gross pollution of firm in country B is always lower than the accepted value of the firm in country A. Therefore, the ranges of possible values are determined based on these assumptions. Table 12.1 represents the simulation values and the ranges of possible values for parameters that will be used to observe the effect of the change in parameters on the optimal policies.

Table 12.1 Simulation values and ranges for parameters

Parameters	Values	Range of values	
		Min	Max
α	15.0	14.5	16.2
b	0.3	0.25	0.45
c	2.02	2.012	2.03
θa	8.02	8.019	8.3
θb	8.01	8.009	8.019
μa	1.012	1.011	1.015
μb	1.01	1.01	1.011
$\phi 1$	1.0	0.99	1.05
$\phi 2$	0.3	0.25	0.31

3.2 Cooperative environmental policies

In this section, we examine the effect on both welfares of cooperative environmental action of the two governments. Like in the non-cooperative case, there is a two-stage game. First, the governments set their pollution quotas cooperatively; second, the firms determine their production level. The cooperative behaviour represents international cooperation to increase welfare in both countries.

Using equations (18) and (19), the welfare function of cooperative equilibrium when differentiated is shown as

$$9bdW = (A1 + A3).dza^{C} + (A2 + A4).dzb^{C} \tag{27}$$

Setting the coefficients of dza^{C} and dzb^{C} equal to zero, we find the cooperative solutions as[4,5]

$$
\begin{aligned}
N\,za^{C} = &\left(12.(\phi 1+\phi 2).(\mu a+\mu b)-28\mu a.\mu b\right).[(\alpha-c).(4\mu b-3(\phi 1+\phi 2)) \\
&+3.(\phi 1+\phi 2).(\mu a.\theta a+2\mu b.\theta b)-\mu b.(11\mu b.\theta b-7\mu a.\theta a)] \\
&-4\mu b.(12.(\phi 1+\phi 2)-11\mu b).[(\alpha-c).(3.(\phi 1+\phi 2)-4\mu a) \\
&-3.(\phi 1+\phi 2).(2\mu a.\theta a-\mu b.\theta b)+\mu a.(11\mu a.\theta a-7\mu b.\theta b)]
\end{aligned} \tag{28}
$$

$$
\begin{aligned}
N\,zb^{C} = &\left(12.(\phi 1+\phi 2).(\mu a+\mu b)-28\mu a.\mu b\right).[(\alpha-c).(4\mu a-3(\phi 1+\phi 2)) \\
&+3.(\phi 1+\phi 2).(2\mu a.\theta a+\mu b.\theta b)-\mu a.(11\mu a.\theta a-7\mu b.\theta b)] \\
&-4\mu a.(12.(\phi 1+\phi 2)-11\mu a).[(\alpha-c).(3.(\phi 1+\phi 2)-4\mu b) \\
&-3.(\phi 1+\phi 2).(2\mu b.\theta b-\mu a.\theta a)+\mu b.(11\mu b.\theta b-7\mu a.\theta a)]
\end{aligned} \tag{29}
$$

The above results shall be used later in the chapter for comparison amongst non-cooperative, cooperative and uniform solutions.

3.3   Uniform policy

In this section, we assume that the cooperative solutions are restricted to be uniform. That is, not only the governments maximize the joint welfare but also set a uniform pollution quota level. First, the governments determine their uniform pollution levels and then the firms determine their production levels.

Using the equations (18), (19) and setting za = zb = z^U, we get the welfare function of uniform equilibrium differentiated as follows:

$$9b\,dW = (A1 + A2 + A3 + A4).dz^U \tag{30}$$

Setting the coefficient of dz^U equal to zero, we find the uniform emission level as[6,7]

$$L\,z^U = (\alpha - c).(6.(\phi1 + \phi2) - 4.(\mu a + \mu b)) - 3(\theta a + \theta b).(\mu a.\theta a + \mu b.\theta b) \tag{31}$$
$$- 7\mu a.\mu b.(\theta a + \theta b) + 11.(\theta a.\mu a^2 + \theta b.\mu b^2)$$

To compare the optimal policies and welfare conditions of countries for non-cooperative, cooperative and uniform solutions, we use the simulation values. Table 12.2 represents the results.

3.4   Policy comparison

The difference between the optimal policies results from the differences in abatement technology and associated gross pollution values of firms given in the simulation. The domestic firm in country A is less efficient and generates higher gross pollution per unit of output on one hand, and has higher abatement cost on the other. Therefore, it produces less output than the rival firm. The government in country A favours the efficient firm (i.e. the foreign firm) by imposing stricter quota than country B. This situation is same when the countries cooperate. In addition, when the countries cooperate, they both apply stricter policies.

In all the three cases (non-cooperative, cooperative and uniform) the welfare in country B is always bigger than in country A, given the parametric values in our simulations. That is, the country with the firm that has more efficient environmental (abatement) technology gets higher welfare values. Table 12.3 (and Table 12.4) may help for the intuition, which examines all the terms in welfare: (i) consumer surplus; (ii) producer surplus; (iii) disutility of pollution. The firms in country B have lower abatement cost. Based on its advantageous position in the market, it produces more and creates higher producer surplus. This high production also leads to more pollution that affects the welfare of country B adversely. However, the positive impact of producer surplus on welfare can dominate the negative impact of pollution. Therefore, country B still has a better welfare in comparison with country A. The results

Table 12.2 The optimal pollution quotas and welfare of non-cooperative, cooperative and uniform solutions

The comparison of the optimal pollution quotas	The comparison of the welfares
$z_a^N < z_b^N$	$W_a^N < W_b^N$
$z_a^C < z_b^C$	$W_a^C < W_b^C$
$z_a^N > z_a^C$	$W_a^U < W_b^U$
$z_b^N > z_b^C$	$W_a^N < W_a^C$
$z_a^N > z^U$	$W_b^N < W_b^C$
$z_b^N > z^U$	$W_a^N < W_a^U$
$z_a^C < z^U$	$W_b^N < W_b^U$
$z_b^C > z^U$	$W_a^C < W_a^U$
	$W_b^C > W_b^U$

Table 12.3 Total welfare for optimal policies under three scenarios

Scenarios	Consumer surplus	Producer surplus	Disutility of pollution	Total welfare
NC	$CS_a^N = CS_b^N$	$PS_a^N < PS_b^N$	$DP_a^N < DP_b^N$	$W_a^N < W_b^N$
C	$CS_a^C = CS_b^C$	$PS_a^C < PS_b^C$	$DP_a^C < DP_b^C$	$W_a^C < W_b^C$
U	$CS_a^U = CS_b^U$	$PS_a^U < PS_b^U$	$DP_a^U < DP_b^U$	$W_a^U < W_b^U$

Table 12.4 Welfare terms of countries under three scenarios

Country	Consumer surplus	Producer surplus	Disutility of pollution	Total welfare
	$CS_a^N > CS_a^C$	$PS_a^N > PS_a^C$	$DP_a^N > DP_a^C$	$W_a^N < W_a^C$
A	$CS_a^N > CS_a^U$	$PS_a^N > PS_a^U$	$DP_a^N > DP_a^U$	$W_a^N < W_a^U$
	$CS_a^C < CS_a^U$	$PS_a^C < PS_a^U$	$DP_a^C < DP_a^U$	$W_a^C < W_a^U$
	$CS_b^N > CS_b^C$	$PS_b^N > PS_b^C$	$DP_b^N > DP_b^C$	$W_b^N < W_b^C$
B	$CS_b^N > CS_b^U$	$PS_b^N > PS_b^U$	$DP_b^N > DP_b^U$	$W_b^N < W_b^U$
	$CS_b^C < CS_b^U$	$PS_b^C > PS_b^U$	$DP_b^C > DP_b^U$	$W_b^C > W_b^U$

show that a country with a more efficient firm in terms of abatement technology may face more pollution because of the stimulated production. This means that technological efficiency is not always associated with the lower pollution level.

When there is cooperation between countries, the allowed pollution levels will be lower than the non-cooperative case and the welfare of both countries will strictly improve. If the governments impose stricter environmental

Table 12.5 The signs of the effects of changes in parameters on equilibrium emission levels

The optimal pollution quotas	Parameters							
	α	c	θa	θb	μa	μb	$\phi 1$	$\phi 2$
za^N	+	–	–	+	+	+	–	+
zb^N	+	–	+	–	+	+	–	+
za^C	+	–	–	+	–	+	–	–
zb^C	+	–	+	–	+	.	–	–
z^U	+	–	–	–	+	+	–	–

policies, the cost of firms will increase so the production and the total pollution generated by domestic and foreign production will decrease. Although the price will increase because of the reduction in production, the gain from lower pollution is larger than the total loss of consumer surplus and producer surplus. Therefore, cooperation allows governments to apply stricter environmental policies because of the negative externalities of pollution.

While cooperative behaviour unambiguously leads higher welfare for each country compared to the non-cooperative case, an interesting result is found when the uniform case is compared with the cooperative for each country (see Table 12.2). In particular, welfare under the cooperative case is bigger than welfare under the uniform case for country B but it is just the opposite for country A. That is, while cooperative behaviour benefits every country, a further attempt to uniformly determine the quotas benefits (harms) the country with the environmentally less (more) efficient firm.

4 Comparative statics

By using the optimal non-cooperative, cooperative and uniform solutions above, we examine the effects of changes in parameters on the equilibrium emission levels. The parameters studied below are market size (α), constant per unit cost (c), per unit gross pollution (θi), disutility of pollution resulted from domestic and foreign production ($\phi 1$, $\phi 2$) and the abatement costs (μi) where i = a, b. Due to enormous size of the equations, we once again run a simulation and use the same values as before. Thus, we keep the analysis at a tractable level. The results are given in Table 12.5.

Pollution quotas and market size: For all the three scenarios, when the market size increases, governments impose less severe pollution quotas in both countries. This is because, an increase in market size creates demand and governments want to meet this growing demand with domestic production. The positive effects of consumer surplus and producer surplus on welfare as a result of increasing output and decreasing price will dominate the negative effect of relaxing pollution standards.

Pollution quotas and marginal cost: Again, under all scenarios, starting from the equilibrium levels an increase in marginal cost decreases the emission quotas in both countries. The intuition is as follows: an increase in marginal cost increases the total cost, and hence leads to a lower level of production and a higher price. This in turn, implies a decline both in consumer surplus and producer surplus. However, a lower level of production also decreases the disutility from pollution. The losses in consumer surplus and producer surplus are more than compensated for by the reduction in disutility from pollution and let the governments impose more severe environmental policies.

Pollution quotas and gross pollution: For the three scenarios, an increase in the level of gross pollution generated by domestic production will increase the negative effect of disutility of pollution on welfare. Hence, governments will decrease their optimal pollution quotas so that the total production and associated pollution will reduce. On the other hand, when the rival firm's gross pollution increases, the government will increase its optimal emission quota. This is because an increase in the level of the rival firm's gross pollution leads the rival government to apply stricter quotas. As a result, the production level will decline. To take advantage of this lack of production in the domestic and foreign markets, the other government will encourage its domestic firm to produce more by increasing allowed emission level.

Pollution quotas and abatement cost: For the non-cooperative solution, when the abatement cost increases, the consumer surplus and the producer surplus will be affected adversely because of the reduction in production. Therefore, governments increase their optimal policy levels since the negative effect of relaxing the pollution standards will be minor compared to the other parts of welfare. Since the governments act non-cooperatively and strategically with self-interest each government relaxes quotas when abatement costs increase. This is also true when the quota is uniformly determined. However, when they act cooperatively, each government tightens (relaxes) local quota level when the abatement cost of the local firm increases (the abatement cost of the foreign firm decreases).

Pollution quotas and the marginal disutility of pollution: When the governments agree to maximize the joint welfare, either through cooperative or uniform policies, the equilibrium level of the pollution quota is decreasing with an increase in marginal disutility levels (for both $\phi 1$, $\phi 2$). That is, when the society cares more about environmental impact (in this model pollution), governments impose more severe policies under cooperation. However, when the governments behave non-cooperatively, given $\phi 1 < \phi 2$, both governments impose severe policies if it is $\phi 1$ that is increasing further; and relax the quota if it is $\phi 2$ that is increasing. For all the cases, when the disutility of pollution increases, the welfare is affected adversely and this negative effect dominates the other parts of welfare so the government sets the stricter environmental standards to mitigate the total pollution level by decrementing total output.

In the case of the non-cooperative solution, an increase in the disutility of pollution generated by foreign production will lead the optimal policy level to increase. This is because when the disutility of transboundary pollution increases, governments may want to encourage domestic production by relaxing emission standards, so that the price of domestic goods decreases. By making their own domestic firm more competitive in the market, governments can reduce the demand for foreign good and so the negative effect of disutility of transboundary pollution on welfare. To conclude, in the cooperative and uniform solutions, an increase in the disutility of pollution generated by foreign production results in a decrease in the optimal pollution level that firms are allowed to emit. Since the higher disutility of pollution causes welfare to deteriorate, both governments impose cooperatively strict pollution standards to mitigate this negative effect by restricting their local production.

5   Conclusion

This chapter examines the optimal environmental standards under the asymmetry in abatement technology. We develop a two-country intra-industry trade model with one domestic firm in each country. Firms are assumed to compete in Cournot-Nash fashion and they serve both domestic and foreign markets. Production generates pollution and there is transboundary pollution between the countries. The firms are also assumed to differ in abatement technology levels. In particular, they generate different levels of gross pollution and incur different abatement costs. The governments impose pollution quota to restrict the emission level and reduce the negative impact of pollution on welfare. We analyse the optimal pollution quotas under three scenarios: (i) non-cooperative solution, (ii) cooperative solution and (iii) uniform solution.

The results show that relatively high-level abatement technology does not always result in lower pollution. This is because: lower abatement cost provides competition advantage and encourages the more efficient firm to produce more. This higher production increases the pollution level. However, the high producer surplus can dominate the negative effect of pollution on welfare. Therefore, the welfare of the country with the more efficient firm in terms of abatement technology has greater pollution but better welfare. When the firm has relatively less efficient abatement technology, the government imposes a more severe emission quota to constrain the pollution level. Since the production is more costly, the domestic firm produces less. In turn, this means less pollution. However, the reductions in producer surplus more than compensate for this effect, and eventually worsen the welfare.

In the case of cooperation, governments set stricter emission quotas because of the negative externalities of pollution. In addition, the welfares of both countries will be better off due to the reduction in pollution levels. The country with the technologically advantageous firm still suffers from more pollution but obtains greater welfare compared to the rival country.

Notes

1 The inverse demand functions are derived from the quasi-linear utility function $U(D^a, D^b, y) = \alpha^a D^a + \alpha^b D^b - [\beta^a D^{a^2} + \beta^b D^{b^2} + 2\gamma D^a D^b]/2 + y$, where y is the consumption of the numeriare good.
2 The concavity conditions hold if $17\mu i < 24\phi 1$ for $i = a, b$ and the stability condition hold if $\mu a \mu b.(17\mu a - 24\phi 1)(17\mu b - 24\phi 1) > (6\mu b.\phi 1 + 6\mu a.\phi 2 - 7\mu a \mu b)(6\mu a.\phi 1 +6\mu b.\phi 2 - 7\mu a.\mu b)$.
3 $M = \mu a.\mu b.(17\mu a - 24\phi 1).(17\mu b - 24\phi 1) - (6\mu a.\phi 1 + 6\mu b.\phi 2 - 7\mu a.\mu b).(6\mu a.\phi 2 + 6\mu b.\phi 1 - 7\mu a.\mu b)$.
4 The concavity conditions hold if $11\mu i < 12.(\phi 1 + \phi 2)$ for $i = a, b$ and the stability condition hold if $4\mu a.\mu b.(11\mu a - 12(\phi 1 + \phi 2)).(11\mu b - 12(\phi 1 + \phi 2)) - (6\mu b.(\phi 1 + \phi 2) +\mu a.(-14\mu a + 6(\phi 1 + \phi 2)))^2 > 0$.
5 $N = 4\mu a.\mu b.(11\mu a - 12(\phi 1 + \phi 2))(11\mu b - 12(\phi 1 + \phi 2)) - (6\mu b.(\phi 1 + \phi 2) + \mu a.(-14\mu a + 6(\phi 1 + \phi 2)))^2$.
6 The concavity conditions hold if $22\left(\mu a^2 + \mu b^2\right) < 12.(\phi 1 + \phi 2).(\mu a + \mu b) + 28.\mu a.\mu b$.
7 $L = 6.(\phi 1 + \phi 2).(\mu a + \mu b) + 14.\mu a.\mu b - 11.(\mu a^2 + \mu b^2)$.

References

Carraro, C. and Siniscalco, D. (1992), 'Environmental Innovation Policy and International Competition', *Environmental and Resource Economics*, 2: 183–200.

Carraro, C. and Soubeyran, A. (1993), *Environmental Policy and the Choice of Production Technology*, Università degli Studi di Udine, Dipartimento di Scienze Economiche, Working Paper MOS.01/93.

Copeland, B. R. and Taylor, M. S. (1995), 'Trade and Transboundary Pollution', *American Economic Review*, 85 (4): 716–737.

Hatzipanayotou, P., Lahiri, S. and Michael, M. S. (2008), 'Cross-Border Pollution, Terms of Trade, and Welfare', *Environmental and Resource Economics*, 41: 327–345.

Kayalica, M. O. and Kayalica, O. (2005), 'Transboundary Pollution from Consumption in a Reciprocal Dumping Model', *Global Economy Journal*, 5(2).

Mathur, A. and Dang, S. (2009), 'Multilateral Environmental Agreements versus World Trade Organization System: A Comprehensive Study', *American Journal of Economics and Business Administration*, 1 (3): 219–224.

Mendez, L. and Trelles, R. (2000), 'The Abatement Market – A Proposal for Environmental Cooperation among Asymmetric Countries', *Environmental and Resource Economics*, 16: 15–30.

Millimet, D. L. (2003), 'Environmental Abatement Costs and Establishment Size', *Contemporary Economic Policy*, 21 (3): 281–296.

Millimet, D. L., Roy, S. and Sengupta, A. (2009), 'Environmental Regulations and Economic Activity: Influence on Market Structure', *Annual Review of Resource Economics*, 1: 99–117.

Montero, J. P. (2002), 'Permits, Standards and Technology Innovation', *Journal of Environmental Economics and Management*, 44: 23–44.

Poyago-Theotoky, J. A. (2007), 'The Organization of R&D and Environmental Policy', *Journal of Economic Behavior and Organization*, 62 : 63–75.

Stenbacka, R. and Tombak, M. M. (1998), 'Technology Policy and the Organization of R&D', *Journal of Economic Behavior and Organization*, 36: 503–520.

Ulph, A. and Ulph. D. (2007) 'Climate Change-environmental and Technology Policies in a Strategic Context', *Environmental and Resource Economics*, 37: 159–180.

Part V
International institutions

13 Challenges of governing international energy transitions

International Renewable Energy Agency as a solution?

Yasemin Atalay

1 Introduction

Consolidation of renewable energy resources is one of the key prerequisites of global sustainability, considering the impact of the energy sector on the environment. The reduction of carbon emissions is a primary target of the sustainable governance of energy. An International Energy Agency (IEA) report suggests that although traditionally, industrialized countries are responsible for the biggest share of anthropogenic greenhouse gases (GHGs), developing countries' emissions are on the rise, and are expected to rise further in the coming years (IEA, 2012: 12). The majority of these emissions stems from the electricity and heating sector, for which fossil resources are widely used all over the world. Indeed, electricity and heat generations' CO_2 emissions, most of which come from coal and peat, natural gas and oil, have increased between 2009 and 2010 (IEA, 2012: 10). Especially China and India stand out as the leading industrial emitters. While China's emissions grew by 9.9 per cent in 2011, those of India grew by 7.5 per cent in the same year (Fogarty, 2012).

The use of fossil fuels, especially in the industry, is so alarming that, for instance, Global Carbon Project's scientists underlined that the expected amount of fossil fuel-related CO_2 emissions will exceed the 1990 emission level by 58 per cent for the year 2012 (Morello, 2012). A few years ago, all these figures could be summarized with one single sentence: 'the problem facing the global community is serious and it should be addressed as soon as possible *before it is too late*'. Today, we do not have the luxury of talking about such conditions, because we are on the verge of facing the worst-case scenario. PricewaterhouseCooper's 2012 Low Carbon Economy Index is one of the many reports that revealed the gloomy future. It states that the global community needs to be prepared for a warming of 'not just 2°C, but 4°C, or even 6°C' (PWC, 2012: 1). Hence, the report calls for 'radical transformations in the ways the global economy functions', such as 'rapid uptake of renewable energy, sharp falls in fossil fuel use or massive deployment of CCS, removal of industrial emissions and halting deforestation' while concluding that business-as-usual is by no means an option any more (PWC, 2012: 9). As for the subject matter of this chapter, it is focused on the rapid uptake of renewable energy, which would require numerous new, technology-intensive and rather unconventional governance and management mechanisms. A large-scale consolidation of renewable energy resource use would mean a paradigm shift in the international energy governance as well, especially when all the embedded characteristics, rules, norms, regulations, actors and institutions of the current international energy regime are considered. An energy transition will also mean a transition in the international institutional structure, in the sense that the dominance of fossil fuel-centred institutions will be broken, and participation and compliance in the renewable energy sector are fostered. This chapter explains how and to what extent the International Renewable Energy Agency (IRENA) is addressing the energy challenges we are facing today. However, before systematically presenting the challenges of the international energy regime, Section 2 tackles the current challenges of fragmented international energy governance. It is then followed by the analysis in Section 3, which tackles how and in what ways IRENA addresses these challenges. How the Agency functions is further highlighted with personal interviews by the author at the IRENA Headquarters in Abu Dhabi during 7–17 April 2015.

2   Challenges of the fragmented international energy governance

The current international energy regime is unsustainable in many ways. Economy-wise, differentiation of the energy mix is inevitable, as depletable resources dominate the current mix. This would lead to significant changes on both production and consumption sides. Policy-wise, this differentiated mix would call for new governance and management mechanisms. This brings us to the idea that energy transition is not a matter of 'if', but is rather a matter of 'how'. The transition process will also include the setting up of a new energy regime.

What is meant by 'energy transition' can be better understood by focusing on the 'transition management' literature. James Meadowcroft defines basic aspects of transition management as follows:

> At the core of 'transition management' is the challenge of orienting long-term change in large socio-technical systems. 'Transitions' are understood as processes of structural change in major societal subsystems. They involve a shift in the dominant 'rules of the game', a transformation of established technologies and societal practices, movement from one dynamic equilibrium to another – typically stretching over several generations (25–50 years).
>
> (Meadowcroft, 2009: 324)

In the case of energy transition, this process can be characterized as 'movement from a fossil fuel based (or dominated) energy system to a non-fossil fuel based (or dominated) energy system', or 'a shift from carbon emitting energy system to a carbon neutral (or low carbon) energy system', or 'a transition from a non-renewable energy system to a renewable energy system' (Meadowcroft, 2009: 327). For the subject matter of this chapter, all these three perspectives are embraced as they go hand in hand with the climate-centric approach to international energy governance. Hence, the post-oil paradigm cannot be defined by a sole renewable energy regime, but it should rather connote a new international energy regime which (unlike the one we have today) would include renewables as one of its primal tenets, thereby challenging the dominance of non-renewable resources. When we look at the international energy regime today, we see an ever-growing tendency towards further fragmentation where the dominance of key energy institutions is challenged with the inclusion of new institutions and actors. This phenomenon is rather predictable, considering certain weaknesses of the previously more integrated character of the international energy regime. However, a number of challenges regarding the current energy governance can be identified.

First, the narrow coverage of a variety of energy issues by IEA has long drawn attention. IEA's focus on renewable energy was considered 'underfinanced and understaffed', making 'training, capacity-building, and technical assistance towards developing countries' very difficult (Van de Graaf, 2013: 26). Indeed, the general overview of many energy institutions reflects the motive to respond to more immediate governance problems, rather than long-term projections such as environmental externalities of production and consumption of energy, or climate change (Meyer, 2013: 2). Furthermore, the global energy mix has changed in the course of time. Just like the increasing amounts of identified unconventional energy resources in recent years, there exist regional and country-based changes in energy supply characteristics. In line with these changes, energy-related institutions face challenges. Concepts like energy security, energy efficiency and clean energy have become more and more complex. Hence they now require a different and more comprehensive approach than ever before. Yet, the main emphasis still seems to be on fossil resources and their international governance. Political and economic power structures of the post-war period, like meeting the growing energy demand through fossil resources and their further discoveries, has overshadowed other policy areas which are equally significant (Fischedick *et al.*, 2011: 2). The management and governance of fossil resources, as it is today, dominate the international energy regime. For most parts of the world, the renewable energy sector is a niche market, where little policy experience is observed. Although the utilization of fossil resources has a long historical background when compared to the renewable resources, their global governance still faces significant challenges. Florini and Sovacool argue that 'there are enormous gaps in the international system's capacity to manage energy commodities, address their externalities, and ensure a successful transition over time to low-carbon resources', especially when the problems regarding public goods and externalities are considered (Florini and Sovacool, 2009: 5240). As a result, many important issue areas like clean energy production, carbon reduction and climate change remained unsolved.

A second weakness of the current international energy regime is that there is a significant division between developed and developing countries. This was especially reflected in the membership structure of the leading international energy institution, IEA. Having its membership exclusively limited to OECD member states, IEA has faced calls for a reform of its institutional structure. However, in the absence of a shared notion of reform among the present members, it would be damaging to do so (Hirst and Froggatt, 2012: 3). Underrepresentation or absence of developing countries in the energy governance is not only observed in IEA, but in some other energy-specific institutions like OPEC and Energy Charter Treaty, where the former mostly deals with the governance of energy in leading oil exporters and the latter's focus area is mainly Europe and Central Asia. Hence, this sort of a differentiated institutional environment which is shaped more by regional and/or country-based characteristics than specific issue areas, leads to the deepening of the divide between developed and developing countries (Hirst and Froggatt, 2012: 9).

Third, there exists a bottleneck in the international energy regime, which is created by certain politically controversial issue areas regarding environmental governance at large, and it acts as a major obstacle for participation and compliance in the field of energy. Distributional conflicts, burden-sharing initiatives and developing countries' discontent over the way negotiation processes are handled can be undermining (Urpelainen and Van de Graaf, 2013). Consequently, many crucial problems that need to be solved are either overlooked or states are deterred from complying with decisions that are agreed upon. This phenomenon is more visible in environmental institutions that aim to address a broad variety of issues. While in one issue area there may be a consensus among participating countries, another issue area can be perceived as a detriment to their interests, and eventually that consensus faces the risk of a breakdown.

These three challenges and/or weaknesses of the current energy governance have been voiced in many scholarly works. New institutions and actors will need to tackle not only these three issues but also a number of other, non-institutional challenges that stem from the centrality of fossil resources in today's energy paradigm.

First and foremost of these urgent problems is that the strength of the conventional fossil resource sector acts as an indirect barrier in front of the development of renewable resources. When we consider the international energy regime, the role played by oil lobbies for instance, seems to outweigh small and medium sized renewable energy companies. This imbalance is also reflected in the preferential treatment of fossil fuels by extensive subsidies. According to IEA, in 2011 while the fossil fuel subsidies reached $523bn with a 30 per cent increase when compared to the previous year, subsidies for renewables totalled only $88bn (RTCC, 2012). When we consider how technology-intensive the renewable energy sector is, this dramatic difference between subsidy amounts stands out as an important problem, which is supported by the dominance of the oil industry. This dominance shapes the rules, norms, regulations and policy experiments within the international energy regime. Kern and Smith emphasize this issue within the framework of Dutch energy transition policy (ETP):

> Firstly, the dominance of regime actors led to the use of selection criteria for the themes, pathways and experiments which do not sufficiently contribute to opening up space for a wide variety of energy practices which could contribute to system innovations ...
>
> (Kern and Smith, 2008: 4101)

> secondly, the dominance of regime actors in the ETP also makes it difficult to combine the nurturing of niches with 'control policies' to put the existing regime under pressure as applying such pressures would 'harm' the energy regime actors, and thus undermine their constructive engagement in the transition process.
>
> (Kern and Smith, 2008: 4102)

Hence, an overarching intergovernmental institution that would regulate these imbalances and give the necessary proportional support to each and every energy resource's utilization is an urgent need. Especially, in the energy transition process, it is the most primal condition that key actors of conventional resource would not impede the development of non-conventional fossil resources and renewable energy resources.

Another challenge is related with the public perception of the urgency of renewable energy uptake. In recent years, more and more unconventional fossil resources are being utilized, and this seems to be reducing the gloominess of the peak oil scenario. That is, so long as these unconventional resources are identified and utilized, then the lifetime of conventional resources can theoretically be expanded. This may be a valid argument from the economic perspective. However, its possible environmental impacts can be striking. Verbruggen and Al Marchohi expressed that 'total carbon emissions from oil may increase at lower oil consumption when substituting non-conventional for conventional resources' (Verbruggen and Al Marchohi, 2010: 5573). Hence, if climate change-based environmental concerns are neglected, substitutions of conventional with unconventional, or oil with gas would result in further CO_2 emissions. What is more, even if a sound climate change policy is set and applied in harmony with global energy policy, if the current share of renewable energy in world energy production remains more or less the same, conventional and non-conventional oil resources are expected to meet the world demand only for 50 years, while natural gas resources are expected to meet that for another 80 years (Jefferson, 2008: 4118). The underlying problem here is that environmental considerations are hardly embedded in the global energy governance, and even if in certain cases green policies are adopted, there are numerous escape routes for those who would rather opt out (van den Bergh, 2012: 531). Hence, the international energy regime's prospective transition cannot go by without the inclusion of sound, effective and efficient policy principles regarding the consolidation of renewable energy resource use, as well as other environment-friendly regulations.

Among the non-institutional challenges, encouraging states to be more willing stands out as an important requirement. Importance of state commitment is one of the commonalities between the oil paradigm and a prospective post-oil paradigm in terms of the regime setting. During the construction of the oil paradigm, the role of state intervention was determinative. Podobnik argues, for example, that 'the periodic intensification of geopolitical competition among advanced industrial nations spurred state intervention in favour of specific energy sectors at particular historical junctures', and that 'the consolidation of a future energy regime based on a cluster of more environmentally sustainable technologies will likely result from a similar convergence of geopolitical, commercial, and social dynamics' (Podobnik, 1999: 166–167). Indeed, when we take human needs as inherent factors within historical system transitions and causes of inter-state and/or inter-regional competitions, we can clearly see how crucial the need for a determined state is. Following up on the emphasis of a new institutional setting, state intervention and strong political will should be considered as conditions which will make the construction of this new setting a feasible one. Especially in renewable energy support mechanisms (e.g. the case of feed-in tariffs in Germany) governmental will play a key role. Business-government cooperation will be one of the most important features of the transition. If demand-side energy efficiency is combined with supply-side renewable energy resource consolidation, it is possible to achieve a 95 per cent sustainable energy supply by 2050 (Deng *et al.*, 2012: 119). In the current setting where there is a divide between developed and developing countries, as well as contextual factors that curb participation and compliance, ensuring states to be more willing and active would require more than just emphasizing immediate human needs. It would also have to offer economically feasible and beneficial opportunities. In other words, complying with rules, norms and regulations of the post-oil paradigm should be perceived as a beneficial initiative rather than a risky endeavour.

Lastly, for a prospective energy transition and the related regime setup, construction of new norms of global energy governance will be necessary. The 'public good' concept of natural resource management has been quite controversial because, for one reason, it does not refer to the totality of issues regarding global energy governance and their implications on many other areas. From the constructivist perspective, the 'public good' concept can no longer address the needs of the global community; therefore it should be deconstructed and reconstructed. It is argued that the concept of 'global

Table 13.1 Guard rails for a sustainable energy system

Ecological guard rails	Socio-economic guard rails
Climate protection	Security of supply and energy security
Resource conservation	Universal, needs-based access to affordable energy
Environmental conservation	Respect for human rights along the process chains
	Avoidance of technological risks

Source: Fischedick *et al.* (2011: 4)

Table 13.2 Institutional and non-institutional challenges of international energy governance

Institutional challenges	Non-institutional challenges
Narrow coverage of demand-side energy issues and environmental externalities	Dominance of conventional fossil resources
Division between developing and developed countries	Public perception of renewable energy deployment's urgency
Bottleneck created by controversial issues	Encouraging states to be more active and willing
	Normative change in the global environmental governance

Source: Data compiled by author from the related literature of Section 2[1]

public good' should be constructed as one of the main norms of energy transition, because 'an energy system that has low or no carbon intensity would be a public good for all humanity because it would give the non-excludable and non-rival benefit of a less dangerous degree of climate change' (Karlsson-Vinkhuyzen *et al.*, 2012: 13). Institutions of the new international energy regime will, therefore, need to embrace this norm in order to lead the way to effective and sustainable energy provisions that can approach the system transformation as a holistic energy transition process.

The overall *guard rails for a sustainable energy system* are presented thoroughly in Fischedick *et al.*'s comprehensive study on global energy governance (Table 13.1). This is one of the many categorizations of agenda items that need to be tackled for consolidating better international energy governance. It is chosen as a reference point for this chapter because unlike the mainstream, holistic sustainability approach, it highlights various aspects of sustainable energy systems, not only in terms of ecological sustainability, but also in terms of social and economic aspects that should be taken into consideration.

To sum up, there exist not only institutional challenges that stem from the current energy governance framework, but also those that can be observed in line with some inherent characteristics of the oil paradigm. In a fragmented institutional setting, new responsibilities and tasks lay ahead for institutions and actors (Table 13.2).

The following section analyses to what IRENA has been able to address the abovementioned challenges.

3   International Renewable Energy Agency: addressing the challenges

While the international energy regime is still heavily dependent on the management and governance of fossil resources, in 2009 there occurred an interesting initiative in a region that has rather negative environmental reputation. The International Renewable Energy Agency (IRENA) came into being in Abu Dhabi, at the heart of a region full of oil-rich rentier states. Subsequently, its establishment attracted a lot of attention especially from the business sector. Some regarded this initiative as a commercial move, which would help the economic diversification process of the Arab Gulf region. However, in time IRENA showed significant signs that it should neither be underestimated nor underrated as a sector-specific energy institution. Its first and foremost aim is the promotion of renewable energy resources at the global level.

3.1   Institutional challenges of international energy governance

Unlike some international energy institutions' and international energy governance's general coverage of certain issues, IRENA has deliberately adopted a narrow focus on renewable energy. While this may seem an initiative that is against what is aimed to be achieved, which is a holistic betterment of international energy governance with respect to principles like sustainability, energy security and access to all, so far it proved otherwise. Downplaying general and controversial issues regarding energy and concentrating specifically on renewable energy and its subsidiary issue areas has so far had three benefits: (i) it enabled IRENA to be effective despite its small budget; (ii) it filled an important gap in the 'contemporary patchwork of global environmental governance' by making renewable energy a priority; (iii) this narrow focus on renewable energy helped overcome controversial situations by putting promising areas of cooperation such as knowledge and technology transfer upfront, rather than approaching the issue from the sole perspective of climate change (Urpelainen and Van de Graaf, 2013: 167–168). With this subject-specific institutional identity, the Agency is able to cover a wide variety of issues regarding renewable energy by demonstrating these issues not as sticks but as carrots.

When energy institutions within the general climate change regime are considered, there have been cases of 'systemic governance risk', where one institution's policies posed the risk of making cooperation more difficult and leading to failures in cooperation in other functionally linked institutions (Meyer, 2013: 4–5). This risk is a significant barrier in front of enabling participation and compliance in these latter functionally linked institutions.

From the perspective of fragmentation too, there were cases of 'conflictive fragmentation' in the climate governance architecture that was shaped by the provisions of climate change governance and the differentiation between industrialized and developing countries (Biermann *et al.*, 2009: 23). In the international climate regime, not only the clashing policy areas of different institutions, but also the divide between developed and developing countries have been acting as detriments to further participation and compliance. How IRENA has been tackling this risk has much to do with its operational character. As one IRENA official puts it, rather than enforcing certain policies, the Agency either aims to support the already adopted renewable energy policies in the member states by providing country and/or region-specific business plans, or if they do not already have a renewable energy policy framework, by helping them make their policy designs first. While doing these, the Agency does not offer conditional support, intervene in national policies and mechanisms, nor does it only foster project-based support (IRENA Official 2015). The Agency carries out its operations within the framework of government-led processes by helping them take easier steps. 'Renewables Readiness Assessment: Design to Action', for example, is a publication that is 'designed for IRENA Member States to help them assess the status and prospects of renewable energy deployment at the national level, dig deeper into issues that need urgent attention or promotion, and define concrete actions' (IRENA 2016a). What needs to be done for a larger renewable energy uptake is framed not as a mandatory environmental duty, but as something that can be economically beneficial by creating further viabilities. Hence, rather than controversial and difficult issues like the need for immediate removal of fossil subsidies, more realistic and achievable tasks are emphasized such as creating more jobs in the renewable energy sector, designing and helping the application of right financial support mechanisms for different sources of renewable energy, country-level mappings of opportunities and challenges of prospective renewable energy initiatives, and publication of helpful data which can be used by policy-makers. When the states see IRENA more and more as a hub that offers economic opportunities rather than as a conventional international institution that imposes certain rules, they are more willing to participate in renewable energy initiatives. This sort of pragmatic approach to the issue creates a more promising atmosphere and helps to facilitate the energy transition towards a more sustainable system.

Unlike the limited membership scheme in some international energy institutions, IRENA is open to membership applications for all countries from all regions. Furthermore, in its areas of operation it designs tailor-made solutions based on specific country characteristics instead of relying on one single governance model. For a variety of countries like Ghana, Peru, South Africa, Poland, Qatar, Fiji and Nicaragua, it has published reports that outline a feasible and achievable roadmap to increased renewable energy uptake at country-level. It also prepares region-specific publications like *Policy Challenges for Renewable Energy Deployment in Pacific Island Countries and*

Territories, Pan-Arab Renewable Energy Strategy 2030: Roadmap of Actions for Implementation and *Africa's Renewable Future: the Path to Sustainable Growth*. Certain important sectors and policy mechanisms are also taken seriously as a part of knowledge dissemination principal of IRENA. *30 Years of Policies for Wind Energy: Lessons from 12 Wind Energy Markets*, for instance, presents best practices in the development of wind energy, while *Renewable Energy Auctions in Developing Countries* highlights important aspects of policy-making from the perspective of developing countries. This welcoming and inclusive attitude of the Agency is also reflected on its collaborations with other international institutions. *IEA/IRENA Global Renewable Energy Policies and Measures Database*, which is prepared with IEA, is a significant example that acts as a comprehensive data set for policy-makers and investors in the renewable energy sector, covering all IEA and IRENA member countries and signatories. Avoiding possible risks of inter-institutional conflicts and focusing on constructive efforts that can be beneficial for a large set of countries has proved to be a win-win scenario for both participating countries and institutions that are involved. While on one hand, developing countries do not feel sidelined when they have access to special information resources and advisory plans that are planned for them; more participation is encouraged on the other hand from the institution's side.

3.2   Non-institutional challenges in the wake of energy transitions

The post-oil paradigm would require intergovernmental institutions with unprecedented organizational structures, terms of references, and missions. The question arises at this point: What needs to be done? The formative phase of energy system transformation calls for four key conditions, which are 'institutional changes, market formation, the formation of technology-specific advocacy coalitions, and the entry of new firms and other organizations' (Jacobsson and Lauber, 2006: 258). If these conditions were to be fulfilled at the global level, then this would mean the construction of a new regime. International regimes, which are composed of their own rules, norms and regulations, shape the policy-making mechanisms at state-level governance. Indeed, the generation of the norms of appropriate behaviour and best practice is what the intergovernmental organizations should be doing (Florini and Sovacool, 2009: 5243). For all these changes to take place smoothly, international governance's importance gains an upper hand. In order to achieve a supra-state harmony in terms of policy mechanisms, financial support systems, easing of technology transfer, policy transfer and policy learning processes, and legal regulations efficient and effective institutions are a must.

The offering of carrots rather than imposing sticks encourages states to be more active and willing in general. One outstanding feature of IRENA, as stated before, is that it embraces an 'open door policy', when it comes to participation:

Numerous international, intergovernmental and non-governmental organisations are natural and indispensable partners, as are many private sector companies who are already seizing the opportunities offered by renewable energy. Civil society groups can also contribute to the IRENA vision by being vocal advocates and observers of actions taken by governments, non-governmental organisations and the private sector. IRENA directs its principal partnership activities towards knowledge sharing, ensuring that existing information and experience is developed, organised, and made accessible in a usable format.

(IRENA, 2013a)

This inclusiveness is a positive characteristic that can pave the way for a large-scale participation in international renewable energy governance. What is more, it can also act as a forum where different stakeholders can raise their voice about different needs, criticisms or suggestions regarding the consolidation of renewables.

Organizational structure of IRENA is also worthy of detailed analysis. It is composed of an Assembly of representatives from member states, which is responsible for the work programme, budget planning, adoption of reports, membership and outlining of the Agency activities (IRENA, 2013c), a Council which is accountable to the Assembly and has 21 members who are elected on two-year terms among both developed and developing country members (IRENA, 2013d) and a Secretariat of the Director General and his staff, which is responsible for administrative and technical support to subsidiary bodies of the organization (IRENA, 2013e). The main tasks of the Secretariat are summarized in three categories (IRENA, 2013e): knowledge management and technology cooperation; policy advice and capacity building; the IRENA Innovation and Technology Centre. These three categories include various important jobs, from expansion of the knowledge base to the creation of the necessary human resource for the sector.

Knowledge management and technology cooperation activities address the establishment of a database, which would collect scattered data on renewable energy technologies in one place, thereby, creating a knowledge hub for those who want to access reliable and accurate data. Under the auspices of this category, country-specific Renewables Readiness Assessments are carried out in order to put forth a detailed, comprehensive and holistic reference for countries that aim to increase the uptake of renewable energy (IRENA, 2013f). Moreover, IRENA also developed the Global Atlas for Solar and Wind Energy, in close cooperation with UNEP, in order to provide an accurate mapping of country-based and region-based potentials and the related information for productive renewable energy project investments (IRENA, 2013b). This project is quite significant, because opponents of renewable energy deployment quite often argue that resources like solar and wind are most of the time unreliable and unstable. The best solution of this problem is a wide-range mapping and data collection of the productive areas with high potentials, with special references to weekly, monthly and yearly trends. In this respect, the Global Atlas for Solar and Wind Energy can be seen as a positive initiative that will fill an important gap during the energy transition process.

Policy advice and capacity building activities, on the other hand, include education, teaching and knowledge transfer opportunities like IRENA's Renewable Energy Learning Partnership (IRELP) and the IRENA Scholarship Programme which provides financial support for graduate students who would like to specialize in renewable energy technologies (IRENA, 2013f). IRENA is engaged in many collaborative activities with the Masdar Institute of Science and Technology of Abu Dhabi, which is a research institution that focuses on renewable energy technology development processes as its preferential research area. Notable academics from reputable universities like Massachusetts Institute of Technology give lectures in Masdar Institute, on innovative policies regarding sustainable energy systems. Hence, this scholarship programme offers substantial opportunities in terms of the development of qualified human resources for the region and beyond. Joint databases on collaborations on knowledge disseminations are some of the main references of governments, private companies, academia and think tanks, along with other significant resources like the Global Atlas for Wind and Solar Energy. The cooperation and harmony between IEA and IRENA on IEA/IRENA Global Renewable Energy Policies and Measures Database is promising also for energy transitions. In the coming years, they are expected to work even closer, combining their resources for efficient and effective global energy governance. This phenomenon can be regarded as inspiring and innovative, since except for a few examples, such major joint actions among organizations of different energy sectors are rarely seen in the global energy governance. Moreover, the production of information that can actually be used is key to consolidating certain energy-related principles at the global level, such as the know-how regarding financial support mechanisms of renewables or sector-specific advisory strategies. UNEP published an evaluation report on IRENA's Global Atlas for Solar and Wind Energy in 2013, based on surveys, interviews and a workshop with potential end-users and concluded that while many important points were already covered, a tool which can address different levels of expertise and analysis capabilities which can also be used offline could make the platform better (IRENA and UNEP, 2013). On April 2015, IRENA launched *RESource* which is an online database that includes maps and publications regarding data, statistics, country information and all types of renewable energy resources (IRENA RESource, 2016). Dissemination of information is a prioritized area of operation for IRENA and its Innovation and Technology Center (IITC) in Bonn is just another outcome of this prioritization. IITC is a substantial programme which is responsible for two main activity areas: 'Assist governments on request in energy planning for more efficient and effective renewable energy technology and innovation strategies', and 'facilitate a better understanding of cost and cost reductions through technology development and market deployment to accelerate renewables uptake' (IRENA, 2013g). This programme is not only functional in fostering technology transfer, but it also promotes entrepreneurship by giving advice on business practices. Such meetings and forums are helpful in clarifying negative preconceptions and biases toward the renewable energy sector by raising awareness and carrying out detailed analyses of success scenarios. This type of activity will be further needed in the future when intra-regional technology transfers increase.

As for public perceptions of the renewable energy uptake, in 2014 IRENA formed a coalition of stakeholders including energy companies, international associations, universities, civil society organizations, regional and international institutions and international non-governmental organizations, called *Coalition for Action to Bolster Public Support for Renewable Energy* (IRENA, 2016b). Having acknowledged 'social acceptance' as a determining factor for renewable energy deployment, the coalition identified four items as prioritized action areas: knowledge base, network of communicators, common communications material and responding to concerns and misconceptions. The last area is especially important as it aims to monitor media coverage and give swift and collective responses where necessary, as well as being engaged with influential journalists and opinion makers (IRENA, 2016c). Bringing together various stakeholders like World Wildlife Foundation, Greenpeace, Japan Renewable Energy Foundation, Arizona State University, European Photovoltaic Industry Association and Vestas Wind Systems, the Coalition is helping the establishment of a common ground that can be embraced by the global public at later stages. One single institution's efforts for convincing the global public about the urgency and importance of further renewable energy deployment may not be adequate by itself. However, for IRENA it can be concluded that it is doing its bit to tackle this challenge.

The dominance of fossil resources in global energy governance can hypothetically be challenged by normative change in the rhetoric that is demonstrated by relevant institutions. IRENA and other institutions' influences alone may not be sufficient at this point. However, the ongoing inevitable fragmentation in global governance can create platforms for re-construction of new norms, rules and regulations. As the consensus over cruciality of norms such as the centrality of knowledge dissemination within renewable energy governance grows, certain behaviours can be more easily consolidated and entrenched within governance structures. Fragmentation, here, can act as an opportunity rather than an obstacle, since 'higher degrees of cooperative fragmentation where key norms are not in conflict may allow for more and different policy approaches, which could facilitate the inclusion of more relevant actors' (Biermann *et al.*, 2009: 29). So long as those who want to make a change in the current structure can find platforms where they can be represented, voice their demands and concerns, and receive constructive feedback from that platform, energy transition can take place more smoothly. So far, there is not sufficient empirical evidence that shows IRENA alone can be a determinant in this process. Future research and analysis about IRENA and its operations can be enlightening in order to see how it further adapts itself to this fragmented system of global governance.

4   Conclusion

Although it is a rather new institution, the number of IRENA's members is continuously increasing. On 14 January, 2013 China announced that it would join IRENA (Gulfnews, 2013). Being one of the leading carbon emitters, its membership is considered as a milestone in the global energy governance that such an important actor voluntarily accepted to take part in IRENA. IRENA indeed has numerous attractions for countries, especially for those who want to explore the niche markets of renewable energy technologies. In most international environmental institutions, lack of binding mechanisms is considered as a problem. In the case of IRENA, however it stands as an advantage with the help of various 'carrots' like technology and knowledge transfer opportunities, pieces of entrepreneurial advice, and education and training support schemes.

This study argues that while governing international energy transitions, certain institutional and non-institutional challenges have arisen. Institutional challenges of the current energy governance are narrow coverage of demand-side energy issues and environmental externalities, division between developed and developing countries in the system, and the bottleneck that is created by controversial contextual issues. Meta-analysis of the relevant literature and personal interviews with IRENA officials by the author showed that IRENA has been addressing these challenges by exclusively focusing on renewable energy issues and avoiding conflictual areas, as well as accepting membership applications from all countries of all regions regardless of any country-characteristic. Thereby, it acts as a productive and constructive platform for information dissemination, policy advisory, mapping of resource potentials and data collection for a large number of member states.

Non-institutional challenges of global energy governance are defined as the dominance of fossil resources within the current structure, the need for a public perception of the urgency of renewable energy deployment, encouraging states to be more active and willing, and a normative change in global energy governance for a more sustainable and comprehensive energy transition. These challenges can also be seen as tasks or missions which are not exclusive to international institutions but all stakeholders from the public and private realms. For its own share of the burden, IRENA has been trying to encourage its member states to be more active and willing in the absence of a binding mechanism by demonstrating its issue areas as promising opportunities for economic benefits, rather than insisting on rather more controversial aspects. Its deliberate focus on solely renewable energy-related agenda items is a concrete reflection of this principle. As for raising awareness and ensuring social acceptance regarding renewables, its multi-stakeholder *Coalition for Action to Bolster Public Support for Renewable Energy* is a noteworthy effort. However, the need for a normative change in global energy governance and a challenge to the dominance of fossil resources in governance structures remain as areas which require broader efforts aside from those of a number of institutions.

The energy price volatility problem is here to stay, hence along with the day-by-day depletion of the fossil resources, more and more states are realizing the high opportunity cost of late investment in renewable energy technologies. More examples of voluntary participation of states indicates their willingness and increasing consensus over this issue. The construction of a new international energy regime cannot go by without state intervention and determination. Hence, so long as these participating states apply what they learn from technology and policy transfers, in their own governmental policy-making, positive results can be expected. IRENA gives substantial project assistance regarding the renewable energy generation in rural off-grid areas for instance. Especially in developing and underdeveloped countries, such activities act as valuable opportunities.

Although we have a few decades before we face significant fossil resource shortages, incremental steps towards a new and more diversified energy regime are already being taken. There exists a common agreement over the idea that the energy transition should also be climate-friendly and sustainable at all costs. Apart from conventional challenges like supply security and energy efficiency, resource diversification and sustainable energy solutions also stand out as important tasks. The global community's performance in tackling these challenges will depend on how determined their state leaders are, as well as to what extent well-designed management and governance institutions are available in the global energy governance structure.

Note

1 For the relevant literature, see Podobnik (1999: 166–167); Kern and Smith (2008: 4101); Hirst and Froggatt (2012: 3); Karlsson-Vinkuyzen *et al.* (2012: 13); and Urpelainen and Van de Graaf (2013).

References

Biermann, F., Pattberg, P., Van Asselt, H. and Zelli, F. (2009), 'The Fragmentation of Global Governance Architectures: A Framework for Analysis', *Global Environmental Politics*, 9 (4): 14–40.

Deng, Y.Y., Blok, K. and van der Leun, K. (2012), 'Transition to a Fully Sustainable Global Energy System', *Energy Strategy Reviews*, 1: 109–121.

Fischedick, M., Borbonus, S. and Scheck, H. (2011), Towards Global Energy Governance: Strategies for Equitable Access to Sustainable Energy, Stiftung Entwicklung und Frieden, Policy Paper, No. 34.

Florini, A. and Sovacool, B.K. (2009), 'Who Governs Energy? The Challenges of Facing Global Energy Governance', *Energy Policy*, 37: 5239–5248.

Fogarty, D. (2012), *India, China Power CO₂ Emissions Growth in 2012 – Study*, Retrieved from Reuters Web site: http://in.reuters.com/article/2012/12/02/climate-emissions-india-china-idINDEE8B107B20121202, published on 2 December 2012.

Gulfnews (2013), *China Announces Decision to Join Irena*, Retrieved from Gulfnews Web site: http://gulfnews.com/business/general/china-announces-decision-to-join-irena-1.1132023, published on 14 January 2013.

Hirst, N. and Froggatt, A. (2012), *The Reform of Global Energy Governance*, Grantham Institute for Climate Change, Discussion Paper, No. 3.

IEA (2012), *CO₂ Emissions from Fuel Combustion: Highlights*, Retrieved from International Energy Agency Web site: www.iea.org/co2highlights.pdf.

IRENA (2013a), *About IRENA*, Retrieved from International Renewable Energy Agency Web site: www.irena.org/menu/index.aspx?mnu=cat&PriMenuID=13&CatID=9.

IRENA (2013b), *Global Atlas for Solar and Wind Energy*, Retrieved from International Renewable Energy Agency Web site: www.irena.org/menu/index.aspx?mnu=Subcat&PriMenuID=35&CatID=109&SubcatID=163.

IRENA (2013c), *Institutional Structure – Assembly*, Retrieved from International Renewable Energy Agency Web site: www.irena.org/menu/index.aspx?mnu=cat&PriMenuID=44&CatID=61.

IRENA (2013d), *Institutional Structure – Council*, Retrieved from International Renewable Energy Agency Web site: www.irena.org/menu/index.aspx?mnu=cat&PriMenuID=44&CatID=62.

IRENA (2013e), *Institutional Structure – Secretariat*, Retrieved from International Renewable Energy Agency Web site: www.irena.org/menu/index.aspx?mnu=cat&PriMenuID=44&CatID=131.

IRENA (2013f), *Policy Advice and Capacity Building*, Retrieved from International Renewable Energy Agency Web site: www.irena.org/menu/index.aspx?mnu=cat&PriMenuID=35&CatID=110.

IRENA (2013g), *IRENA Innovation and Technology Centre*, Retrieved from International Renewable Energy Agency Web site: www.irena.org/menu/index.aspx?mnu=cat&PriMenuID=35&CatID=112.

IRENA (2016a), *Renewables Readiness Assessment: Design to Action*, Retrieved from International Renewable Energy Agency Web site: www.irena.org/menu/index.aspx?mnu=Subcat&PriMenuID=36&CatID=141&SubcatID=335.

IRENA (2016b), *Bolstering Public Support for Renewable Energy*, Retrieved from International Renewable Energy Agency Web site: www.irena.org/menu/index.aspx?mnu=Subcat&PriMenuID=35&CatID=109&SubcatID=376.

IRENA (2016c), *Coalition Activities*, Retrieved from International Renewable Energy Agency Web site: www.irena.org/menu/index.aspx?mnu=Subcat&PriMenuID=35&CatID=109&SubcatID=376&RefID=376&SubID=382&MenuType=Q.

IRENA Official (2015), *Personal Interview*, 14 April, IRENA Headquarters, Abu Dhabi, United Arab Emirates.

IRENA RESource (2016), *RESource: Your Source for Renewable Energy Information*, Retrieved from International Renewable Energy Agency Web site: http://resourceirena.irena.org/gateway/.

IRENA and UNEP (2013), *Insights from Interviews, a Survey, and a Workshop with Potential End-Users of the Global Atlas for Solar and Wind Energy*, Retrieved from International Renewable Energy Agency Web site: www.irena.org/DocumentDownloads/Publications/IRENA_UNEP_Insights_Global_Atlas.pdf.

Jacobsson, S. and Lauber, V. (2006), 'The Politics and Policy of Energy System Transformation: Explaining the German Diffusion of Renewable Energy Technology', *Energy Policy*, 34: 256–276.

Jefferson, M. (2008), 'Accelerating the Transition to Sustainable Energy Systems', *Energy Policy*, 36: 4116–4125.

Karlsson-Vinkhuyzen, S.I., Jollands, N. and Staudt, L. (2012), 'Global Governance for Sustainable Energy: The Contribution of a Global Public Goods Approach', *Ecological Economics*, 83: 11–18.

Kern, F. and Smith, A. (2008), 'Restructuring Energy Systems for Sustainability? Energy Transition Policy in the Netherlands', *Energy Policy*, 36: 4093–4103.

Meadowcroft, J. (2009), 'What About Politics? Sustainable Development, Transition Management, and Long Term Energy Transitions', *Policy Science*, 42: 323–340.

Meyer, T.L. (2013), 'The Architecture of International Energy Governance', *Proceedings of the Annual Meeting (American Society of International Law)*, 106, 389–394.

Morello, L. (2012), 'Global CO_2 Emissions from Fossil-Fuel Burning Into High-Risk Zone', *Scientific American*, Retrieved from Scientific American Web site: www.scientificamerican.com/article.cfm?id=global-co2-emissions-from, published on 3 December 2012.

Podobnik, B. (1999), 'Toward a Sustainable Energy Regime: A Long-Wave Interpretation of Global Energy Shifts', *Technological Forecasting and Social Change*, 62: 155–172.

PWC (2012), *Too Late for Two Degrees? Low Carbon Economy Index 2012*, Retrieved from PricewaterhouseCoopers Web site: http://pdf.pwc.co.uk/low-carbon-economy-index-nov12.pdf, published in November 2012.

RTCC (2012), *IEA: Fossil Fuel Subsidies Increased 30% in 2011. Responding to Climate Change*, Retrieved from RTCC Web site: www.rtcc.org/iea-fossil-fuel-subsidies-increase-30-in-2011/, published on 14 November 2012.

Urpelainen, J. and Van de Graaf, T. (2013), 'The International Renewable Energy Agency: A Success Story in Institutional Innovation?', *International Environmental Agreements*, 15 (2): 159–177.

Van de Graaf, T. (2013), 'Fragmentation in Global Environmental Governance: Explaining the Creation of IRENA', *Global Environmental Politics*, 13 (3): 14–33.

Van den Bergh, J.C.J.M. (2012), 'Effective Climate-energy Solutions, Escape Routes and Peak Oil', *Energy Policy*, 46: 530–536.

Verbruggen, A. and Al Marchohi, M. (2010), 'Views on Peak Oil and its Relation to Climate Change Policy', *Energy Policy*, 38: 5572–5581.

Viguier, L.L. (2004), 'A Proposal to Increase Developing Country Participation in International Climate Policy', *Environmental Science and Policy*, 7: 195–204.

14 Carbon dioxide emissions in the carbon cycle frame

What will the future look like?

Onur Tutulmaz and Selim Çağatay

1 Introduction

The climate change problem the world is facing today is crucial for the future of the planet. Despite a great deal of political, academic and international endeavour activated to control emissions, very little success has been achieved so far. Our study tries to bring a critical look on this issue.

The fast industrial development and expansion after the destruction of the World Wars caused a rising pressure on the environment. Meanwhile, society started to pay an increasing attention to environmental issues. In this framework, the role of limited but significant academic and activist studies in this increasing public attention should be underlined. *Silent Spring* (Carson 1962), *The Limits to Growth* (Meadows *et al.* 1972), *Our Common Future* (or *Brundtland Report*[1]) (WCED 1987) and the other studies of the Club of Rome can be regarded in the same vein. The ozone layer depletion was the first important global level environmental problem the world encountered. The satellite photos of the ozone layer, which detected destruction in the layer, caused a sudden turmoil. That bitter surprise led to a fast international reaction that eventually produced the Montreal Protocol, and CFC (chloro-fluorocarbon) emissions depleting the ozone layer were taken under control. Ozone layer depletion and the Montreal Protocol are still deemed as the most successful cases in environmental issues (EC 2007: 5).[2] Today, human beings are facing another global level environmental problem: global warming and climate change. However, we cannot observe similar success in dealing with this vital global problem so far. Of course, there are a few reasons behind this current failure. Nevertheless, the most important one is its complexity.

Further reasons can also be counted for that lack of success. First of all, the climate change issue did not have such a clear proof as the ozone layer issue had, especially at the beginning. Despite a large majority among scientists now agreeing that climate change is an imminent problem for the world, some are still not convinced. Moreover, it rapidly turned into a political dispute, especially in North America.

If we concern ourselves with the last point in more detail, one should mention that some of the scientific realities that are used as arguments in that dispute need to be clarified. One is that the earth had different climate ages in its past geological time scale.[3] Another one connected to the first is that planet earth and the life on it has survived and adapted. This is because geological time scaled climate changes can give enough time for evolutionary adaptation processes. The main problem in this discussion is the *human causation* in climate change and global warming. Human caused emissions are often called *anthropogenic emissions*. Anthropogenic emissions have been emerging for more than two centuries after the occurrence of the industrial revolution, and they are estimated to continue in an increasing way at least for the near future. Initial results of the *Paris Climate Conference*[4] indicate ambitious targets, but even in the best scenarios, we still need some time to see the peak in emissions and only after reaching the peak can a net decrease in global emissions be possible, as shown in Figure 14.4.

We can look at the institutional timeline of climate change briefly. The first Climate Change Conference was held in 1979. One of the most important results of that conference was realized 11 years later and IPCC, Intergovernmental Panel on Climate Change, was established in 1988. After years of uninterrupted efforts, three Conventions,[5] to deal with the negative effects of economic development, were established at the Rio summit in 1992. The environmental problems in the three different fronts which those conventions are built to deal with can be deemed as the results of exceeding carrying capacities of the planet in various areas. Despite the interconnectivity of various natural cycles and processes in different areas, the climate change problem places carbon dioxide emissions as the most urgent. United Nations Framework Convention on Climate Change (UNFCCC) was established under the UN roof at the Rio summit and came into force in 1994, becoming the first fundamental treaty to be the base for all subsequent diplomacy to deal with the climate change problem. As a next step, Kyoto Protocol was generated to legally frame UNFCCC convention, and therefore, it became the first solid base in struggling with GHG emissions. Kyoto Protocol was signed by 195 countries including European Union in 1997, and came into force in 2005. Kyoto Protocol required from the signatory countries to reduce the greenhouse gases (GHG) emissions 5.2 per cent below their 1990 emission levels.

Despite the whole efforts, not any significant success has been achieved to create a positive impact on the greenhouse effect in the atmosphere of the planet. This chapter aims to analyze the current structure, mostly pre-Paris situation, and speculate about the results and methods to deal with it. Second section tries to analyze the carbon emissions situation which is the most important among GHG emissions in terms of their total impact in greenhouse effect. Third section takes the carrying capacity issue into account. Fourth section evaluates the situation of carbon emission and its effects on the carbon cycle. Fifth section concludes the analysis and speculates about future developments or methods that should be searched for.

2   Carbon dioxide emissions

The global economy still depends on carbon fuels with more than 80 per cent dependency level. Therefore, fossil fuels, which are oil, natural gas and coal, are today still unrivalled large-scale energy sources that power the world economies. The nuclear energy, solar and other renewable energy sources, having about 10 per cent share combined, which constitutes an unacceptably small share for sustainable environmental concerns; especially the capacity of renewable energy needs to be improved much further. This current structure, however, has created today's global economy emitting a huge amount of carbon and other greenhouse gases (GHG).

Among GHGs,[6] carbon dioxide emissions take the leading concern, which we scrutinize in this paper. There can be several reasons for such a priority. First, the total effect of carbon dioxide, as it is shown in Figure 14.1, is dominant among other GHGs; actually, it is called 'the single most important anthropogenic greenhouse gas in the atmosphere' (WMO, 2014: 3). Second, the most significant threat posed against the natural cycles is the one that affects the carbon cycle. In that sense, carbon dioxide, once again, is placed in an unchallenged position. The heavy threat becomes obvious if we take into account that methane (CH_4), having the second biggest portion in Figure 14.1, is another carbon including gas.

Third, CO_2 emissions are directly related with the energy sector which constitutes directly the base for the whole economy; therefore, the main driver of the increase of radiative forcing, as given in Figure 14.2, is coming from CO_2. Eighty-three per cent of the radiative increase in the last ten years comes from CO_2 emissions. Figure 14.2 shows that the NOAA[7] greenhouse gas index

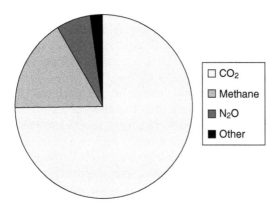

Figure 14.1 Share of CO_2 among greenhouse gases in 2010 (in terms of CO_2 e-tons which reflect the greenhouse effect effectiveness)

Source: WDI (2015: Table 3.9).

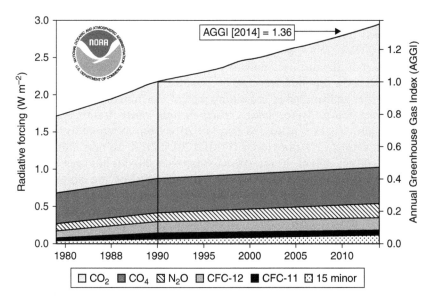

Figure 14.2 Atmospheric radiative forcing of long lived GHGs and 2014 NOAA Annual Greenhouse Gas Index

Source: WMO (2015: 2).

has risen to 1.36 from the 1990 level of 1, which means a 36 per cent increase (WMO, 2015: 2).

Other items, which should be mentioned at this point, are water vapour and aerosols. Water vapour, after carbon dioxide, is the second most important in terms of the greenhouse effect; however, it is not anthropogenic, it has generally short-term effects, and a complex relationship with other greenhouse gases. For example, when the carbon intensity reaches twice the pre-industrial levels water vapour can increase the warming effect of CO_2 three times more than it would do without water vapour (see Figure 14.6). Therefore, this vapour accelerative effect must also be added to the warming effects of carbon emissions to make a proper assessment of the greenhouse effect. Aerosol is also warming effective like the water vapour; on the other hand, it is one of the anthropogenic gases unlike the water vapour. Aerosol, like water vapour, is not counted among the GHGs or in climate change calculations because its adverse effect is assumed to neutralize its heating effects.

After explaining the single dominant position of carbon dioxide among other GHGs, we can focus on the sink and source ends of the carbon cycle, which is a strategic ecosystem structure to supply very critical ecosystem services related with absorption capacity, climate regulation and regulation of the energy budget of the planet. Starting from the macro level, total CO_2 emission has been emitted so far amounting to 555 GtC[8] (±85 GtC). About

40 per cent of that amount (240 ± 10 GtC) has remained in the atmosphere, and the rest has been removed by the oceans (about 30 per cent or 160 GtC) and natural terrestrial systems (about 30 per cent or 155 GtC) between 1750 and 2011 (Ciais *et al.*, 2013: 486).

Total carbon dioxide accumulation in the atmosphere has risen from 550 GtC, which is the pre-industrialization era value, to 800 GtC. This increase is caused by the unabsorbed or remaining part of the human caused emissions as presented above. Atmospheric carbon dioxide concentrations have risen by more than 40 per cent to 398 ppm[9] in 2014 from its pre-industrial mid-eighteenth century 278 ppm levels (WMO, 2015: 2). If we take into account that about 60 per cent of the human caused carbon dioxide has been absorbed by the terrestrial systems and oceans,[10] the real level of the emissions can be evaluated in a better way. Emissions are not therefore just piling up posing a threat to climate but they also increasingly continue to pile up in the atmosphere. Figure 14.3(a) shows the majority of the CO_2 accumulation in the atmosphere that has been created in the last 60 years.

Figure 14.3(b) shows a direct relationship between the dissolved carbon dioxide levels and in-situ pH[11] levels in the last 20 years, as an indication of acidification. In turn, this acidification caused by ocean absorption of the total carbon dioxide emissions could be considered as an important side effect of the regenerative activity of the globe.

Meanwhile, the rising atmospheric GHG levels increase the amount of heat absorbed by the earth in unit time, called the *greenhouse effect*, and cause continuous warming of the globe. This rising heat intake of the globe has resulted in a warming up about 0.85 °C so far (IPCC, 2013: 5). It must be underlined that the suspension of CO_2 molecules in the atmosphere will continue to contribute to global warming by absorbing sunlight; this warming effect prevails for centuries even after new emissions stop. Calculating the long endurance of CO_2 in the atmosphere,[12] the existing amount of CO_2 would lead to a 0.5 °C further warming relative to the present surface temperature which would mean almost 1.5 °C above the pre-industrial levels (Flannery 2015). Figure 14.4 shows two important enduring effects of existing CO_2 in the atmosphere. First, it takes time to reach CO_2 stabilization levels after starting to curb emissions; and this time lag causes a significant temperature rise to happen in this transition period.

Second, it can be seen from Figure 14.4 that even after eliminating CO_2 emissions and reaching stabilization levels, the temperature rise continues slowly, however the rise continues for longer than a century.

Additionally, the estimates show that two-thirds of the overall amount emitted so far comes from fossil fuel usage and the remaining third could be attributed to the change in land usage which mainly represents the effects of deforestation (Ciais *et al.*, 2013: 474; IPCC, 2013: 12).

With today's annual 10 GtC (in terms of nearly 40 $GtCO_2$) global emissions level (Flannery 2015), the total cumulative emission of the last two and

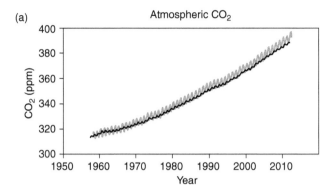

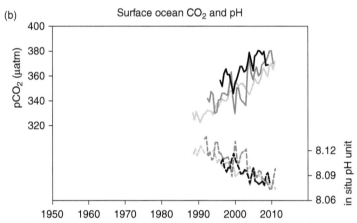

Figure 14.3 Some measured indicators of changing carbon cycle: (a) atmospheric CO$_2$
concentrations from Mauna Loa and South Pole; (b) partial pressure of
dissolved CO$_2$ at ocean surface (solid curves) and in-situ pH levels (dashed
curves), an acidity measure (taken from three stations on the Atlantic and
Pacific Oceans)

Source: IPCC (2013: 12).

half centuries could be reached in only 55 years. Moreover, a decrease in the
sink capacity or the dynamic effects of the natural cycles might play an accel-
erator role in the near future and therefore should be closely observed.

Observing the recent trends in annual emissions reveals the argument that
the geographical and nationwide properties of global emissions seem to exer-
cise a non-negligible role in the future. While the two major emitters, the US
and Europe, have been trying to slow down their emissions, other main emitters, the prominent developing economies of China and India, are experienc-
ing acceleration in their own. In brief, the momentum in developing economies
seems to be a big challenge for post-Paris curbing emissions efforts.

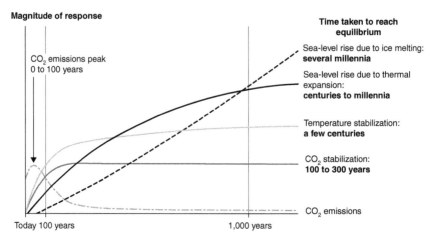

Figure 14.4 Time taken to reach equilibrium
Source: UNEP (2011: 18).

3   Carrying capacity

Unlike the ozone layer depletion case we mentioned in Section 1, little success has been achieved in dealing with carbon emissions and the climate change problem so far. We have already pointed out a few reasons for the unsuccessful route but the most important one is the complexity of the problem creating difficulties in framing the current situation. The systematic approach to frame down that problem should take both source and sink sides. Accordingly, the regenerative and carrying capacity concepts must be used to frame emissions.

The ecosystem of the planet is composed of different natural cycles. The carbon cycle, an important cycle for the ecosystem, is directly related with the energy sector and global warming. Actually there are different dimensions of the carbon cycle and those dimensions have different time scales as well. For instance, while geological processes are scaled over thousands of years, the photosynthesis cycle takes place on a daily basis. In order to define a regenerative capacity of a subsystem, we should have a common time frame; therefore, the effect of the natural cycles must be expressed in terms of the same unit. The annual basis is commonly used when dealing with emissions; hence, we should take the carbon cycle at an annual scale. Apart from the time scale, other factors such as geography and ambience also have effects on the natural cycles. Those different environments determine the properties of the sink and source parts of cycles. Back to the carbon cycle, terrestrial and ocean sinks have very different capacity and dynamic properties.

The regenerative capacity of the world actually refers to that of its subsystems. Although it can be approximated using the vector of subsystem capacities, as Wackernagel *et al.* (2002) did, the overpassing capacity is defined as the vulnerable dimension using the analogy of the weakest link of a chain. Researchers used different terms to describe the regeneration capacities of individual cycles such as planetary boundaries (Rockstrom *et al.*, 2009), carbon footprint (Yang *et al.*, 2014) and also Daly used the terms 'carrying capacity' and 'ecological footprints' in relation to the concept of the regeneration capacity (Daly and Farley, 2004: 34–35).

As carbon dioxide emissions are our primary concern, regenerative capacity should be taken into account as part of the whole global carbon cycle (Ciais *et al.*, 2013: 470–475). Because it is directly related to the global warming issue, other GHG emissions should also be included in the calculations. On the other hand, separating out the carbon cycle alone, we can build simplified carbon dioxide emissions calculations. Then it can be compared in terms of average weight in global warming. For the sake of simplicity we have tried to isolate the CO_2 emissions boundary of the planet below. We can also justify our focus on CO_2 emissions because the positive and negative effects of the aerosol and non-CO_2 emissions can currently be assumed to stabilize each other (Rockstrom *et al.*, 2009: 10).

3.1 Threshold criteria for carbon dioxide emissions

Rockstrom *et al.* (2009) described a dual boundary depending on the extent of land ice. The first criterion is calculated as 350 ppm for CO_2 concentration. The second criteria is calculated for radioactive forcing and set at 1 W/m^2 for its threshold value. Since the current concentration of CO_2 has reached 400 ppm levels, we notify that the first threshold has been passed (Flannery, 2015).

Similar to the ecological footprint concept, the carbon footprint threshold would be unity, or 1.0, in global concept. Wackernagel *et al.* (2002) calculated an annual regenerative capacity for carbon dioxide emissions using the ecological footprint concept. The regenerative capacity was exceeded around 16 per cent (i.e. the average global area demand is calculated as 1.16 gha (global hectares) for fossil fuel and nuclear energy usage); and more importantly this 1.16 gha constitutes half of the overall global area demand (which was calculated as 2.33 in 1999), after separating oceans intake of one third of total CO_2 emissions. One should note that this amount represents very rough calculations and depends on several assumptions. On the other hand, IPCC (2013) has a similar calculation stating that 15–30 per cent of annual emissions accumulate in the atmosphere after all the carbon has been fixed by natural ways.

As for the carbon fixation capacity of the planet, about 258[13] GtCO2 (approximately 70 GtC) carbon dioxide is fixed by photosynthesis. Oceanic photosynthesis is responsible for about half of it (47 per cent of total amount; roughly 120 GtCO2 or 33 GtC) and the rest of the photosynthetic transformation fixation is conducted by the terrestrial organisms and plants. These numbers are comparable in level terms with today's carbon cycle realizations given in the United States' Department of Environment in Figure 14.5: 120 GtC carbon gases are annually cycled in the terrestrial carbon cycle and about

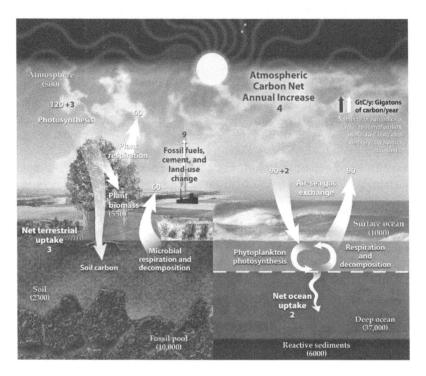

Figure 14.5 Simplified representation of the global fast carbon cycle
Source: US DOE (2008: 1).

90 GtC are annually sequestered in the oceanic carbon cycle. These figures here are representing an equilibrium that can be reached in a geological time scale, which is at least a hundred thousand years (Rockstrom *et al.*, 2009: 2–3). Anthropogenic, or human caused, emissions experienced in the last two centuries represent a very fast change, almost equal to a shock in terms of geological time scale. An excessive 10 GtC annual anthropogenic emission comes as a burden for the carbon cycle, shown as added numbers in Figure 14.5. The terrestrial and oceanic natural systems increase the intake part carbon cycle as a defensive response but still more than 40 per cent of anthropogenic emissions are piled up in the atmosphere.

An important point about this emission flow is the intake capacity of the carbon cycle. An increasing intake is the response of nature to the emissions and it definitely helps to requester a part of human caused carbon emissions. But still half of those emissions has created today's problem of a substantial rise in atmospheric carbon levels, as well as increased acidification in oceans as a side effect. If there is a limit to increase this intake capacity, the carbon piling rates will become a more serious problem than expected. The complex relationship between separate natural systems and interconnectedness of natural cycles can serve as an *acceleration effect*.

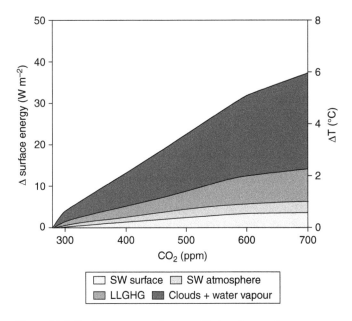

Figure 14.6 Surface energy change effects of greenhouse gases according to CO_2 intensity in the atmosphere

Source: WMO (2015: 1).

Figure 14.6 presents a good example for that acceleration effect. At the pre-industrial levels of the atmospheric carbon concentration, the radiative force, and therefore, the surface temperature, is at balance. When we surpass the planetary boundary of atmospheric carbon concentration, the warming effect of GHGs, mainly carbon dioxide, is increasing proportionally with the increasing atmospheric concentration; but the interaction of water vapour with these long lived greenhouse gases (LLGHGs) can triple this effect. To sum up, the planetary boundaries reflect a very complex balance of natural systems; when we surpass the carbon threshold and break the natural balance of radiative forcing, not just direct effect of emissions, as an unbalancing factor, but the interaction of other interconnected cycles and their acceleration effects come into the scene, and hence, they should also be taken into account.

3.2 General threshold criteria for the world

The ecological footprint concept tries to express regenerative boundaries of the planet in a manner easier to understand. In this sense the threshold criterion of the ecological footprint must be 1.0 for the global ecological system. The concept of ecological footprints has a direct connection with the carrying capacity and/or appropriated carrying capacity concepts (Rees, 1992; Daly and Farley, 2004: 35).

Similarly Rockstrom *et al.* (2009) proposed another term to define regenerative boundaries of the world: *planetary boundaries.* They calculated nine sub-planetary boundaries in order to define global thresholds, which are likened to 'planetary playing-fields' in their study.

On the other hand, Wackernagel *et al.* (2002) produced a measurement of 'ecological overshoot' based on regenerative capacities of the biosphere including six human activities. The research found that nature's supply was 20 per cent *overshot* by human demand (Wackernagel *et al.*, 2002: 9269).

4   Evaluation of the emissions and human effect on the carbon cycle

Several methods, such as the cap-and-trade system, carbon tax and carbon credit systems, have been used to deal with CO_2 emissions and the climate change problem so far. However, their applications are still at trial levels; and the current results are not reliable and the ongoing discussion on that issue is not mature in the literature yet. In spite of individual encouraging examples, the impact of emission controlling policies on the carbon emissions has been minor so far.

The practice of the Kyoto Protocol, whose even very mild goals have not been met, has been very discouraging so far. Nevertheless, we are gradually witnessing the recognition of increasing effects of climate change forcing countries to take serious steps to curb their carbon emissions. Valuable efforts have been noticed from leading economies in reducing the carbon emissions. Especially in the last year, before the occurrence of the Paris Climate Change Conference, these efforts seemed accelerated: the EU prepared to propose a 60 per cent cut by 2050 (Neslen, 2015); the US proposed a 30 per cent cut by 2025, and China is undergoing significant promises (Parlapiano, 2014). Those endeavours have the potential to bring significant change to the gloomy route the Kyoto Protocol has followed so far. On the contrary, there is still a big gap for a 2 °C warming threshold (UNEP, 2015b). Moreover, as another imminent challenge, we are expecting the share of developing economies to overtake the dominance in the global emissions. This will be another difficulty for the post-Paris efforts to control the carbon emissions.

If we add the interconnectedness and acceleration effects of planetary boundaries, the severity of the situation would be clearer. Figure 14.6 in the previous section shows that the greenhouse effect of carbon emissions can be tripled by the effect of water vapour when carbon concentrations reached twice the pre-industrial levels. In fact, this *acceleration effect* shows how things can get worse much faster than expected before.

Analysing the overall situation, on the positive side we observe that by the severity of the climate change problem becoming clearer, the world showed a real intention to deal with the problem maybe for the first time at the Paris Climate Conference (December 2015). Some of the leading economies and global institutions are stepping in and announcing significant thresholds for their economies and INDCs[14] (Intended Nationally Determined

Contributions) to reduce emissions. Those steps are in favour of giving the private sector and technology developers the necessary incentives to accelerate their efforts. On the negative side, however, newly applied strategies and the complexity of applying international targets create vulnerability for the success of the post-Paris global endeavour of controlling carbon emissions. More importantly, even if the successful scenario case of emission reductions can be achieved, its insufficiency has already been discussed (Revkin, 2015; UNEP, 2015b).

Our basic analysis on carrying capacity and carbon cycle shows that the problem is bigger than controlling and easing the emissions now. Above 40 per cent of the human caused emissions are continuing to pile up in the atmosphere. Accumulation of the human caused emissions have raised the carbon levels in the atmosphere by about 45 per cent, from 289 ppm to almost 400 ppm in terms of intensity, or from 550 GtC to 800 GtC in terms of total sink accumulation in the atmosphere.

The slow or enduring effects of emissions, interconnectedness and accelerating effects of other global boundaries are often omitted in the calculations. However, some studies show that the expected results of the global warming can even rise from 3 °C to 6 °C at the end of the century taking into account such slow cycle effects or 'slow feedbacks' (Rockstrom *et al.*, 2009: 10). Calculations for decreasing carbon emissions generally do not take slow cycle effects into account, but when we go out of the natural cycle's planetary boundaries, these slow feedbacks can bring forward the interconnectedness and acceleration effects of unforeseen interaction of different natural cycles.

In conclusion, it is remarkably clear for us that the world cannot continue in business-as-usual in atmospheric carbon emissions. The world might probably have to undergo a significant transformation in its energy structure in the next 50 years independent of the success in application of the Kyoto Protocol and Paris Agreement. Therefore, bringing into the agenda the transition methods and strategies for our economies to conform to the carbon cycle boundaries is at least as important as curbing carbon emissions.

Decarbonization has been used as a widespread term in recent literature and in the institutional endeavour of curbing and decreasing carbon emissions. Decarbonization is defined as the declining carbon intensity ratio of primary energy by the IPCC (2007). On the other hand, countries have focused on decreasing emissions by changing the combination of fossil fuels instead of decreasing the total percentage of the fossil fuels usage. We will differentiate those two tracks; calling the former channel 1 and the latter channel 2. In doing so, we will separate *decarbonization* methods. Channel 1 can be realized by forcing out the dirty sources or by forcing old technologies out. Channel 2 can be achieved rather by phasing out fossil fuels and replacing them with non-emission sources such as renewable energy sources. To underline the structural differences between them it has to be made clear that undergoing the second channel is not about the limited mitigation but more about the real transformation of the energy sector.

5   Conclusion and speculation on future prospects

The economic development of the last two centuries after industrialization has created an important challenge for the world. Despite important steps taken aiming to control carbon emissions lately, very little success has been achieved so far. Some institutional attempts and INDCs of 119 countries (see Section 4) preceding the highly anticipated COP21 Paris Conference are good examples for increasing attempts to control climate change.

On the other hand, a significant rise in average surface temperature is almost inevitable for our century regarding the structure of emissions; and accordingly, our economies have to undergo important transitions. Moreover, apart from the success in application of the Kyoto Protocol or Paris Agreement, the current accumulated carbon amount in the atmosphere poses a necessity of radical transformation for the energy sector in the near future. This acceleration of the second channel, as we call it, will probably soon turn out to be an inevitably clear step for the world to take. Consequently, the countries which prepare themselves for this transformation sooner might have a bigger opportunity. Actually, we have seen signs of the starting of another historical competition in this field called green economy and green energy. The Paris agreement seems also to shackle this issue, but it is too early to see the dimensions and implications of this grand theme.

In investigating the current situation, we propose that channel 1 cannot be the right humanitarian response that we are looking for in endeavouring with climate change. Having more than 80 per cent dependency in the world economy on them, fossil fuels will continue to be a vital energy source at least for the near future. Decarbonization by real transformation of the energy sector, which we called channel 2, will have to get priority to transform the sector; as far as it can be achieved.

Furthermore, we can speculate that even the crucial channel 2 might not be enough because the current 4–5 per cent contribution of renewable energy (including bio-energy) does not seem to be improvable fast enough. Therefore, other radical steps, under the name of channel 3, have to be brought to the table without further delay. This group includes; first, technologies for fossil fuel usage such as emission catching methods for ongoing emissions or pumping carbon emissions underground, which might be obligatory regulations for fossil fuel usage when we pass the 2 °C threshold; second, carbon capturing methods to draw carbon from the atmosphere (which does not exist yet); third, the more fantasy level technologies for the moment, such as injecting sulphur into the atmosphere. Our speculation proposes that the world will find itself talking about those radical steps faster than expected; therefore bringing them into our agenda will not be unrealistic.

Notes

1   The report is commonly known as the *Brundtland Report*, with the name of the head of the commission, Gro Harlem Brundtland, the former Prime Minister of Norway.

2 For more details about the Montreal Protocol, see UNEP (2015a).
3 The geological time scale shows a much longer time period than the historical one. The stress in this scientific fact should be on *time scale* rather than *changes* not to be misleading. The change in short historical time scale shows a connection to human activity in global warming when compared to other climate changes that happened in the geological time scaled history of the planet.
4 The official name of the conference is COP 21: 21st Conference of Parties to UNFCCC. The conference, held annually as the most important body of UNFCCC, is also known as *Climate Conference* or *Climate Change Conference*.
5 The three conventions are: UNFCC, Framework Convention on Climate Change; UNCBD, Convention on Biological Diversity; UNCCD, United Nations Convention to Combat Desertification (see, www.unfccc.int; www.cbd.int; www.unccd.int).
6 In the Kyoto Protocol only six GHGs are counted, as follows: Carbon dioxide (CO_2), methane (CH_4), nitrous oxide (N_2O), phosphate flora carbons (PFCs), hydro flora carbons (HFCs) and sulphur hexafluoride (SF_6) gases. Some of the GHG have a much more warming effect on the environment than CO_2. Nevertheless, CO_2 emissions have the biggest detrimental impact in terms of total effect on climate change.
7 NOAA: National and Oceanic and Atmospheric Administration.
8 1 Gigatonne of carbon = 1 GtC = 10^{12} kilograms carbon. This is equal to 3.667 GtCO₂.
9 ppm: particules per million, used as a measure of emissions intensity in the atmosphere. ppm (ppb, parts per billion, also used depending on the scale of emissions) indicates the ratio of the number of gas molecules to the total number of molecules of dry air. For example, 300 ppm means 300 molecules of a gas per million molecules of dry air.
10 Additionally, the ocean acidification is accepted as an important side effect of the carbon emissions (IPCC, 2013: 11).
11 pH is a logarithmic measure of hydrogen ion concentration, and is used to indicate the acidity or alkalinity of a liquid solution. It shows acidity if pH is less than 7.
12 It is estimated that 15–40 per cent of the carbon emitted until 2100 will stay in the atmosphere more than a thousand years (Ciais *et al.*, 2013: 472).
13 This number does not include the respiration consumption following photosynthesis, therefore, the gross number of carbon fixation can be calculated as higher by as much as 50 per cent.
14 119 countries have submitted their commitments before the Paris Conference (see http://unfccc.int/focus/indc_portal/items/8766.php; http://uneplive.unep.org/media/docs/theme/13/EGR_2015_Presentation.pdf).

References

Carson, R. (1962), *Silent Spring*. Boston, MA: Houghton Mifflin.

Ciais, P., Sabine, C., Bala, G., Bopp, L., Brovkin, V., Canadell, J., Chhabra, A., DeFries, R., Galloway, J., Heimann, M., Jones, C., Le Quéré, C., Myneni, R. B., Piao, S. and Thornton , P. (2013), Carbon and Other Biogeochemical Cycles. In: *Climate Change 2013: The Physical Science Basis. Contribution of Working Group I to the Fifth Assessment Report of the Intergovernmental Panel on Climate Change*, T.F. Stocker, D. Qin, G.-K. Plattner, M. Tignor, S.K. Allen, J. Boschung, A. Nauels, Y. Xia, V. Bex and P.M. Midgley (eds), Cambridge, United Kingdom and New York, USA: Cambridge University Press, 465–570.

Daly, H.E. and Farley, J. (2004), *Ecological Economics: Principles and Applications*, Washington, DC: Island Press.

EC (2007), *The Montreal Protocol*, Belgium European Commission.

Flannery, T. (2015), 'A "Third Way" to Fight Climate Change', *The New York Times*. 24 July. Retrieved from New York Times Web site: www.nytimes.com/2015/07/24/opinion/a-third-way-to-fight-climate-change.html?ref=topics.

IPCC (2007), *Contribution of Working Group III to the Fourth Assessment Report of the Intergovernmental Panel on Climate Change*, B. Metz, O.R. Davidson, P.R. Bosch, R. Dave and L.A. Meyer (eds), Cambridge, United Kingdom and New York, USA: Cambridge University Press.

IPCC (2013), Summary for Policymakers. In: *Climate Change 2013: The Physical Science Basis. Contribution of Working Group I to the Fifth Assessment Report of the Intergovernmental Panel on Climate Change*, T.F. Stocker, D. Qin, G.-K. Plattner, M. Tignor, S.K. Allen, J. Boschung, A. Nauels, Y. Xia, V. Bex and P.M. Midgley (eds), Cambridge, United Kingdom and New York, USA: Cambridge University Press, 3–29.

Meadows, D.H., Meadows, D.L., Randers, J. and Behrens, W. (1972), *The Limits to Growth*, New York: Universe Books.

Neslen, A. (2015), 'EU Wants Paris Climate Deal to Cut Carbon Emissions 60% by 2050', *The Guardian*. 23 February. Retrieved from Guardian Web site: www.theguardian.com/environment/2015/feb/23/eu-wants-paris-climate-deal-to-cut-carbon-emissions-60-by-2050.

Parlapiano, A. (2014). 'Climate Goals Pledged by China and the U.S.', *The New York Times*, 12 November.

Rees, P. (1992), 'Ecological Footprints and Appropriated Carrying Capacity: What Urban Economics Leaves Out', *Environment and Urbanization*, 4: 121–130.

Revkin, A.C. (2015), 'The Reality Gap in the Push to Close the Global Warming "Emissions Gap" in Paris', *The New York Times*. 6 November. Retrieved from New York Times Web site: www.dotearth.blogs.nytimes.com/ 2015/11/06/ the-reality-gap-in-the-push-to-close-the-global-warming-emissions-gap-in-paris.html.

Rockstrom, J., Steffen, W., Noone, K., Persson, A. and Chapin, F.S. (2009), 'Planetary Boundaries: Exploring the Operating Space for Humanity', *Ecology and Society*, 14(2), Retrieved from Ecology and Society Web site: www.ecologyandsociety.org/vol14/iss2/art32.

UNEP (2011), *Introduction to UNFCC and Kyoto Protocol, Session 4*, Retrieved from UNEP Web site: www.google.com/url?sa=t&rct=j&q=&esrc=s&source=web&cd=1&ved=0CCAQFjAAahUKEwj2uaGwm4HIAhXMEywKHTaDASA&url=http%3A%2F%2Fwww.unep.fr%2Fshared%2Fpublications%2Fcdrom%2FDTIx0899xPA%2Fsession04_UNFCCC.ppt&usg=AFQjCNGKvJ_aOWjWGcpZ9vkJzSJup3jEQA&sig2=GUVwW2myCTQ8YRqqEikJTg.

UNEP (2015a), *The Montreal Protocol on Substances That Deplete the Ozone Layer,* UNEP Ozone Secretariat, Retrieved from UNEP Web site: http://ozone.unep.org/en/treaties-and-decisions/montreal-protocol-substances-deplete-ozone-layer.

UNEP (2015b), *The Emissions Gap Report 2015, Executive Summary.* UNEP-United Nations Environment Programme, Retrieved from UNEP Web site: http://uneplive.unep.org/media/docs/theme/13/EGR_2015_ES_English_Embargoed.pdf. Retrieved on 2015-12-14.

US DOE (2008), *Climate Placemat: Energy-Climate Nexus*, Report from the March 2008 Workshop, DOE/SC-108, U.S. Department of Energy Office of Science.

Wackernagel, M., Schulz, N.B., Deumling, D., Linares, A.C., Jennkins, M. and Kapos, V. (2002), 'Tracking the Ecological Overshoot of the Human Economy', *PNAS*, 99 (14): 9266–9271. Doi: 10.1073/pnas.142033699.

WCED (World Commission on Environment and Development) (1987), *Our Common Future*, New York: Oxford University Press.

WDI (2015), *Trends in Greenhouse Gas Emissions, Table 3.9*, World Development Indicators, World Bank, Retrieved from World Bank web site: http://worldbank.org.

WMO (2014), *WMO Greenhouse Gas Bulletin, No 10*. World Meteorological Organization, Retrieved from WMO Web site: www.wmo.int/pages/prog/arep/gaw/ghg/GHGbulletin.html.

WMO (2015), *WMO Greenhouse Gas Bulletin, No 11*. World Meteorological Organization, Retrieved from WMO Web site: www.wmo.int/pages/prog/arep/gaw/ghg/GHGbulletin.html.

Yang, H., Lantao, S. and Chen, G. (2014), 'Separating the Mechanisms of Transient Responses to Stratospheric Ozone Depletion: Like Cooling in an Idealized Atmospheric Model', *J. Atmos. Sci.*, 72 (2): 763–773.

Concluding remarks

*M. Özgür Kayalıca, Selim Çağatay
and Hakan Mıhçı*

Nil Volentibus Arduum
Nothing arduous for the willing

Climate change is a major threat to nature and the damage continues. Life, as we know it, will never be the same again unless it is stopped. Countries have been rounding tables for the last half-century as parties to international cooperation with the beliefs of being able to solve the environmental problems, curb the emissions, etc., and/or simply just be a part of such global initiatives whether or not a solution will be eventually achieved. How could one be sure? Not only compliance costs but also assessment of the implementation, compliance and effectiveness of IEAs are quite complex. Concerned with global and transboundary negative externalities, this book thoroughly discusses how performance of IEAs can be improved and aims to bring the main challenges of international agreements in sharper focus. In this context, the book attempts to analyse the most probable factors that cause IEAs to fail in achieving the proposed outcomes of such IEAs.

The first factor is considered to be the stability of IEAs. The book explores various aspects of 'stability of IEAs'. One aspect is the heterogeneity of countries, which is presented in Chapter 1. After surveying vast literature from the perspective of political economy, the authors reach the conclusion that reputational effects and IEA design on the international level, and domestic institutions and actors on the national level, are major determinants of IEA compliance. They noted that peculiar country characteristics like employment situation, household incomes or level of education seem to influence national preferences and interests. Two points became clear from their literature survey: First, systematic evidence on the determinants of compliance with IEAs is restricted. Therefore, major findings and derived conclusions from such studies should be handled with caution and quickstep generalization should be prevented. Major difficulties are associated with quantification of compliance. To find an appropriate indicator for compliance proves to be extremely complicated in cases where there is no precise compliance goal that the behaviour of IEA parties can be compared to.

Second, the literature on autocratic compliance with international agreements is often limited, and especially in the case of IEAs, one may even argue its non-existence. For the time being, the literature is mostly concerned only with non-IEA issues or ratification behaviour and domestic environmental policies in general.

Moreover, IEAs and their implementation have to be evaluated with respect to efficiency perspective. IEAs and national compliance strategies are generally resulted with various types of economic inefficiencies. There may be two main reasons for such unexpected outputs: First, national policy-makers are inclined to pursue control policies instead of fallowing marked oriented tools. Second, although market oriented instruments are used to comply, policy targets are predetermined on non-optimal levels. Inefficiencies might also originate from the design of the IEAs. Therefore, one should closely scrutinize the design of the IEAs. Last but not least, IEAs can only be efficient if there is compliance.

Another aspect is the endogenous and exogenous factors that determine stability. Endogenous determinants are internal and heavily depend on national institutions. Exogenous determinants are dependent on factors that are external to individual countries' decision-making processes. Under such circumstances, the main findings in Chapter 2 suggest that a multi-step process is less likely to give rise to a global international environmental agreement than a one-step process. Moreover, a global agreement is less likely to form if a sub-global agreement between two countries is already in place. The enlargement of the initial coalition may be blocked, not only by the outsider, but also by the insider depending on the size of the pollution externality and on the country-size asymmetry. Overall, the grand coalition is less likely to emerge when sub-coalitions are profitable which implies a strong country-size asymmetry.

The last aspect in stability of IEAs is related to preferences of individuals regarding inequality-aversion that affects stability of coalitions. This study examines the impacts of inequality-averse attitudes on the individual incentives of participating in international environmental agreements using a laboratory experiment. The theoretical assumption is that when countries are self-interested, stable coalitions exist if signatories have no incentive to leave and non-signatories have no incentive to join. The experiments in Chapter 3 focus on a coalition with a unique equilibrium and the individuals' attitudes toward inequality-aversion are considered. A set of experiments are conducted that measure the individuals' attitudes towards inequality-aversion and in which subjects are given different payoff tables and asked whether or not they would join a coalition.

The findings suggest that the inequality-averse attitudes have significant positive impacts on the incentives of participation, and especially, when the subjects are non-critical players, the egalitarians are likely to give up the free-riding benefit by joining a coalition. Individual inequality-averse attitudes could be the reason for large coalition formation and no matter whether they are critical players or not, a stronger attitude towards inequality-aversion leads to more willingness to participate in a coalition. The results of Chapter 3 also suggest that the individual motivation could be affected by their political and religious attitudes.

The game theoretic analysis of IEAs with heterogeneous countries is a largely unresolved issue. Regarding effects of 'country heterogeneity' on performance of IEAs, the book identifies three factors. The first one is the transnational approach that might become a necessity in case of heterogeneous countries. Chapter 4 provides an exploration of some transnational initiatives for climate cooperation by claiming that considering only nation state governments can provide a partial explanation and instead strategic interaction of heterogeneous actors should be taken into account. To underpin this claim, the chapter extends already existing game theoretic approaches to international environmental agreements to analyse the strategic effects of transnational environmental agreements.

The two created examples show that climate clubs offer an opportunity to cooperate in more than one agreement at the same time and cities can form alliances in which they agree to mitigate greenhouse gases. The effectiveness of such transnational environmental agreements is found to depend on the political influence that cities have on national governments. They find that cooperation can be individually rational, even in the presence of free-rider incentives. Both examples of transnational environmental agreements have shown that such agreements may indeed be effective and improve over the standard single international environmental agreement consisting only of nation states. Furthermore, the chapter offers various other settings of heterogeneous actors that might be conducive to tackle climate change. Finally, limitations of the game theoretic analysis such as the re-legitimation of the climate regime or potentially irrational behaviour of agents are summarized which might shine a light for future research.

The second factor in country heterogeneity arises in case of transboundary pollution. In Chapter 5, Baksi and Chaudhuri examine the impacts of trade liberalization and border tax adjustment on the incentives of heterogeneous countries to cooperate when regulating emissions of a global pollutant. They use an oligopolistic model of trade between two countries, North and South, where production generates transboundary pollution and the pollution damage parameter is higher in the North. Each country imposes a pollution tax on its domestic firm, where the tax rate can be chosen either cooperatively or non-cooperatively. The authors analyse the sustainability of environmental cooperation between the countries within an infinitely repeated game framework using trigger strategies.

While the North has a stronger incentive to cooperate than the South, it is shown that an increase in the degree of heterogeneity between the two countries in terms of their pollution damage parameter reduces the likelihood of cooperation between them. Trade liberalization increases both the global gains from cooperation as well as the likelihood of cooperation between the countries. The chapter also considers the use of a border tax adjustment under non-cooperation, where the North imposes a tariff on imports of the polluting good from the South, and the tariff rate reflects the difference in pollution tax rates across the two countries. The analysis provides that imposing the BTA (Border Tax Adjustments) makes the North less likely to cooperate, while the South is more likely to cooperate provided the countries are sufficiently heterogeneous.

The third factor in country heterogeneity is the case where a developed country faces a developing one, which is the case in Chapter 6. Using an intra industry trade framework with a two-country (North-South), two-firm model, Orbay and Erkol investigate the effects of labour intensity of production and marginal damage of pollution on government policies as well as location choice of a foreign firm. Both firms pollute the local environment. North Firm decides where to locate first, among the choices of staying at home, moving the production entirely to the South country. South and North countries reveal the government policies afterwards. Firms decide their country specific production levels à la Cournot in the third stage. They find that subsidization is the optimal policy choice for the case where North Firm produces at home, whereas taxing is the South government's optimal choice when North Firm locates in South. Due to these policy choices, producing at home is always the best location choice for the North Firm. With higher (lower) employment effect of the North (South) Firm and lower marginal pollution damage, producing at home becomes even more attractive.

After observing that producing in its country of origin is a more attractive location choice for the North Firm, the authors analyse how the social welfare levels of the countries and environmental pollution levels change if governments attempt to have an IEA, i.e. cooperative behaviour. Given the above specification, subsidization is a better policy option for the governments at both non-cooperative and uniform cooperative equilibrium in spite of the pollution. In both the cooperative and non-cooperative case, subsidization has positive effects on profits, consumer surplus and employment effect of production, and clearly these positive effects are dominating. Although the total environmental pollution is lower, unfortunately, the uniform cooperative equilibrium is not welfare improving.

Under the title of 'firm heterogeneity', one of the issues that the book focuses on is the presence of foreign penetration in Chapter 7. There has always been a fierce competition amongst countries for foreign firms, especially amongst the developing countries. USD billions worth of inflow of FDI into countries with low controls on emissions has been alleged to create pollution havens. This may hamper the potential cooperation and IEAs on a larger scale, as it will discourage governments from signing treaties. The relationship between FDI and environment is, hence, an important one. While many see FDI inflows as the result of low standards, one can also ask if the FDI inflows may also be the reason for low standards. Lahiri and Tsai examine the latter in Chapter 7. They use a partial equilibrium model with n

number of identical foreign firms and m number of identical domestic firms competing in the market for a non-tradeable commodity in a host country. The government is assumed to have a pollution control policy, i.e. quota (standard), which allows only a certain amount of units of pollution per unit of output produced.

Both sets of firms create pollution while producing and possess an abatement technology. The chapter considers two scenarios depending on whether there is free entry and exit of domestic firms or not. They show that the results depend crucially on whether there is free entry and exit of domestic firms. For example, under free entry and exit of domestic firms, FDI does not affect the level of optimal emission standards, but it does when the number of domestic firms is exogenous. Even under the latter scenario, FDI may not make environmental policies less stringent.

The second issue regarding the firm heterogeneity is the abatement levels in agreements, which is the topic of Chapter 8. According to Gautier, international cooperation should be concerned at least with three points to achieve lower global emission. The first one is the asymmetry in pollution intensities and marginal abatement costs across countries. The second one is the fear of losing competitive edge due to stricter environmental policies. The third is the type of reform imposed. Given the aforementioned background, Chapter 8 deals with the elements of strategic environmental policy, with particular attention to policy reform and its impact on global emissions in the presence of heterogeneous abatement costs across countries. The chapter considers a two-country model where firms behave in a Cournot fashion and face an emission tax. Countries are assumed to undertake policy reform of emissions taxes and cost-related regulations associated with production costs and pollution abatement costs.

The model allows for asymmetries in abatement cost functions, thereby capturing differences in pollution intensities (i.e. emissions per unit of output) and marginal abatement costs. The chapter argues that the ability of countries to reduce local and global emissions via policy reform depends crucially on these asymmetries. For example, unilateral policy consisting of higher taxes and lower costs by the pollution-intensive country may reduce global emissions. Other multilateral policies are analysed where the presence of an emission tax to reduce emissions, via the incentives created by the marginal abatement cost function, is crucial in reducing emissions.

In Chapter 9, the book concentrates on the production generated pollution externalities and optimal emission standards in case of heterogeneous firms as well as heterogeneous countries. The analysis indicates that optimal environmental policy depends on country size, marginal abatement cost and firm efficiency. It is shown, among others, that in the non-cooperative equilibrium and with sufficient differences in country size, the relatively smaller country sets a stringent pollution quota as long as the marginal disutility from pollution is sufficiently large. More generally, a relatively stringent quota is set as long as the damage from pollution is sufficiently large regardless of country size. In the cooperative equilibrium, a relatively stringent environmental policy benefits the smaller country because in this way pollution damages are addressed, but also, there are gains from trading with the larger country. In this case, the larger country also benefits from a stringent environmental policy as long as firms operating in that country are sufficiently efficient.

'The relationship between environmental technology and international cooperation' is covered in three different contexts. In the first one, in Chapter 10, firms decide whether to sign an agreement and to conduct R&D collectively where the role of R&D is to reduce the cost of technology adoption. This chapter analysed the effectiveness of an international technology agreement in which the signatories collectively decide whether to conduct R&D that reduces the cost of technology adoption. Findings suggest that there is a threshold regarding R&D costs which has a positive relationship with the number of countries that share the resources such that the value of the threshold is high (low) when the number of countries that share the resources is large (small). The threshold determines the effectiveness of an international technology agreement, and if R&D costs are lower than the threshold, an international technology agreement is functional, otherwise it is not. Furthermore, findings insist the effectiveness of an international technology agreement in the real world.

As the second context of the 'relationship between environmental technology and international cooperation', Chapter 11 studies the 'relationship between adoption technology and free riding'. The framework presented in Chapter 11 assumes that countries undertake adaptation and emission decisions simultaneously. This model is equivalent to one in which adaptation occurs after emission decisions are undertaken. Benchekroun, Marrouch and Chaudhuri investigate the free-riding incentives of individual countries from a given coalition where all coalition members jointly mitigate emissions. Pollution is considered as a transboundary one. To ensure that their results are not driven by specific non-standard assumptions about the properties of the effective damage function, they use the standard framework used in this literature where pollution damage is quadratic in emissions. Thus, the model yields emission strategies that are strategic substitutes, in line with the standard result in the literature on transboundary pollution games. This, in turn, facilitates comparison of the results to the existing literature examining free-riding incentives from IEAs. Finally, they consider an exogenous decrease in the marginal cost of adaptation.

Furthermore, the chapter also indicates that an increase in the efficiency of adaptation technology may result in a reduction of individual countries' incentives to free ride on an IEA, and an increase in the gains from forming the IEA. Benchekroun, Marrouch and Chaudhuri clearly show that the more efficient is adaptation at reducing marginal damage from emissions, the flatter the best response functions of each country in terms of emissions. This means that non-cooperative equilibrium will yield to lower levels of global emissions, which in turn makes cooperation on emission strategies easier.

Chapter 12 presents the final work regarding the relationship between environmental technology and international cooperation. The aim of this chapter is to show that relatively high-level abatement technology does not always result in lower pollution. This is because lower abatement cost provides competition advantage and encourages the more efficient firm to produce more. However, the high producer surplus can dominate the negative effect of pollution on welfare. Therefore, the welfare of the country with more efficient firm in terms of abatement technology has greater pollution but better welfare. When the firm has relatively less efficient abatement technology, the government imposes more severe emission quotas to constrain the pollution level. In the case of cooperation, governments set stricter emission quotas because of the negative externalities of pollution. In addition, the welfares of both countries will be better off due to the reduction in pollution levels. The country with the technologically advantageous firm still suffers from more pollution but obtains greater welfare compared to the rival country.

The last part of the book starts with Chapter 13 and explores a case study to understand how successfully international energy is governed. This part also examines what sort of an institutional framework will be efficient and effective during the inevitable energy transition. This study argues that while governing international energy transitions, certain institutional and non-institutional challenges have arisen. Institutional challenges of the current energy governance are narrow coverage of demand-side energy issues and environmental externalities, division between developed and developing countries in the system, and the bottleneck that is created by controversial contextual issues. Non-institutional challenges of global energy governance are defined as the dominance of fossil resources within the current structure, the need for a public perception of the urgency of renewable energy deployment, encouraging states to be more active and willing, and a normative change in global energy governance for a more sustainable and comprehensive energy transition.

Meta-analysis of the relevant literature and personal interviews with International Renewable Energy Agency (IRENA) officials by the author showed that IRENA has been addressing these challenges by exclusively focusing on renewable energy issues and avoiding conflictual areas, as well as accepting membership applications from all countries of all regions regardless of any country-characteristic. For its own share of the burden, IRENA has been trying to encourage its member states to be more active and willing in the absence of a binding mechanism by demonstrating its issue areas as promising opportunities for economic benefits, rather than insisting on rather more controversial aspects. Its deliberate focus on solely renewable energy-related agenda items is a concrete reflection of this principle. As for raising awareness and ensuring social acceptance regarding renewables, its multi-stakeholder *Coalition for Action to Bolster Public Support for Renewable Energy* is a noteworthy effort.

Furthermore, IRENA gives substantial project assistance regarding the renewable energy generation in rural off-grid areas. There exists a common agreement over the idea that the energy transition should also be climate-friendly and sustainable at all costs. Apart from conventional challenges like supply security and energy efficiency, resource diversification and sustainable energy solutions also stand out as crucial tasks.

Then, in Chapter 14, the impact of 'international institutions' on IEAs with a general and forward-looking approach is introduced. The past experience is evaluated to create messages to improve performance of IEAs in the future. The chapter emphasizes the failure with regard to controlling carbon emissions despite various important steps particularly imposed by bilateral and multilateral environmental agreements. Various measures taken to reduce fossil fuel use are proposed as the first channel to fight against carbon emissions. Nonetheless, no further success is expected in using this channel as currently about 80 per cent of energy use is supplied by fossil fuels. The chapter highlights decarbonization by real transformation of the energy sector, and proposes this to be the second channel. Consequently, the countries that prepare themselves for this transformation sooner might have a bigger opportunity. However, this channel might be unsatisfactory because the current 4–5 per cent contribution of renewable energy (including bio-energy) does not seem to be improvable fast enough. The third channel which the chapter focuses on for future scientific research is, though, quite radical: development of emission catching methods for ongoing emissions or pumping carbon emissions underground, which might be obligatory regulations for fossil fuel usage when we pass the 2 °C threshold; development of the carbon capturing methods to draw carbon from the atmosphere; the more fantasy level technologies for the moment, such as injecting sulphur into the atmosphere. The authors' speculation proposes that the world would find itself talking about those radical steps faster than expected; therefore bringing them into our agenda will not be unrealistic.

At this point, we might ask the question 'whether international environmental agreements can ever succeed' given the variety of firm, country, technology and industry-based conflicts as elaborated in the above chapters. At least one has to understand that, from its nature, an international environmental agreement is about a trade-off as such whether it will establish strict commitments and limit flexibility of participants or it will allow rather more flexibility and in this way increase level of participation and compliances by countries. Taking into account what has been found in the above game theoretical analyses there is a thin line just in between two edges of this trade-off and establishing an agreement which is just and inclusive is not an easy task. No surprises should be expected from the future as small countries will converge to large ones and developing ones will converge to developed ones. The gap between economies will always exist and trigger the conflicts.

All in all, laborious researches elaborated for the present edited volume clearly indicate that the danger of environmental destruction not only attained to unprecedented levels for the globe but also forced the regions, nation states and firms to cooperate without reservation and extra delay. In this respect, reaching comprehensive multi-party IEAs seems to be a prerequisite for the sustainable development of the world economy and even the coexistence of human beings with other living creatures. Nonetheless, the problem is not limited to the legal and institutional framework; the willingness of the associated parties to ensure long-lasting accomplishment of the IEAs is vital as well. Therefore, the design and the successful implementation of the IEAs should go beyond the complex nature of game theoretical approaches and current limits of international political economy.

To conclude, we believe the solution of environmental problems rests on a trivet; the earth still needs: international environmental agreements; feasible technologies that use alternative energy sources; more sensitive and responsible human behaviour.

Index